SCRIPTURE AND ETHICS

SCRIPTURE AND ETHICS

• *Twentieth-Century Portraits* •

JEFFREY S. SIKER

New York   Oxford
Oxford University Press
1997

Oxford University Press

Oxford   New York
Athens   Auckland   Bangkok   Bogota   Bombay
Buenos Aires   Calcutta   Cape Town   Dar es Salaam
Delhi   Florence   Hong Kong   Istanbul   Karachi
Kuala Lumpur   Madras   Madrid   Melbourne
Mexico City   Nairobi   Paris   Singapore
Taipei   Tokyo   Toronto

and associated companies in
Berlin   Ibadan

Copyright © 1997 by Jeffrey S. Siker

Published by Oxford University Press, Inc.
198 Madison Avenue, New York, New York 10016

Library of Congress Cataloging-in-Publication Data
Siker, Jeffery S.
Scripture and ethics : twentieth-century portraits /
Jeffrey S. Siker.
p.   cm.
Includes bibliographical references and index.
ISBN 0-19-510104-9; ISBN 0-19-511099-4 (pbk.)
1. Christian ethics—History—20th century.   2. Bible—Use.
3. Christian ethics—Methodology.   4. Ethics in the Bible.
5. Bible—Criticism, interpretation, etc.—History—20th century.
I. Title.
BJ1231.S45   1997
241—dc20   96-8899

A shorter version of chapter 7 previously appeared as "Uses of the Bible in
the Theology of Gustavo Gutiérrez: Liberating Scriptures of the Poor" in
Biblical Interpretation 4, no. 1 (1996): 40–71. The author and publisher are
grateful to the editors for permission to revise this article.

1 3 5 7 9 8 6 4 2

Printed in the United States of America
on acid-free paper

For Paul and Sally Sampley, with love and thanks.

ACKNOWLEDGMENTS

*I*am indebted far more than I can say to the suggestions and critiques of many people who have read various parts of this book. In particular, I would like to thank Bernard Häring, Stanley Hauerwas, James Cone, and Rosemary Ruether for their gracious and helpful comments on the chapters dealing with their respective uses of Scripture. I also thank Michael Cartwright, Steve Crocco, Charles Curran, Richard Hays, Bill Spohn, Allen Verhey, and my colleague John Popiden for their comments on several chapters of this book in various stages of repair. I would further like to thank Larry Rasmussen, John Bennett, and Robert McAfee Brown for their comments on the Reinhold Niebuhr chapter; Carolyn Osiek, Mary Hembrow Snyder, and my colleague Marie Anne Mayeski for their comments on the Rosemary Ruether chapter; Jim Nickoloff, Robert McAfee Brown, and Curt Cadorette for their comments on the Gustavo Gutiérrez chapter; and the anonymous reader for Oxford University Press.

I am grateful to the National Endowment for Humanities, to the Catholic Biblical Association, and especially to Loyola Marymount University for various grants and fellowships that enabled me to complete work on this book. My thanks to two students, Midge Gonzales and Pam Contreras, for all their help as research assistants. I owe a special word of thanks to my colleagues in the Department of Theological Studies at Loyola Marymount University for creating such a marvelous collegial community in which to teach and write. I am especially grateful to the "lunch crowd" of Doug Burton-Christie, Jim Fredericks, Michael Horan, Lizette Larson-Miller, and Louke van Wensveen.

Throughout the process of writing this book, my children, Derek and Ursula, have continued to be a refreshing and joyful reminder of what matters most in life. I also thank my parents, Dr. E. S. and Eileen Siker, for their gracious and continuous love in all things. Bart Ehrman and Steve Crocco have been constant and encouraging friends, albeit from afar. Judy Yates Ellis has been a great love, friend, and critic—mere words cannot express my gratitude. Finally, I thank Paul and Sally Sampley for their love, care, and play from Indiana to Charlemont. I dedicate this book to them as but a token of my thanks.

Los Angeles   J.S.S.
October 1995

CONTENTS

SCRIPTURE AND ETHICS

one

INTRODUCTION

*M*y goal in this book is to bring together two significant aspects of biblical interpretation: the history of biblical interpretation and the appropriation of the Bible for Christian ethics. In both instances my focus is on the twentieth century, particularly on how the Bible has been used in constructing Christian theological ethics. Although many books and articles have been written describing how the Bible *should* be used in Christian theological ethics,[1] very little research has been done on how the Bible actually *has* been used in the work of twentieth-century Christian theological ethicists.[2] (The work that has been done comes almost exclusively from those with primary formal training in Christian theological ethics rather than from those whose primary formal training is in biblical studies.) Further, although many studies have examined the ethics of Scripture,[3] that is, the various moral visions and moral worlds of the different biblical writers, relatively little work has been devoted to what might be called the scriptures of ethics—namely, an assessment of construals of the Bible for contemporary theological ethics.

I intend to focus attention on a series of related questions revolving around how Christian ethicists and moral theologians have made use of Scripture in their constructive work. Specifically, I use five guiding questions to explore ways in which the Bible has been used and approached by various theological ethicists. There are other questions one could ask, but to me these seem to be among the most important.[4]

First, what biblical texts are used? This question seems to me to be the most obvious starting point, and yet it is surprisingly almost never asked. Before one can talk about how Scripture is used, one first has to determine where and when an author uses the Bible. In making constructive use of the Bible every theologian/ethicist necessarily chooses to highlight certain parts over others. For a variety of reasons, theologians operate out of a working biblical canon with specific contours. My first task is to identify the shape of the working biblical canon for the various theological ethicists surveyed in this book.

Second, how does the author use Scripture? While it is important to be aware of which biblical texts an author uses—especially in seeking to discern each author's working biblical canon—the mere use of a passage in itself is not necessarily self-explanatory. The appeal to a biblical passage only makes sense, of course, in the larger context in which it appears. To ask how an author uses the Bible, then, is to ask a very broad question, since all the authors studied here appeal to the Bible in a variety of contexts. Rather than limiting myself to prefabricated notions of "use," I have attempted to describe and analyze the various authors' "uses" of Scripture in keeping with the larger contexts and purposes of their writings. This is not to say that I have no presuppositions about ways in which the Bible is used or construed in constructive theological ethics. Rather, my aim has been to describe as clearly and as thoroughly as possible— in ways recognizable both to the authors themselves and to the larger communities of ecclesial and academic discourse—how the various authors appear to be employing Scripture. In almost all cases, this is the longest and most fully developed section of each chapter.

Third, how is the authority of Scripture envisioned? To ask this question necessarily raises many others. What is the relation of biblical authority to other moral norms? In what ways, if any, is Scripture normative? How does one distinguish among competing interpretations of Scripture? In addition to making significant use of Scripture, all the authors studied have something to say about the authority of Scripture for moral discourse; in construing Scripture for Christian theological ethics, it is important to articulate clearly each author's understanding of biblical authority.

Fourth, what kind of hermeneutic is employed in approaching the Bible? In selecting and using biblical passages in their constructive theological ethics, each author has a set of implicit or explicit, hermeneutical convictions for understanding the Bible. My goal is to describe as clearly as possible the hermeneutical method(s) evident in each author's handling of Scripture, especially as this relates to their constructive theological and ethical programs.

Fifth, what is the relationship between the Bible and Christian ethics? To a degree, this question is related to the second question, but here I am primarily interested in seeing how each author construes the significance of Scripture for practical and constructive Christian ethics. In part, this can be illustrated by seeing how the Bible is related to specific issues in theological ethics.

After asking these five questions of each author, I then conclude each chapter with comments by way of critical evaluation, highlighting what I believe to be the strengths and weaknesses of each author's "use" of Scripture for constructive Christian theological ethics, as well as posing questions for further consideration.

But of whom am I asking these guiding questions and why have I chosen to concentrate on the works of these authors and not others? Why have I opted to focus on discrete authors at all rather than on larger "movements" within Christian theological ethics?

I have selected eight of the most important contributors to theological ethics in the twentieth century: Reinhold Niebuhr, H. Richard Niebuhr, Bernard

Häring, Paul Ramsey, Stanley Hauerwas, Gustavo Gutiérrez, James Cone, and Rosemary Radford Ruether. My criteria for choosing the works of these authors are fourfold. First, I particularly wanted to study the writings of twentieth-century Christian theologians whose work has been among the most influential for moral discourse within the larger Christian community. Second, the authors chosen needed to have produced a sufficient body of work to allow for an in-depth analysis. Third, it was important to select authors who make repeated and significant use of the Bible in their constructive work. And, fourth, I wanted to choose authors who, considered collectively, present various (if not necessarily representative) ways in which the Bible has been appropriated for Christian theological ethics in the twentieth century.

The writings of each of the eight authors selected continue to exercise a tremendous influence on contemporary Christian theological and ethical reflection: Reinhold Niebuhr for his "Christian realism" in all aspects of Christian ethics; H. Richard Niebuhr for his ethics of response and his work in narrative theological ethics; Bernard Häring for his pioneering work as a Roman Catholic moral theologian in recasting the natural law tradition and in leading the renewal of a more biblically grounded moral theology; Paul Ramsey for his emphasis on covenantal ethics and his contributions to just war theory and medical ethics; Stanley Hauerwas for his emphasis on the communal context of interpreting the Christian story and his forceful articulation of a nonviolent Christian ethics; Gustavo Gutiérrez for his foundational contribution to Latin American liberation theology; James Cone for his fundamental and formative work in the black theology of liberation; and Rosemary Radford Ruether for her constructive work in feminist theology and ethics.

The use of the Bible in the constructive work of other prominent twentieth-century Christian theological ethicists might also be examined (e.g., Walter Rauschenbusch, James Gustafson, John Howard Yoder, Charles Curran, and Beverly Harrison, to name but a few).[5] Limiting this study to those chosen is largely pragmatic, in that I want to examine in depth a sufficiently broad and significant group of Christian theological ethicists. I consider the chapters that follow to be exegetical probes, as it were—an exegetical analysis of the writings of various theologians and ethicists with a focus on their uses of Scripture.

A brief word about the relation and distinction between "theology" and "ethics" is in order. The disciplines of systematic theology and theological ethics are obviously very closely related and overlap to a significant degree. In practice, however—especially on the American scene—systematic theology has focused on what would be considered classical questions of theology revolving around the identity and actions of God, (e.g., doctrines of God, creation, sin, redemption, Christology, and revelation), whereas theological ethics has grown out of theology and has placed greater emphasis on human responses to God, as well as to other people, on what it means to be faithful to God and to one another in practical terms. Though theology and ethics are inseparable, for better or worse they have come to be relatively distinct, if closely related, fields of discourse. The writings of all the authors examined here could be—and, to some degree, have been—considered within the field of systematic theology rather than theological ethics (especially those of H. Richard Niebuhr). The three liberation theologians (Gutiérrez, Cone, and Ruether) have all argued that the distinction between theology and ethics is a false one (as has Hauerwas on other grounds) and that all theology is best seen as critical reflection on Christian praxis, on activity in the world. All this is to acknowledge that a sharp distinction between theology and ethics is inappropriate. However, for the purposes of this study I am more interested in what has come to be the area of theological ethics than I am in systematic theology, especially as it has been traditionally and classically defined.[6]

Why have I chosen to study the writings of individual authors rather than seek to discern various "types" of construing Scripture for ethics? One of the aspects with which I am most concerned is the specificity of an author's uses of Scripture. To this end, I am convinced that the only responsible way to describe and analyze an author's uses of the Bible is to undertake a thorough reading of each author's writings and then see how the Bible is used within the context of each author's larger constructive theology and ethics. Among other things, this means taking into account the ecclesial tradition and the social location within which each author stands and out of which each author writes, as well as the broader currents in theology and ethics to which the various authors are responding. However, to abstract from all this a series of types into which each author might fit seems to me somewhat artificial and would detract from my focus on the specific uses of specific biblical passages in the constructive work of the eight theologians/ethicists I have chosen.[7]

This brings me to the topic of my own identity as the author of this study, which is not irrelevant. I write from a confessional (Christian) perspective and as a white, upper-middle-class, professional male working as a professor at a Roman Catholic university shaped by the Jesuit and Marymount traditions (specifically, Loyola Marymount University in Los Angeles). I am an ordained minister in the Presbyterian Church (USA), in which I actively participate. I am a biblical scholar (New Testament) trained in the traditional historical-critical approach, but with strong leanings in the direction of literary, narrative, and sociological approaches to biblical studies (like most of my peers at other institutions). I write as one committed to dealing with biblical writings honestly and openly, recognizing the tremendous influence they have had—and continue to have—yet also recognizing significant problems both in understanding the writings themselves and in assessing how they have been appropriated and (mis)-used.

In my own view, the Bible is a collection of writings by various people and communities that have sought to give voice both to their perceptions of God's workings and to their understanding of what it means to live faithfully before God and with one another. I write as a Christian moved by these (and other) testimonies to discern God's continued working in and about our midst. I have no doubt that these aspects of my own identity (together with others) have shaped my approach to the writings of the different authors considered in this book, my attempts to attain some critical distance notwithstanding. Nonetheless, I believe it possible to carry out a descriptive analysis of the appropriations of Scripture in the writings of the various authors considered in a manner that is recognizable both to the authors themselves and to the larger communities of ecclesial and academic discourse.

I am convinced that more clarity can be gained about the relationship(s) we pursue between Scripture and Christian ethics if we have a better understanding of how Scripture and ethics have been related by those who have made crucial contributions to constructive theological ethics in the twentieth century. Simply stated, we will have a better idea of where we are and where we are going if we have a clearer conception of where we have been. To that end, I have written this book in the hope of contributing both to the modern history of biblical interpretation and, in particular, to discussions regarding the use(s) of the Bible in constructive Christian theological ethics.[8]

two

REINHOLD NIEBUHR

Scripture as Symbol

On 8 March 1948, Reinhold Niebuhr (1892–1971) appeared on the cover of *Time* magazine, its twenty-fifth anniversary issue. The article inside referred to Reinhold Niebuhr as the number one theologian in America, a statement that could find little dispute in the 1940s. Niebuhr's powerful writings together with memories of his personal presence have continued to exercise considerable influence on theological and ethical discussions to the present time. His legacy has been enormous. One indication of his influence can be seen from the number of volumes on Niebuhr that have appeared from the 1950s through the 1980s and into the 1990s.[1]

There is, however, a surprising and significant lacuna in the many studies on Reinhold Niebuhr's theology and ethics: his use of Scripture. To a large degree Niebuhr grounded his theology and ethics in Scripture,[2] and yet the relationship between his use of Scripture and his theological ethics has received almost no attention, despite renewed interest in the use of Scripture in Christian ethics.[3] Since Reinhold Niebuhr and his brand of Christian realism have made such a significant mark on contemporary Christian theologians and ethicists, it is important to be aware of how he used Scripture. Indeed, commenting on the enduring influence of Niebuhr's approach to Scripture, Michael Cartwright has observed that "scholars in the field of Christian ethics have rarely noted the extent of Niebuhr's influence with respect to the use of Scripture in Christian ethics. . . . Christian ethicists writing *after* Niebuhr may not even realize how much they have been influenced by his use of Scripture."[4] Here I seek to describe and assess Niebuhr's use of the Bible in his theological ethics.

At the outset, three preliminary comments are appropriate. First, by way of reiteration, I should state clearly that I am approaching Reinhold Niebuhr's use of Scripture, not as an ethicist, but as a biblical scholar interested in the interaction between Scripture and ethics. Second, my analysis of Niebuhr's use of Scripture is drawn from an extensive but not exhaustive examination of Niebuhr's writings. The vast extent and often occasional character of his writings makes it practically impossible to do other than assess but a part of his literary

8

output.[5] I am drawing my analysis principally from a few central and representative writings: his most systematic and extensive work, the two-volume *The Nature and Destiny of Man*; his essays in *An Interpretation of Christian Ethics*; a collection of his sermons edited by his wife, Ursula Niebuhr, entitled *Justice and Mercy*; and four collections of his essays (*Essays in Applied Christianity: The Church and the New World* and *Love and Justice: Selections from the Shorter Writings of Reinhold Niebuhr*, both edited by D. B. Robertson; *The Essential Reinhold Niebuhr*, edited by R. M. Brown; and *Reinhold Niebuhr: Theologian of Public Life*, edited by L. Rasmussen). I have also used other, occasional writings.

Third, it is important to note that nowhere in his writings does Niebuhr articulate a self-conscious or explicit "method" for using Scripture.[6] He does not clearly give any governing "hermeneutic." Thus, one has to draw out from his extensive writings an explicit description and analysis of his use of Scripture. There is a danger here, because Niebuhr tended not to be terribly systematic in his writings. Indeed, he was uneasy with being called a "theologian" because it implied doing more thoroughgoing and comprehensive systematics than he found of interest.[7] He thought of himself as more of a preacher than a professional theologian. As his wife, Ursula Niebuhr, reported, Reinhold Niebuhr remarked to some theological students in 1955 that "he was 'one who loves preaching more than teaching, a sort of a preacher by instinct—no, I won't say by instinct, but by preference.' "[8] Thus it is somewhat artificial to look for a "system" or "method" of using Scripture in Niebuhr's work. Nevertheless, because of Niebuhr's tremendous influence, it remains a significant endeavor to describe the contours of Niebuhr's use of Scripture.

As was noted in the Introduction, my descriptive analysis will proceed by asking five related questions: What biblical texts does Niebuhr use? How does he use the texts to which he appeals? How does he envision the authority of Scripture? What kind of hermeneutic does he employ? And how does he envision the constructive relationship between Scripture and ethics? I will then conclude with a brief evaluation of Niebuhr's use of Scripture in ethics.

Biblical Texts Used by Reinhold Niebuhr

By way of a general observation, one striking feature of Niebuhr's writings is the frequency with which he refers in rather generic terms to the "biblical conception" of this, the "biblical doctrine" of that, or the "biblical view" of something else. Indeed, Niebuhr characterizes his own work as a "Biblical-Christian" approach, although he never defines exactly what this means.[9] Even a casual perusal of Niebuhr's writings reveals his habit of referring to "biblical" notions. To take, for example, one short segment from the first volume of *The Nature and Destiny of Man*, the section "Creation as Revelation" (pp. 131–36), one finds references to "Biblical faith" (pp. 131, 133), "Biblical religion" (pp. 132, 134), "the Biblical doctrine of creation" (pp. 133, 134), "the Biblical emphasis upon the meaningfulness of human history" (p. 134), "the Biblical idea of Creator" (p.

135), and "the Biblical conception of God" (p. 135). Significantly, in this same section the only explicit reference to a specific text is to Rom. 1:19–20. Indeed, Niebuhr often does not cite specific biblical texts to support his general characterization of an idea or conception as "biblical."

Sometimes, however, Niebuhr does refer to various specific texts in a relatively short span. In the section "Historical and Special Revelation" in *The Nature and Destiny of Man* (vol. 1, pp. 136–49), for example, the section immediately following "Creation as Revelation," Niebuhr again refers generically to "the Biblical idea of the character of human history" (p. 137), "the Biblical interpretation of sin" (p. 139), "the emphasis of Biblical faith upon history as a revelation of the wrath of God" (p. 141), and the like, but he also explicitly cites Isa. 44:6, 45, 47:10; Ezek. 28:2–9; Psalm 49; Luke 12:19–20; and Rom. 1:18–23 in support of his assertions.

When one examines Niebuhr's work as a whole, one finds that he tends to make more frequent references to specific biblical texts in his more overtly theological writings, even if often in passing. For example, in *The Nature and Destiny of Man* the Scripture index lists about two hundred passages cited over the course of about six hundred pages of text. In his more socially and politically oriented writings, however, Niebuhr rarely cites Scripture, perhaps because of the more public forum he was seeking to influence.[10]

Although one rarely finds a Scripture index in Niebuhr's works, one can make several observations regarding which specific texts he uses. Not surprisingly for a Christian ethicist, Niebuhr tends to favor the New Testament over the Old Testament, but in no way does he have Marcionite leanings. Regarding the Old Testament, Niebuhr once gave the following appreciative statement:

> Nothing gives Biblical faith a greater consistency than this subordination of the struggle between good and evil men to the more significant struggle between all men and God in "whose sight no man living is justified." If there was any inconsistency in the Old Testament upon these two strains of interpretation, it is certainly overcome in the New Testament. There only the one conflict is dealt with so consistently that one sometimes wonders whether the conflict between justice and injustice in history is considered at all. This is why in times of such conflicts, as in the recent war, we turn with a certain relief to the Old Testament and thank God that it is a part of the Bible.[11]

From the Old Testament he has a definite preference for the prophets (especially Isaiah and Amos) and for the Psalms. Aside from Genesis 1–3, the Pentateuch receives almost no attention at all, as can be seen from *The Nature and Destiny of Man*, where Niebuhr refers explicitly to texts from the Torah only ten times (eight of them from Gen. 1–3, the other two from Gen. 28:12 and Deut. 5:6–7).

Among the writings of the New Testament, Niebuhr prefers the Gospel of Matthew and Paul's letter to the Romans. In his use of Matthew, he has a slight preference for the Sermon on the Mount (Matt. 5–7), as well as for the apocalyptic judgment texts from Matthew 24–25. In his use of Romans he draws heavily on the discussion of sin in Romans 1–2 and especially on Paul's treatment of sin and law in Romans 7. He also makes regular use of 1 Corinthians. As for the rest of the New Testament, he rarely refers to the Gospel of Mark or to the Gospel of John, and the other documents receive only sporadic use (e.g., only three references to the Acts of the Apostles in all the writings surveyed).

How Reinhold Niebuhr Uses Scripture

Niebuhr uses the Bible in essentially three different but closely related ways. First, Niebuhr uses the Bible to create symbolic constructs that guide his overall approach to and use of Scripture. Second, Niebuhr employs a relatively standard "biblical concept" approach. And, third, Niebuhr makes "illustrative" use of the Bible. We will look at each of these in turn.

Symbolic Constructs: Prophetic Religion and the Love Ethic of Jesus

Niebuhr did not, of course, approach the Bible with a blank slate. Rather, he had been thoroughly schooled in the late-nineteenth and early-twentieth-century liberal understanding of the Bible, and despite his sharp criticisms of liberalism, his thought remained deeply influenced by it, especially by such figures as Troeltsch and Harnack. In his essay "How My Mind Has Changed," Niebuhr acknowledged, "I find that I am a liberal at heart, and that many of my [earlier] broadsides against liberalism were indiscriminate."[12]

Thus, Niebuhr already had an interpretive framework for approaching the Bible as a whole. This framework is characterized by two fundamental constructs that Niebuhr derived in a general way from liberalism's reading of the Bible, constructs that he used both for interpreting the Bible and for relating the Bible to moral life in the twentieth century. These two symbolic constructs of the Bible are "prophetic religion" and "the love ethic of Jesus." Both of these constructs recur throughout Niebuhr's writings. Indeed, they represent for Niebuhr the highest and most noble expressions of humanity's attempts in history to be faithful to God. The notion of prophetic religion, of course, has to do primarily with the witness of the Old Testament, while the love ethic of Jesus deals with the New Testament. But the two are very closely related, as we shall see.

Niebuhr never really gives a specific definition of "prophetic religion," but it is relatively clear what he means by the phrase.[13] Prophetic religion acknowledges God as the transcendent creator and judge of the world. It trusts God as the unity, ground, and goal of all existence. Prophetic religion, or "Hebraic Prophetism" as he sometimes calls it, is significant because it

> is the beginning of revelation in the history of religion. It is the beginning of revelation because here, for the first time, in the history of culture the eternal

and divine is not regarded as the extension and fulfillment of the highest human possibilities. . . . God's word is spoken *against* both his favored nation and against all nations. This means that prophetism has the first understanding of the fact that the real problem of history is not the finiteness of all human endeavors, which must await for their completion by divine power. The real problem of history is the proud pretension of all human endeavors, which seeks to obscure their finite and partial character and thereby involves history in evil and sin.[14]

Prophetic religion recognizes the true identity of God as the transcendent ground of being and the true identity of humanity as utterly dependent upon and rebellious against God. As he puts it elsewhere, "It is the genius and the task of prophetic religion to insist on the organic relation between historic human existence and that which is both the ground and the fulfillment of this existence, the transcendent."[15] Thus, for Niebuhr, prophetic religion emphasizes God as the source and sustainer of all things and humanity's sinful pride in the face of God. Especially important for Niebuhr in this regard is that the Old Testament prophets spoke against Israel as well as against the nations. True prophetic religion does not give in to the sin of nationalistic pride. Indeed, when he appeals to prophetic religion, Niebuhr regularly refers to the prophets Amos and Isaiah (especially First Isaiah), famous for speaking God's word of judgment against Israel.[16]

For Niebuhr, the construct of prophetic religion serves a crucial, and primarily negative, role in any legitimate expression of Christian faith. Prophetic religion provides a basis for criticizing false developments in Christian thought, especially in discussing the Christian conception of sin. As Niebuhr puts it in the closing comments of his early book *An Interpretation of Christian Ethics*:

> [T]he truth of prophetic religion, and of Christianity in so far as Christianity is truly prophetic, must survive the tempests of a dying civilization as an ark surviving the flood. . . . It is the life in this ark of prophetic religion, therefore, which must generate the spirituality of any culture of an age in which human vitality is brought under a decent discipline. (p. 146)

It is significant to note here Niebuhr's characterization of prophetic religion as an "ark" that survives the flood of a dying and sinful civilization. By referring to prophetic religion as a symbolic ark, Niebuhr invokes the language of the faithful remnant that endures despite human sinfulness. What is more striking, however, is that prophetic religion is not a remnant or an ark of Israel per se, of God's covenant community called out from the peoples of the world; rather, prophetic religion is that which generates "the spirituality of any culture" of apparently any age that has lost its "human vitality." Thus, prophetic religion extends well beyond the religious boundaries within which it arises, and it functions on a much larger scale of human culture than was the case for the prophets in ancient Israel.

I suspect that one reason the construct of prophetic religion especially appealed to Niebuhr was because he saw himself as something of a prophetic figure in the United States, seeking to generate a renewed and realist spirituality on the American scene. Just as Amos and Isaiah warned Israel about God's impending judgment because of Israel's pride, so Niebuhr constantly warned the leaders of the United States, along with those of Germany and the former Soviet Union, not to be too self-righteous in domestic and international affairs.[17] Niebuhr's primary community, then, was not so much the church as it was the forum of national and international policy debates addressed in light of his Christian convictions.

If prophetic religion provides a critical perspective on human existence, pointing simultaneously to God's transcendence and human sinfulness, then the construct of the love ethic of Jesus provides for Niebuhr a positive basis, an ideal, for the construction of a Christian ethic. Indeed, he sees the love ethic of Jesus as the fruition of prophetic religion. Thus Niebuhr begins his lecture on "The Ethic of Jesus" with this statement: "The ethic of Jesus is the perfect fruit of prophetic religion. Its ideal of love has the same relation to the facts and necessities of human experience as the God of prophetic faith has to the world. . . . The ethic proceeds logically from the presuppositions of prophetic religion."[18]

The love ethic of Jesus is an ideal for Niebuhr because Jesus' love was oriented to the other, primarily to God and then to other people, both neighbor and enemy. His love was not self-love. According to Niebuhr, the love ethic of Jesus is ultimately expressed in his sacrificial love as he accepted death on the cross for others. Human beings constrained by history can thus most nearly approximate the love ethic of Jesus by practicing sacrificial love. Closely related to sacrificial love is "love as forgiveness," forbearing with the shortcomings and sins of another. Within history, it is possible for humans to realize only these two "pinnacles of love," as Niebuhr calls them: sacrificial love and love as forgiveness.[19] Because of human sinfulness, the transcendent character of love as universal actuality will only be expressed beyond history.

With regard to the love ethic, it is also crucial for Niebuhr to argue that the love ethic of Jesus is an impossible ethical ideal. It presents a transcendent absolute and radical ideal that is beyond the striving of human potential constrained by history. But it remains an absolutely essential ideal because it points to the individual's relationship with God, a relationship that God initiates and that is finally consummated beyond history. It is also essential because within history it places human pretensions in stark relief by showing the self-seeking and self-justifying behavior that inevitably characterizes and undermines human actions.[20]

These two constructs—prophetic religion and the love ethic of Jesus—provided Niebuhr with symbolic constructs for understanding the significance of the Bible as a whole and for relating the biblical witness to the moral life of humanity in the modern age.

Biblical Concepts

A second way in which Niebuhr uses the Bible can be described as a "biblical concept" approach.[21] A biblical concept approach is simply an attempt to discern what the Bible says about this or that subject. Thus the cohesive theology and ethics of the biblical witness itself are sought regarding various concepts, an endeavor that presupposes that the Bible in fact contains such cohesive concepts.[22] In the course of *The Nature and Destiny of Man*, for example, Niebuhr devotes different sections to various biblical concepts. In one place he discusses the biblical basis of the doctrine that humanity was made in the image of God (vol. 1, pp. 151–66) and the biblical "doctrine of man as creature" (vol. 1, pp. 167–77). He appeals extensively to the Bible in his analysis of "man as sinner" (vol. 1, pp. 178–207) and discusses the biblical concept of "original sin and man's responsibility" (vol. 1, pp. 241–64). Niebuhr presents the biblical concept of "prophetic messianism" and seeks to show how Jesus reinterpreted this concept (vol. 2, pp. 23–34). He also has sections addressing "the biblical doctrine of grace" (vol. 2, pp. 100–107) and "the NT idea of the end" (vol. 2, pp. 289–98).

On two occasions he uses passages from Paul's letters to provide section headings for his discussions in the second volume of *The Nature and Destiny of Man*. From 1 Cor. 1:24 Niebuhr uses Paul's language of Christ as the "wisdom of God" and the "power of God" to discuss what the concepts of wisdom and power mean (pp. 54–62), as well as Paul's references (1 Cor. 1:25) to the "foolishness of God" and the "wisdom of man" (pp. 62–67). And in his development of the theme of grace as God's power in and mercy toward humanity, Niebuhr uses Paul's statement from Gal. 2:20 to provide section headings: "I am crucified with Christ; nevertheless I live; yet not I, but Christ liveth in me" (pp. 107–26). Thus we can see that various biblical concepts, especially from the New Testament, are very important for Niebuhr's analysis of the human situation and his exposition of human destiny.

In addition to these examples from *The Nature and Destiny of Man*, Niebuhr's other writings also contain endless generic references to the biblical doctrine of this or the biblical concept of that, as we have seen. Yet almost never does he provide any exegetical analysis to support his assertions. Nevertheless, it seems important for Niebuhr to develop such concepts and doctrines in order to show that his own theological analyses are clearly grounded in the Bible. On the whole, then, Niebuhr seems more interested simply in calling attention to the biblical basis of his thought than in demonstrating it. Perhaps being the pragmatist that he was, he thought that he was merely explicating what to him appeared the obvious meaning of the texts. Perhaps this tendency also supports Niebuhr's contention that he was more at home as a preacher than as an academician concerned with scholarly exegesis of biblical texts.

Indeed, Niebuhr seems little interested or even much aware of what was going on in biblical studies from the 1930s through the 1950s. He occasionally refers to the work of biblical scholars, especially from the early twentieth century, such as S. J. Case, C. C. Torrey, H. W. Robinson, B. Weiss, P. Wernle, A. Schlatter, and R. H. Charles, though he also occasionally uses the work of C. H. Dodd and R. Bultmann. By and large, however, he makes little constructive use of biblical studies in his writings.[23]

Niebuhr also tends to view the Bible as a cohesive and coherent witness that speaks more often than not with one voice. He is certainly aware of tensions between different biblical writers, but he downplays such tensions and instead lifts up various biblical concepts as if the Bible has a relatively clear and consistent position on them. Niebuhr was criticized for this by E. A. Burtt in his 1956 essay "Some Questions About Niebuhr's Theology." Burtt asks:

> If we take any major theological theme and examine the relevant facts objectively, do we not find, first that in the Bible itself there is a diversity of beliefs with respect to that theme; and second, that Niebuhr's interpretation of any one of them is contradicted by many other interpretations that have just as good a claim as his own to constitute the "Biblical view"? . . . The crucial point . . . is whether the evidence really supports the idea that there is any such thing as *the* Biblical view, and whether therefore any theology which assumes that there is does not inevitably project into the teachings of the Bible a selection, an emphasis, and an organizing unity that are in the theologian and not in the Bible.[24]

In his own "Reply to Interpretation and Criticism," Niebuhr admits that the Bible does contain some conflicting ideas, but he goes on to state, "I believe nevertheless that there is a 'Biblical' faith of great consistency and uniqueness."[25] This tendency in Niebuhr to stress the consistency of various biblical concepts is somewhat surprising, because elsewhere he is very concerned to let the tensions stand as dialectics.[26]

The Bible as Illustrative Source

A third way in which Niebuhr uses the Bible can be called "illustrative." Throughout his writings, Niebuhr cites the Bible, sometimes exactly and sometimes loosely, to illustrate and/or to confirm an argument he has been making, almost by way of proof texts added to flavor the substance of an argument.[27] As Ursula Niebuhr comments, the Bible "gave him illustration[s] for his exposition of the faith."[28] Thus, for example, Niebuhr states that the genius of the Bible is that it shows "the ultimate and transcendent character of God [which] challenges man's own conception of piety and goodness. 'My thoughts are not your thoughts,' etc."[29]

Niebuhr's appeal to Scripture often comes at the end of a discussion or section. For example, Niebuhr uses Rom. 14:8 to illustrate a general observation that individuals often must disregard their own personal success and failure for the sake of the common good. As Niebuhr cites him, Paul states, "Whether we live, we live unto the Lord; and whether we die, we die unto the Lord; whether we live therefore, or die, we are the Lord's."[30]

Elsewhere he uses Paul to criticize Barth's polemic against natural law, citing Paul's statement in Rom. 2:14 that "when the Gentiles . . . do by nature the things contained in the law, these . . . are a law unto themselves."[31] Along similar lines, Niebuhr states: "Karl Barth's belief that the moral life of man would possess no valid principles of guidance, if the Ten Commandments had not introduced such principles by revelation, is as absurd as it is unscriptural."[32]

Beyond using specific and isolated texts to illustrate and corroborate a point, Niebuhr also often uses biblical images and metaphors. His writings are generously seasoned with such images. For example, in a discussion about the relationship between philosophy and theology Niebuhr notes that

> in practice philosophy sometimes achieves a greater spirit of humility than theology. It is saved from *hybris* by its lack of any quick means of escape from the obvious limitations of human knowing. It has no Jacob's ladder upon which the angels of grace rightly ascend and descend, but which is used falsely when the theological Jacob imagines it an instrument for climbing into heaven.[33]

Niebuhr will also often use biblical phrases to complete a sentence expressing his own thought. For example, in a discussion regarding the rise and fall in history of the world's many cultures and civilizations, Niebuhr comments: "In their weakness and youth, while making their way in history against all the perils of life, they are revelations of the power of God who 'hath chosen . . . things which are not, to bring to nought things that are' " (using 1 Cor. 1:28).[34] Niebuhr also frequently invites the reader to participate in various confessions and questionings found in the Bible. For example, he leads the reader to "declare with Paul" or to "ask with the Fourth Ezra."[35] These confessions and questions are used to corroborate human experiences. Moreover, as preachers often do, Niebuhr regularly strings together biblical citations from different contexts (although he rarely cites more than two verses at a time, except from the Psalms).

Although Niebuhr often used the Bible as a source for illustrations, it would be unfair to say that the Bible was peripheral to the *substance* of his thought. Niebuhr's language was so infused with biblical imagery and biblical phrases that clearly the Bible was not an afterthought for him; rather, these biblical images, as he appropriated them, formed part of the very fabric of his thinking, however much they were transformed in the process.

Reinhold Niebuhr's View of the Authority of Scripture

Despite the generous use Niebuhr makes of Scripture, he clearly sees the Bible's authority in relative terms. At best, the Bible can have only relative authority because of its historically contingent character. As Niebuhr puts it, "Biblical observations upon life are made in a living relation to living history. When they are falsely given an eminence which obscures this relation, they become the source of error and confusion."[36] Or, as he put it more succinctly, "You cannot teach the Bible without understanding its historical character."[37] Thus, in principle, Niebuhr had a healthy respect for the need to understand the historical and social context of the biblical writings.

This respect can also be seen in his understanding of the biblical canon. According to Niebuhr, the inclusion of certain writings in the canon is "sometimes quite fortuitous."[38] Or, as Niebuhr observes elsewhere, the Bible contains "relative standards of knowledge and virtue *which happen to be* enshrined in a religious canon."[39] Thus, for Niebuhr, the formation of the canon appears to be more historical accident than divine inspiration. And so the authority of Scripture would seem to have no necessary dependence on the canonical status of Scripture.

Nevertheless, Niebuhr also felt that the value and significance of the Bible could be obscured by focusing too much on the historical relativities it contains. And so Niebuhr sharply criticized such liberal biblical scholars as Shirley Jackson Case, for example, for attributing the rigor of Jesus' ethic to "the peculiar circumstances of time and place—agrarian simplicity . . . as contrasted with the industrial complexities of our own day."[40] For Niebuhr such an analysis was the result of the liberal illusion that in the gospel ethic of Jesus "we are dealing with a possible and prudential ethic."[41] According to Niebuhr, the authority of the Bible, though relativized by its historical contingencies, is also enduring, because the Bible alone relates the drama of Israel and the Christ, which best reveals the human situation in light of God's love and justice. The authority of the Bible thus derives from its capacity to reflect God's transcendent character amid the historical constraints which characterize human existence.

Overall, however, Niebuhr seems to be most concerned with those who have too lofty a view of Scripture, and so he tends to address the issue of scriptural authority in a largely negative way, pointing out when appeals to biblical authority are inappropriate. To see Scripture with much of orthodox Christianity as "an authoritative compendium of social, economic, political, and scientific knowledge" is to use it as a "vehicle of the sinful sanctification and scientific knowledge of relative standards."[42] Along the same lines, he mourns the fateful influence of the authority of such passages as Rom. 13:1 upon Christian political thought, because naive Christian appropriations of this biblical text fail to see the perils of power and uncritically accept "the virtues of social power" reflected in a biblical text that is "a less prophetic type of religious thought."[43] He comments further on the problems of Paul's "very 'undialectical' appreciation of government" in Rom. 13:1–3 by stating: "This unqualified endorsement of government and the unqualified prohibition of resistance to its authority is justified by the mistaken assertion that government is no peril to virtue but only to vice. History proves that the power of government is morally ambiguous."[44] Though in Niebuhr's view Paul is mistaken in his sentiments about the goodness of government, still Niebuhr does go on to excuse Paul by saying that "the Pauline justification of government was valid enough in the particular historical context in which it was made. It was undoubtedly a warning against the irresponsibility towards government which the eschatological mood of the early church encouraged."[45] In any event, the "misuse" of Romans 13 in later church tradition is, for Niebuhr, a prime example of the "perils of Biblicism."[46]

Niebuhr continues to call into question too ready an appeal to biblical authority in his essay "An Answer to Karl Barth," where Niebuhr addresses the issue of "what is 'time bound' " in Scripture, stating against Barth that "I should certainly regard St. Paul's absolute subordination of women to man as more obviously time-bound than the word, 'In Christ there is neither male nor female.' "[47] Niebuhr worries about Barth's seeming blindness to the time-bound character of much of the biblical witness. And so he asks:

> Or does the modern Continental [i.e., Barthian] conception of Biblical author-
> ity exclude the possibility that echoes and accents of the culture of an age
> appear in the Scripture? If this is excluded, Biblical authority may indeed
> emancipate us from the prejudices of our own age, but at the price of binding
> us to the prejudices of bygone ages. Furthermore, the Bible may thus become
> the instrument of, rather than the source of judgment upon, the sinful preten-
> sions of men—in this case of the sinful pretensions of the male toward the
> female.[48]

Niebuhr charges Barth with so overstating the authority of the Bible that it becomes as oppressive as it is liberating.

Another factor that emerges in Niebuhr's response to Barth is a criterion for regarding some biblical texts as more authoritative than others. In part, he has already hinted at an aspect of the criterion. Those texts that are less clearly time bound express, by definition, truths that are more timeless, and so authoritative, than texts that are heavily laden with cultural and historical sentiments. A case in point is the issue in 1 Cor. 11, concerning women praying with uncovered heads, clearly a time-bound practice (conceded even by Barth) that no longer applies—that is, that no longer has authority.[49] Niebuhr goes on to conclude: "There are in short very good reasons for preferring some texts of Scripture to others and for judging them all from the standpoint of 'the mind of Christ.' We do that at our hazard of course; but the hazards of Biblical literalism are certainly greater."[50] The criterion for assigning more or less authority to biblical texts is articulated by Niebuhr as "the mind of Christ," a Pauline phrase (see Rom. 8:6, 12:2; 1 Cor. 1:10; Phil. 2:1–5) that Niebuhr recognized is not easily applied as a general principle, although it was one with which he was willing to live.

For Niebuhr, "rightly conceived Scriptural authority is meant *merely* to guard the truth of the gospel in which all truth is fulfilled and all corruptions of truth are negated."[51] Thus, in Niebuhr's view, both orthodox Christianity and liberal Christianity have extreme positions in regard to the authority of Scripture, for the former fails to take adequate account of the historical relativity of the writings of Scripture and thus makes absolutes out of relativities, while the latter fails to recognize adequately the extent to which through Scripture God discloses God's self and God's actions in and among human beings in a way that transcends all historical relativities. Scripture is meant to uphold the truth of the gospel, and the truth of the gospel concerns, not the authority of Scripture, but the transcendent power of God's love in Christ.

Reinhold Niebuhr's Hermeneutics

Nowhere in his writings does Niebuhr explicitly present his hermeneutics, his principles of interpretating the Bible.[52] Still, I would propose that the overall approach Niebuhr uses to interpret Scripture can be summarized in the term "symbolic." Niebuhr uses this word incessantly when talking about Scripture, but getting a handle on what he means by "symbolic" is another matter. Niebuhr's approach reminds one of Tillich's symbolic interpretation of Scripture. Both emphasize the need to "deliteralize" Scripture in order to get at its meaning. For Tillich, Scripture contains symbolic language in that the meaning of Scripture lies over and above what it says. Scripture is symbolic and not merely a sign, for in pointing beyond itself, it also participates in that to which it points.[53]

For Niebuhr, biblical symbols "deal with the relation of time and eternity, and seek to point to the ultimate from the standpoint of the conditioned."[54] For example, the second coming of Christ is symbolic of "faith in the sufficiency of God's sovereignty over the world and history, and in the final supremacy of life over all the forces of self-love."[55] The resurrection is symbolic of the significance of nature in human individuality and in all of history past and future.[56]

For Niebuhr, it is important to take the biblical symbols "seriously but not literally,"[57] and he points out the dangers of either taking them literally or not seriously enough. The symbols cannot be taken literally because, as finite creatures, our minds cannot comprehend the eternal God who transcends and fulfills history. If the symbols are taken literally, then the proper dialectic relation between time and eternity is falsified, and the fulfillment of history in Christ's return becomes simply another point in time rather than the vindication of God over all of time and history. And yet the symbols must be taken seriously because as pointers they express "the self-transcendent character of historical existence and point to its eternal ground."[58] If the symbols are not taken seriously enough, then the biblical dialectic is destroyed, for then the eternal does not fulfill history but rather destroys history.[59] In short, if the symbols are taken literally, then history is not taken seriously enough.

For Niebuhr, this hermeneutic of symbolic interpretation is most appropriate to the character of the Bible itself. Since the Bible is both historically relative and yet "the record of those events in history in which faith discerns the self-disclosure of God," a hermeneutic is needed that takes into account both of these factors, and he sees symbolic interpretation as the best tool by which to achieve this goal.[60] Any hermeneutic that flattens out a serious but nonliteral interpretation of the Bible endangers the "biblical dialectic" of time and eternity, history and superhistory.[61]

From Niebuhr's perspective, Scripture itself testifies to the primacy of symbolic interpretation. For example, regarding Eph. 4:1–10, which talks about Christ descending to the lower parts of the earth and ascending above all heavens, Niebuhr writes that the "conception of the relation of history to the perfection of Christ is stated symbolically in very clear terms."[62] Peter's reaction to Jesus' prediction of his suffering in Matt. 16:22, "God forbid, Lord! This shall never happen to you," may also "be regarded as symbolic of the resistance to the truth of Christianity which develops not only outside, but inside of, the Christian faith."[63] In addition, Niebuhr sees the irony that is present throughout the Bible as "the symbol of the potential contradiction between all historic achievement and the final meaning of life."[64] Since, for Niebuhr, Scripture itself is self-interpretive in symbolic terms, it only follows that symbolic interpretation of Scripture is the most appropriate hermeneutic.

Perhaps he best articulates his convictions regarding symbolic interpretation in his sermon "As Deceivers, Yet True," taking the sermon title from Paul's remarks in 2 Cor. 6:8.[65] Here, Niebuhr states that "what is true in the Christian religion can be expressed only in symbols which contain a certain degree of provisional and superficial deception."[66] This observation applies also to the Bible, the primary sourcebook of Christian religious symbols. All the central Christian doctrines which Niebuhr sees grounded in the biblical account—creation, the fall, incarnation, redemption, last judgment, and resurrection—are symbols that point beyond themselves to God's transcendent presence in human history. The danger is in construing these dynamic symbols as static rational truths. Thus, for instance, "the Christian religion is always tempted to insist that belief in creation also involves belief in an actual forming of man out of a lump of clay, or in an actual creative activity of six days. It is to this temptation that biblical literalism succumbs."[67]

Niebuhr's interpretive approach, then, stresses the symbolic character of the Bible. The Bible relates the truth about God's dealings with humanity, and humanity's responses to God, but this truth is also deceptive, for biblical symbols are polyvalent and never capture the full truth of what they symbolize. They point to the truth, but they also have the capacity to deceive. They are and they are not truthful, much like a house of mirrors. For Niebuhr, then, the most appropriate hermeneutic in approaching the Bible is one that is commensurate with the character of the biblical account, a symbolic hermeneutic for a symbolic witness.

One additional note regarding Niebuhr's interpretive approach is significant here. Niebuhr states that what the Bible "discerns are actions of God which clarify the confrontation of man by God in the realm of the personal and individual moral life."[68] What stands out is Niebuhr's emphasis on the "personal and individual moral life," the relationship between God and individual persons, especially as persons find themselves confronted by God through God's actions. This relationship between God and individuals brings to mind the ideal love ethic of Jesus, which is attainable only by individuals in terms of sacrifice and forgiveness. Completely lacking in Niebuhr's hermeneutical approach to the Bible, then, is any sense of the Bible as an expression of a community of believers or of contemporary Christians as forming an interpretive community that reads and uses the Bible together. When it comes to the Bible, for Niebuhr, everything revolves around "personal and individual moral life." Indeed, in the essay "Reinhold Niebuhr's Contribution to Christian Social Ethics," John Bennett, Niebuhr's longtime colleague at Union Theological Seminary in New York, comments: "Niebuhr is basically a theologian who sees the implications of his theology for Christian ethics, but he has never addressed himself primarily to the Church as Church."[69]

For Niebuhr, the primary forum of discourse about Christian ethics is, not the Christian community per se, but public discourse about ethics in general. As Michael Cartwright rightly observes: "Niebuhr effectively moves the *locus* of Christian ethics *outside* the context of the Church as a historic community."[70] Niebuhr emphasizes the individual and personal moral implications of Scripture, then, in a way that disembodies the believer from the communal context of Christian moral discourse.

Reinhold Niebuhr and the Significance of Scripture for Ethics

As we have seen, Niebuhr is very clear about inappropriate ways of appealing to Scripture for ethical guidelines. Scripture is not a sourcebook of social, economic, political, and scientific knowledge that can be flatly applied to a given situation. Scripture does not provide a set of moral codes Christians can follow, although throughout the history of Christianity attempts to force Scripture into this mold have been made repeatedly. Given these limitations, what would be an appropriate way of appealing to Scripture for ethical guidance? According to Niebuhr, Scripture is ethically most relevant insofar as it points to the *ideal* of the love ethic of Jesus, from which Christian ethics derives its starting point.

Throughout his writings, and particularly in *An Interpretation of Christian Ethics*, Niebuhr appeals to Jesus as portrayed in the Gospels as the source of the Christian understanding of love, pointing especially to Jesus' sacrificial love for others, so clearly demonstrated by the symbol of the cross. And yet Niebuhr's appeals to Jesus tend to be much more abstract than concrete. Because he is so convinced that Jesus did not provide a prudential ethic, he says very little by way of the practical implications of Jesus' love ethic for the everyday life of the Christian. What he does say is put almost entirely in negative terms. Indeed, he states that "the ethic of Jesus does not deal at all with the immediate moral problem of every human life."[71]

Far from addressing the day-to-day ethical problems faced by the Christian, for Niebuhr the love ethic of Jesus "has only a vertical dimension between the loving will of God and the will of man."[72] Thus the love ethic points only to the individual's relationship with the transcendent God beyond history. It has nothing to say about the horizontal dimension of human existence, the social and communal dimension. It does have practical implications, but these cannot be readily spelled out in concrete terms, for to do so is to threaten the ideal character of this impossible ethic. For example, in commenting upon Jesus' admonitions to love one's enemies, to forgive "seventy times seven," and the like, Niebuhr says: "The modern pulpit would be saved from much sentimentality if the thousands of sermons which are annually preached upon these texts would contain some suggestions of the impossibility of these ethical demands for natural man in his immediate situations."[73] Or again, as he puts it rather clearly, "The ethic of Jesus may offer valuable insights to and sources of criticism for a prudential social ethic which deals with present realities; but no such social ethic can be directly derived from a pure religious ethic."[74]

Yet, although Niebuhr sees the starting point of Christian ethics in general terms as the love ethic of Jesus, he also makes clear the necessity of developing Christian ethics beyond the solitary confines of the biblical materials. For Niebuhr, this is simply a matter of course. An adequate Christian ethic "naturally . . . must avail itself of non-Biblical instruments of calculation, chiefly a rational calculation of competing rights and interests and an empirical analysis of the structures of nature, the configurations of history and the complexities of a given situation in which decisions must be made."[75] Thus, the viewpoint of the Bible has, as Niebuhr puts it, "perpetual relevance"[76] but not exclusive or necessarily primary relevance for Christian ethics.

From Niebuhr's perspective, there was a real and present danger in the neo-orthodox theology, especially from such theologians as Barth, who sought to dispense with nonbiblical sources of judgment in providing guidelines for Christian ethics. According to Niebuhr, "the primary peril is that the wisdom of the Gospel is emptied of meaning by setting it into contradiction to the wisdom of the world and denying that the coherences and realms of meaning which the cultural disciplines rightfully analyze and establish have any relation to the gospel."[77] Niebuhr sharply criticized Barth's approach to Scripture. From Niebuhr's perspective, Barth exhibited "a kind of irresponsibility toward the problems of interpreting the Scriptures honestly in terms of the knowledge which historical sciences had brought to the analysis of the books of the Old and New Testaments."[78]

Niebuhr viewed the error of exclusive Biblicism as far more dangerous than the failure to focus sufficiently on the Bible. He even termed such misuse of the Bible as "Bibliolatry"—worship of the book instead of the God to whom the book pointed.[79] It is telling that in the subject index to Niebuhr's *The Nature and Destiny of Man*, one finds no entry for "Scripture" or "Bible" but only an entry for "Bibliolatry"!

Far from detracting from the proper development of Christian ethics, non-biblical sources, and particularly philosophical and sociological ones, provide a richness and depth to Christian ethical discussions. As Niebuhr observes, "A vital Christian faith must undertake a constant commerce with the culture of its day, borrowing and rejecting according to its best judgment."[80] The question that arises here, of course, is what the criteria are that determine the "best judgment" of Christian faith.[81] By pointing to experience as a source of judgment, Niebuhr answers this question only in part. The relevance of both biblical and nonbiblical insights about life is in part determined by human experience.[82] Does experience validate these insights? Is one led to a more faithful life through their application? Thus, experience helps the believer sift through non-biblical as well as biblical materials in formulating Christian ethics.

Overall, then, the Bible functions as one resource for Christian ethics, providing abstract and symbolic ideals that serve to inspire and to judge proximate attempts to embody and live out the gospel in everyday life. As with his use of nonbiblical materials, Niebuhr is extremely eclectic in his use of biblical texts in this regard.

Critical Evaluation

Niebuhr's use of the Bible elicits both admiration and frustration when viewed from a perspective at the end of the twentieth century. In general, one admires his emphasis on the historically conditioned character of the biblical texts and his endeavor to take the Bible seriously through his symbolic interpretation. One also admires his poetic and often powerful use of biblical images. He is at his best as a preacher.

But the limitations of his use of the Bible are, in my estimate, somewhat greater. I would identify three serious problems in his use of the Bible. First, and most serious, is the artificial character of the symbolic constructs he employs, prophetic religion and the love ethic of Jesus. As for his notion of prophetic religion, he tends to emphasize the judging and transcendent aspects of the prophets to the neglect of their messages of mercy and grace, which stress God's closeness.[83] He overlooks the hopefulness and vision of a prophet like Hosea or Ezekiel. Thus, his monochrome portrait of prophetic religion neglects the wider and more diverse character of the prophetic witnesses. Even more problematic, Niebuhr focuses on the prophets to the exclusion of all else within the Hebrew Scriptures. His canon within the canon is very narrow and selective in this regard. To be sure, one reason for Niebuhr's emphasis on the texts of prophetic judgment can be found in the audience he was addressing, generally those in positions of power and authority rather than those who were the downtrodden and the poor of his day (his Detroit parish days notwithstanding). But it remains striking how little he drew on the legal materials from the Hebrew Scriptures.

As for his notion of the love ethic of Jesus, several concerns arise. To begin, Niebuhr seems to have a monolithic view of Jesus that is not borne out by the New Testament witness. He shows little to no awareness of the very different portraits of Jesus that emerge from the different Gospels. Rather, he lumps them all together in a rather artificial manner (as was admittedly characteristic of early-twentieth-century liberal interpretations of the Gospels). Further, he tends to fuse the historical Jesus with belief in Jesus as the Christ, showing an insufficient awareness of how even the Jesus of the Gospels is already an ideal figure redacted from earlier tradition. While it is important not to be anachronistic in criticizing Niebuhr, it does appear that he paid very little attention to the substance of most biblical scholarship of his day.

Still more serious is Niebuhr's portrait of Jesus in singularly individualistic terms. He completely ignores the social dimension of Jesus' ministry, even among the disciples. And so Niebuhr wrongly construes Jesus' love ethic in exclusively vertical terms. The result is a liberal caricature of the heroic individualism of Jesus as he dies on the cross. One final problem here is that Niebuhr flattens out the eschatological character of Jesus' ministry, interpreting it in symbolic terms that obscure the historical concreteness of Jesus' ministry.

In short, for all of Niebuhr's emphasis on history, he has an insufficiently historical awareness of the biblical texts. Ironically, he did not emphasize history enough. If he had, he would have been more aware of the tremendous problems with his constructs of prophetic religion and the love ethic of Jesus. As it is, if these constructs are undermined as being too artificial, then the value of Niebuhr's appropriation of Scripture for ethics is seriously limited.

The second problem with Niebuhr's use of the Bible is that he engages too often in what amounts to prooftexting. Of course, he has much company here. He tends not to allow the biblical writers to speak on their own behalf, due largely to his lack of attention to exegesis of texts. In a similar vein, H. N. Wieman makes the following sharp criticism of Niebuhr:

> Niebuhr claims to base his faith upon the Bible and calls it Biblical faith. But a careful examination shows that he corrects the Bible according to his own convictions. According to Niebuhr many truths of the Bible are presented in the form of myths. But myths are deceptive, he admits, and even Jesus and Paul were deceived by them, although he claims that he has penetrated the deception and found the hidden truth. His tendency for developing general notions from biblical texts with little or no specific analysis of the nuances of the texts results in readings of texts that subvert his appeals to the Bible.[84]

Finally, a third problem is that there appear to be few controls for determining the symbolic character of biblical texts.[85] By speaking so often about biblical symbols, Niebuhr introduces a rather arbitrary construal of the meaning of biblical texts. Niebuhr does not appeal to the Christian community, neither in general nor to any specific church or denomination, as a forum that might exercise some control over the interpretation and appropriation of biblical symbols. In addition, Niebuhr again pays insufficient attention to the historic and social communal contexts that gave rise to the present shape of the biblical texts in the first place.

To conclude, although Niebuhr argued that one should take the Bible seriously but not literally, he perhaps did not take the Bible seriously enough when using it in his reflections on Christian ethics, a tendency evidenced especially in his reluctance to allow the diversity and historicity of the biblical witness to stand.

three

H. RICHARD NIEBUHR

Confessing with Scripture

H. Richard Niebuhr (1894–1962) is generally recognized as one of the foremost Protestant theologians/ethicists in the twentieth century, and his
continuing influence is readily apparent as we come to its close.[1] Niebuhr
sought to reflect on Christian faith and on the Christian Scriptures, quite self-
consciously, from where he perceived himself to be situated, as a twentieth-
century Christian moral philosopher convinced in a fundamental way of God's
sovereignty, of humanity's lostness, sinfulness, and idolatry in response to God,
and of God's graciousness toward human beings made manifest in the person of
Jesus Christ. Another fundamental conviction Niebuhr held was the radically
historical character of all human existence, including his own existence and the
existence of Christianity in all its variations.[2] Niebuhr approached Scripture as
a witness to God's sovereignty and grace and to human sinfulness, and as witness
to and participant in the radically historical character of human existence in all
its faithfulness and sinfulness alike.[3]

Niebuhr knew Scripture not only as a Christian academic moral philosopher but also as one who was dedicated to the church. This dedication can be
seen in his own time as a local church pastor at Walnut Park Evangelical
Church in St. Louis, Missouri, from 1916 to 1919, and especially in his commitment to training Christian ministers. From 1919 to 1922 he served as a professor
of theology at Eden Theological Seminary.[4] In 1922 he moved to New Haven,
Connecticut, and in two years earned his bachelor of divinity and his Ph.D.
from Yale University (his dissertation was on "Ernst Troeltsch's Philosophy of
Religion"). During this time he also pastored a Congregational church in neighboring Clinton, Connecticut. Upon graduation, he was invited to stay at Yale
Divinity School and to teach—of all things—New Testament theology, and so
to take over some of F. C. Porter's courses. He chose instead to become Presi-
dent of Elmhurst College in Illinois (his undergraduate alma mater), where he
stayed from 1924 to 1927, after which he returned as professor of theology to
Eden Theological Seminary (1927–31). In 1931, Niebuhr made his final move, to

Yale Divinity School, where he remained until his unexpected death on 5 July 1962, a year before he expected to retire.

In addition to spending most of his career teaching in a seminary and training future clergypersons, Niebuhr showed his added commitment to the church by accepting the role of director for the study of theological education in the United States and Canada (1954–56). This appointment involved visits (by him or by his staff) to more than ninety theological seminaries, the supervision of the writing of two books from the project,[5] and his own writing of the seminal volume for the project, *The Purpose of the Church and Its Ministry: Reflections on the Aims of Theological Education.*

Niebuhr was thus at the forefront of offering critical reflections on the Christian faith and on the training of church leaders in the mid–twentieth century. These reflections have continued to shape in significant ways theological and ethical thinking at the end of the twentieth century, including reflection on Scripture and ethics.[6]

Biblical Texts Used by H. Richard Niebuhr

We may begin with an editorial note by H. Richard Niebuhr's son, Richard R. Niebuhr, in the posthumously published book *Faith on Earth*. The note reads as follows: "It seems that in the draft stage of writing the author quoted the Bible from memory and drew upon several translations, including Luther's translation into the German, the Authorized (King James) Version and the Revised Standard Version (RSV)."[7] One may presume that Niebuhr's style of quoting Scripture for *Faith on Earth* was similar to his manner of referring to Scripture in most of his other writings. Significantly, Niebuhr appears to have quoted the Bible often from memory. Indeed, many times Niebuhr quotes a biblical passage and refers to the biblical book (or not) without reference to chapter and verse.[8] That Niebuhr often quoted from memory, especially when he does not give a specific reference, indicates that he knew the Bible, or at least certain sections of it, very well. This observation also indicates perhaps that Niebuhr's reflections on the Bible fell into a certain pattern of citing favorite texts, some evidence of which we will see here.[9]

Niebuhr seldom refers to Old Testament texts outside his "Introduction to Biblical Ethics" essay, and then mostly in his book *Radical Monotheism and Western Culture.*[10] Niebuhr's relatively infrequent use of the Old Testament in no way indicates any depreciation or devaluation of the Hebrew Scriptures. Indeed, the Hebrew Scriptures are crucial for Niebuhr in several respects. First, the Old Testament bears witness in fundamental ways to the character and identity of God as experienced by the Israelites. In his book on theological education, *The Purpose of the Church and Its Ministry*, for example, when discussing signs of new vitality in seminary education (writing in 1956), Niebuhr states:

[T]he study of the Old Testament has become a fascinating and exciting busi-
ness in school after school. . . . Perhaps the explanation is to be found in the
hints some students give of the extent to which the Old Testament has become
for them an introduction to the fundamental problems of man's life before
God, a revelation of the greatness, freedom and power of the Sovereign Lord,
of the meaning of the people of God and of human history.[11]

Although Niebuhr reports this as an observation about seminary students, it also
represents, I would argue, Niebuhr's own assessment of the significance of the
Old Testament. This becomes clear in his book *The Responsible Self*, where,
reflecting on "the logic of Hebrew ethics as that ethics runs through all the
pages of Hebrew Scriptures and through the tragic, yet wonderful story of this
people of God," and reflecting specifically on Isaiah 10, he writes:

It is an ethos of laws, to be sure, but an ethos which centers even more in
responsiveness to omnificense, to the all-doer. There is no evil in the city but
the Lord has done it. No nation exists that he has not called into being. . . .
To discern the ways of God not in supernatural but in all natural and historic
events, to respond to his intention present in and beyond and through all finite
intentions, that is the way of responsibility to God.[12]

Though he infrequently makes direct reference to the Hebrew Scriptures, then,
Niebuhr does see a generic character to these writings that points faithfully to
God and God's presence in the world, which calls forth human response.

Second, for Niebuhr it is significant that Christians believe in a Jewish
messianic figure for whom the Hebrew Scriptures were the only Scriptures. He
recognizes that he can only interpret the Hebrew Scriptures with the eyes of the
Christian that he is, but he goes on to say that his interpretation

is that of a Christian who is indebted to the Jew, because his Christ was a Jew;
who must understand his Christ with the aid of the Hebrew Scriptures; and
who, when he asks what God is intending now in preserving this people against
Christian and pseudo-Christian and pagan attacks, must answer: They are given
to us for a sign; they point us to universal responsibility. They are, whatever
their own intentions may be, our saviors from a polytheism into which we
Gentile nations are forever tempted to fall.[13]

Thus, for Niebuhr it is not just the continuing significance of the Hebrew Scriptures that is important for Christians and Christian faith, it is also the continuing
presence of the Jewish people, the "descendants" of these Scriptures, that is of
great theological and sociohistorical significance. Here, then, we already have a
hint of the close relationship Niebuhr sees between the Scriptures and specific
communities of faith in history, a point to be addressed at greater length below.

Even given the significance Niebuhr attributes to the Old Testament, however, I think it fair to say that in the face of the biblical interpretation current
from the 1930s through the 1950s, which was especially under the sway of and
in response to Barth and Bultmann, Niebuhr tended to shy away somewhat from
using the Old Testament. In particular, the reduction of the Old Testament to

law, especially in the German Lutheran tradition, with a resultant emphasis on an ethics of obedience, on deontology, is a tradition Niebuhr resisted but did not fully overcome. Thus, on the one hand, he criticized Barth and Bultmann for reading the Bible, and especially the Old Testament, in terms of law and obedience (notwithstanding Barth's efforts to transform law into gospel and commandment into permission and Bultmann's attempt to transform eschatology into an ethics of radical obedience).[14] On the other hand, however, Niebuhr himself saw much of the Old Testament (as well as some of the New Testament) as the expression of ancient Israelite (and early Christian) communities who assumed—from Niebuhr's perspective wrongly—that an ethics of obedience was the most faithful response to God. They assumed that

> [r]ight life is obedient life, obedient to right rules; sin is transgression. . . . With the symbol of law and transgression firmly established, the development of ideas of universal law and of a universal judgment and of an eternal punishment or reward seem logically to follow, when the scene of our human action is understood as that of the universal society under law in infinite time. . . . And yet it is notorious that paradoxes accumulate for us as we try to understand ourselves in society and time before God, with the use of this symbolism.[15]

And so, for Niebuhr, the problem of overemphasis on a legalist deontological reading of the Old Testament rests both with contemporary interpreters and with the text itself, with the ancient Israelite communities who expressed their understanding of God and of themselves in the Hebrew Scriptures.[16]

As for the New Testament, Niebuhr's emphasis falls clearly on Matthew (47 citations), John (47 citations), Romans (31 citations), and 1 John (47 citations), as references to these writings make up 172 of his 229 references to the New Testament. In Matthew, Niebuhr refers primarily to the Sermon on the Mount (Matt. 5–7: 30 references), especially in his essay "Introduction to Biblical Ethics," where he offers his interpretation of the Sermon on the Mount.[17] From Paul's Letter to the Romans, Niebuhr focuses on 3:21–8:39 and on chapter 13. Most significant, however, is the heavy emphasis Niebuhr places on the Johannine writings, particularly on 1 John and the Gospel of John, in both cases especially in constructing typologies for his book *Christ and Culture*. For Niebuhr, 1 John represents the type of "Christ Against Culture," whereas the Gospel of John represents the type of "Christ the Transformer of Culture," the latter clearly representing Niebuhr's own understanding of the most appropriate model.

In the Gospel of John, it is noteworthy that Niebuhr draws most heavily on the last discourse material in John 13–17 (16 references), primarily because he sees this material as pointing to the kind of inward personal and communal transformation that will lead to the transformation of culture. I will return to a discussion of his use of Romans, 1 John, and John in a further consideration of the use of the Bible in *Christ and Culture*.

How H. Richard Niebuhr Uses Scripture

One of the hallmarks of Niebuhr's approach to theology and ethics (especially in contrast to deontological or teleological theological ethics) is his constant insistence that the first question and indeed the last question is always What is going on? (What is happening? What is God doing?), not What *should* I/we do?[18] To ask what one should do before one has reflected on what is going on is to ask a premature question, for one can only have some sense of what is fitting or responsible in light of an understanding of what is happening in any given present situation. I mention this significant feature of Niebuhr's theology here because the question of what is going on is applicable also to Niebuhr's understanding of and uses of Scripture. Niebuhr never makes the argument that Scripture says "x" and so we should do "x" without further reflection. Instead, Niebuhr begins with reflection on historical situations, the situations that gave rise to Scripture in the first place, and the subsequent history of situations in which Scripture was read and employed. With Niebuhr, then, the first question is not How should Scripture be used? but instead, What is going on? What is God doing in Scripture? And in light of what is going on, how do we respond in radical faith?

Indeed, Niebuhr saw Scripture itself as having the same approach, asking first what was going on and only secondly what one should do in response. For example, regarding the prophet Amos, Niebuhr states: "Amos' ethics begins with consideration of God's nature and activity. . . . this divine determinist begins with 'what is' rather than with 'what ought to be' and derives his 'ought' from his convictions about reality."[19] In the same vein, the "mind of Jesus" was

> directed not in the first instance to what man ought to do and in the second place to what aid he might receive from God in doing what he ought to do, but rather toward what God was doing and what man ought to do in the light of God's doing. God's doing—not what God ought to do in order that he might live up to the expectations men had of him—stands in the center of Jesus' mind.[20]

Niebuhr's viewing of Scripture with these questions in mind, of what God was doing and how humans should then respond, I would argue, is central to his approach to and use of Scripture.

What Is Happening in and with Scripture?

To ask what is happening in and with Scripture is to ask about the character of Scripture. It is surely to ask about the Bible's contents, but even more it is to ask about the function of Scripture. What is happening with Scripture? What is the Bible? Only when one has a sense of what is going on with Scripture can one then begin to address the question of how to use Scripture, or of how it has been used.

WHAT SCRIPTURE IS NOT

Niebuhr spends nearly as much time stating what Scripture is not as he does addressing the question in a more positive and constructive vein. That Niebuhr felt so obliged to criticize various approaches to Scripture indicates how problematic he found many of the perspectives of his day, especially in the 1940s and 1950s and in response both to classic liberalism and to neo-orthodoxy. As James Gustafson has pointed out in a brief section on Niebuhr's understanding of the place of Scripture in Christian ethics in his well-known introduction to Niebuhr's *The Responsible Self,* Niebuhr was critical of two forms of Biblicism: the approaches to Scripture of both classic liberalism and of neo-orthodoxy.[21] He criticized the former for offering an abstracted and romanticized love ethic drawn in a narrow way from the teachings of Jesus. (And here Niebuhr clearly included the theological appropriation of the Bible by his more famous brother, Reinhold Niebuhr.)[22] He criticized the latter for raising up the Bible too highly as the exclusive source of knowledge for human moral responsibility. (Here Niebuhr had especially the work of Karl Barth in mind.) Niebuhr was particularly concerned with this latter form of Biblicism, for it tended toward a theology which "does not make God so much as Scriptures the object of its interest, and which depends for law and grace not on Father, Son and Holy Spirit but on Bible."[23]

Perhaps Niebuhr was particularly both aware and wary of uncritically Biblicist views of Scripture because of his commitment to and intensive study of theological education. In his book *The Purpose of the Church and Its Ministry,* Niebuhr observes that while some theological education "suffers from inadequate attention to the Biblical history of divine words and deeds[,] there is more that suffers from so close a concentration on these that the One to whom Scriptures bear witness is overshadowed by the witness" (p. 43). That there are significant relations between Scripture and revelation Niebuhr is sure, but, he argues:

> it is not necessary to await the outcome of a long debate before one arrives at the conclusion that whatever else is true about these relations, the identification of the Scriptures with God is an error, a denial of the content of the Scriptures themselves. To give final devotion to the book is to deny the final claim of God; to look for the mighty deeds of God only in the records of the past is to deny that he is the living God; to love the book as the source of strength and of salvation is to practice an idolatry that can bring only confusion into life. Without the Bible, as without the Church, Christians do not exist and cannot carry on their work; but it is one thing to recognize the indispensability of these means, another thing to make means into ends. (pp. 43–44)

In Niebuhr's view, the danger of Biblicism was so acute in theological education, in contemporary theology, and in the (Protestant) church in general that he saw Biblicism as one of the foremost distortions of genuine Christian faith in the church and in theology. "Denominationalism not the denominations; ecclesiasticism not the churches; Biblicism not the Bible; Christism not Jesus

Christ; these represent the chief present perversions and confusions in Church and theology" (p. 46).

SCRIPTURE AS INTERNAL HISTORY OF FAITH

To understand the significance of Scripture for Niebuhr, it is necessary to begin with his understanding of history and of faith, and of the relation between the two. Scripture is a historical document, but it is also a document of faith. Niebuhr correlates history and faith in his important development of the distinction between internal history and external history, especially in his book *The Meaning of Revelation.*[24] An extended discussion is not necessary here, but simply put, internal history means to look with, to participate with, the subject being considered, whereas external history means to look at, to objectify, a given subject.

For Niebuhr, internal history signifies an I–Thou relationship, borrowing (as Niebuhr does) Buber's language, whereas external history signifies an I–it relationship.[25] Internal history is personal and involves selves; external history is impersonal and involves things. Internal history is a matter of participation; external history is a matter of being a spectator and a relatively dispassionate observer. Internal history revolves around one's immediate experiences; external history deals with mediated perceptions of others' experiences. Internal history is the realm of faith and revelation; external history is the realm of objective and detached reporting.

The distinction between internal and external history should not, however, be overdrawn, since each is necessary to the other, and both are but different aspects or perspectives for approaching the same subject. An appreciation of internal history is essential for getting at the heart of the subject, but external history is an important reality check, as it were, on the claims of internal history.[26]

The significance of Niebuhr's distinction between internal and external history for understanding his approach to Scripture is that for Niebuhr, Scripture is a record, an embodiment of internal history. Scripture has certainly been the object of historical-critical investigation, and thus has been approached especially over the last two hundred years with the perspective of external history. But to understand and to appreciate the actual character of Scripture is to recognize Scripture as internal history. As Niebuhr puts it:

> The relevance of this distinction between two histories to the subject of revelation must now have become apparent. When the evangelists of the New Testament and their successors pointed to history as the starting point of their faith and of their understanding of the world it was internal history that they indicated. They did not speak of events, as impersonally apprehended, but rather of what had happened to them in their community. . . . Such history, to be sure, can only be confessed by the community, and in this sense it is esoteric. One cannot point to historic events in the lives of selves as though they were visible to any external point of view. Isaiah cannot say that in the year King

> Uzziah died God became visible in the temple nor Paul affirm that Jesus the
> Lord appears to travelers on the Damascus road. Neither will any concentration
> of attention on Isaiah and Paul, any detailed understanding of their historical
> situation, enable the observer to see what they saw. One must look with them
> and not at them to verify their visions, participate in their history rather than
> regard it if one would apprehend what they apprehended. The history of the
> inner life can only be confessed by selves who speak of what happened to them
> in the community of other selves.[27]

Thus Scripture records the internal history of various communities of faith as
they have encountered God in their histories. In the case of the Old Testament,
of course, the internal history stretches over hundreds of years and across rather
different forms of communities, whereas in the case of the New Testament, the
internal history expresses a much more cohesive set of faith communities over a
much shorter period of time.

The variety of faith communities across time and space and culture represented in Scripture begs the question as to the unity of the Bible as a whole,
and so the unity of the internal history found there. Niebuhr is well aware of
the problem of the cohesiveness of the different inner histories present in the
Bible, but he is much more impressed with the unity of Scripture overall than
he is bothered by its great diversity. In his essay "Introduction to Biblical Ethics,"
Niebuhr addresses this question directly:

> The question has often been raised whether there is enough unity in the
> thought of the Scriptures on any subject, including morality, to permit a sum-
> mary statement of Biblical ideas. . . . Both uncritical worshippers of the Bible
> and equally uncritical detractors have made such uses of this variety that the
> impression of diversity in scriptural ethics has been exaggerated. . . . Yet the
> unity of Scriptures in moral teaching, as well as in other respects, is more
> impressive and effective than its diversity. Understanding of that unity doubtless
> requires repeated and careful reading of these writings.[28]

Niebuhr does not go on to say exactly wherein lies the unity of the inner
history recorded in the biblical record, and yet from his writings as a whole, he
clearly sees unity in such notions as radical monotheism, the overwhelming
transcendence and grace of God, and God's continued call for internal human
transformation in the face of human sinfulness. Perhaps in part, Niebuhr emphasized the unity of the Bible because without some semblance of unity, there
would be no embodied internal history for Christian faith to look to.

> Without the Bible and the rites of the institutional church the inner history of
> the Christian community could not continue, however impossible it is to iden-
> tify the memory of that community with the documents. Though we cannot
> point to what we mean by revelation by directing attention to the historic facts
> as embodied and as regarded from without, we can have no continuing inner
> history through which to point without embodiment.[29]

The Bible is thus essential to the continuation of the story of Christian faith's
internal history, both communally and personally, even though the Bible is not

to be confused with the living story, the living faith itself, and especially not with the living God.

It is one thing, however, to talk about Scripture as the embodiment of the internal history of Christian faith; it is another to present the actual substance of this internal history. Of course, according to Niebuhr, the internal history of faith is truly accessible only to those who stand within that history themselves, who identify with it and take it on as their own rather than standing outside, for one cannot get at the substance of internal history through the approach of external history. With this caveat in mind, what then, for Niebuhr, is the substantive content of Christian faith's internal history, and how does this story relate to what may be learned by looking at this faith with the additional eyes of external history? What does he see when he looks *with* Isaiah, *with* Amos, *with* Jesus, *with* Scripture?

He sees, first of all, a glimpse of God's dealings with human beings, and thus a glimpse of God's dealings with himself as a believer in a community of believers along with Isaiah and Paul. In Scripture, he encounters with Isaiah the sovereignty of God, God's desire to save Israel, and God's call for Israel to reform in the face of the Assyrian invasion (Isa. 10).[30] In Scripture, he understands with Amos "that God rules and that he is one, universal and intensely active. He is one, that is to say, is constant, unwavering, reliable."[31] With the Mosaic covenant recorded in Exodus, he sees that God is on the side of the weak (as with the Israelites in slavery), and that God's justice means ultimate destruction for those who oppress the poor and the weak.[32]

With Jesus, he shares the conviction that "God now rules and that the actuality of his rule and its justice will therefore be made quite evident."[33] With Jesus, he sees God's utter mercy and grace poured out upon the entire creation, upon the just and the unjust alike.[34] He sees God's call to embrace one's neighbor, even one's enemy, in God's grace; and he sees an emphasis on the inward transformation of human beings in their attitudes toward one another. In short, looking with Jesus as he is presented in the Gospels means recognizing God's spirit at work for radical transformation among people in the world, for "the image of the world economy that is in Jesus' mind is never that of the market place where men must pay for all they receive; it is that of the home where gifts are given before they are deserved and where the same spirit of graciousness is expected in the recipients."[35]

In looking with Jesus to God, it is important to point out that Niebuhr primarily looks both at and with the Christ of faith, not the historical Jesus. The Christ of faith is a significant aspect of the dynamic of internal history, whereas the historical Jesus is a matter of external history. Though there is a relationship between the Christ of faith and the historical Jesus, and though a real particular individual historical figure stands behind the Christ of faith, Niebuhr believes we have access only to the Christ of faith and not to the historical Jesus. Indeed, Niebuhr states, one of the results of historical-critical research on the Bible is "that we cannot know an historical Jesus save as we look through the history and with the history of the community that loved and worshipped him."[36] When one reflects on the life of faith in and with Jesus, "we find that what is present is not a Jesus of history but the Christ of faith, not Jesus incarnate, but the risen Lord."[37]

And yet Niebuhr is not in any way docetic in his approach to Jesus. Jesus was a real historical person who lived, but what we know of him is the effect he had on others, reflected in their faith in God through him and in their witness to his faithfulness. Thus, writes Niebuhr in *Faith on Earth*:

> The Christ of faith, that is, the Christ who has been introduced into our personal histories by the faith of those who trust him and are loyal to him in his loyalty, is a specific individual figure. We meet him in the company of those who believe in him: not as an empty point on which their eyes are focused in trust and faithfulness, not as an indefinable companion, but as a specific figure.[38]

When Niebuhr looks at this specific figure of Christ along with Paul, for example, he finds a faith that makes no claims to universal empire but, with Christ, empties itself out in obedience and service to God for the sake of others.[39] Paul, like Christ (and like Isaiah and Jeremiah), stresses radical internal transformation of the believer before God and neighbor. Such transformation is made fully possible, though, because of Christ.[40]

Such is the substance of Scripture as the internal history of faith's experience of God's revelation. Although Niebuhr uses Scripture as witness to faith's internal history, he still sees an important role for approaching Scripture with the eyes of external history as well, for looking *at* Scripture in addition to looking *with* it. Historical-critical approaches to the Bible in particular have helped to remind reasoning faith that the Scriptures are fundamentally human documents with human foibles. As he puts it in *The Meaning of Revelation*: "[E]xternal histories have helped to keep the church from exalting itself as though its inner life rather than the God of that inner life were the center of its attention and the ground of its faith. They have reminded the church of the earthen nature of the vessel in which the treasure of faith existed."[41] In short, external history helps to keep faith honest and self-critical.

SCRIPTURE AS COMMUNAL VOICE

As we have seen, a common motif in the biblical witness according to Niebuhr is the internal transformation of the believer that faith brings about. Such an emphasis on inward transformation, however, should not suggest a merely pietistic and overly personalistic/individualistic sense of religious experience and appropriation of Scripture for Niebuhr. Indeed, though he stresses internal personal transformation and sees this as thoroughly grounded in the biblical witness itself, for Niebuhr this inward transformation is part of the story of faith's internal history, a history which is fundamentally communal in character. Thus, personal transformation is a function of communal transformation. The same

Scriptures that point to the conversion of one's inward being are the Scriptures that point to the communal witness and the communal character of faith.

For Niebuhr, the witness of the community of faith and the witness of Scripture are so closely related that they begin to fuse. To speak of one is by definition to speak of the other: "[I]t becomes apparent that one cannot know the Scriptures without knowing the community which recorded what it had seen and heard; and that one cannot know the mind of the community without knowing the Scriptures."[42] As he puts it in *Faith on Earth*:

> The community of faith speaks to us preeminently through the voice of the Holy Scriptures. When we deal with the church as the community of faith and the Scriptures we are not dealing with two different companions of ours in the life of faith but with one. For what are the Scriptures except the confession of trust in God and loyalty to him and the report of what happened to those who believed in him and were not put to shame? What are they but the interpretation of the words of God given directly to generations of men? They speak of what these men of faith have heard and seen, what their hands have handled of the word of life. They give us their prayers and confessions of sin. They are the present incarnation of generations of the community of faith. . . . Scriptures and church are one and the same principle, the community of faith at our side, interpreting the word of God, presenting the living Christ of faith.[43]

But the community of faith represented in the Bible is not to be confused with the visible institutional church, according to Niebuhr. The community of faith may overlap with the visible church, but the two are not the same. This can be seen from Scripture itself:

> [T]he men of faith who speak in the Scriptures are often not recognized members of the visible organization. As prophets they are mostly unofficial, nonordained, irregular, amateur spokesmen for the visible church. Jesus himself is rejected by it. Paul establishes his credentials with difficulty. The visible church gives fictitious names to the writers of the Gospels in order to make them regular. The visible church establishes its distinctions from the community of faith by the anxiety of its life, by its fear of death, by its compromises with lies, by its efforts to induce men to put their confidence in it or in its rites, or in its Bible.[44]

Whenever the visible church uses the Bible to point not to God but to itself, it ceases to be the authentic community of faith.

Scripture is the collective voice of the formative communities of faith, from ancient Israel through the churches of the first century. To participate in the Christian community is to understand the "early and most creative periods" of these communities.[45] Indeed, the task of the present community of faith is to enter into conversation with the formative communities of faith embodied in Scripture.

> There is no other way to learn, organize and apprehend experience, think and speak Christianly, than by long and continuous participation in the life of the Biblical communities. In this conversation with those who being dead yet speak

we learn the logic as well as the language of the community that centers in God.[46]

He hastens to add, however, that such communication is not a one-way monologue, with the communities of faith represented in the Bible speaking and the contemporary communities of faith only listening. Rather, the present faith communities pose new questions and new concerns to the formative faith communities, which in turn yields new understandings and still further questions.[47]

A final aspect of Scripture's communal character involves the faith community's reinterpretation of internal history. This process of reinterpretation and reconstruction can be seen in Scripture itself and continues to take place as communities of faith interpret Scripture anew from their present situations. If internal history bears witness to the communal experience of revelation, then the embodiment of that experience in Scripture is an attempt to make sense of the past in light of the present revelation. Thus, for example:

> When Israel focused its varied and disordered recollections of a nomad past, of tribal bickerings and alien tyrannies in the revelatory event of its deliverance and choice to be a holy people, then it found there hitherto unguessed meaning and unity. What had been a "tale told by an idiot" . . . became a grand epic. . . . The tribal chants, the legends of the unheroic past were not forgotten; they were remembered in a new connection; meanings hitherto hidden became clear.[48]

Likewise, those who encountered Jesus were compelled to reinterpret their communal identity and their internal history, especially in light of his death and resurrection. "Through Jesus Christ, through his life, death, resurrection, and reign in power, we have been led and are being led to *metanoia*, to the reinterpretation of all our interpretations of life and death."[49] This process of reinterpretation and reconstruction necessarily continues in the present as the communities of faith seek to relate their present faith experiences to the formative experiences recorded by past faith communities in Scripture. In this sense, Scripture demonstrates and participates in the ongoing process of discerning "what is going on" and how to respond in faith. Since Scripture is the faith record of the formative faith communities, it has a special place in all ongoing reflections, because it functions as a common touchstone for all subsequent faith communities who claim this internal history as their own.

Scripture as Witness to Faith Responding to God

If, as I argue, Niebuhr views Scripture fundamentally as the embodied internal history of faith's communal voice, if that is what is going on in Scripture, then it is perhaps not surprising that Niebuhr uses Scripture primarily as a witness to the faith responses of ancient Israel and the earliest church, responses which in turn point beyond themselves to the God who has made Godself known and present in these communities.[50] By emphasizing the faith responses of the biblical communities, Niebuhr closely links Scripture to his own development of an "ethics of response," elaborated most fully in his book *The Responsible Self*. Here, he highlights two biblical examples that show the kind of ethics of response he seeks to articulate. One example is the Joseph story from Genesis and the other comes from Isaiah 10. In particular, Niebuhr is concerned in both of these biblical texts to present the contrast between finite human actions (and their underlying intentions) and the transcendent intentions of God underlying all human actions, divine intentions which are seen only in retrospect.

In the case of Joseph, his brothers simply intend to get rid of him and to make a little money on the side by selling him into slavery (Gen. 37). But God made Joseph great in Egypt. Niebuhr sees Gen. 50:20 as summarizing the distinction between limited (and malicious) human intentions on the one hand and the transcendent (and gracious) intentions of God on the other hand. "One may take as an example of responsibility to the one and universal God the kind of thinking presented in the Joseph story and summarized in Joseph's statement to his brothers: 'You thought to do evil but God thought to do good, to bring it about that many people should be kept alive'" (pp. 168–69).[51]

The case of Isaiah 10 is "[a]nother clear paradigm of the ethics of response to divine action behind, in, and through all finite activity" (p. 169). In this instance Israel faces an impending invasion by the Assyrians. How are they to respond to this threat? What guidance does the prophet Isaiah have to give? As Niebuhr puts it, "What the prophet offers is first of all an interpretation of what is going on. The invasion is to be understood, as he makes quite clear, as act of God. Israel is to ask, What is *God* doing?" (p. 169). Isaiah makes it clear that God is about to use Assyria to punish an unfaithful Israel (Isa. 10:1–6) and to call a rebellious Israel to repentance and to internal transformation. This is what God is doing, but, as Niebuhr stresses, Assyria sees itself as doing something rather different. As Isaiah writes: "But this is not what he [Assyria] intends, nor does he have this in mind" (Isa. 10:7). Assyria's intention is to extend its power and to show its greatness, not in any way to serve God consciously.

What Assyria intends with its finite actions, then, and what God intends in God's use of Assyria are radically different. Indeed, after God has used Assyria to chastise Israel, then will God "punish the arrogant boasting of the king of Assyria and his haughty pride" (Isa. 10:12), for Assyria mistakenly presumes to have conquered Israel by means of its own power; but "in a little while my indignation will come to an end, and my anger will be directed to their destruction" (Isa. 10:25).

As Niebuhr reads this passage, he sees a paradigmatic example of responding faith, here in Isaiah's vision of what is going on and of what Israel is to do as a result:

> The destructive intentions of Assyria are one thing; the holy, saving intentions of God are another. The meet, the fitting response of Israel, must be to the infinite intention in the first place, to the finite intention only secondarily. That means that the first response, the fitting action in the critical hour, is to be internal reformation; defense against Assyria is the secondary thing. (pp. 169–70)[52]

Niebuhr does not say whether defense against Assyria is appropriate, only that it is secondary to the internal reformation for which Isaiah calls.

For Niebuhr, then, Scripture functions to point away from preoccupation with finite human intentions and instead to point towards the ultimate intentions of God. In the examples from the Joseph story and Isaiah 10, the ultimate intention of God is human salvation, even though in both cases it appears that human destruction (Joseph's and Israel's) is the immediate consequence. Such destruction is not, however, the ultimate end or result that God seeks and accomplishes.

The epitome of the faithful response to God, according to Niebuhr, is, of course, embodied in the person of Jesus. From the perspective of Niebuhr's ethics of response, Jesus "is the responsible man who in all his responses to alteractions did what fitted into the divine action. . . . He responded to all action upon him as one who anticipated the divine answer to his answers" (p. 164). By way of example, Niebuhr points to Jesus' response to natural happenings. Along with others of his day, Jesus sees that it rains and shines upon the just and the unjust alike. The question, though, is how to respond to this observation, how to interpret it. Is this a sign that the universe is unjust and unconcerned with whether human conduct is right or wrong? That was the response of many. In contrast to this interpretation, however, "Jesus interprets the common phenomena in another way: here are the signs of cosmic generosity. The response to the weather so interpreted leads then also to a response to criminals and outcasts, who have not been cast out by the infinite Lord" (pp. 165–66). Similarly, the birds and the flowers are signs of God's overflowing creativity and artistry that rejoices in creation. In short, "there is a righteousness of God for Jesus; there is a universal ordering for good" (p. 166). Jesus does not look only at finite human intentions or finite human responses; instead, for Niebuhr, Jesus responds to the infinite purposes of God underlying all finite situations:

> If then we try to summarize the ethos of Jesus in a formula we may do so by saying that he interprets all actions upon him as signs of the divine action of creation, government, and salvation and so responds to them as to respond to divine action. He does that act which fits into the divine action and looks forward to the infinite response to his response. (p. 167)

For Niebuhr, then, Jesus' response to God is an "ethos of universal responsibility" (p. 167),[53] for Jesus trusts that God is working for salvation, even in the face of what appears to be destruction, even Jesus' own destruction. By beginning with the premise of God's affirmation of creation rather than God's indifference to creation, Jesus points again and again to God's grace, which redeems and transforms humanity and the world with it (pp. 175–76).[54]

Scripture as Witness to Faith Responding to the World

In addition to using Scripture as witness to appropriate models of faith responding to God, Niebuhr also uses Scripture to illustrate how formative faith communities responded to being in the world. In his classic study *Christ and Culture*, Niebuhr draws especially on 1 John, Paul, and the Gospel of John to illustrate different attitudes of Christian faith to the world, correlating these responses with others taken from Christian history.

After an opening chapter in which he defines "Christ"[55] and "culture," Niebuhr proceeds to discuss the type of "Christ Against Culture." For Niebuhr, among the writings of the New Testament, 1 John "contains the least ambiguous presentation of this point of view" (p. 46),[56] though 1 John's position is not the most radical or purest form of this perspective. Although 1 John emphasizes radical love among brothers and sisters in Christ and faith in Christ, the "counterpart of loyalty to Christ and the brothers is the rejection of cultural society" (p. 47). Thus, for 1 John "the world" is a negative term referring to society outside the church, and 1 John enjoins Christians not to love the world or the things of the world (1 John 2:15), for the world is passing away while those who are faithful are being saved (1 John 2:17).

In addition to 1 John, Niebuhr presents Tertullian as the most radical example of the Christ Against Culture type, along with Tolstoy in the modern period. That Niebuhr felt a deep sympathy with this position, and thus with 1 John, is indicated by his own advocacy early on in his career of the church's withdrawal from society, evident from his 1925 essay "Back to Benedict" and his coauthorship in 1935 of *The Church Against the World*.[57] From his perspective in 1951, however, when he wrote *Christ and Culture*, Niebuhr came to believe that this type of approach, even with its necessary warning against the church's co-optation by culture, was ultimately inadequate. Although if "Romans 13 is not balanced by I John, the church becomes an instrument of state," it is even more true that "there is no escape from culture," and so Christians should not pretend to be able to do so.[58] Radical separatist Christians, including the author of 1 John, always make use of culture. "The writer of I John employs the terms of that Gnostic philosophy to whose pagan use he objects."[59] In short, it is impossible to be a Christian without reference to culture, and since that is so, another approach must be found other than simply denying culture.[60]

After surveying the "Christ of Culture" type, where Niebuhr finds no affinities with the biblical witness,[61] and the synthesist approach of "Christ Above Culture," where he likewise concludes that the "New Testament contains no document that clearly expresses the synthetic view,"[62] Niebuhr turns his attention to the type of "Christ and Culture in Paradox," where he considers various "dualist" approaches to relating Christ and culture. Here he treats the apostle Paul.[63]

For Niebuhr, Paul represents a dualist approach in several respects. Since Paul had died with Christ to the world, he knew only Christ and him crucified, as well as the seeming foolishness and weakness of the cross, over against the supposed wisdom and power of the world. Thus, all cultural institutions and values are radically relativized for Paul in Christ; all are under the power of sin. And yet, God's redemption in Christ was offered to all, and Paul felt both called and compelled to carry out his evangelizing because of this.

In addition, God was at work in Christ creating a "new kind of humanity" here and now, though this work would only be completed at the eschaton (*Christ and Culture*, p. 162). Christians lived, thus, between the times, taking on new life in Christ here and now, yet knowing that the culmination of this new life would not take place in this world. Thus, "Paul could not take the way of the radical Christian with his new Christian law by attempting to remove himself and other disciples out of the cultural world into an isolated community of the saved," for the presence of sin was not confined to the world but could also readily manifest itself even in the midst of Christian community, as he knew from experience with the Corinthians and the Galatians (p. 163).

According to Niebuhr, however, Paul did add to his proclamation of the gospel "a cultural Christian ethics," an ethics of how to live within a Christian community (dealing with, e.g., marriage and divorce, household relations, quarrels between Christians) and an ethics of how to relate to the culture encountered in the world (e.g., church/state relations, slavery, table fellowship with non-Christians; p. 164). As Niebuhr puts it, "Paul seems to move in the direction of a synthetic answer to the Christ-and-culture problem," albeit in a different direction from a Clement or a Thomas, for the synthesists move "from Christ the instructor to Christ the redeemer, whereas Paul moves from Christ the judge of culture and the redeemer to Christian culture" (p. 165).

In the end, then, Niebuhr views Paul as a dualist who advocates two ethics that refer to contradictory tendencies in life. On the one hand is the "ethics of regeneration and eternal life," and on the other the "ethics for the prevention of degeneration," with the result that at its best the "ethics of Christian culture, and of the culture in which Christians live . . . is the ethics of nonviciousness — though there are no neutral points in a life always subject to sin and to grace" (p. 166). The one ethics has a view to God's overabundant grace; the other has a view to God's wrath against sin.[64]

In evaluating "the virtues and vices of dualism," Niebuhr concludes that dualistic motifs do give legitimate expression to the experience of living between the times. He is critical, however, of the static character of Paul's (and Luther's) dualism, which does not promote cultural reform in any substantive way, so that there is an inbred conservatism in the dualistic approach which allows hierarchical structures of power, including patriarchalism, to continue unchallenged.[65]

Finally, Niebuhr turns to the last type, "Christ the Transformer of Culture." He begins by outlining three theological convictions of the "conversionist" position, clearly Niebuhr's own position. Briefly stated, the three theological convictions are (1) a more positive view of the creation than that in the dualist approach; (2) an understanding of humanity's "fall" as radically distinct from creation and of humanity as perverted good rather than as completely evil; and (3) a more positive view of history where one lives not so much between the times as in the divine "now," where the eschatological future has become an eschatological present, all focused on "the divine possibility of a present renewal" (p. 195).

Niebuhr then presents a section entitled "The Conversion Motif in the

Fourth Gospel" (pp. 196–206). Although he sees aspects of the conversionist approach in 1 John and in Paul, Niebuhr sees this motif most clearly present in the Gospel of John, though he is quick to acknowledge John's separatist leanings. Thus, for Niebuhr, the

> basic ideas of conversionist thought are . . . all present in it; and the work itself is a partial demonstration of cultural conversion, for it undertakes not only to translate the gospel of Jesus Christ into the concepts of its Hellenistic readers, but also lifts these ideas about Logos and knowledge, truth and eternity, to new levels of meaning by interpreting them through Christ. (pp. 196–97)[66]

According to Niebuhr's reading of John's Gospel, one finds a positive view of the world, since creation came about through the Logos and since God loved the world so much, God gave the Son of God on behalf of its salvation (John 3:16). Similarly, Niebuhr sees as implicit in John a recognition of the fall of humanity into sin and the perversion of created good. And finally, John's view of history is far less future oriented than it is oriented to the present, where God is acting. Indeed, "the great point of the Gospel is that the new beginning, the new birth, the new life, is not an event that depends on a change in temporal history or in the life of the flesh. It is the beginning with God, from above, from heaven, in the spirit" (p. 201). And so John has largely substituted the teaching about the coming of the Paraclete for the doctrine of the return of Christ.

For Niebuhr, John's conversionist approach can be seen in what the evangelist says about human culture, especially in relation to Judaism and to Gnosticism. On the one hand John "presents Judaism as anti-Christian; on the other he emphasizes that 'salvation is from the Jews' " (p. 202). Although this tension can be explained by reference to the historical tensions between early Judaism and early Christianity, according to Niebuhr "it may also be maintained that such an attitude is consonant in all times and places with the view that Christ . . . is the hope, the true meaning, the new beginning of a Judaism that accepts his *transformation* of itself not into a Gentile religion but into a nondefensive worship of the Father" (p. 202, emphasis mine). In other words, Jesus shows what genuine Jewish faith looks like, and he seeks the conversion of Judaism away from its overly particularist self-understanding as the chosen people of God.

John's approach to Gnosticism shows a similar tension. On the one hand, John emphasizes the incarnation of Jesus in the flesh and a positive view of creation over against Gnostic views (and in keeping with 1 John), but on the other hand, John shares with the Gnostics a deep interest in matters of the spirit and a concern for knowledge. Again, this tension may be explained by referring to the historical conflict between early Christianity and Gnosticism, but "this dual attitude is more intelligible in conversionist terms as a Christian transformation of cultural religious thought" (p. 202).

Overall, Niebuhr sees John as preeminently concerned with the conversion of one's spirit, one's heart, and not with external observances, even Christian ones such as baptism and eucharist. As Niebuhr puts it, John "is concerned

throughout his book with the transformation by the spirit of Christ of the spirit
that expresses itself in external acts of religion. He is concerned that each symbolic act should have the true source and the true direction toward its true
object" (p. 203). John is interested in the participation of the believer in Christ
and Christ's spirit, without at the same time denying the significance of the
material world or of external actions. Thus, as far as

> the religious culture and institutions of men are concerned, it seems clear that
> the Fourth Gospel thinks of Christ as the converter and transformer of human
> actions. . . . in general John's interest is directed toward the spiritual transfor-
> mation of man's life in the world, not toward the substitution of a wholly spiri-
> tual existence for a temporal one. (pp. 203–204)

Niebuhr does recognize that there are limits to seeing John as having a wholly
conversionist approach, however. Niebuhr saw that John's "universalistic note is
accompanied by a particularist tendency" (p. 204). Thus, the Gospel of John
"has combined the conversionist motif with the separatism of the Christ-against-
culture school of thought" (p. 205), though Niebuhr sees John as leaning clearly
more in the direction of conversion and transformation than of separatism.[67]

Niebuhr offers no criticisms of the "Christ the Transformer of Culture" type
(though he did not consider it beyond critique), and indeed, his other writings
leading up to *Christ and Culture* clearly indicate that he viewed this approach
as the most appropriate stance for Christian faith in relation to the world. As L.
Kliever has indicated, Niebuhr's *Kingdom of God in America* (1937) showed Niebuhr's attempt to understand Christianity, and especially "constructive Protestantism" in America, as a force that molds culture in positive ways instead of
being merely molded by culture (a view that Niebuhr had already demonstrated
in his 1929 book *The Social Sources of Denominationalism*).[68] It is no accident
that Niebuhr was especially impressed with and influenced by Jonathan Edwards and his efforts in America's Great Awakening, perhaps for Niebuhr a
prime example of Christ transforming culture. Indeed, regarding the use of the
Bible in the Great Awakening, Niebuhr writes:

> As we have seen, in the dialectic between the objective criterion of the Word
> of God in Scriptures and the subjective criterion of the testimony of the Holy
> Spirit orthodoxy had tended to emphasize the former, separatism the latter,
> while each needed to recognize the principle represented by the other. In the
> Awakening the two principles were combined. Practically, the Awakening stim-
> ulated very great interest in and reading of the Scriptures while insisting upon
> the necessity of personal experience of the truth taught in Scriptures. . . . If we
> may adapt a later philosophical formula we can state their general position
> thus: Scripture without experience is empty, but experience without Scripture
> is blind. Hence, though they used the Bible with far greater freedom than their
> immediate orthodox predecessors had done, they used it with greater fidelity
> and keener recognition of the problem involved than had the exponents of the
> "inner light."[69]

Niebuhr's immense respect for the use of Scripture in personal and cultural transformation during the Great Awakening is unmistakable here. In 1946 Niebuhr wrote an essay, "The Responsibility of the Church for Society," for a volume edited by K. S. Latourette, *The Gospel, the Church, and the World,* a significant shift from his earlier more separatist writings (e.g., *The Church Against the World* in 1935).[70] And in reflecting on how his mind had changed, especially in light of the ethics of response he had developed, Niebuhr wrote an essay, entitled "Reformation: Continuing Imperative," in which he again sounded the call for permanent *metanoia,* perpetual conversion and transformation.

That Niebuhr linked the Gospel of John in particular to a conversionist approach indicates that Niebuhr felt a special kinship with the vision of this Gospel as he understood it, for the evangelist called for the kind of internal transformation of persons and community in the world that Niebuhr saw as being at the core of responses of Christian faith to God's actions and presence in and through Christ in the world. Niebuhr's attachment to the Fourth Evangelist can also be understood as an expression of his own personal theological movement from a more separatist approach to Christian faith in the world to the more conversionist approach he articulated in his mature theological statements. Like the Gospel of John, however, Niebuhr's transformist faith retained aspects of separatist leanings.

H. Richard Niebuhr's View of the Authority of Scripture

For Niebuhr the authority of Scripture is a function of what is happening in and with Scripture, and the meaning and limits of biblical authority are already evident in his uses of Scripture as witness to the dialectic between faith responding to God and faith responding to the world.

That the Bible has authority in the Christian community goes almost without saying for Niebuhr. Indeed, he writes: "The Bible is not . . . only the book of Christian beginnings. It is an authority for Christians in many and unique ways."[71] Niebuhr compares its authority to that of a written constitution for a national community. Its authority is also closely connected with the Christian experience and understanding of revelation, since the Bible points to God's revelation and Christians identify their own experience of God's continuing revelation with that to which Scripture bears witness.[72] In order to flesh out the issue of biblical authority in Niebuhr's writings, I would point to two concerns: Scripture as the companion of faith and the problem of the canon.

Scripture as Indispensable Companion

For Niebuhr the authority of Scripture does not rest in itself; rather, it rests in its capacity to bear witness to God's redemptive acts in the internal history of faith. Niebuhr is wary of approaches to Scripture which invest, from his perspective, too much authority in the Bible and so distract and detract from the God to whom Scripture points. Scripture does not stand *over* the Christian community as an authority; rather, it stands alongside the Christian community, reminding ever successive communities of faith about the formative experiences of God's revelation among the formative communities of faith. Thus, for example, in *Faith on Earth*, Niebuhr states that the Scriptures

> are preeminently the Scriptures of faith. They are the report of the dialogue of divine faithfulness with human distrust and trust. They are the reflections of the Promise of God, of the word that God has given, and of man's acceptance, rejection and reenactment of that promise. They are the books of the Covenant. The Promise of God does not come to us through them, it is made directly to created man, but the community of faith through this record, through this report of its acceptance of the divine promise, interprets for us the encounter in which we stand directly. Jesus Christ does not come to us through the Scriptures; he presents himself to us in the whole community of faith as the risen Lord; but without this testimony of the Scriptures all our interpretation of who this is whom we encounter would be confused and full of error. The Word of God, God's address to us, calling us to repentance and to faith in him, does not come through the Scriptures, but directly in all the encounters of our life with immovable reality, but how should we understand these words or know who it is who is speaking did we not have the interpreter at our side, the community of faith represented by the Scriptures, speaking to us through them?[73]

And so, for Niebuhr, Scripture itself does not directly mediate God's promise, Jesus Christ, or even the Word of God. It does not have this kind of authority or capacity, for then God's present activity would be undermined. But Scripture is indispensable in helping the believing community to interpret and to understand God's promises, Jesus Christ, and the Word of God. As James Gustafson has written, for Niebuhr Scripture has a " 'corroborative authority.' It is a court of validation for the judgments and actions of the Christian community and its members." It also has an " 'educational authority.' It is like the role of the teacher, which is to lead to a direct relationship of the student to the more ultimate authority of reality that the teacher mediates." But even in mediation the Bible's "authority is a 'mediate derived authority.' "[74] It is a unique authority, but not an exclusive one. It functions alongside the community of faith's experience of and witness to God's revelation in Christ.

Niebuhr is so concerned with Protestant doctrines of Scripture that elevate Scripture to a position of being an intermediary between God and humanity that he tends to shy away from discussing the authority of Scripture. Indeed, he strongly opposes any notion of hierarchical mediation between God and humanity, whether it be Scripture, church, or nature. In response to such hierarchical notions Niebuhr writes:

> This view seems fallacious. A mediator who establishes our trust in God must stand alongside of us as our companion before Him, not between us. So long as my trust is in the church and I believe what it tells me about God, so

long I distrust him as one who has not accepted me as his child. Mediation is companionate and neighborly, not hierarchical and aristocratic. The Scriptures are the indispensable handbook, the indispensable companion, the interpreting community of faith at my side in all my encounters with God, with Christ, with my neighbors.[75]

Scripture stands alongside the community of faith as "the indispensable companion," not as some demiurgic authority wielding power on its own. Scripture is the handbook of faith. Elsewhere, he refers to "the dictionary of the Scriptures," which is essential to understanding what God is doing and declaring in public and private experience.[76] Indeed, to see Scripture as somehow standing between God and the believer evidences a failure to understand Scripture itself, which points, along with the church, to the immediate relationship God establishes directly with the believer and the community of faith.[77]

Changing Canons

For Niebuhr, having identified the witness of Scripture very closely with the witness of the church, "the chief question which arises is that of the canon."[78] The problem is that even if the official canon of Scripture is fixed and unchanging, the working canon of Scripture for individuals and for churches alike is ever changing:

For any specific individual person the canon of Scriptures which have authority, interpreting and in this sense revealing authority, will differ from that of other persons. The canon of sacred Scriptures will differ from period to period in his life. The same thing is true of groups of Christians. As in the second century the canon differed somewhat from place to place, so in the modern world.[79]

And it is not just that one part of Scripture will be interpreted as having more authority than another part. Different biblical writings do not simply compete, as it were, for authority with other biblical writings. Instead, scriptural authority vies with other witnesses that the church experiences as equally or even more authoritative, so that scriptural authority can become a function of another authority.

There can be little doubt that the Westminster Confession has been actually more powerful as interpreter of God's words and acts than the Book of Proverbs for many Presbyterian Christians. Luther's Catechism, the Book of Common Prayer, the Heidelberg Catechism, Pascal's *Pensées*, Augustine's *Confessions* have often exercised greater influence in the community of faith as testimonies of faith than have Leviticus and Jude.[80]

Niebuhr does not see this as necessarily a problem for Christian faith. Indeed, as God works through Scripture to bear witness to God's revelation, so God works through other vehicles as well, though certainly none are so widely accepted as authoritative as is Scripture, and none can take the place of Scripture. Augustine's *Confessions* and the Book of Common Prayer, like Scripture, have been experienced by various communities of faith across time and culture as companions given by God. To quote Niebuhr at length:

> We are dealing here not with arbitrary selection but with the fact that God in his faithfulness provides us with companions who interpret his word for us. Some of these companions are so representative of the community of faith that they are rarely without power, such as the Psalms, the Gospels and Paul's letters. They always seem to speak to faith out of faith. They are established by no human decision. They have been put into our history by a process of selection in the community of faith which is at least as irreversible as the process whereby Plato's *Dialogues* and Kant's *Critiques* have been selected and established in the community of thought. They are simply acknowledged, received and consulted with gratitude. They are gifts of God through the community of faith. Others are less established. If we now accept as canon of sacred writings a list narrower and broader than that which functions for us individually and in groups as the indispensable interpreting representatives of the community of faith this is because we seek to realize roughly but as best we can in our visible church the structure of the invisible but known and real community of faith.[81]

Of course, this view of changing canons raises the question of how decisions are made in the face of competing authoritative canons that lead individual believers and the church in different and conflicting directions. Unfortunately, Niebuhr does not answer this question directly. If I may surmise from Niebuhr's writings, however, I imagine he would call on communities of faith to recognize and to understand how others experience different or overlapping sets of writings as companions bearing witness to God and, in light of this understanding, to engage in constructive dialogue; for better to become friends with new companions than through defensive exclusivism to find oneself or one's community clinging to but a single witness as if it exhausted both the ways in which God speaks to humanity and the ways in which humanity responds to God. Further, different canons can serve as correctives one to the other. That is why, for Niebuhr, it is crucial that Romans 13 be balanced by the witness of 1 John, lest the church become a mere vassal of the state.

Having said this, however, it is important to note that Niebuhr believed there is something unique about the biblical witness that makes it in fact irreplaceable, even if it may be supplemented by other witnesses. Thus, although Niebuhr recognized that from a historical perspective (external history), there is a certain arbitrariness and certainly a historically conditioned character to the process of the formation of the biblical canon, nonetheless, as one looks in faith *with* the biblical witness to God (internal history), both the believer and the community of faith realize that especially here is found access to the primary story of God's encounters with Israel and through Jesus Christ with the early church. Even though canons change, then, the biblical canon is never a replaceable witness for the believer in the context of the community of faith.

H. Richard Niebuhr's Hermeneutics

What can be said regarding Niebuhr's hermeneutics, or his principles of biblical interpretation? Niebuhr himself says very little directly about the way in which he approaches Scripture (indeed, I have not found even one example of his use of the term "hermeneutics"). In light of what has already been said, however, I would emphasize two aspects of Niebuhr's interpretive philosophy: his historical hermeneutics, and his thoroughly confessional hermeneutics.

A Historical Hermeneutics

For Niebuhr, being aware of one's own and of others' contingent historical existence is paramount. If one is not aware of the historically conditioned character of one's life and times, one is liable to be deceived. Niebuhr saw nonhistorical thinking as very dangerous, for it tended to treat historically conditioned embodiments of human experience as if they were somehow transhistorical and eternally true, as if they were not expressed in contingent terms. Nonhistorical thinking (and believing) tends to absolutize the relative, which for Niebuhr is "the great source of evil in life." [82] As he states in his prologue to *The Responsible Self*:

> If I dissent from those philosophers who undertake to analyze the moral life as though that life were nonhistorical, as though the ideas and words of the English moral language referred to the pure emotions of nonhistorical beings or to pure concepts, I find myself equally ill at ease with theologians who deal with the Scriptures as a nonhistorical book and undertake to explain it as though they were nonhistorical men. [83]

If human existence shows anything, it shows how past history is constantly reinterpreted in light of present historical understanding and experience. Niebuhr thus took the relativity of history extremely seriously. This outlook applies also to the Bible. The Bible is as radically historically conditioned as any other human writing. Having said this, however, it is also important to note that the biblical writers sought to bear witness even in their limited historical situations to the one eternal and true God. Thus, to read the Bible is to hear various historically conditioned encounters between God and the people of God across time. And across time, certain patterns emerge that testify to the constancy of God in relation to humanity. Such cohesiveness provides the necessary unity to the biblical witness to God and to the community of faith even across time.

A Confessional Hermeneutics

Precisely because all human attempts to speak of God are historically conditioned and thus relative, Niebuhr believed that the only responsible way to express Christian faith and Christian ideas was confessionally. Christians are called to bear witness to God by referring to what they have experienced of God and what they believe about God, giving at the same time a rationale for their understanding as best they can. But in no way can Christians do more than testify and confess. Niebuhr articulates his confessional approach most clearly in *The Meaning of Revelation*. In his preface to the book, he is concerned to make explicit some of his convictions that are of fundamental importance to him. His first conviction is "that self-defense is the most prevalent source of error in all thinking and perhaps especially in theology and ethics. I cannot hope to have avoided this error in my effort to state Christian ideas in confessional terms only, but I have at least tried to guard against it." [84]

The character of human existence as historically conditioned necessitates a confessional hermeneutic. "As we begin with revelation only because we are forced to do so by our limited standpoint in history and faith so we can proceed only by stating in simple, confessional form what has happened to us in our community, how we came to believe, how we reason about things and what we see from our point of view" (p. 29). Niebuhr sees this confessional approach as grounded in Scripture itself, for the early Christians did not argue for the existence of God, nor did they admonish people to follow some suprahistorical dictates from on high. Rather, they primarily recited what they had experienced of God through their encounter with Jesus Christ in his historical appearance. They gave their "confession of what had happened to the community of disciples. . . . The confession referred to history and was consciously made in history" (p. 32).

And yet the confession of the early Christians was no idle "oh by the way" confession. Their confession was indeed passionate; they felt they had to tell what had happened among them. As Niebuhr puts it:

> [W]hat prompted Christians in the past to confess their faith by telling the story of their life was more than a need for vivid illustration or for analogical reasoning; it was irreplaceable and untranslatable. An internal compulsion rather than free choice led them to speak of what they knew by telling about Jesus Christ and their relation to God through him. Today we think and speak under the same compulsion. (pp. 34–35) [85]

Thus, Niebuhr's confessional hermeneutic is not an expression of apologetic Christianity, but it is an expression of a felt compulsion. The evangelists of the New Testament had to speak of what God had done; they had no choice but to tell of their experiences. And so Niebuhr identifies with them in their compulsion to bear witness to God's redeeming presence. Regarding this compulsion, Niebuhr also writes: "Whatever other men say we can only confess, as men who live in history, that through our history a compulsion has been placed upon us and a new beginning offered us which we cannot evade" (p. 139).

Since the Bible is nothing but the confessions of the formative communities of faith, and subsequent generations of Christians have identified with these confessions, so here and now, according to Niebuhr, Christians feel called to testify to their experience and understanding of God's salvific acts. [86] Again, a description of what God has done cannot be related as a dogmatic statement of what all people in all times must believe. Rather, "[s]uch a description must once more be given confessionally, not as a statement of what all men ought to do but as a statement of what we have found it necessary to do in the Christian community on the basis of the faith which is our starting point."[87]

A historical hermeneutics and a confessional hermeneutics thus define the only approach to Scripture and to Christian experience that Niebuhr believed to be possible for Christians acting responsibly in the world. That both aspects of this hermeneutical approach were grounded in the community of faith was also of great importance to Niebuhr, so that one might even speak of a communal hermeneutic for Niebuhr. One does not come to see what God has done and is doing in history save through the community of faith past and present, and one does not understand the context and significance of believing in God apart from the community of faith. Niebuhr's emphasis on history and on confession is closely related to the communal character of Christian faith.

H. Richard Niebuhr and the Significance of Scripture for Ethics

Having examined Niebuhr's uses of Scripture along with his understanding of biblical authority and the most appropriate hermeneutical approach to Scripture, what can be said about how Niebuhr correlates Scripture and contemporary constructive ethical reflection? To begin with, it is important to point out that Niebuhr made a significant distinction between the ethics of Scripture and the appropriation of Scripture for ethics. The ethics of Scripture refer to how the various biblical authors correlated their understanding of faith in God with their understanding of what it meant to live this faith out appropriately in the world. Thus, to ask about the ethics of Scripture is to ask in large part a historical question. But to speak of using Scripture for constructive ethics today refers to how contemporary Christians in their own specific historical contexts are to relate the formative Christian visions embodied in Scripture to the question of what faithful existence means in rather different historical circumstances.

Describing the Ethics of Scripture

As we have seen, Niebuhr emphasized time and again the historically contingent character of the biblical writings, despite his confidence at the same time that Scripture related in a fundamental way the enduring internal history of Christian faith. For Niebuhr, then, to ask about Scripture and ethics meant first of all to be aware of the various ways in which Scripture presented ethical reflection and action. In part, his answer to this question is reflected in *Christ and Culture*, where he discussed the historical responses of 1 John, Paul, and the Gospel of John to the cultural world outside the Christian community. His most direct presentation of biblical ethics, however, is to be found in his chapter

"Introduction to Biblical Ethics," his only extended commentary on biblical texts, which he wrote in 1955 as the first chapter for the sourcebook coedited with Waldo Beach, *Christian Ethics: Sources of the Living Tradition.*

Faced with the task of reducing "biblical ethics" to its most essential form, Niebuhr seeks to relate what he considers to be "some of the main ideas and themes of Biblical ethics" and then to trace "their development in a few great documents representative of various periods of Biblical history" (p. 13). Niebuhr begins with various summaries of biblical ethics contained in the Bible itself, such as the Ten Commandments from Exodus 20 and Deuteronomy 5, as well as Jesus' summary statements regarding the Great Commandment in Mark 12:28–31 (and parallels).

In discussing these summaries, Niebuhr highlights several recurring themes. The most important observation is that "Biblical ethics begins with God and ends with him" (p. 15). God is the source of all moral requirements and is the highest value. Various themes flow from this emphasis. First, much of biblical ethics has an imperative tone. The Bible refers not so much to humanity's chief good as to people's duties to God and to one another. Second, biblical ethics concentrates on acts which affect one's neighbor or companion. And third, biblical ethics emphasizes the "close connection between attitudes and actions toward God with attitudes and actions toward the neighbor" (p. 16).

Having looked at some of the summaries of biblical ethics, Niebuhr then proceeds to treat two sections from the Old Testament (the Book of the Covenant and the prophet Amos) and two sections from the New Testament (the Sermon on the Mount and Paul's Letter to the Romans). In the Book of the Covenant (Exod. 20:22–23:33), Niebuhr notes the imperative tone throughout, the emphasis on responsibility toward one's neighbor, and the interrelation of loyalty to God with loyalty to neighbor. In particular, Niebuhr highlights the concern of God for the weak and the distressed and the general demands for justice, all grounded in the reminder that God freed the Israelites from slavery in Egypt and stands on the side of the poor and the oppressed (pp. 19–21).

Niebuhr turns to the Book of Amos as representative of the prophetic literature coming from the time of the monarchy and focusing on the contexts of urban life and temple cult. As Niebuhr reads Amos, he stresses two inseparable convictions found there: "the conviction about God and the conviction about the supreme importance of justice" (p. 22). Amos's ethics begin with a consideration of the character and identity of God and God's actions. God is one; God is universal; and God calls a rebellious humanity to repentance and to respond in obedience and in faith to God by doing away with injustice and oppression toward other human beings.

In tracing the development of biblical ethics from the time of Amos to the time of the New Testament writings, Niebuhr stresses four transitions: from a more social to a more individualized view of life; greater wrestling with the problem of God's justice; deepened convictions about the rule of evil in the world; and the development of law (p. 27). Especially amid questions regarding the justice of God, various biblical authors after Amos struggled to give voice to

God's faithfulness, God's oneness, and God's integrity (e.g., Jeremiah, Job, Psalms, Isaiah). Indeed, it "is in the struggle with such questions that the heart of Biblical religion and ethics is revealed" (p. 28).

Among the New Testament writings, according to Niebuhr, the Sermon on the Mount (Matt. 5–7) "represents in the briefest form available the essence of the ethical teaching of Jesus" (p. 31). It shares with other summaries of biblical ethics an emphasis on direct imperatives addressed to the believing community. And yet the Sermon on the Mount does not prescribe static and unchanging rules without regard to people's actual situations. "These apparently arbitrary commandments are the rational corollaries of a pronounced and definite conviction about the character of the human situation. The conviction may be briefly stated: God rules and his rule will soon become manifest" (p. 32). As Niebuhr interprets the Sermon on the Mount, Jesus' fundamental conviction is, not that God will rule sometime in the future, but that God rules already now, and the actuality of this rule will be made evident. God's rule is characterized by justice and mercy; indeed, the Sermon on the Mount shows that for Jesus God is "holy love" (p. 33).

Niebuhr does see, however, some distinctive aspects in Jesus' view of God and his consequent ethics. Three things stand out. First, whereas most of the prophets of old addressed the strong and the influential in the community and called upon them to do justice to the poor, Jesus addresses the poor directly. Jesus' viewpoint is that of the poor and the oppressed themselves. Second, Jesus' conception of the neighbor shows significant development beyond the prophets of Israel, for Jesus counts the enemy as "among those to whom men have an obligation under the rule of God. The neighbor is no longer the member of a closed society whose citizens support each other by rendering mutual services, but any member of that community of which the universal God is the head" (pp. 34–35). Beyond the Sermon on the Mount, Niebuhr sees this theme especially in the parable of the Good Samaritan (Luke 10:29–37). Third, and probably most important for Niebuhr, Jesus emphasized the character of the attitudes one has toward the neighbor (here in its expanded sense of including the enemy). Jesus "discerns that the relations between men in the great community are matters not of obvious, external behavior but of psychological, internal attitudes" (p. 35). Here, Niebuhr clearly has in mind the "new law," where by Jesus condemns, not just murder and adultery, but anger and lust as well (Matt. 5:21–48). In sum, according to Niebuhr, "[t]he ethics of Jesus is the ethics of a single community, the community of which God, the Father, is author and ruler and in which relations to him are always of decisive importance. But these relations can never be severed from one's relations to the neighbor" (p. 36). This is the heart of Jesus' teachings about the actual, not ideal, community in the Sermon on the Mount and elsewhere.

Niebuhr chooses, finally, Paul's Letter to the Romans because in his estimate, next to the Sermon on the Mount, "no other Biblical document has had greater influence on the ethical reflection of the Christian church" (p. 36). Far from representing a form of speculative theology, Niebuhr views Romans as deeply interested in ethical concerns. For Paul, the great moral problem is not one of knowledge but of will. Paul's "point of departure is, therefore, the situation of mankind in revolt against the moral law that it acknowledges, of man in revolt against himself" (p. 38). Humanity as a whole is morally ill and needs to be made well before it can act as God intends. God provides a solution in Christ: "What is most signifiant for Paul's ethics in this connection is his conviction and experience that in and through Jesus Christ, not simply through his teachings but through his character and fate, God has made himself known to men in such a way that a new relation to him is possible" (p. 41). Jesus' coming also marks a new age in human history characterized by the presence of the spirit of God's sonship as revealed in Jesus.

Because of this new relationship to God through Christ, with believers being internally empowered by the spirit of being children of God, Paul criticizes the imperative moral law as something external to human beings. As Niebuhr sees it, "This criticism of imperative moral law is one of Paul's great contributions to moral thought, though he makes explicit here only what was present in Jesus' teaching and conduct and what a Jeremiah had sensed" (pp. 41–42). In describing Christian existence as "dying and rising" with Christ (Rom. 6), Paul stresses how becoming a Christian "involves a complete inner transformation of the fundamental attitudes of men toward God, their world, themselves, and their neighbors" (p. 42). In sum, then, Paul's Christian ethics is the ethics of the believer who participates in the community of faith, where God-in-Christ is ever present and ever inspiring, and in which all persons are members of one another (p. 44).

In describing the character of biblical ethics, Niebuhr increasingly emphasizes the transformative aspect of biblical faith, a faith that builds new communities and is based upon the internal renewal of persons who embrace even the enemy as neighbor in the spirit of God-in-Christ. This understanding of biblical ethics provides Niebuhr with some central foundations as he then seeks to use biblical ethics in constructing his own ethics for contemporary communities of Christian faith.

Constructing Ethics with Scripture

It is one thing to describe the ethics of Scripture, but for Niebuhr it is quite another to construct a contemporary Christian ethic in light of the ethics of Scripture. Since all ethical constructions are inseparably linked to specific historical contexts, it is not possible simply to adopt the ethics articulated within Scripture and apply them to the various contemporary historical situations in which Christian communities find themselves. Indeed, in what is undoubtedly his most significant attempt at constructive Christian ethics, *The Responsible Self*, Niebuhr quite consciously states at the outset that "my approach is not Bible-centered, though I think it is Bible-informed" (p. 46). Niebuhr was concerned that other attempts to construct Bible-centered theology and ethics resulted in ahistorical approaches both to the Bible and to the contemporary situation. Still, he sees his approach as significantly influenced by the biblical witness.

Niebuhr developed his ethics of response with the Bible clearly in view. Indeed, he sees the Bible as in large measure taking the same approach to ethical questions. Further, Niebuhr thinks that his approach helps one to see aspects of the biblical witness itself that have been masked by other approaches. As Niebuhr puts it in *The Responsible Self*:

> The idea of the moral life as the responsible life in this sense not only has affinities with much modern thinking but it also offers us, I believe, a key—not *the* key—to the understanding of that Biblical ethos which represents the historic norm of the Christian life. In the past many efforts have been made to understand the ethos of the Old and the New Testaments with the aid of the teleological theory and its image of man-the-maker. . . . Each of these interpretations has been buttressed by collections of proof texts, and doubtless much that is valid about the Bible and about the Christian life which continues the Scriptural ethos has been said within the limits of this interpretation. But much that is in Scriptures has been omitted by the interpreters who followed this method, and much material of another sort—the eschatological, for instance— has had to be rather violently wrenched out of its context or laid aside as irrelevant in order to make the Scriptures speak in this fashion about the self. (pp. 65–66)

It is important to see the limited claims Niebuhr makes for approaching Scripture in light of his ethics of response. He sees his approach as *a* key, not *the* key. It is one significant way to appropriate the biblical witness in keeping with the character of that witness itself. But Niebuhr knows that all attempts at constructive Chistian ethics are at best partial efforts that always need to be corrected and supplemented, and sometimes abandoned for a time.[88]

Nonetheless, Niebuhr thinks his approach resonates with Scripture in pointing to God and to ethical human responses:

> If now we approach the Scriptures with the idea of responsibility we shall find, I think, that the particular character of this ethics can be more fully if not wholly adequately interpreted. At the critical junctures in the history of Israel and of the early Christian community the decisive question men raised was not "What is the goal?" nor yet "What is the law?" but "What is happening?" and then "What is the fitting response to what is happening?" When an Isaiah counsels his people, he does not remind them of the law they are required to obey nor yet of the goal toward which they are directed but calls to their attention the intentions of God present in hiddenness in the actions of Israel's enemies. . . . Israel is the people that is to see and understand the action of God in everything that happens and to make a fitting reply. So it is in the New Testament also. The God to whom Jesus points is not the commander who gives laws but the doer of small and of mighty deeds, the creator of sparrows and clother of lilies, the ultimate giver of blindness and of sight, the ruler whose rule is hidden in the manifold activities of plural agencies but is yet in a way visible to those who know how to interpret the signs of the times. (pp. 66–67)

Niebuhr sees in Scripture itself the very questions with which he begins: What is going on? What is God doing? What is the fitting response to what is happening? The task of the Christian is to discern the signs of the times, to understand the possible ways in which contemporary happenings can be interpreted in light of faith in the one God, who is at work in all human affairs. Thus, it is perhaps best to say that for Niebuhr Scripture provides patterns for approaching what is going on in the world in light of belonging to the community of believers who look to God. The task is one of interpretation, which forms the beginning of faithful response.

In approaching the Bible as a source for constructing an appropriate ethics of response, Niebuhr turns to Christ as the most fitting "paradigm of responsibility."[89] As we have seen above, Niebuhr identified Jesus' faithfulness to God especially in terms of his identity with the poor and the oppressed of the world, his inclusion of the enemy as neighbor, and his emphasis on the transformation of internal attitudes toward one's neighbor. For Niebuhr, these are characteristic of faithful responses of Christian communities in the world.

Perhaps a specific example will show how Niebuhr's appropriation of Scripture in an ethics of response works in practice. In the midst of World War II, Niebuhr wrote three seminal essays in *The Christian Century:* "War as the Judgment of God," "Is God in the War?" and "War as Crucifixion."[90] For Niebuhr, Isaiah's response to Assyria's threat and the death of Jesus on the cross provide two powerful biblical symbols that he finds helpful in discerning what is going on in the war, and especially what God is doing in the war. These biblical symbols are war as God's judgment and war as crucifixion. Both Isaiah and Jesus looked at their respective situations in light of what the one universal transcendant God was doing. Isaiah saw God's judgment as ultimately God's act of seeking the repentance and thus salvation of a faithless and rebellious Israel. God was using Assyria's impending destruction of Israel in fact to call Israel to repentance and to internal reform. Similarly, in facing his own crucifixion, Jesus saw not the power of Pilate but the power of God pointing to human sinfulness and calling for the recognition of human brokenness, and so ultimate reliance on the God who seeks and accomplishes human transformation in the death and resurrection of Christ. As Niebuhr puts it:

> To see the act of God in war is to stand where Isaiah stood when he discerned that Assyria was the rod of divine anger and where Jesus stood when he saw in the crucifixion not Pilate's nor the Jews' activity but that of the Father who gave Pilate the power to crucify and whose will rather than Pilate's or Jesus' was being done.[91]

Indeed, the responses of Isaiah and Jesus to God's actions show how God's judgment of Israel and God's crucifixion of Jesus lead, if only tragically, to human repentance and then to reconciliation. Niebuhr asks those claiming to be Christians to see in the war God's judgment of all human claims to special privilege at the expense of others and to see the war as the crucifixion of so many countless innocents; only then perhaps in repentance and in subsequent healing, would people realize and embody God's gracious love for the whole human family.[92]

In responding to God's actions, both Isaiah and Jesus "built new community in the midst of tragedy, cleaned themselves and society of egoism, fear and hatred, and opened up a productive future in which the tragedy was made the foundation of new life."[93] As restoration came eventually to a chastened Israel, and especially as resurrection came to the crucified Jesus, so Niebuhr analogously envisioned World War II as God's judgment of a world bent on crucifying the innocent and the weak for self-gain, with the potentiality that humans might repent and seek out the good for the dispossessed in the process of transforming human community.[94]

We can see a link, finally, between Niebuhr's conception of World War II as judgment and crucifixion and his understanding of the biblical ethics of Jesus in particular. For Niebuhr, Jesus redefined the meaning of "neighbor" so that it included even, and perhaps especially, those persons traditionally thought of as enemies. World War II showed God's judgment upon the destructive and idolatrous nationalisms that permeated the world order. For Christians, such nationalism is a gross perversion; not only does it fail to see the "enemy" as beloved neighbor but also it demonizes the neighbor as a pretense for justifying war. Furthermore, Jesus spoke from the standpoint of the poor and the oppressed and identified himself completely with them, calling on his followers to do the same. But in the war, far from aligning themselves with the suffering poor, many identifying themselves as followers of Jesus in fact took part in crucifying Jesus again along with so many innocents. This suffering of the innocent becomes, in turn, a call to repentance and to conversion. As Niebuhr puts it:

> Interpreted through the cross of Jesus Christ the suffering of the innocent is seen not as the suffering of temporal men but of the eternal victim "slain from the foundations of the world." If the Son of God is being crucified in this war along with the malefactors—and he is being crucified on many an obscure hill—then the graciousness of God, the self-giving love, is more manifest here than in all the years of peace.[95]

The redemptive grace of God given in the death and resurrection of Christ can lead to the transformation of internal human attitudes, the third hallmark of Jesus' ethic according to Niebuhr. Such a process of conversion, then, is ever taking place.

Critical Evaluation

How are we to evaluate H. Richard Niebuhr's approach to and uses of Scripture? In offering a critical evaluation, I would raise three concerns in particular. The first question revolves around Niebuhr's portrait of the Bible in general and his view of several biblical writings in particular. In general, one may ask if Niebuhr's characterization of the Bible as primarily a confessional witness is fair. Clearly, Niebuhr is concerned with Christianity's tendency toward a naive triumphalism, but is it not also evident that much of the biblical witness presents itself not only in confessional terms but often with an exclusivist and triumphalistic voice (e.g., the perspectives of Matthew, John, or Luke–Acts toward Judaism)? John Cobb, for example, has criticized Niebuhr:

> There is certainly a strong confessional element in the New Testament in that men are directly testifying to their apprehension of God in Jesus Christ and not attempting to demonstrate his existence or his presence. But we must also recognize that the New Testament writers do not understand their faith as one among several ways in which God may be encountered. Neither do they understand their theological utterances as having validity only in the community of shared revelation. . . . They seem to think that those who do not believe in Christ are objectively rejecting truth and barring themselves from the one salvation.[96]

In other words, many of the biblical writings, and especially the New Testament writings, seem to present themselves precisely in the kind of defensive and apologetic terms that Niebuhr found troubling. Even if one understands the historical contexts that gave rise to such a theological understanding of Christian faith, as Niebuhr clearly did, is it perhaps not overly generous to characterize Scripture on the whole as primarily confessional in tone?

Regarding Niebuhr's understanding and exegesis of several specific biblical books, I would also raise some concerns. Niebuhr sees the Gospel of John as maintaining a mediating position between the types Christ Transforming Culture and Christ Against Culture, but leaning toward the former. When Niebuhr wrote *Christ and Culture* in 1951, he relied heavily upon the work of the leading New Testament scholars of the day, most notably from the British school (E. Hoskyns on John, C. H. Dodd on 1 John). In the 1940s and 1950s it was commonplace to see the Gospel of John as primarily Hellenistic in outlook, an adaptation of the gospel message for Greek (and Gentile) Christianity. Thus, as Niebuhr writes, the Gospel of John "undertakes not only to translate the gospel of Jesus Christ into the concepts of its Hellenistic readers, but also lifts these ideas about Logos and knowledge, truth and eternity, to new levels of meaning by interpreting them through Christ."[97]

Since the time that Niebuhr did his work, however, the Gospel of John has increasingly been understood by New Testament scholars (especially through the work of R. E. Brown, J. L. Martyn, and R. Schnackenburg, among others) as a relatively separatist Jewish-Christian Gospel, indeed a Gospel that became increasingly separatist as it went through various editions. Thus, the view of the Gospel of John at the end of the twentieth century is rather different from Niebuhr's, so that the Gospel of John appears as rather ill-suited to serve as an illustration for the type of Christ Transforming Culture.

In addition, from the perspective of hindsight, it must be said that Niebuhr's reading of Paul is rather heavily influenced by Luther and falls clearly in the category of an introspective reading of Paul via Augustine and Luther, in contrast to the understanding of Paul and his robust conscience at the end of the twentieth century, thanks to the pioneering work of such scholars as K. Stendahl and E. P. Sanders. Though Paul may still fit Niebuhr's type of Christ and Culture in Paradox, one can also imagine him fitting equally well into Niebuhr's type of Christ Transforming Culture.

A second question has to do with the relationship between the embodiment of the faith expressions of the formative faith communities in Scripture and the faith expressions of contemporary Christian communities. I wonder if Niebuhr's emphasis on the constructive dialogue that takes place between the internal histories of faith as discerned then and now, does not play down discontinuities that contemporary faith communities experience when reading and seeking to appropriate Scripture anew. Perhaps this is more the case at the end of the twentieth century than it was in the middle of the century, but Niebuhr's confessional approach does make the present experience of God as significant as past faith experiences embodied in Scripture, which opens up the possibility that present understandings are not just shaped by the formative understandings of the biblical communities, but that present experiences of God actually challenge the adequacy and thus the normativity of the formulations found in Scripture. This can be especially seen, for example, in ethical questions about the status of women in the Christian community or about the eschatology of the earliest Christians (Niebuhr makes no references to 1 or 2 Thess.). Clearly, Niebuhr saw some biblical formulations as more adequate than others, and he was aware of how working canons change. But what does Niebuhr do, for example, with the hierarchalism of the Pastoral Epistles (to which I have found no reference in his writings) or with the triumphalism of Revelation? In the end, does not Niebuhr himself reject the theological vision and adequacy of some biblical writings in favor of those of others? To what extent, then, does Niebuhr truly see Scripture as a whole as having a normative function for Christian theology and ethics?

A final question I would pose has, perhaps, as much to do with Niebuhr's overall theological vision as it does with his approach to and use of Scripture. Put sharply, Niebuhr's presentation of the biblical witness so stresses God's involvement in and control of human history as to raise questions both about God's ultimate power and about God's goodness. Niebuhr himself is aware of potential problems here. In anticipating possible criticisms of his portrait of Jesus in *The Responsible Self*, Niebuhr asks: "Does not this way of understanding him, and so of understanding the model Christian life, make of this life an affair of pure resignation to the will of God? Is not this interpretation one of fatalism?"[98] Niebuhr's response is as follows:

> When this One [God] is understood, with the use of the symbols of making and of design, as the predesigner, the foreordainer of all that happens, then indeed nothing but fatalism could result from an ethics of response to God. . . . But such a Determiner of Destiny is not the One to whom Jesus Christ made his responses; nor is he the God of Isaiah; nor would he be One to whom we have access. The God and Father of our Lord Jesus Christ is the

loving dynamic One, who does new things, whose relation to his world is more like that of father to his children than like that of the maker to his manufactures. . . . The symbols fatalism uses to interpret what is happening do not fit the situation. The [images] of the kingdom and of the family are, to be sure, symbols also, but they do greater justice to our actual experience of life.[99]

For Niebuhr, God is not the predeterminer of all things; rather, God is the loving parent who seeks the good of God's children in the world. Thus, in the Assyrian destruction of Israel, Isaiah saw God working for Israel's good. In his own death on the cross, Jesus trusted God was working for the good of humanity despite the tragedy and injustice of his own death. But how did Isaiah and Jesus go about discerning divine intention? How does one know, for example, whether Hananiah's or Jeremiah's reading of God's purposes is on target?

In his war essays, Niebuhr states: "Interpreted through the cross of Jesus Christ the suffering of the innocent is seen not as the suffering of temporal men but of the eternal victim 'slain from the foundations of the world.' "[100] In saying this, is not Niebuhr open to the charge of downplaying the real suffering of people in real history? If such suffering is supposed to prick the consciences of human beings to the point that they repent of their sinful self-centeredness and idolatry, if this is what is going on and what God is doing, are not both the goodness of God and the power of God called into question? Niebuhr believed that God used the Assyrians to bring judgment upon a stubborn Israel. Was God also doing the same in visiting the Babylonians upon Judah? Was God doing the same in visiting the Romans upon Palestine? Was God doing the same in visiting the Germans upon European Jews during the Holocaust? Is this Niebuhr's only vision and understanding of why the innocents suffer, and if so, does it find as much support in the biblical witness as Niebuhr supposes?

Clearly, Niebuhr is convinced that notwithstanding appearances to the contrary, God is in fact at work saving the world despite itself, evidenced in the life, death, and resurrection of Jesus Christ. And so let me give Niebuhr the last word:

> However adequate or inadequate our theories of atonement or reconciliation may be, the fact remains: the movement beyond resignation to reconciliation is the movement inaugurated and maintained in Christians by Jesus Christ. By Jesus Christ men have been and are empowered to become sons of God—not as those who are saved out of a perishing world but as those who know that the world is being saved.[101]

four

BERNARD HÄRING

The Freedom of Responsive Love

*B*ernard Häring, C.SS.R., a Redemptorist priest (b. 1912), is generally considered to be one of the most significant (and arguably *the* most significant) Roman Catholic moral theologians of the twentieth century.[1] The reasons for this appraisal are not difficult to see. During the early 1950s well before Vatican II was convened, Häring had already moved in a sharply different direction from the manual tradition in moral theology that had endured for over three hundred years.[2] Indeed, most scholars consider his three-volume work *The Law of Christ*, first published in 1954, to have been pivotal for the renewal of moral theology during the generation following Vatican II.[3] In many ways, this book already initiated changes that Vatican II sought to bring about a decade later.[4] Twenty-five years after the appearance of *The Law of Christ*, Häring published another monumental three-volume work, *Free and Faithful in Christ* (1978–81), which sought to address significantly different situations in the Roman Catholic church after Vatican II, in theological ethics, and in the general world scene.

One of the changes that has characterized the renewal movement in moral theology has been greater attention to the Bible,[5] as indeed the Vatican II decree *Optatam totius* (Decree on Priestly Formation) called for in paragraph 16: "Special attention needs to be given to the development of moral theology. Its scientific exposition should be more thoroughly nourished by scriptural teaching."[6] Perhaps it should not come as a surprise that Häring himself was responsible for the formulation of this statement. Writing about his role in drafting this document, he states:

> When in the next-to-last vote on priestly formation (*Optatam totius*), many Council Fathers demanded a clear prohibition of legalistic books on moral theology, the responsible Commission asked me to try to deal with these requests. At first I presented my doubts about condemnations: for then one would have to carefully describe what one was condemning, and not much would be gained thereby. Thus I formulated the following constructive suggestion: "Special care should be given to the perfecting of moral theology. Its scientific presentation should draw more fully on the teaching of Holy Scripture and should

throw light upon the exalted vocation of the faithful in Christ and their mission to bear fruit in love for the life of the world" (No. 16). The text was presented for its own vote and was almost unanimously approved.[7]

Häring regularly refers to this call from Vatican II in his writings after 1965,[8] though he had already emphasized the need for renewed attention to the Bible in his foreword to *The Law of Christ*. There, Häring states that in contrast to other approaches to moral theology, the "present work attempts to expound the most central truths in the light of the inspired word of the Bible."[9] In general, it must be said that he appears to be rather self-conscious about drawing more fully on the Bible in presenting his own moral theology, although he clearly does a better job of this in *Free and Faithful in Christ* than in *The Law of Christ*, as we shall see. And so it comes as somewhat of a surprise that to date Häring's use of Scripture in moral theology has received very little attention, and then only from moral theologians and not from biblical scholars.[10]

Two brief comments are appropriate here to set the stage for the discussion that follows. First, my analysis of Häring's use of Scripture is drawn from an extensive but not exhaustive examination of his writings. (To date, Häring has written over sixty-seven volumes and countless articles.) I have concentrated on several central and representative writings: his two most systematic and extensive works, both consisting of three volumes, *The Law of Christ* and *Free and Faithful in Christ*; his essays in *Toward a Christian Moral Theology*; and other selected essays. Second, I should again stress that although I teach at a Roman Catholic university, I myself come from the Protestant tradition (Presbyterian to be exact), and this perspective should not be forgotten as I look at Bernard Häring's use of Scripture in his moral theology. My understanding of moral theology in the Roman Catholic tradition has been mediated more through reading about it than through direct personal experience of the tradition.

Biblical Texts Used by Häring

Häring refers to over thirty-four hundred specific biblical texts in his two three-volume works, *The Law of Christ* and *Free and Faithful in Christ*, which themselves total a little over thirty-four hundred pages. In keeping with his radically christocentric approach, one finds relatively little use of the Old Testament (only about six hundred of the thirty-four hundred references come from the Old Testament). His tendency to downplay the Old Testament can be illustrated by a defensive comment he makes about Ambrose in his historical survey of moral theology from the first volume of *The Law of Christ*: "Though one is astonished at his predilection for the Old Testament and his admiration for the exalted morality of the patriarchs, the preference may be explained by his penchant for concrete examples in pastoral instruction."[11]

When Häring does use the Old Testament, he draws primarily upon four kinds of material: the creation story in Genesis 1–3, the theophany and legal

matter in Exodus, the wisdom literature of Proverbs and Sirach, and the Servant
Songs of Second Isaiah. Apart from that, there is very little. Most striking is the
relatively minor attention given to the prophetic literature. For example, Hosea
and Amos are mentioned only eleven times.

Häring's overall neglect of most of the Old Testament may in part be due
to his reaction against the older manual tradition of centering on the Decalogue
as a point of departure for moral reflection. Indeed, in the foreword to *The Law
of Christ*, he explicitly states that the "reader of the text need scarcely be reminded that the point of departure in our study is not the decalog, but the life
of Christ."[12] Further, in a private letter responding to some questions I had
asked him about his use of Scripture, Father Häring wrote, "Since my youth I
was wrestling with so many cruelties done in God's name in the Old Testament.
The newer exegesis has helped me greatly to see the main line of divine revelation and opposing human forces and traditions."[13]

As for the New Testament, it is clear that by far Häring prefers the Gospel
of John, and particularly the last discourse material of John 13–17. Well over 10
percent of all Häring's biblical references are to the Gospel of John. He also
makes extensive use, as one might expect, of the Sermon on the Mount in
Matthew 5–7. Indeed, Häring explicitly states: "Especially in the Sermon on the
Mount (Mt 5:1 ff), the high-priestly prayer [John 17], and in the farewell discourse to His apostles (Jn 13:31–17:26), He [Christ] expressed in words charged
with all the majesty of His divine authority the inner compulsion of the 'law of
the spirit.'"[14] The core of his working canon is thus John 13–17 and Matthew
5–7.

As for the Pauline writings, one finds frequent reference to Romans, especially Romans 5–8, and significant use of 1 Corinthians. The deutero-Pauline
writings are also heavily represented, particularly Ephesians 4–5 and Colossians,
although it is interesting that Häring never raises the question of Pauline author-
ship and refers to these writings as if Paul wrote them. Hebrews also gets a fair
amount of attention, although proportionally, the five chapters of 1 John are
cited more often than any other document of the New Testament (143 references).

Is there a discernible change of emphasis in which biblical texts Häring
uses in moving from *The Law of Christ* to *Free and Faithful in Christ* twenty-
five years later? In a word, no. There is some difference in *how* he uses biblical
texts, but I was able to discern only two shifts regarding *which* biblical texts
Häring uses between the two works. First, and this came as somewhat of a
surprise, Häring refers to about half the number of biblical texts in *Free and
Faithful in Christ* as he does in *The Law of Christ* (about twelve hundred references compared to about twenty-two hundred references). Second, there is a
sharp move away from the wisdom literature in *Free and Faithful in Christ*.[15]
To explain these two shifts, I suggest the following. Part of the reason for more
biblical references in *The Law of Christ* is that this work is over 400 pages longer
than *Free and Faithful in Christ* (1,923 pages compared to 1,509). But part of the
reason may be due to Häring's increasing departure from proof texting in *Free*

and Faithful when compared to *The Law of Christ*, which I will comment on further later. I would suggest that Häring's move away from the wisdom litera-ture can be attributed to his increasing move away from a focus on "what to do" to a focus on "how to be"—a move away from parenesis per se to an emphasis on dynamic relationships of creative freedom, one of the hallmarks of Häring's approach to moral theology.[16]

If one asks whether Häring has favorite texts that are repeatedly cited, the answer is yes. From the Old Testament Häring's favorite passage is clearly Jer. 31:31–34, which, of course, speaks about God's promise to write a covenant upon the human heart.[17] Given Häring's emphasis on the need for the renewal of the heart, this preference is understandable. As for the New Testament, there are several texts that Häring returns to over and over. And it comes as no surprise that again the Gospel of John takes precedence here. The most frequently cited texts are John 15:12 and Rom. 8:2. Häring uses John 15:12, "This is my command-ment, that you love one another as I have loved you," as a theme that guides his fundamental understanding of Christian life and the focus of moral theol-ogy. He calls John 15:12 the "supreme norm which Jesus formulated at the Last Supper"[18] and identifies this text as the synthesis of "all the goal command-ments of covenant morality" along with Matt. 5:48, "Be perfect, therefore, as your heavenly Father is perfect."[19]

In the same connection, Häring highlights Luke 6:36 ("Be merciful, even as your Father is merciful") as "an all embracing law" and as "the main pattern of the Bible."[20] In his contribution to the *festschrift* for Richard McCormick, Häring writes that the "core of the New Testament's moral message is: 'Be mer-ciful as your heavenly Father is merciful' (Lk 6:36). I can fulfill the difficult mission of a moral theologian only insofar as I orient, not only my private life, but also my theological ethos and activity, according to the beatitude: 'How blest are those who show mercy; mercy shall be shown to them' (Mt 5:7)."[21] Indeed, the focus on these texts goes hand in hand with Häring's move away from moral theology's traditional concern about sins and negative prohibitions to the re-newal concern about life in the Spirit and positive goal commandments.

Häring's repeated references to Rom. 8:2 ("For the law of the Spirit of life in Christ has set you free from the law of sin and of death") undergird his constant emphasis on freedom in one's life in Christ.[22] Along the same lines, Häring refers regularly to Gal. 6:2 ("Bear one another's burdens, and in this way you will fulfill the law of Christ"), from whence comes the title for his first major work, *The Law of Christ*, again emphasizing the positive aspects of the Christian moral life and vision.[23]

Other texts that are often cited cohere around themes of humility (Matt. 5:3; 6:6, 16; 11:25; Luke 10:21), mercy (Luke 6:36), sacrifice and suffering (Rom. 8:17, Gal. 6:14, Col. 1:24), truthfulness (John 8:44, Eph. 4:15), mutual love (John 13:34, Gal. 5:6, 1 John 4:8), and the constant call to renewal and conversion in Christ (Rom. 12:2), all of which Häring sees as dominant features of moral life in the kingdom of God, a motif that he also stresses with many references to

Mark 1:15 and Matt. 4:17. Further, Häring refers frequently to texts that speak of Jesus (whom Häring always calls "Christ") in lofty christological and incarnational terms, especially from the Gospel of John and from Colossians (John 1:14; Col. 1:15, 3:1).[24]

It is also noteworthy that Häring refers primarily to isolated sayings of Jesus and Paul and relatively rarely to narratives about Jesus, although clearly for Häring the ministry, death, and resurrection of Jesus are crucial. Although he is aware of larger narrative contexts, he rarely pays much attention to them.[25]

Finally, an interesting feature of Häring's use of biblical texts is his awareness of text-critical and translation problems, something I have rarely found in the writings of other theological ethicists.[26] For example, in a discussion of sexual self-stimulation and masturbation, Häring refers to 1 Cor. 6:10, where Paul gives a list regarding vices that exclude people from God's kingdom. Häring comments:

> The writings of the Old Testament have no direct word on self-stimulation. The same is probably true of the New Testament. 1 Cor 6:10 was sometimes given this meaning, but the translation of The New English Bible expresses the mind of most of today's biblical scholars: "No fornicator or idolator, none who are guilty either of adultery or homosexual perversion . . . will possess the kingdom of God." ("Homosexual perversion" includes the latin *"mollis."*) The Jerusalem Bible has the same thought, translating "catamites, sodomites." Manualists not infrequently translated "masturbators."[27]

The implication of Häring's comment is that 1 Cor. 6:10 really does not address the issue of masturbation, even though earlier manualists thought it did. Rather, Paul in this text is discussing some form of "homosexuality," for lack of a better word, which he considered perverse. Although Häring correctly calls attention to the difficulties in translating 1 Cor. 6:10, it is surprising that when he discusses homosexuality a few pages later, he only refers to Rom. 1:24–27 and does not pick up on 1 Cor. 6:10.[28]

How Häring Uses Scripture

Overall, I would suggest that four basic uses of Scripture can be found in Häring's writings: (1) proof texting, (2) a biblical concept approach, (3) Scripture as providing examples, and (4) Scripture as illuminating.

Proof Texting

One of the problems that Häring identifies with the manual tradition of moral theology is its tendency to use Scripture as a secondary source of moral guidance, so that as divine revelation it was only brought into a discussion in order to support conclusions that had been arrived at on the basis of rational arguments in the natural-law tradition. Indeed, Häring states: "In earlier years it was an unfortunate custom to refer to Scripture only after having presented one's own system, and to do so particularly in order to present proof-texts for the norms already established once and forever." [29] Or again, he argues that "it is not correct to quote discrete biblical texts as proof texts, unless proper care is taken to discern the dynamics of historical development of ethical knowledge and the very diversity within the books of the Bible." [30] The problem is that Häring himself falls prey to proof texting, especially throughout *The Law of Christ*, a general observation that has been made by Raymond Collins, among others, [31] and that has been documented by Vincent Macnamara in his book *Faith and Ethics: Recent Roman Catholicism.* [32]

Macnamara shows how Häring at times uses Scripture "quite literally and argues from the words of Scripture directly to moral values and rules." [33] For example, Häring ties the argument for fruitfulness in marriage directly to Gen. 1:28 ("Increase and multiply"). [34] Or again, Häring argues for the indissolubility of marriage on the basis that it "was instituted in paradise as an indissoluble union," an assertion that finds no clear support in Scripture, and yet an assertion that Häring indirectly backs up with a reference to Gen. 2:24: "For this reason a man leaves his father and mother, and clings to his wife, and the two become one flesh." [35]

But to be fair to Häring, it must be acknowledged that in retrospect he himself is aware of considerable proof texting in *The Law of Christ*, and that there is a significant move away from proof texting in *Free and Faithful in Christ*. In private correspondence, he has stated:

> There is a great difference between my use of scripture in *The Law of Christ* and in later publications. . . . When I published the German text *Das Gesetz Christi* [in] 1954 two biblical scholars had read the text and approved. The influence of *Divino Afflante Spiritu* [1943] was not yet fully visible. There was still a tendency towards "proof-texts" also with moderation and still with an increasing emphasis on the main lines of revelation. [36]

Although Häring did engage in much proof texting in *The Law of Christ*, he was at the time already clearly aware of the need to move beyond this approach in moral theology and to use the Bible in more responsible ways. This awareness seems to lie behind a somewhat defensive comment he makes at the beginning of volume 2 of *The Law of Christ* in which he remarks on his procedure of correlating love of God with love of one's neighbor and appeals to the authority of a respected biblical scholar in the process: "Our arrangement is exegetically sound and correct, according to C. Spicq in his exposition of Pauline theology." [37] Thus, *The Law of Christ* shows both a clear movement away from the older manual appropriation of Scripture as secondary and yet retains many of the elements of the older approach's use of Scripture in proof texting. But, as we will see, it is not quite correct to say that *The Law of Christ* engages in little more than proof texting, for already there we can see the beginnings of the other uses of Scripture that would typify Häring's more mature work in moral theology.

The Biblical Concept Approach

A second use of Scripture that can be found throughout both *The Law of Christ* and *Free and Faithful in Christ* is what can best be termed the "biblical concept approach."[38] In this use, Häring devotes discrete sections to the biblical concept of a theme or idea. For example, in *The Law of Christ*, Häring has sections entitled "Conscience in Holy Scripture" (1:137–39), "The 'Heart' in Scripture and Tradition" (1:208–11), the "Scriptures and the Natural Moral Law" (1:244–45), "Positive Divine Law" (1:250–57), "The Biblical Delineation of Sin" (1:342–48), "The Words of Scripture" on mortal and venial sin (1:354–55), "The Inspired Concepts of Prudence" (1:499–501), "Divine Glory in the Old Testament" (2:111–13), "Worship of God in the New Testament" (2:113–17), and "The Biblical Use of the Term Scandal" (2:474–77).[39] These sections usually come at the beginning of larger discussions and, it must be said, have little clear relation to the general discussions that follow. These sections on biblical concepts amount to little more than word studies along the lines of Kittel's *Theological Dictionary*, to which frequent reference is made.[40] But this was a dominant style of doing biblical exegesis and biblical theology in the 1950s.

In turning to *Free and Faithful in Christ*, one again finds some treatments of biblical concepts, although not nearly as many as are found in *The Law of Christ*. In *Free and Faithful*, biblical concept studies are found in the sections "The Biblical Vision of Conscience" (1:225–29), "Reciprocity of Consciences in Paul's Letters" (1:267–70), "Hope in the Bible" (2:380–91), "The Complexity of the Biblical Concept of 'World'" (3:116–17), and "War and Peace in the New Testament" (3:398–99). These sections are again primarily word studies, but with much more nuance and awareness of the difficulties of talking generically about "biblical concepts" per se. This awareness is illustrated by Häring's comment regarding what the Bible says about hope: "to understand the message of hope in the Bible, it is not enough to look just for texts mentioning the word 'hope.' "[41]

Häring never explicitly states why he has chosen to develop some biblical concepts and not others. One has to assume that he devoted discrete sections to those concepts he found most significant—especially on conscience and sin.

Scripture as a Source of Examples

Häring repeatedly refers to examples from Scripture. He does this in two ways. On the one hand, he refers to various biblical examples in order to illustrate a general principle. On the other hand, he draws on biblical examples by way of analogy in order to suggest a more specific contemporary application of a text. I will look at each in turn.

A few instances will show this use of Scripture. In a section where Häring is discussing the place of humility in repentance, he states that "the typical examples of conversion found in the Bible teach the same lesson of the importance of humility for true repentance," going on to refer to Jesus' story in Luke 18 contrasting the Pharisee and the tax collector who both go up to pray.[42] He also refers to the general example of Paul's sensitivity to the diversity of the audiences he addressed in his missionary work, thus illustrating the general principle of the need to be aware of how the gospel takes different shapes in different social and cultural contexts.[43] Or again, Häring presents biblical "examples of creative liberty and fidelity,"[44] in which he calls attention to how the earliest Christians dealt with conflict, drawing specifically on the new ministry of deacons in Acts 6, the extension of the gospel to the Gentiles in Acts 10, and the conflict between Paul and Peter rehearsed by Paul in Galatians 2. Häring comments:

> Because of the prophetic word of Paul, the prophetical initiative of Stephen, Philip and the other deacons, and the charismatic leadership in the apostolic Church, Christianity could spread all over the known world of that time. The gospel was not impeded by a canon law like the one which hindered the Church's mission work from the sixteenth to the twentieth century in Asia and Africa.[45]

Thus, for Häring, the early Christians provide a paradigmatic example of how to resolve conflict in a way that maintains fidelity to the character of the gospel, and this example in turn can serve as a critique of mistakes made by the modern church.

Häring repeatedly seeks to make analogous connections between the situations addressed in the Bible and similar contemporary situations in the church. For instance, in a section on the use of mass media for presenting the gospel, he draws the following analogy: "The kingdom of God is a public reality. 'You must shout from the housetops' (Mt 10:27). Are not the modern mass-media today's housetops?"[46] A second instance no doubt generates more controversy. In a section on potential conflict between culture and Christian ethics Häring raises the difficult situation of the church's handling of the levirate marriage custom in various African contexts. He reflects back on the practice of levirate marriage as recorded in the Old Testament and goes on to state that

> in my opinion, this vision [from the Old Testament] could be helpful . . . for facing realistically the problem of baptizing African polygamists without destroying a healthy and socially approved and sanctioned family unit. Cannot the levirate marriage, which in the Old Testament was one of the most "sanctioned" moral duties, be temporarily tolerated in newly converted African communities in which this institution has the same function and the same sense of

obligation as in Old Israel? The same is true for the stages of the customary marriage, which cannot be changed suddenly without damage to all involved and to the life of the young church.[47]

In a different place, Häring makes a similar comment regarding the interpretation of Genesis 38: "[I]t should not be excluded that the text might be a challenge to the Church when she prohibits the fulfilment of the levirate duty to African tribes who are, as much as were the sons of Abraham, convinced that this is their duty."[48]

Häring's use of the Old Testament to argue for allowing a practice that clearly goes against official church teaching and tradition is quite intriguing. Because the Bible presents a situation that really is analogous to a contemporary problem faced by the church, Häring suggests that the biblical example can provide the church with a viable way out of the dilemma.

The Illuminative Use of Scripture

This last use of Scripture is somewhat slippery. Throughout *The Law of Christ* and *Free and Faithful in Christ*, Häring generously seasons his discussions with references to specific biblical texts that appear to add insight to the argument but receive no development. Perhaps this could be called an ornamental use of Scripture. It is not really proof texting in the traditional sense, because Häring does not appeal to the biblical text as added support for an argument. Rather, he draws in Scripture almost in a homiletical style, as if to invite the reader to reflect further on the matter from the perspective of a biblical citation. Almost without exception, Häring will cite one or two verses with no reference to context.

Along the same lines, Häring frequently makes use of what I call "cluster citations." A cluster citation is a reference to three or more biblical texts, often citing them partly or completely, to add to the discussion, although it must be admitted that at times Häring appears to do little more than pile one text upon another without comment. He seems to assume that the meaning of the texts and the reason for reference to them is obvious.[49] The primary purpose of these cluster citations is apparently to give a biblical flavor to the general discussion by seasoning it with generous biblical citations, without substantive appeal to or development of the citations made.[50]

Häring's View of the Authority of Scripture

Although Häring never offers any explicit comments about the authority of Scripture, he does make several indirect comments. One indication of his view of Scripture's authority is a not so subtle shift that he makes from *The Law of Christ* to *Free and Faithful in Christ*. In volume 2 of *The Law of Christ*, Häring had written a brief "Prelude," as he called it, on the Bible as a source for moral reflection. Interestingly, this "Prelude" was not part of the main text of the volume but appeared more as a preface to the volume. In *Free and Faithful in Christ*, however, the very first section of volume 1 is entitled "Biblical Perspectives" and is clearly incorporated into the main body of the volume. Over Häring's career, Scripture takes on more and more authority for his understanding and development of moral reflection.

One significant feature of Häring's view of biblical authority is the great distinction he makes between the authority of the Old Testament and the authority of the New Testament, especially in *The Law of Christ*. In particular, he characterizes the law of the Old Testament as completely transcended by the law of the New Testament, to such a degree that the Old Testament really does not figure in the task of moral theology: "To present the specific characteristics and the content of the New Testament law is the task of moral theology as a whole." [51]

In one section, "Law of the Old Testament," Häring states that three different kinds of law are found in the Old Testament: cultic law, judiciary law, and moral law. Both cultic and judiciary law are made obsolete in Christ and thus emptied of all authority. Indeed, "with the founding of the universal Church, the spiritual norms of her law replaced the juridical norms, temporal and spiritual, of the Israelitic theocracy." [52] All that remains in any way authoritative from the Old Testament is the moral law. Häring completely identifies this moral law with natural law, which is available to all humans, Israelite or not, by means of human reason.

According to Häring, such statements as that found in Deut. 30:11, 14 ("This commandment, that I command thee this day is not above thee . . . but the word is very nigh unto thee, in thy mouth and in thy heart, that thou mayest do it"), "are probably an indication that the law conforms to reason and is naturally knowable. In any case, the content of the second table of the decalog does not transcend the law of nature." [53] As Häring puts it elsewhere in *The Law of Christ*:

> The moral law of the Old Testament as the clear revelation of the natural law is without doubt more specific and precise in its determinations and enjoys a loftier sanction because of the loving alliance between God and His people. The moral norms of the Old Testament are summed up in the decalog and in the great commandment. Their binding force as natural law rested on the rational nature of man, who can grasp them by use of his natural endowment of reason. [54]

Häring goes on, however, to state that the continuing authority of the Old Testament's moral law comes not from the status of the Old Testament as Scripture but instead from the New Testament endorsement of this moral law. The authority of the Old Testament moral law is mediated by the New Testament.

> As to their substance, the moral laws of the Old Testament preserve their binding force also in the New Testament, both in virtue of the natural law and in virtue of the positive specification of this law through the revelation of the Old Testament. The Old Testament revelation surely preserves its character as

revelation also in the New Testament. However, its binding force, interpretation, and sanction no longer derives from the Old Testament, but from the
New.[55]

What becomes increasingly clear in *The Law of Christ* is that for Häring the
Old Testament has no revelatory, and thus no authoritative, capacity apart from
its corroboration in the New Testament. The Old Testament appears to contain
no substantive revelation of moral significance apart from the "moral law,"
which is actually accessible to human reason as natural law.

The degree to which the Old Testament has been completely displaced and
outmoded, then, can hardly be overstated. Its sole function appears to be that
of pointing to and anticipating what is to be revealed in Christ, as indeed Häring
argues: "Christ, even before the Incarnation, is the center toward which the Old
Testament law tends (Rom 10:4; Gal 3:24)."[56] The law of the Old Testament,
and even its moral law, which is all that remains, is inferior to the new law
revealed by and in Christ. "The new law demands of the individual . . . a much
higher perfection than the Old Testament."[57] Indeed, the "negative precepts of
the decalog, the two tables of the law, are not a perfect and adequate expression
of the inner law written in the heart through our assimilation to Christ."[58]

An example of the inferiority of the Old Testament law (not the moral law,
but in this instance the judicial law) may be seen in the right of the state to
punish some crimes with the death penalty (and here Häring lists Gen. 9:6 and
Num. 35:16 ff.). Although such texts would seem to legitimate the right of the
state to carry out capital punishment for the larger common good, Häring comments:

> A word of caution regarding these texts: at best these texts from the Old Testa-
> ment taken in themselves alone show that the death penalty could be justified
> and necessary before men had received the fulness of the redemption. How-
> ever, it would not at all be in harmony with the unique fulness of salvation [in
> Christ] and its loving kindness to apply these drastic directives without any
> qualification as obligatory in the present order of salvation and grace.[59]

Thus, for Häring, the moral teachings of the Old Testament have no binding
authority on their own and must be revisioned in light of the fullness of redemption in Christ, to which the New Testament bears direct witness.

The relatively negative approach to the Old Testament found in *The Law
of Christ* finds significant revision in Häring's later three-volume moral theology,
Free and Faithful in Christ, where he assigns a greater authority to the Old
Testament than he had in his previous work. In his opening section "Biblical
Perspectives" (vol. 1, chap. 1), he states: "Moral theology has much to learn from
the great and all-pervading perspectives of the Old Testament. There, the great
themes that are particularly fruitful for ethics overlap and integrate each
other."[60] Häring especially highlights the notion of God's creative word and
God's calling found throughout the Old Testament. Thus, there is God's call to
repentance and salvation (Noah), God's call of election and promise (Abraham),
God's call of liberation and covenant (Moses), God's call of charismatic leaders

(Judges), and finally God's call of the prophets, which "ethical prophetism" is, in Häring's view, "the summit of the Old Testament."[61]

In addition to the motifs of creation and call, Häring draws particularly on the Servant Songs of Second Isaiah, which, for Häring, point clearly in the direction of Christ:

> To my mind the summit of the Old Testament, and especially of the history of the ethical and religious prophetism, is Second Isaiah, who presents the "Servant of Yahweh" (Isa. 40 ff). . . . This is the heart of the prophetic message: that God will finally call and send One who is fully, faithfully, and creatively the Servant of God and men. This is the messianic hope.[62]

The significance of the Old Testament here, then, is in its anticipation of the New Covenant in Christ.

Similarly, Häring calls attention to the covenant written on one's heart in Jeremiah 31 and Ezekiel 36, concluding that the central themes of the Old Testament point directly to the gospel message of salvation in the New Testament. Thus, although ultimately the Old Testament remains for Häring primarily a precursor and pointer to Christ, he moves significantly away from the overall negative characterization of the Old Testament found in *The Law of Christ* to a more positive appreciation for the Old Testament, and the unity and authority of the biblical witness as a whole, in *Free and Faithful in Christ*.

Beyond his characterization of the relatively inferior authority of the Old Testament in comparison to the New, his indirect comments on the authority of Scripture have mostly to do with the process of distinguishing between time-bound statements, which no longer have authority, and normative statements, which continue to have authority. Häring devotes considerable attention to how one differentiates time-bound statements in the Bible from normative statements that remain authoritative. He writes, "Surely, we must carefully distinguish what is an abiding orientation and normative ideal from what is time-bound moral or religious exhortation in a particular situation."[63]

In principle, Häring proceeds by identifying the more general moral statements as authoritative and binding while seeing the more concrete and specific statements as more likely to be time-bound and not authoritative in the same sense. According to Häring, "the more concrete some biblical norms are the more carefully must the question of concrete historical circumstances be raised; and the universality of norms binding for all time is not to be asserted on the basis of one or two texts."[64] To give an example, Häring states:

> The first impression, and the rightful presumption, is that the general material norms derived from the main perspectives of faith are meant to be abiding and binding teaching for all times. . . . [However, n]ot infrequently the context and the formulation of the inspired authors indicate that it is a matter of guidance in a unique historical context or even a response to a very special local problem. The latter is evidently the case in Paul's argumentation about the women's veil in Corinth (1 Cor 11:33–36 . . .). However, this does not at all mean that these passages are irrelevant for the moral teaching of today; on the contrary,

they are very helpful as "models" of how to deal with particular traditions and how to incarnate the Gospel morality in other cultural contexts.[65]

Thus, even when specific biblical moral statements are considered time-bound and not authoritative in a primary sense, they are authoritative in a secondary sense insofar as they provide models, or prototypes (but not archetypes), for how the Christian and the church should proceed in different cultural situations.

What are the normative biblical statements that remain authoritative? Häring identifies what he calls the "eschatological virtues"—faith, hope, and love—as authoritative for Christianity in all times and places. According to Häring, these virtues "are originally biblical, emphasized at all times and normative for Christian ethics."[66] He states that "the emphasis of the Bible is on the eschatological virtues" and goes on to say: "My intention, here, is to show that a return to the biblical vision can generate and release energies of creative liberty and fidelity in today's world."[67]

Of particular interest in this regard is an essay Häring published in 1967, "The Normative Value of the Sermon on the Mount," in the leading Roman Catholic journal of biblical studies in the United States, *The Catholic Biblical Quarterly*.[68] He begins the essay by asking: "Is the Sermon on the Mount a collection of pious counsels without binding power? Or is it merely a question of casuistic solutions to concrete questions or of legal directives which claim validity for all times and places?" (p. 69). His answer is to highlight the character of the Sermon on the Mount as normative covenant law and on the basis of the sermon's literary form and construction to portray this covenant law character of the sermon as Matthew's intention. In particular, Häring notes how Matthew clearly "intends to set off the New Law against the OT covenant law" (p. 69). Indeed, already in *The Law of Christ*, Häring had emphasized the normative status of the Sermon on the Mount over against the Old Testament:

> The negative precepts of the decalog, the two tables of the law, are not a perfect and adequate expression of the inner law written in the heart through our assimilation to Christ. This is manifested rather by the Sermon on the Mount, the new law of the kingdom of God promulgated by Christ, the law of disinterested and unbounded love, humility, and love of the cross. . . . The Sermon on the Mount determines the ideals and goals toward which we must strive (purposive precepts).[69]

In his 1967 essay, he develops in more detail the authoritative character of the Sermon on the Mount over against the Mosaic law. Whereas the revelation of the law to Moses on Sinai took place at a distance from the rebellious Israelites (Exod. 19:17–25; 34:1–3), God's revelation of the New Law through Jesus stands in sharp contrast, because Matthew emphasizes "Jesus' proximity to his disciples and the great crowds of people. The announcement of the Beatitudes does not merely replace the thunder and lightning. Rather the whole setting serves to feature the New Covenant which comes to us in Immanuel as the promised New Covenant" (p. 70). For Häring, the closeness of Jesus to the people in contrast to the distance of God from the Israelites is one of the most significant features of the Sermon on the Mount. While both theophanies emphasize the authority of the lawgiver and the law given, for Häring it is the combination of authority and closeness in Jesus that is remarkable. "The marvelous harmonious tension between the authority and the proximity of Jesus to his disciples and also to the crowds of the people is uniquely expressed in Mt's whole literary composition of the Sermon on the Mount" (p. 71).

Häring hastens to add a comparison of the closeness seen in the Sermon on the Mount with the closeness of Jesus to his disciples seen in the last discourse of John's Gospel.

> The Johannine synthesis of Jesus' moral proclamation (13–17) provides a basis for comparison. Jesus, the bearer of salvation, the herald of the salvific message, and the giver of the New Law, appears there in another image, in unsurpassable proximity, in a revelation of boundless love and, at the same time, in absolute authority: Jesus as the master of the house washes the feet of the Apostles and explains: "You call me 'Master' and 'Lord,' and rightly so, for that is what I am" (Jn 13,13). (p. 71)

Like the Sermon on the Mount, for Häring the last discourse of John highlights the new and normative connection in Jesus of closeness and authority, so that authority comes not from Jesus lording over the disciples but from his approaching them with compassion and serving them. For Häring, Jesus' authoritative command arises from the gift of his saving presence with the disciples. "The sublimity of the demand corresponds to the sublimity of the gift and call. The unity of indicative and imperative, however, the total incorporation of the command into the gift, also confirms the normative value of the Sermon on the Mount" (p. 72).

What is the central authoritative message of the Sermon on the Mount? According to Häring, the high point of the sermon comes in Matt. 5:43–48, which he cites as follows: " 'Love your enemies and pray for your persecutors; only so can you be children of your heavenly Father, who makes his sun rise on good and bad alike. . . . you must therefore be all goodness [perfect], just as your heavenly Father is all good' (Mt 5,43–48)" (p. 72). For Häring, this indicates that by the fact of the New Covenant, "by the inner proximity of God to his People, there arises the grace-founded possibility, and from this the norm for imitating precisely God's mercy" (p. 72). Häring sees the same motif of God's unmerited love in Luke's version of the sermon (especially in Luke 6:36: "Be compassionate as your Father is compassionate") and especially in Jesus' command in John 15:12, "This is my commandment: love one another, as I have loved you."

But what is specifically and authoritatively normative from the Sermon on the Mount? Häring argues that Matthew leaves intact "the validity of minimal limits" (do not murder, do not commit adultery, etc.), so that Christian ethics cannot ultimately be reduced to situation ethics (p. 74). There is a bottom line of minimal standards, but in the New Law much more has been indicated. The Sermon on the Mount does not so much add additional limitations as it completely shifts the balance and point of view of the law. "The disciple of Christ as such is not confronted with the tablets telling him what not to do. If he still has need of them, then it is due to the fact that he has not yet perfected the change of outlook with sufficient energy. He who has accepted the new form of the covenant commandment of the Beatitudes is far removed from transgressing the negative directive 'Thou shalt not kill! Thou shalt not commit adultery' " (p. 74). From Häring's perspective, the Sermon on the Mount points to the complete renewal and sanctification of the believer as the goal toward which the believer is directed.

> It is unmistakably clear from the Sermon on the Mount that the decisive directive for the disciple of Christ is that of the goal commandments, which are "commandments" of beatitude, the Good News, grace, and the kingdom of God which draws near with power. The goal commandments, which are all summed up in: "You therefore must be all goodness, just as your heavenly Father is all good," are no less serious than the fulfillment commandments (limitative commandments) of the Decalogue; they are absolutely normative in their seriousness. However, the word "norm" attains a new, analogous meaning here. It looks to a dynamic propulsion, an initiated movement, an organized action toward clearly defined goals. (p. 74)

Here Häring lifts up the goal commandments of perfection, of direction toward a goal, as being at the heart of the Sermon on the Mount.

He seeks to illustrate his point by appealing to the parable of the talents (Matt. 25:14–30). The servants who use their talents to the full receive equal praise from the master. For Häring, this indicates: "In every case it is a question of that grateful affirmation and acceptance of God's grace in Christ Jesus which liberates the person in the dimension of true freedom" (p. 75). Jesus' statement in the Sermon on the Mount "But this is what I tell you" provides a "dynamic norm which can be 'fulfilled' only in the manner of perpetual conversion, unrelenting effort, somewhat like Paul's way of expressing it in the Epistle to the Philippians. 'It is not to be thought that I have already achieved all this. I have not yet reached perfection, but I press on' " (Phil. 3:12–15) (p. 75).

What are the ongoing criteria for discerning the authoritative norm articulated in the goal commandments of the Sermon on the Mount? For Häring, the sermon itself provides several criteria: love of enemy as the "fully characteristic criterion of the newness of life," the Golden Rule of Matt. 7:12, and finally the criterion of fruitfulness (Matt. 7:20). "The Sermon on the Mount is an ethic of attitude, a directive drawn from the power of the Good News. At the same time it makes it clear that the change of attitude transforms one's whole life" (p. 76). Häring agrees with Matthew, who

> sees in the Sermon on the Mount the absolutely binding and liberating directive of the New Covenant. . . . The goal commandments are not an optional piece of advice. Each one must acquire for himself that spirit which is described here and with all the power at his command start out in the direction which is shown here. (p. 76)

Still, even given the authoritative and binding character of the Sermon on the Mount, Häring also argues that the directives of the sermon cannot be construed as "casuistic solutions" for all imaginable cases, such as never taking an oath (Matt. 5:33–37), or always offering the other cheek (5:39) or even the saying that "whoever marries a divorced woman commits adultery" (5:32). Alongside this last statement, Häring places the Pauline sayings on divorce and remarriage as indications that the saying in the Sermon on the Mount (5:32) cannot be taken as an absolute and exceptionless directive (p. 77).

Häring concludes his essay with a statement that summarizes the overall balance he seeks to articulate regarding the normative and authoritative character of the Sermon on the Mount and the more general directives of the goal commandments, which point toward the freedom of the believer to pursue all goodness as best he or she can:

> The Sermon on the Mount does not allow any legal minimalism which acts as if everything else were mere optional counsel. However, it gives just as little room to legal harshness. It refers to the noble reply to God's love and beckons to the mature Christian who grows in the knowledge of Christ and thus in sound judgment also. From this knowledge, therefore, of the true physiognomy of love he is to advance in the best possible way at the time in the direction of perfect love. (p. 78)

As we have already seen, Häring's working authoritative canon revolves around the farewell discourse of John 13–17 and the Sermon on the Mount in Matthew 5–7. The overall authority of this working canon, in turn, is that of giving normative, positive direction for Christian discipleship, a discipleship grounded in the love and grace of God in Christ.

Häring further develops the normative value of Scripture for Christian ethics in the section "The Bible and Normative Ethics" in the first volume of *Free and Faithful in Christ*:

> A moral theology of creative liberty and fidelity finds its distinctively Christian quality in the light of the dynamic dimensions and perspectives which we find in the Bible. Their normative value is quite different from any kind of norms fitting external controls. They are, however, binding—and at the same time liberating—guidelines, norms in a very broad but real sense. (1:23)

Häring argues for the binding and normative character of Scripture in theological ethics, though he sees Scripture as offering guidelines and direction more than it does rules or limits. "In all these perspectives of the Old and especially of the New Testament, there is no place for a mere code morality or an allowance to confine oneself to static norms. It is always the dynamics of salvation truth" (1:24). But the "dynamics of salvation truth" presented in Scripture remain very broad and general when it comes to the authority of Scripture for normative Christian ethics.

Häring's Hermeneutics

Häring has relatively little to say about his hermeneutical approach to Scripture. In *The Law of Christ* he has absolutely nothing explicit to say. As Macnamara has observed in his book *Faith and Ethics*: "[A]t this stage of his theology he had not produced a cogent and convincing moral methodology: this is compounded by a considerable looseness of style. One cannot find that in *The Law of Christ* he even once adverts to the exegetical or hermeneutical problems of the use of Scripture."[70] In *Free and Faithful in Christ*, however, he does devote a small section in the first volume to his hermeneutical principles, which is the source of my comments here.

The guiding principle for Häring's hermeneutics is to be exegetically aware, to take the historical contexts and literary forms of Scripture very seriously, and only then proceed to apply what Scripture says to the contemporary scene.

> [W]hile exegesis is principally concerned with discovering what really happened and was said in those times . . . , theological hermeneutics seeks to answer the question: What does the Bible teach us in order to understand God's will here and now, in our time? Hermeneutics requires knowledge both of that time and our time, sharp awareness of the biblical horizon for understanding, including the time-bound worldview of the inspired writers, and of our own culturally conditioned way of approaching the problems.[71]

Thus for Häring, historical awareness is paramount in one's approach to Scripture, awareness of the Bible's contextual settings and of the varied contextual settings in which Christians have sought and seek to use the Bible for moral reflection.

Aside from this, Häring really says little more in concrete terms. In several places, he states the need to have the "appropriate approach to . . . hermeneutics"[72] but then does not go on to say what that approach means apart from historical, social, and cultural sensitivity. Trying to get a firmer picture of Häring's hermeneutical methodology reminds one of a comment made by Richard McCormick in his "Notes on Moral Theology" about an article by Häring. McCormick writes that "the essay is vintage Häring, which is to say that it is characterized by obvious Christlike kindness and compassion, pastoral prudence, a shrewd sense of the direction of things, and a generous amount of haziness"![73]

There are, however, some additional observations one can make about Häring's hermeneutics. In his approach to Scripture, Häring emphasizes the general unity of the Bible rather than its diversity. This unity is important for providing a holistic view of Christian existence, as Häring is concerned to focus on main themes and patterns within the biblical witness. As he puts it in the first chapter of *Free and Faithful in Christ* ("Biblical Perspectives: Vision of Wholeness"):

> We can gain the necessary vision of wholeness only by listening to the word of God and, in the light of his word, searching the signs of the times. Hence, I present first the main perspectives of the Old and New Testaments as biblical

theology and a biblically oriented moral theology have worked them out. Only
then do I try to discern the main patterns that respond faithfully to the biblical
perspectives and, at the same time, creatively meet the signs of the times. (1:6)

Rather than highlighting differences between the various biblical writings, and
their different visions of embodied faith, Häring seeks to present a general and
somewhat homogeneous "vision of wholeness" discerned from the main patterns
of the Bible, even while paying attention to the historical contexts of the various
biblical writings. For Häring, such a unified approach to Scripture has the capacity to elicit dynamic responses from those faithful to God. "My intention . . .
is to show that a return to *the biblical vision* can generate and release energies
of creative liberty and fidelity in today's world"(1:201, emphasis mine).

In addition to an emphasis on the unity of Scripture, Häring repeatedly
refers to the role of the Holy Spirit in the appropriation of Scripture, and it is
clear that he sees God's Spirit as part of the hermeneutical circle. For example,
in a section on ecumenism, Häring writes that "the basis and starting point of
our common search for unity and greater fullness of truth is holy Scripture. But
immediately we must add that this is so because we believe in the Holy Spirit
who not only has inspired the sacred authors but who will also guide us in our
common search if we trust in him" (2:276). Or again: "The Spirit introduces us
not only to an understanding of the Bible but . . . to an understanding of 'things
that are coming' " (1:331). Thus, according to Häring, the central feature of good
hermeneutics is a combination of trust in historical-critical exegesis with trust
in God's Spirit at work in the church, for Häring also argues that the Bible only
really functions appropriately when it is read and interpreted in the context of
Christian community.[74]

Finally, Häring's hermeneutics stresses the dialogic character of Scripture,
lifting up God's call and human response as the basic pattern of Christian existence. As he puts it in the preface to the second volume of *The Law of Christ*,
the basic question of Christian morality is always the same: "How can we respond to the incomprehensible love which the Father has spoken to us in His
Incarnate Son, the Word, Jesus Christ?" (2:xvii).[75] In the "Prelude" that follows,
in a section entitled "The Biblical Source," Häring states that Christian existence "is essentially dialog-response, which means that it springs from the response of man to the redemptive word of God committed to him. In consequence moral theology in all its considerations must flow from the word of God"
(2:xxi), which bears witness to the ethics of response at the core of Christian
moral reflection and action.[76]

This ethics of response continues in *Free and Faithful in Christ*, as Häring
states in the introduction: "I also feel a strong sense of continuity in my effort
to present responsibility and co-responsibility as key concepts in a Christian
ethics for people of today" (1:1). And, in Scripture, he sees the pattern of God's
call and the believer's response repeated over and over again, from the Old
Testament to the New. Indeed, "the main perspectives of the Old Testament
merge into the one 'Good News' of conversion as God's gracious word and work

and the people's grateful acceptance and response. It is a message and call for each of them and all of them"(1:15).

In choosing a leitmotif for presenting Christian ethics as creative liberty and fidelity, Häring states that a leitmotif should only be chosen

> after having carefully studied the biblical patterns and after discerning, in view of those patterns, the special signs of God's present action and call in history. . . . It is therefore a distinctively Christian approach to emphasize *responsibility* as a leitmotif, but in a way that shows it as expression of creative freedom and fidelity.[77]

This emphasis on an ethics of response, then, permeates Häring's approach both to moral theology in general and to the Bible in particular.

Häring and the Significance of Scripture for Moral Theology and Christian Ethics

Häring sees Scripture as providing a holistic vision of Christian life that gives general normative guidelines and examples of how faith is lived out in the world. But Scripture does not provide many specific moral directives that can be applied without taking historical and social contexts into account. Scripture must always be correlated again and again with contemporary situations, for there is no permanently lasting interpretation, just as there is no once and for all exposition of moral theology.

For Häring, it is sufficient to use Scripture to point in general directions, to describe main principles of the Christian life, to provide goals and a unified vision toward which Christians strive together in community. Such directions, principles, and goals are normative and binding, but how they find expression in concrete terms in the everyday life of Christians is primarily up to the capacity of each Christian as he or she responds out of creative freedom in fidelity to God's call and claim upon his or her life.

Häring came from the tradition of manuals in moral theology that sought to enumerate all possible specific cases and to articulate rules that applied in each case, appealing to Scripture rarely and then merely for proof texting one conclusion or another. Häring breaks free both from this approach to moral theology in general and from its use of Scripture in particular. He does so by stressing Christian freedom in God's love and grace made manifest in Christ. He sees such freedom in the biblical witness and seems determined to avoid portraying the Bible as merely a series of constraints. Instead, he uses Scripture to give broad shape to a vision of authentic Christian existence that is responsive both to God and to people. In keeping with his personalist approach, he allows generous leeway for how Christians appropriate and pursue the goal commands laid out in Scripture. It is thus difficult to develop in any more than the general terms already spelled out regarding the Sermon on the Mount how Häring construes Scripture for constructing Christian ethics.[78] When it comes to using

Scripture for Christian ethics, he is content to talk about "clear perspectives, a most relevant vision and basic principles."[79]

Critical Evaluation

In assessing Häring's use of Scripture in moral theology, I would call attention to four concerns. First, although Häring regularly calls the reader to pay attention to the historical and social concreteness of Scripture, Häring himself ironically often exhibits little sensitivity to the historically conditioned character of Scripture. This is an interesting oversight, because he does display a sophisticated and critical awareness of how moral theology has been conditioned by various historical contexts.[80] It appears that in his enthusiasm for Scripture, he is often insufficiently critically attentive to historical situations that gave shape and substance to the various biblical writings. For example, he refers more to the Gospel of John than to any other document, but not once does he ever discuss the historical and theological context in which this rather polemical Gospel developed. (Häring has a way of ignoring those aspects of Scripture that are problematic; e.g., the demonic portrayal of Jews in John 8 becomes symbolic for Häring of a larger point regarding lies.)[81] He does refer regularly to specific contexts of Paul's letters—1 Corinthians, Galatians, and sometimes Romans. But he does not do this with any other biblical material. He is aware of historical problems (e.g., he states clearly that Adam and Eve were not real historical persons but represent human collectives), but he is not very consistent in his use of historical readings of Scripture. The effect of his somewhat ahistorical approach to Scripture is that his appeals to Scripture often appear to be rather loose and insufficiently grounded.

A second concern is related to the first. Häring rarely engages in what would be considered actual exegesis of texts, and in particular, he generally neglects any consideration of the literary contexts of the passages he cites. This leaves the impression that with most of his biblical citations there is little concern (and little need for concern) for how well his appropriation of the biblical writings accords with the larger framework and purposes of the various writings he uses. (Perhaps an exception here is his discussion of the Sermon on the Mount, where he is quite interested in the literary development of the sermon and in the social-historical context underlying Matthew's theology.) Häring is clearly quite familiar with the work of various biblical scholars (e.g., R. Schnackenburg, J. Dupont, E. Käsemann, and W. Eichrodt), as evidenced especially in *Free and Faithful in Christ*, but he does not often incorporate the findings of biblical scholars in his many appeals to biblical texts.[82]

A third concern has to do with his approach to and use of the Old Testament. What does it mean for Christians to have a unified biblical canon containing two testaments? Häring's thoroughly christological approach to the Bible nearly renders the Old Testament nonfunctional for Christian theological ethics. He appears to find the Old Testament useful only insofar as it illumines

God's revelation in Christ in the New Testament. Indeed, Häring seems almost to suggest that there really is no revelation per se in the Old Testament law, since the moral law is accessible through natural reasoning. And Häring does little to develop any other positive evaluation of the moral vision found in the Old Testament, especially among the prophets. In short, Häring's approach to the Bible lacks an integrated vision of how the Old Testament continues to function along with the New Testament as Scripture that is useful for constructing Christian ethics.

Fourth and finally, one of the strengths of Häring's approach to Scripture also raises various questions. Häring quite consciously seeks to present a rather general and unified picture of Christian existence in biblical terms. He is content with broad principles, with John 15:12 providing the basic vision: "Love one another as I have loved you." Häring's very open-ended approach has been a refreshing change in the tradition of Roman Catholic moral theology, as we have seen. And yet it is so general in scope that it begs for sharper definition. In particular, Häring is so concerned with presenting a unified biblical "vision of wholeness" that one wonders about the tremendous diversity of approaches found within the biblical witness. How are these different moral visions to be construed in relation to one another? This is a question that Häring does not ask, let alone answer. For him, the answers come in the freedom of Christians as they seek faithfully to respond to God and to one another in Christ.

five

PAUL RAMSEY

Obedient Covenant Love

*P*aul Ramsey (1913–88) is generally recognized as one of the foremost Christian ethicists of the twentieth century. His career spanned some forty years, most of it teaching in the religion department at Princeton University from the 1940s to the 1980s. He is probably best known for his contributions to just war theory and to medical ethics, but he has also exercised a tremendous influence upon the field of religious ethics in general, both in Protestant ethics and in Catholic moral theology.[1] A good deal of attention has been given to Ramsey's thought, resulting in, for example, a 1973 book on Ramsey by Charles Curran; a book of essays by various scholars, *Love and Society: Essays in the Ethics of Paul Ramsey* (1974); and an entire issue (fall 1991) of the *Journal of Religious Ethics* devoted to essays on Ramsey.[2] But Ramsey's use of the Bible has not been treated in any of these analyses, and very little on this subject can be found elsewhere.[3]

My analysis of Ramsey's use of Scripture is based on only a part of his literary output. Ramsey wrote thirteen books, edited twelve others, and wrote over 180 articles and chapters. In this regard, it is worth citing a comment made by the Catholic moral theologian Richard McCormick in his response to a lengthy critique Ramsey had written of a much shorter article by McCormick. McCormick begins by saying: "It was to be expected that only heroic efforts by the prodigious Paul Ramsey could reduce his manuscript to a lean one hundred and twenty manuscript pages. 'Increase and multiply' is a biblical mandate Ramsey has taken over and spoken to his typewriter with a real vengeance, or, if I may, with a finality disallowing any exceptions by proportionate reason. Amidst it all, I am never sure I have him down pat."[4] One cannot but empathize with McCormick, for the extent of Ramsey's writings and his often rather cumbersome style make it difficult for the reader to have full confidence that she or he really knows what Ramsey is saying.[5] Ramsey's writings provide no easy handles.

To set reasonable limits for this examination, then, I have concentrated my analysis on several central and, I think, representative writings: his books *Basic Christian Ethics* (1950),[6] *Deeds and Rules in Christian Ethics* (1967), *The Patient as Person* (1970), and *Speak Up for Just War or Pacifism* (1988), along with many of his articles, especially "Beyond the Confusion of Tongues" (1947) and "The Biblical Norm of Righteousness" (1970).[7] Perhaps more so than any other author considered in this book (with the possible exception of Reinhold Niebuhr), Paul Ramsey's influence is due to the many topical essays and articles he wrote as much as to his books. I have also examined his other books, though seldom does one find in them much significant use of the Bible.

Biblical Texts Used by Ramsey

In the writings I have surveyed, Ramsey refers to the Bible a little more than 300 times (314 to be exact), with about twice as many references to the New Testament as to the Old Testament (215 New Testament references to 99 Old Testament references). Of these, about two-thirds come from his earliest book, and his only comprehensive and foundational work, *Basic Christian Ethics* (61 Old Testament and 147 New Testament references).[8]

From the Hebrew Scriptures, Ramsey appeals primarily to Genesis (22 citations; all from Gen. 1–14) and to the prophetic literature, particularly Isaiah and Jeremiah (17 and 12 citations, respectively). Most of the Old Testament citations appear in his discussion of the righteousness of God, a central notion for Ramsey (see *BCE*, pp. 2–24). Ramsey's selection of Old Testament texts, however, is clearly and self-consciously guided by his christocentric approach to Christian ethics, and so to the Bible. Indeed, Ramsey characterizes his *Basic Christian Ethics* as "an essay in the Christocentric ethics of the Reformation" (p. xiv). This christocentric approach is easy to see. For example, he states that "Old Testament ethics reaches perhaps its highest expression in the book of Hosea, in the Suffering Servant passages in Isaiah, and in Job's 'negative confession,'" where Job defends his life by saying he has extended mercy to others (see Job 31; *BCE*, p. 11). According to Ramsey, Hosea and the Suffering Servant Songs of Isaiah, along with other prophetic materials, show God's righteousness, which is definitively expressed in Jesus. For Christians, Jesus has become the righteousness of God.[9]

Further, Ramsey openly distinguishes between the creation stories in Genesis and the Christian creation story, which he identifies with the prologue to John's Gospel. For example, in the context of discussion on procreation, Ramsey states in his book *Fabricated Man*: "The Prologue of John's Gospel (not Genesis) is the Christian story of creation which provides the source and standard for responsible procreation."[10] Christians identify their creation by God with their creation in Christ.

Finally, another indication of Ramsey's conviction that Christians should read the Old Testament through the New Testament comes in his discussion of the United Methodist Bishops' pastoral on peace. Ramsey acknowledges that his own theology is "more Augustinian than Hebraic," but then he goes on to wonder why the bishops' pastoral "is more *Hebraic* than New Testament."[11] Ramsey thus chooses Old Testament texts which resonate with his reading of the New Testament. In principle, for Ramsey, "Christians read their Bibles *backward*, first the New Testament, then the Old" (*BCE*, p. 292). At least this is the way it should be in his view.

In addition to Ramsey's emphasis on Genesis, Isaiah, and Jeremiah, one also finds significant references to Deuteronomy and to the Psalms. He tends to discount the legal materials of the Old Testament as code morality that stands in tension with the righteousness in Christ that God manifests and requires. From Ramsey's perspective, along with much of early-twentieth-century Lutheran and Reformed theology, "legalism finally triumphed over righteousness in official Judaism after the Exile and in the days of Jesus" (*BCE*, p. 13). Ramsey bought into the now defunct view of the "decline" of "late Judaism." (Ironically, what biblical scholars at the beginning of the twentieth century termed "late Judaism" is termed "early Judaism" by most biblical scholars at the end of the twentieth century!) Thus, for Ramsey, the prophetic literature represents the high point of Old Testament ethics, whereas the postexilic writings show Judaism's decline into legalism.

When it comes to the New Testament, Ramsey himself states that he appeals "especially to the teachings of Jesus and St. Paul" (*BCE*, p. xiii). While this is certainly borne out by a look at the texts Ramsey employs, he clearly has a preference for the synoptic Gospels over John. And yet Ramsey appears to be somewhat suspicious of Matthew's Gospel, because it "tells us more about the rebirth of legalism within early Christianity than it does about Jesus" (*BCE*, p. 64).[12] For example, regarding the famous saying in Matt. 5:18–19 that "not an iota, not a dot will pass from the law until all is accomplished," Ramsey suggests that they are likely not the original words of Jesus, "or else they are sorely in need of a loose interpretation" since, from Ramsey's perspective, Jesus opposes all expressions of Jewish "legalism" (*BCE*, p. 54). Likewise, Ramsey points out that Luke preserves the original words of Jesus' saying on divorce, whereas Matthew adds the exception clause and so gives in to Jewish legalism (*BCE*, p. 71). Ramsey trusts Mark's and Luke's accounts of Jesus' approach to the Jewish law, and so to Jesus' ministry, more than Matthew's.[13] Ramsey's reading, then, is that "Jesus stands entirely outside the evolution of Jewish legalism" (*BCE*, p. 65). For Ramsey, Jewish ethics was code ethics, whereas Jesus' ethics was without rules, without a code. In this way, Jesus overcame the Jewish law.[14] Ramsey does use Matthew, particularly the Sermon on the Mount material, but he makes equal use of Luke's Gospel. He makes relatively little use of John's Gospel but does draw upon John to develop his notion of obedient love, which is central to Ramsey's ethics.

As for the writings of Paul, Ramsey appeals especially to 1 Corinthians (forty references), and there particularly to 1 Corinthians 13 on love. He also makes significant reference to Romans 5–8, particularly in regard to human sin. Finally, Ramsey regularly uses Ephesians 5 in the context of addressing Christian views of marriage.

Ramsey's working canon, then, consists of Genesis 1–14, Isaiah and Jeremiah, and a sanitized (i.e., de-legalized) Matthew and Luke, along with Romans 5–8, 1 Corinthians, and Ephesians.

How Ramsey Uses Scripture

It is worth noting that Ramsey began his career at Princeton University by teaching courses on the Old and New Testaments. Indeed, he says that the foundational images he chose for developing his theological ethics were the fruit that resulted from this teaching experience.[15] Throughout his writings, Ramsey often refers rather generically to biblical ethics (namely, the ethics articulated within Scripture) as the fundamental source for his ethical reflection. Of the four standard sources for theological reflection (Scripture, tradition, reason, and experience), Ramsey clearly sees Scripture as the most important source.

In the introduction to his first book, *Basic Christian Ethics*, Ramsey states that, "As a treatise on basic Christian ethics, this book endeavors to stand within the way the Bible views morality" (*BCE*, p. xi).[16] Ramsey's reference here to "the way the Bible views morality" is of interest because it apparently indicates that he understands "biblical morality" in singular and rather unified terms, an observation to which we will return. Ramsey very clearly sees himself writing within the larger Protestant traditional approach to biblical morality, and so he self-consciously uses the Bible as a primary source in "setting forth a constructive theory of Christian ethics" (*BCE*, p. xiv).[17]

In using the Bible as an authoritative source for Christian ethics, Ramsey makes rather general use of the biblical witness as a whole. He sees the Bible as providing a fundamental grounding for moral discourse and as supplying normative language for Christian ethics. That normative language is derived directly from Ramsey's understanding of biblical ethics, or biblical morality.[18] Always fighting against "situation ethics" and what he perceived to be the relativist ethics of the 1960s and 1970s in particular, Ramsey argued that the Bible provides normative models, principles, and rules of practice for Christian conduct in the world. As far as he was concerned, all he was doing in making constructive use of the Bible in his own contemporary Christian ethics was articulating what he saw as a fairly clear "biblical ethic."

The Biblical Model

In an essay entitled "Christian Ethics Today," written to refute situation ethics, Ramsey develops what he identifies as "the heart and soul of Biblical ethics."[19] From Ramsey's perspective, the central message of the Bible as a whole "is that God means to mold human life into the action of God, human righteousness into God's righteousness, man's frequent faithlessness or maybe his fragile faithfulness into the faithfulness of God Himself."[20] This biblical message then finds articulation in a fundamental model of biblical ethics. This model is the same for both the Old and the New Testaments, though couched in different language. The basic model and measure is found, not in human behavior, but in how God acts toward humanity. For Ramsey the only appropriate starting point is with God, from whence one then moves to humanity, rather than starting with humanity and then moving to God.[21]

In the Old Testament the "source and at the same time measure of human righteousness" is the Exodus story. In commenting on the significance of the Exodus story, Ramsey states:

> Expressly excluded from the heart and soul of Biblical ethics is the notion that we should deal with people only according to their merits, earned or unearned; or that we are simply to treat all men as their manhood intrinsically deserves. Not corrective justice or distributive justice or any other humanitarian standard is the measure, but a *contributory* justice, a helpful, redeeming, caring justice, since the day God began to form the consciences of men and to shape their lives to the measure of God's own righteousness that stooped to conquer wrong. (*BCE*, p. 3)

In support of this interpretation of the Exodus, Ramsey quotes Deut. 7:6–8:

> It was not because you were more in number than any other people that the Lord set his love upon you and chose you, for you were the fewest of all people; but it is because the Lord loves you, and is keeping the oath which he swore to your father, that the Lord has brought you out with a mighty hand and redeemed you from the house of bondage.

For Ramsey this shows that God's righteousness is the model and norm for humanity. Thus, whoever remembers that God rescued him or her from the house of bondage knows both what kind of God God is and what it means to be faithful to God. Whoever remembers the manifestation of God's righteousness in the Exodus knows how to answer moral questions like How should I treat a helpless or an alien or an insignificant needy person? As Ramsey puts it: "He answers that question by reference to no human measurement, but by faith in the faithfulness and love of God manifest in his own life. By this he becomes what he is, and is what he is becoming. So likewise in his life and with other men" ("Christian Ethics Today," p. 4).

The model from the New Testament is essentially the same. It is not to be found, Ramsey argues, in the Golden Rule ("Do unto others as you would have them do unto you"); nor is it found in the maxim "Love your neighbor as yourself"; for in both cases the standard of measure is a human standard. Rather,

> the New Testament does not take from man himself the measure of what it means to be a mature or righteous man. Instead this standard is taken from the man Christ Jesus. The Commandment, the model, the organizing principle of all New Testament ethics are Jesus' words: "Love one another *as I have loved you!*" [John 15:12] ("Christian Ethics Today," p. 4).

As the Exodus event shows the meaning of God's unmerited love for Israel in the Old Testament, so the Christ event shows the meaning of God's love for all humanity in the New Testament. Ramsey puts this another way by citing Paul's statement in Rom. 5:6–8, 10, that Christ died for the ungodly, that "God shows his love for us in that while we were yet sinners, Christ died for us; while we were enemies we were reconciled to God." Thus, while the Exodus of the Old Testament shows God delivering the Israelites out of physical bondage in Egypt, God's actions in Christ show God delivering humanity "from the Egypt of sin and death." As Ramsey puts it: "he who for himself remembers of himself that Jesus Christ actually saved him from the Egypt of sin and death, he becomes a man on exodus from any natural or human standard, a man whose conscience and life are destined to be formed in accordance with the saving righteousness and faithfulness of God" ("Christian Ethics Today," p. 4). Therefore, Ramsey sees in John 15:12 ("Love one another as I have loved you") the ultimate commandment given by Christ to his followers. Christ himself is the normative model of Christian existence.

Ramsey's "Biblical Covenant Ethics"

Another way in which Ramsey gives voice to his understanding of the basic model of biblical ethics can be seen in his constant reference to the notion of obedient love in covenant, which expresses God's righteousness.[22] Ramsey uses a cluster of terms to develop this motif. As he puts it, "a biblical ethical idea is rightly grasped only when we succeed in reducing it to a simple corollary of (1) God's righteousness (*tsedeq*) and love (*hesed, agape*) and (2) the reign of this righteousness in the Kingdom of God—or of 'the idea of the covenant between God and man from which they both stem.' "[23] These two sources of Christian ethics, God's loving righteousness and God's reigning righteousness, are two sides of the same coin, and Ramsey often invokes this cluster of images by appealing to the central motif of covenant.

Covenant is *the* biblical theme around which he chooses to organize his appropriation of biblical ethics since covenant "is not only frequently mentioned in the Bible but is its main theme" (*BCE*, p. 2).[24] Ramsey's "interpretative principle" is "the Biblical norm of *fidelity to covenant*, with the meaning it gives to *righteousness* between man and man."[25] Ramsey's notion of righteousness in covenant relationship thus serves as the fundamental biblical norm that permeates his work and is at the core of his theological ethics and his appropriation of the Bible.[26] This emphasis can be seen throughout his writings. Already in his 1949 essay "Elements of a Biblical Political Theory," Ramsey presents the concept of covenant as a central and pervasive biblical motif. Much of the material developed in that essay can be found in Ramsey's 1950 *Basic Christian Ethics*.

Some years later, in his important essay "The Case of the Curious Exception," Ramsey continues to maintain that "in Christian ethics we are mainly concerned about the requirements of loyalty to covenants among men."[27] In his work on medical ethics, the notion of biblical covenant again stands out.[28] In *Fabricated Man*, Ramsey comments: "Men and women are created in covenant, to covenant, and for covenant."[29] Again, in the preface to his landmark book *The Patient as Person,* Ramsey states that "in the following chapters I undertake to explore a number of medical covenants among men."[30]

What, then, does Ramsey understand by God's covenant righteousness as expressed in the Bible? He sums it up by putting it as a principle: "To each according to the measure of his real need, not because of anything human reason can discern inherent in the needy, but because his need alone is the measure of God's righteousness toward him" (*BCE,* p. 14). Thus, God's righteousness and justice are neither corrective nor distributive. Rather, God's righteousness is redemptive love.[31]

Divine love, then, as revealed in the Bible, becomes the model and basis for Ramsey's theological ethics.[32] This love is best seen in Jesus' life and death, which show that God's love means turning to one's neighbor, even to one's enemy, according to their real needs. "Using the measure of divine love inverts self-love and discovers the neighbor" (*BCE,* p. 21). The pattern of God's love for human beings expressed in Jesus becomes the pattern for how human beings should love one another, namely, disinterested, obedient love for the neighbor. This is what it means, for Ramsey, to "love one another as I have loved you" (John 15:12).

Another way in which Ramsey expresses the heart of this obedient covenant love is by speaking of "neighbor-love" as the new principle of Christian ethics in the aftermath of Jesus and Paul. Ramsey is wary of fixed principles which might lead to fixed rules and codes, but he nevertheless characterizes "neighbor-love" responding to "neighbor-need" as "a new 'principle' for morality only in the sense that here all morality governed by principles, rules, customs, and laws goes to pieces and is given another sovereign test" (*BCE,* p. 57).

The first-century Jewish context in which Jesus taught was, according to Ramsey, one of code morality, where what mattered was abiding by the legal code, almost regardless of all else. Jesus did away with code morality, since it too often sacrificed human need to a legal code rather than having the legal code serve human need. "A faithful Jew stayed as close as possible to observance of the law even when he had to depart from it. Jesus stayed as close as possible to the fulfillment of human need, no matter how wide of the sabbath law this led him" (*BCE,* p. 56).

The need of the neighbor and consequent neighbor-love were the governing factors in Jesus' ethic, not the relationship of his actions to any given code morality. Ramsey sees this principle demonstrated in Jesus' ministry through such stories as his healing on the Sabbath of the woman who had been bent over for eighteen years (Luke 13:10–17; *BCE,* pp. 55–56). Similarly, the parable of the Good Samaritan (Luke 10:25–37) demonstrates what neighbor-love looks like. As Ramsey points out regarding this parable, Jesus does not answer the question that had been asked, "Who is my neighbor?"

> The parable tells us something about neighbor-love, nothing about the neighbor. What the parable does is to demand that the questioner revise entirely his

point of view, reformulating the question first asked so as to require neighborli-
ness of himself rather than anything of his neighbor. . . . The parable actually
shows the nature and meaning of Christian love which alone of all ethical
standpoints discovers the neighbor because it alone begins with neighborly love
and not with discriminating between worthy and unworthy people according to
the qualities they possess. (*BCE*, p. 93)

In short, obedient covenant love means being disinterestedly attuned to the
needs of the neighbor above all else, and certainly above any kind of code
morality (see *BCE*, p. 59).

The apostle Paul also demonstrates for Ramsey this emphasis on neighbor-
need and neighbor-love apart from a legal code. Indeed, Ramsey appeals to Paul
to explain "what the Christian does without a code" (*BCE*, pp. 74–91). Ramsey
emphasizes Gal. 5:6 as a guiding principle or slogan ("For in Christ Jesus neither circumcision nor uncircumcision is of any avail, but faith working through
love"), and especially the last phrase ("faith working through love"). In stating
this, Paul goes beyond any kind of code morality, to such a degree that "Galatians was Paul's great declaration of Christian independence from legalism,"
reflecting a perspective that was "essentially the same as Jesus" (*BCE*, p. 75).

On the basis of the slogan "faith working through love," Ramsey proceeds
to ask whether "an entirely Christocentric ethic can be elaborated" (*BCE*, p.
76), to which he responds affirmatively. In essence, Paul's position is that "by
definition Christian love will be pleased only by doing what the neighbor needs"
(*BCE*, p. 78). This is why Paul says with some satisfaction that he has become
"all things to all people" (1 Cor. 9:22; see *BCE*, p. 79), for his principle of action
is not the written Jewish law, nor is it what nature teaches (though, according
to Ramsey, Paul can unfortunately "slip" into this kind of language),[33] but it is
solely the needs of one's neighbor which shape one's loving response.

By being immoderate about this one thing, namely Christian care for the
neighbor's needs, Christian ethics is *on principle* alternatively more lenient
(more free from regulation) and more severe with itself (more subject to command) than any other ethic. Thus Paul sometimes became "as one under the
law," at other times "as one outside the law" (I Cor. 9:20, 21). (*BCE*, p. 79)

Drawing on Galatians and 1 Corinthians, then, Ramsey sees Paul as continuing
and developing what Jesus had initiated, an ethic based on God's covenant righteousness and God's concern for humans that responds to neighbor-need with
appropriate neighbor-love. Just how one determines what a neighbor truly needs,
however, is not always self-evident, nor is the appropriate response of neighbor-
love always clear. Ramsey acknowledges this problem but does not develop
much of an answer to it.

Beyond this emphasis on disinterested love for one's neighbor as a fundamental expression of covenant obedience, it is important to point out two closely
related aspects of Ramsey's appropriation of biblical covenant language. The
first has to do with Ramsey's view that covenant righteousness is made vital only
in light of Jesus' apocalyptic eschatological orientation.[34] He asserts that "obedi-

ent love for neighbor, which is the distinctive 'primitive idea' of Christian ethics, had its origin and *genesis* in apocalypticism" (*BCE*, p. 39). In an important section on the eschatological character of all of Jesus' teachings, Ramsey asks the crucial question about the relation between Jesus' kingdom expectation and his ethical teachings (*BCE*, pp. 24–45). He surveys three approaches to this issue and rejects the first two, namely, the notion of Jesus' teachings as an "interim ethic," most forcefully articulated by Albert Schweitzer, and the notion that Jesus' radical ethic is valid only when the future kingdom of God is fully established, a position that Ramsey attributes to Martin Dibelius.

The third position is the one Ramsey himself adopts and is as follows. Jesus' teachings can be divided into two groups. The first are eschatological teachings stressing urgency that can be stated in noneschatological terms *without* any essential change in meaning (e.g., do not be angry, do not lust, be single-minded) (*BCE*, pp. 31–34). For example, Jesus' teachings regarding Sabbath observance have an eschatological edge, as Jesus refers to the Son of Man being lord even of the Sabbath (Mark 2:28). Although there is a connection between Jesus' teaching regarding the Sabbath and his apocalyptic expectations, still, according to Ramsey,

> Jesus' teaching concerning the sabbath may be translated from its original eschatological setting and language without any change or loss of what this means for morality. . . . the ethical principle which summarizes Jesus' teaching and practice in relation to the law of sabbath observance may be stated in general, non-eschatological terms: the infinite superiority of neighbor-need in comparison with legal righteousness in determining the meaning of human obligation. (*BCE*, pp. 33–34)

For Ramsey, general ethical principles can be discerned from those teachings of Jesus that do not have an *essentially* apocalyptic eschatological character.

The second type of eschatological teachings are qualitatively more rigorous in content, not just in urgency, and so cannot be expressed adequately in noneschatological terms (e.g., nonresisting love, unlimited forgiveness, unconditional giving to every need) (*BCE*, pp. 34–35). In this instance, "the radical content of Jesus' strenuous sayings depends . . . on his apocalyptic expectation" (*BCE*, p. 35).

The problem, Ramsey notes, is that today, almost two thousand years after Jesus, we no longer share the apocalyptic eschatological orientation that so shaped Jesus' teachings. What to do, then? (And, indeed, Ramsey entitles one section of *BCE*, pp. 35–45, "In What Way, Then, Are the Teachings of Jesus Valid?") One option is to extend Jesus' radical apocalyptic ethic to all aspects of life, even in our nonapocalyptic setting. But this will not do for Ramsey. He asserts, "Making the strenuous teachings of Jesus cover the whole ground of action necessary to restrain or eliminate evil was simply not the religious ethic of Jesus" (*BCE*, p. 38).

The other option, and the one Ramsey advocates, is the limitation of Jesus' strenuous ethic to its appropriate sphere, namely, relations between individuals on a one-to-one basis. Apparently, the strenuous ethic is appropriate only to relations between individuals because in a noneschatological setting such a vigorous ethic is neither possible nor prudential on a social scale beyond one-on-one relationships. Thus, Jesus' ethic of nonresistant love is not an appropriate response to all forms of evil but only to the evil exerted by one individual upon another.

Beyond relations between individuals, then, this means that force (would Ramsey call this "resistant love"?) may be used in dealing with "tyrannical structures of evil" (*BCE*, p. 38). As Ramsey puts it, "The first step to an understanding of the validity of Jesus' strenuous teachings must involve putting a limitation upon the area of their intended application" (*BCE*, p. 39). The "area of intended application" extends only to the neighbor, from one individual to another.[35] It is easy to see how Ramsey can then go on to extrapolate from this understanding of biblical ethics in the teaching of Jesus to support the just war tradition as in fact having a biblical foundation.

A second significant aspect of Ramsey's biblical covenant language has to do with covenant righteousness as covenant between persons. This can be presented more briefly. Because Jesus' strenuous ethical teachings are applicable only between individuals, Ramsey stresses the requirements of covenant righteousness between persons. Ramsey's ethic, then, is person centered, in large part because he sees Jesus' ethics, the biblical ethics, as an expression of such a person-centered approach. God has expressed love for human beings by sending the person Jesus, a person who paradigmatically sought out the needs of other persons, a person who gave the same obligation of obedient love to his disciples. It is no accident, then, that Ramsey constantly speaks about covenants between persons, or the "patient as person."

Ramsey's reading of the Bible, and especially of Jesus' ministry, is that one explicitly finds there only personal ethics, the ethics of person to neighbor. David Smith has put this well:

> The root of Ramsey's argument . . . is his view of the relationship between eschatology and ethics in the teachings of Jesus. His basic idea is that the message and ethic of Jesus were apocalyptic which means that they were directed to the one-to-one situation, the relationship between only two individuals. Jesus' commandment to love was concerned only with the proper form of this bipolar relationship.[36]

In person-to-person relations, Jesus' strenuous ethics of nonresistant love, of seeking the need of the neighbor, holds for the Christian.

However, when more than one neighbor is involved, individuals often have to choose between competing claims, and in this case a "neighbor-centered preferential love" is appropriate (*BCE*, p. 159). Indeed, relations between more than two individuals may necessitate a change in tactics from nonresistant love to resistance against one neighbor on behalf of another neighbor.[37] Ramsey again grounds this "preferential ethic of protection" (*BCE*, p. 169) in the ministry of Jesus, who protected some individuals from the injustices of other individuals. For example, Jesus denounced the practices of the Pharisees for unnecessarily burdening the people with external forms of law observance. As Ramsey puts it:

> Yet without distorting the text, the beginnings of a multilateral ethics of protection, certainly a multilateral neighbor-centered preferential love, may be found in Jesus' own attitudes and example. On occasion he showed indignation, even wrath, over injustice, using vitriolic words as weapons against the devourers of widows' houses (Luke 20:47). He was unsparing in his condemnation of the complacency of Israel's religious leaders. (*BCE*, p. 167)[38]

Significant here is Ramsey's implicit argument that Jesus' use of words as "weapons" against one set of neighbors (Pharisees) on behalf of another set of neighbors (poor widows) is not too far away from legitimate use of physical force to defend an oppressed neighbor against an oppressing neighbor.

Thus, already in Jesus' own ministry, Ramsey sees the beginnings not only of an ethics of preferential neighbor-centered love but also of an ethics of active resistance on behalf of a neighbor (or group of neighbors) being wronged. Indeed, to have an ethics of preferential love for one neighbor over against another neighbor necessitates resisting one neighbor on behalf of another, which, Ramsey argues, is precisely what Jesus did. Ramsey appeals to the scene of Jesus "cleansing the Temple" in Jerusalem as the basis for a Christian ethics of resistance.

> Whether the whip Jesus used in driving the money-changers out of the Temple was plaited of straw or of leather, whether he applied it to animals or to men, whether the decisive factor that day was the force of his own powerful personality justifiably indignant on behalf of a righteous cause or the threatening multitude of people gathered in Jerusalem who forestalled the immediate use of the Temple police, in any case some form of resistance was raised that day not only against perverse practices but also against the men who engaged in them. Force does not become any less resistant because of its "spirituality," or resistance wrong to a greater degree because it takes material form. Circumstances similar to those which warranted a change from Jesus' announced ethic of non-resistance to any manner of resistance he may have used in cleansing the Temple may not only permit but even on occasion require Christian love to adopt physical methods of resistance. (*BCE*, p. 169)

Ramsey continues to develop the notion of a Christian preferential ethics of protection (and resistance) by appealing to Jesus' parable of the unforgiving servant (Matt. 18:23–35). In the parable, after a servant begs a king to whom he is indebted for patience and mercy, the king releases the servant from the equivalent of a multimillion-dollar debt. In turn, however, this same servant is unwilling to forgive another servant a small amount of money owed to him. When the king hears about this incident, he responds with anger (as Ramsey cites the text): "Then his lord summoned him and said to him, 'You wicked servant! I forgave you all that debt because you besought me; and should not you have had mercy on your fellow servant, as I had mercy on you?' And in anger his lord delivered him to the jailers, till he should pay all his debt" (Matt. 18:32–33). For Ramsey, because the king allowed the debt owed him to be forgiven, he does not allow the forgiven servant to act unmercifully to another servant who is indebted to the forgiven servant. Through his own failure to show mercy, the servant who had been forgiven in turn loses the mercy he had received. Regarding this parable, Ramsey states:

> From this story it is evident that love which for itself claims nothing may yet for the sake of another claim everything, that any one who unhesitatingly and times without number renounces "what is due" when he himself alone bears the brunt of such a decision may nevertheless turn full circle and insist with utter severity upon full payment of what is due to others; and what is due to others is never simply just payment but full forgiveness "as I had mercy on you," never exact justice alone but Christian love. (*BCE*, p. 171)

In all but one-on-one relationships, then, Ramsey sees in Jesus' ethics the basis for a preferential ethics of protection and a Christian ethics of resistance. And all of this is grounded in his understanding of the obedient covenant love established through Jesus.[39]

Ramsey's View of the Authority of Scripture

I have already mentioned something about Ramsey's view of biblical authority, namely, that he saw the Bible as the primary authority for reflection on theological ethics. Ramsey's view of the Bible and its authority was very much influenced by Karl Barth, to whom Ramsey regularly appeals, and by H. Richard Niebuhr, Ramsey's mentor at Yale. For Barth and Niebuhr, the Bible does not contain a set of propositions about God, nor does the Bible present a relatively static morality. Rather, the Bible reveals God Godself and God's self-sacrificial love expressed in the cross. James Gustafson has described the approaches of Barth and Niebuhr well: "for Karl Barth, the Bible first of all points toward the living God, known in Jesus Christ, and thus what is required of ethics is obedience to a Person, not a proposition, or, in the language of H. Richard Niebuhr, *response* to a Person, and not a rule."[40]

Already in a 1947 article in *Theology Today* entitled "Beyond the Confusion of Tongues," Ramsey used very similar language in describing his view of God in the Bible: "The Bible's conception of God is that he is beyond all conceptualization and requires of men not so much ideas as obedience."[41] This view stands out even more clearly in the following citation:

> The world desperately needs a return to Biblical religion, to an apprehension of the Word of God in the Bible. This does not mean an exaltation of the objective authority of the literal words of Scripture "up to heaven." That way lies confusion of tongues as surely as from any other human way of affirming that God is objectively with us in a set of authoritative words. . . . But without falling into the error and the arrogance of Biblical literalism, it may neverthe-

less be said that some comprehension of the Word of God in the Bible speaking to and against this generation is our last, best hope.

This is true precisely because in the Bible men meet God, not simply a conception of God. . . . Individuals or nations stand within the Biblical heritage when they are able to say of contemporary events and responsibilities that come upon them that here the God of Abraham, Isaac, and Jacob, the God of Babel and of Jesus, speaks to them. There needs to be an end to the attitude of saying to the God who meets us in the pages of Scripture, "Oh, thou One-of-the-world's-greatest-notions-of-God, speak and thy servant will think it over." . . . in the Bible God uses the medium of words to confront us, to confront us as God and not as an idea, to confront not simply our minds but also our selves.[42]

For Ramsey, the Bible is the primary arena of an encounter between God as Person and humans as persons.[43]

Ramsey is rather critical of any theological ethics that does not see the Bible as the basic authority. In the preface to his *Basic Christian Ethics*, Ramsey submits "that it would never occur to an unprejudiced mind . . . to look for the meaning of Christian ethics anywhere else than in the biblical record and in the writings of men of the past whose thinking about morality has been profoundly disturbed and influenced by what they found there [in the Bible]" (p. xiii). Ramsey also states: "In Christian theological ethics . . . one invokes, for warrants, backing, and foundation, both the *person* and the *works* of Christ, appealing both to Bible and tradition as source and authority."[44]

The Bible does function in relation to other sources of authority for Christians, especially the other classic sources of tradition, reason, and experience. But if the Bible is not the primary source, and thus the primary authority, then from Ramsey's perspective, the point of reference is no longer God but humanity: "I suggest that, no matter how we strive to reach Him [God], we speak of man, and not God, if (to say the least) the revelation in Scripture traditioned to us falls *below* scientific or philosophical reason and human experience broadly conceived as sources."[45]

What kind of authority does Ramsey attribute to the Bible? In sum, the Bible is the touchstone for all Christian ethics, insofar as it is the preeminent place where the believer encounters God in Christ.

Ramsey's Hermeneutics

Ramsey says very little explicitly about his hermeneutics. Indeed, the prominent ethicist Paul Lehmann comments that in Ramsey's book *Basic Christian Ethics*, he has "ignored the hermeneutical problem and . . . consequently disregarded the basic question of what Christian ethics really is."[46] Similarly, James Gustafson notes that Ramsey has a confessional approach to the Bible and ethics, but that Ramsey nowhere "makes an extended defense of it against alternative theological positions, nor does he spell out a view of biblical revelation to support it."[47]

The most Ramsey says about his hermeneutics is that "the principles of hermeneutics (or the science of interpretation) can best be exhibited in the course of actually interpreting Scripture and in debates about its theological meaning. . . . This seems to me to be an altogether correct procedure, and the only fruitful one," because "hermeneutical principles . . . are empty until Scripture is interpreted."[48] This leads us back, of course, to how Ramsey interprets Scripture. And as we have seen, his working principle appears to assume that Scripture speaks with a rather unified voice about obedient love in covenant with the God whose righteousness is revealed in Christ.

Another relatively clear hermeneutical principle at work in Ramsey's approach to the Bible, then, has to do with his view of the unity of Scripture. He recognizes the diversity of the New Testament writers, even in their notions about love (see *BCE*, p. 20). Nonetheless, Ramsey avers: "Differences in New Testament theology, however, should not be emphasized, since in getting to know the origin, and more decisively the meaning, of Christian love the important point to see is the unanimity with which men of the Bible applied a supernatural measure to all obedient love" (*BCE*, p. 21).[49]

Ramsey and the Significance of Scripture for Ethics

I now turn to Ramsey's understanding of the constructive relationship between Scripture and ethics. Ramsey states that "an ethician must be his own exegete," and that indeed it cannot be otherwise, since biblical scholars "never come to the end of their task, at least not with packaged agreements that we can work with."[50] To examine Ramsey's biblical exegesis, I will analyze his use of the Bible in formulating his stance on the controversial issue of abortion, a position he claims in fact to ground in his biblical exegesis.

Ramsey articulates his view of abortion in his 1979 article "Liturgy and Ethics."[51] There he emphasizes that any legitimate Christian ethics pays attention to the whole of the biblical narrative. Commenting on the relation of liturgy and morality, he states, "The notion of steadfast 'covenant' love, or *agape*, in Christian ethics must obviously be constantly nourished by liturgy, and the entirety of the Biblical narrative, or else it loses its meaning and becomes a mere 'concept.' "[52] Biblical narratives, then, the biblical story, provide substance and meaning to Christian ethics and come alive especially in liturgical contexts. The interplay of Bible and liturgy informs moral discourse. Ramsey goes on to give specific examples of such interplay, focusing at length on marriage and abortion. Ramsey argues that the shape of the biblical narrative clearly argues against abortion. The narrative of the creation story and the narrative of the Exodus from Egypt point to God's creating a world and a people out of nothing. Likewise, this pattern of God's purposeful creation from nothing is expressed by

Jeremiah in his famous statement: "Before I formed thee in the belly I knew thee; and before thou camest forth from the womb I sanctified thee" (Jer. 1:5).[53] From this pattern, Ramsey goes on to say, and I quote at length:

> It is simply stupid for anyone to say that the Bible gives no point of departure for addressing the question of the morality of abortion. Note that in saying this I am not simply lighting upon the verses in *Jeremiah* . . . If these verses were not there, a prophet or poet could still write them if he or she had any religious sensibility for the *Exodus* and the *Genesis* stories of creation, and within these embracing contexts wished to say whence and how came the creation of our particular, individual lives.
>
> If we do not exclude Scripture from the liturgy, from all eternity God resolved not to be God without our particular human life from its microscopic origins. . . . Thus in all three creations—of his people Israel and the second Israel by the new covenant, of the entire cosmos, and of each one of us in particular—God calls into existence the things that are from things that are not. This is the shape of Biblical thought. And it is the shape of Christian liturgies so far as the Bible has not been excluded from them.
>
> Yet there are multitudes of sincere contemporary Christian people who seem to believe that the Bible says nothing definitive to the abortion question. I can only conclude that they have not heard Biblical sermons; or else have responded: "Speak Lord, and thy servant will think it over!"[54]

For Ramsey, then, the pattern of God's creation as expressed in the biblical narratives provides a starting point for clear discourse about the morality of abortion and shows that abortion is not moral.

Ramsey continues to develop this position from another appeal to biblical narrative, this time drawing on the birth stories of Jesus to argue against abortion. Ramsey argues that from the perspective of biblical narrative, it is clear at what point God was made a human being—not in the stable in Bethlehem but at conception.

> Far more than any argument, it was surely the power of the Nativity Stories and their place in ritual and celebration and song that tempered the conscience of the West to its audacious effort to wipe out the practice of abortion and infanticide. As the hold of the stories over the minds and imaginations of millions upon millions of men and women recedes, it is clear that both abortion and infanticide are becoming "thinkable" again as permissible practices, even good.
>
> After the Annunciation it is recorded in St. Luke's Gospel that "Mary rose in those days and went into the hill country with haste, into a city of Judea; and entered into the house of Zacharias, and saluted Elizabeth. "Hi, Liz," she said; "I am 'with embryo.' " And Elizabeth responded, "Hail, Mary, didn't you know? I'm 'carrying a fetus.' . . . Lo, as soon as the voice of thy salutation sounded in mine ears, the babe leaped in my womb for joy" (*Luke* 1:39–44, slightly revised). So did John the Baptist, the Forerunner, first point to the Christ.
>
> But that is not how the story goes. From the correct version heard and sung and dramatized generations of men and women learned to feel and think

of their own unborn children in a very special way. The Nativity Narratives served as a model for human beginnings, just as the creation of a people out of Egypt did for *Genesis, Jeremiah,* and the *Psalms.*[55]

For Ramsey, the birth stories of Jesus are formative in shaping the Christian approach to abortion. These biblical stories show, according to Ramsey's reading, that the fetus is already a person, already a real human being. End of argument.

Critical Evaluation

I have examined various dimensions of Paul Ramsey's uses of Scripture. How may his understanding and uses of Scripture in Christian ethics be evaluated? In brief, I would offer five comments. First, in general, and I think positively, Ramsey clearly takes Scripture very seriously as the primary source for Christian faith and ethics. He is concerned about fidelity to the guiding images provided in Scripture.

Second, however, Ramsey's understanding of the fundamental theological motif in Scripture can be rightly challenged. His emphasis on covenant expressed in obedient love can surely be found throughout Scripture, but even this overarching theme is extremely reductionistic when used as the lens for reading and appropriating the Bible as a whole.[56] This is too monochromatic an approach and does not allow for the full richness of the biblical witness, tensions and all. Ramsey does see the tensions between biblical writings, but he is uncomfortable letting them be. He thus often fails to take into account the full range of what Scripture has to say.[57]

Third, Ramsey's reading of Scripture is oddly personalistic and individualistic. He sees Jesus' strenuous ethics as applying only in relations between individuals and so distorts, I would argue, the centrality of community and communal ethics expressed in the teachings of Jesus and Paul alike. Is the community Jesus establishes with his disciples, and the community established in Jesus' name following his death and resurrection, not significant in a constructive appropriation of Jesus' teaching? Does Jesus speak only regarding individuals or primarily within the context of a believing community?

Fourth, despite Ramsey's claim to ground his moral reasoning in Scripture, he tends to engage in what can only be called special pleading and proof texting when it comes to particular applications of biblical texts to ethical issues. A good example of this is his use of biblical narratives to argue against abortion. He takes Luke's birth story of Jesus, which for Luke apparently related something about the special significance of Jesus, and uses it as a warrant to show that personhood begins at conception. Ramsey's literalist reading of the birth narrative reflects an uncritical approach to the birth story genre and is not in principle far from the argument (which Ramsey does not make) that on the basis of Genesis 1 and 2 the earth was in fact created in seven days. Or again, in a discussion of marriage, Ramsey justifies monogamy on the basis of God's covenant with one people, Israel, and Christ's covenant with one church. Ramsey simply ignores the irony that even after the covenant many in Israel practiced polygamy. Indeed, James Gustafson laments that "Ramsey turns out to be more of a Barthian and biblicist than I had thought."[58]

Fifth, I would call into question Ramsey's distinction between two different kinds of eschatology in the sayings of Jesus, those that can be understood apart from an apocalyptic framework and those more strenuous sayings of Jesus that can only be understood within an apocalyptic setting. How does Ramsey discern which sayings fit into which category? This is not as easy to do as Ramsey makes it appear. Further, and this is not something Ramsey could have foreseen, how would Ramsey's understanding of an apocalyptic eschatological Jesus be affected by a new school of New Testament interpretation that portrays Jesus as a non-apocalyptic preacher? What happens then to the distinction between prudential and nonprudential teachings of Jesus?

In closing, at one point Ramsey makes an interesting statement regarding Augustine's interpretation of Paul's comments about natural law in Rom. 2:14–16. Ramsey states that Augustine's interpretation "is poor exegesis but good Christian ethics" (*BCE*, p. 86). (In order to defend the distinctiveness and necessity of the New Law revealed in Christ, Augustine held that in Paul's reference to Gentiles having a natural law unto themselves he meant Gentiles who had now become Christians. Ramsey recognizes that Paul was likely referring to the voice of natural conscience, quite apart from one's identity as Christian or non-Christian.) Ramsey's comment raises the obvious question of how Scripture and Christian ethics are related, especially when poor exegesis can go hand in hand with good Christian ethics. In Ramsey's case, I would argue that his own problematic biblical exegesis leads to significant questions regarding his construction of Christian ethics, especially since he puts so much emphasis on the biblical ground of Christian ethics. Still, Ramsey's covenant ethics should not be discounted entirely. Perhaps he at times shares company with Augustine, who engaged in poor exegesis but good Christian ethics. Would good exegesis (how defined?) lead to better Christian ethics?

six

STANLEY HAUERWAS

The Community Story
of Israel and Jesus

S tanley Hauerwas (b. 1940) is currently among the most prolific and significant theological ethicists.[1] His work has exercised a tremendous influence
in theological ethics from the 1970s through the 1990s, and one imagines well
beyond. A significant feature of Hauerwas' writing has been his self-conscious
concern with Scripture as a touchstone for reflecting on theological ethics. For
example, he introduces his book A *Community of Character* (1981) with the
following statement: "My wish is that this book might help Christians rediscover
that their most important social task is nothing less than to be a community
capable of hearing the story of God we find in the scripture and living in a
manner that is faithful to that story."[2] For Hauerwas, all theological reflection
necessarily entails hearing the stories of Scripture and performing these stories.
At the same time, Scripture is a function and derivative of Christian community,
which means that the story of God related in Scripture can only be truly heard
and enacted in the broader context of such community. Hauerwas's approach to
the Bible, then, reflects an appreciation for how the Christian community interprets Scripture and how, in turn, Scripture interprets the Christian community.
This dynamic conversation between Scripture and community lies at the heart
of Hauerwas's approach to the Bible.[3]

Biblical Texts Used by Hauerwas

An examination of Hauerwas's explicit appeals to specific biblical texts results in
several observations. First, given the extent of his writing, he makes relatively
few direct references to discrete texts, at least in comparison to the work of
others addressed in this book. But the relative lack of references should not be
misconstrued to suggest that the specificity of biblical stories is unimportant to
Hauerwas. Indeed, one of the hallmarks of Hauerwas's work is his concern with
hearing the biblical stories themselves, and not just hearing about them. Overall, Hauerwas has made increasingly explicit use of specific biblical texts as his

writing has progressed. His early work—e.g., *Vision and Virtue* (1974), *Character and the Christian Life* (1975), *Truthfulness and Tragedy* (1977)—makes relatively limited use of the Bible.[4] His more recent writings—especially *The Peaceable Kingdom* (1983), *Resident Aliens* (1989), and most notably *Unleashing the Scripture* (1993)—contain more references to specific biblical texts, as well as offer more development of these texts.[5] Also significant is the relative lack of references to biblical texts in his works on medical ethics, in which he is by no means alone.[6]

Second, Hauerwas clearly leans heavily in the direction of the New Testament, no surprise for a Christian theologian (58 indexed citations from the Old Testament and 177 indexed citations from the New Testament). For his Old Testament references, Hauerwas draws mostly on the Pentateuch, Isaiah, and the Psalms. For Hauerwas, the story about Israel as the people God freed from bondage in Egypt, recorded in Deut. 6:21–25, is a formative story that lies at the heart of Israel's identity. Similarly, Hauerwas seizes upon Deut. 5:6 as a central characterization of Israel: "How does God deal with human fear, confusion, and paralysis? God tells a story: I am none other than the God who 'brought you out of the land of Egypt, out of the house of bondage.' "[7] Hauerwas draws on the Psalms particularly in the context of lamenting in the face of illness, suffering, and death. Such laments both reflect and help form experiences of despair.[8]

Despite his relatively few references to the Old Testament, Hauerwas never denigrates it or downplays its significance. Rather, the reader senses that he simply does not know it all that well, which he concedes in *Unleashing the Scripture*.[9] Hauerwas talks incessantly about the story of Israel and the story of Jesus,[10] emphasizing the continuity between the two. For example, the whole notion of *imitatio Dei* begins "not with Jesus but with Israel. For Jesus brought no new insights into the law or God's nature that Israel had not already known and revealed."[11]

Along the same lines, one striking aspect of Hauerwas's approach to the Bible is his apparent preference for referring to the story of Israel as the "Hebrew Scriptures" rather than as the "Old Testament."[12] Similarly, despite his strong emphasis on Jesus' story as paradigmatic for Christian existence, Hauerwas appears to maintain the continued validity of Judaism apart from Jewish belief in Jesus as the Messiah. He puts it in the following way:

> No conversation over differences is more important than that between Israel and the church. For it is from Israel that we learn of the God who is present to us in the life, cross, and resurrection of Jesus. It is from Israel's continuing willingness to wait for the Messiah that we learn better how we must wait between the times. The church and Israel are two people walking in the path provided by God; they cannot walk independently of one another, for if they do they both risk becoming lost.[13]

For Hauerwas, the story of Jesus, and so the story Christians claim, cannot be separated from the story of Israel expressed in the Hebrew Scriptures of the Christian canon.

As for the New Testament, Hauerwas has a strong preference for the synoptic Gospels. From these Gospels, particular attention is given to the Sermon on the Mount in Matthew 5–7 (especially Matt. 5),[14] the Passion predictions in Mark 8–10 with their emphasis on the cross,[15] and passages in Luke that stress how God works through the poor and the weak.[16] Aside from a sermon in *Unleashing the Scripture,* one finds only four passing references to the Gospel of John in all of Hauerwas's fourteen books (as of 1994), giving the appearance of a studied avoidance of John's Gospel, conscious or unconscious.[17] This apparent reluctance to appeal to John raises the question, of course, as to why this is the case. Given Hauerwas's emphasis on the down-to-earth and gritty life Jesus led in community with the disciples and in ministry to the outcast, my own hunch is that he has found John a bit too otherworldly, and Jesus too glorified therein, to allow it any significant place in his appeal to the Gospel traditions.[18]

Beyond the centrality of the synoptic Gospels, Hauerwas also makes significant use of the Pauline writings, in particular Romans, 1 Corinthians, and especially Ephesians. Hauerwas cites a whole cluster of passages from Romans (3:21–26, 5:1–5, 6:5–11, 12:9–19, all full citations) to show the connections between the pronouncement of justification by faith, ethical admonitions, fidelity to Jesus, and communal life in Christ.[19] Similarly, he draws heavily on the household codes of Ephesians 5 in an effort to rehabilitate their status in theological reflection because they point to how Christians in general "should be subject to one another as faithful disciples of Christ."[20]

A third observation has to do with Hauerwas's style of drawing on biblical passages. Although it may appear inconsequential, I find it notable that Hauerwas rarely refers to a biblical text without at the same time citing the passage in full. This practice engenders the reader's direct engagement with the biblical passage, and not just with Hauerwas's comments upon the text. Thus, his habit of citing in full the texts to which he appeals has a way of making such appeals more substantive.

Finally, in keeping with Hauerwas's notion that the Bible is the church's book, it is significant that his appeals to Scripture often come in liturgical contexts and draw on the given lectionary readings of the church year. This is especially the case in the twelve sermons published in *Unleashing the Scripture* and in his responses to Willimon's sermons in *Preaching to Strangers.*

How Hauerwas Uses Scripture

Hauerwas's use of the Bible arises from his understanding of the character of the Bible as the Christian community's living Scripture that tells the basic story (the "sustaining story") of the community's, and so each believer's, identity in relation to God and to the world.[21] The "Bible is fundamentally a story of a people's journey with their God."[22] Hauerwas appeals to the Bible as the primary resource for reminding us of who and whose we are. The Bible "provides the resources necessary for the church to be a community sufficiently truthful

so that our conversation with one another and God can continue across generations."[23] The Bible thus forms the arena for Christian conversation across both
time and space. Accordingly, Christian theological "[e]thics, as an academic
discipline, is simply the task of assembling reminders that enable us to remember how to speak and to live the language of the gospel."[24] For Hauerwas, such
speaking and living are essentially activities of Christian community. I have chosen to develop five interrelated and recurring motifs that, I think, best characterize his appeals to Scripture in a communal context: (1) a storied and remembered people, (2) a cruciform people, (3) a people between the times, (4)
a worshiping people, and (5) a people set apart. I will examine each in turn.

A Storied and Re-membered People

For Hauerwas, the Bible functions as the collective generative story of God's
people. By providing accounts of the originating identity of God's people
through the story of Israel and the life, death, and resurrection of Jesus, the
Bible gives direction and shape to the ongoing identity of those who claim this
story as their own. As Hauerwas puts it, "the Christian's task is nothing other
than to make the story that we find in Israel and Christ our story."[25] The Bible
becomes a kind of map that shows the path along which God's people move
and the boundaries that God's people observe along the way. The Bible provides
a sense of orientation so that Christians have a clearer understanding of who
they are and how they are to be in life, as well as in death.

    This orientation arises from the story of God's people, a story articulated in
two movements, namely, in Israel and in Jesus. What is the content and substance of this story? This is really the central question, because as Hauerwas
observes, "we need to ask what kind of story is it that we have told in Israel and
Christ that should become our story."[26] First, what it is not. It is not a story that
can be reduced to less than the story. One cannot derive principles and rules
from the story, only to leave behind the story itself, without at the same time
distorting the story.[27] The story of Israel and Jesus must be told and heard in all
its particularity before it can be embraced and enacted by the people of God
who claim their identity in this story. To say this, however, is not yet to tell the
story but only to call attention to the importance of how one approaches the
story, an aspect that will receive further attention in my treatment of Hauerwas's
hermeneutics.

    Second, it is a story that begins with God and God's calling together a
people, Israel. Although Hauerwas does not have much to say about Israel, he
does emphasize Israel as a called and chosen people.[28] This chosen status finds
expression in the covenants initiated by God with Israel, covenants that show
Israel the way and the path, the *torah*, so that they might walk faithfully with
God.[29] According to Hauerwas,

> the task for Israel, indeed the very thing that makes Israel Israel, is to walk in
> the way of the Lord, that is, to imitate God through the means of the prophet

(Torah), the king (Sonship), and the priest (Knowledge). To walk in the way of God meant that Israel must be obedient to the commands (Deut. 8:6); to fear the Lord (Deut. 10:12); to love the Lord (Deut. 11:22); and thus to be perfect in the way (Gen. 17:1). But the way of obedience is also the way of intimacy, for Israel is nothing less than God's "first-born son" (Ex. 4:22). Moreover Israel has the knowledge of the Lord as a just and compassionate God and so Israel too must act justly and with compassion (Jer. 22:16).

Israel is Israel, therefore, just to the extent that she "remembers" the "way of the Lord," for by that remembering she in fact imitates God.[30]

God does not impose God's will on Israel, rather God calls Israel "time and time again to his way, to be faithful to the covenant, but always gives Israel the possibility of disobedience."[31] For Hauerwas, the notion of God *inviting* relationship and fidelity is crucial, for it shows that faith is not coercive. God does not coerce relational fidelity, and so Israel (and all humanity) has the constant capacity and temptation of breaking the covenants. I should hasten to add that although God's collective covenant with Israel is important, it does not exhaust the ways, or even provide the central way, in which Israel's relation to God can be characterized. Hauerwas is extremely wary of settling upon any single biblical theme as a controlling motif for understanding God's interaction with humanity.[32]

Another aspect of Israel's identity on which Hauerwas draws is Israel's response to adversity and suffering. Here, the literature of lament comes into view. Hauerwas calls attention to the psalms of lament, and also Job, as indications of the need, not so much to explain suffering, as to make a response to suffering: "not only did Israel think it legitimate to complain, but she also developed an entire genre for lament. . . . the suffering is simply acknowledged for what it is with no explanation given for it."[33]

Hauerwas has little more to say about Israel's story with and about God, save that he strongly emphasizes continuity between the story of Israel and the story of Jesus. The story of Israel is a necessary part of Christian identity: "understanding the story of God as found in Israel and Jesus is the necessary basis for any moral development that is Christianly significant."[34] For Hauerwas, the story of Israel is inseparable from the story of Jesus, since the story of Jesus is rendered senseless apart from the story of Israel. The story of Israel points to Jesus just as the story of Jesus points to Israel, all of which finds further reflection in the Christian church. Hauerwas describes this relationship between Israel, Jesus, and the church as "recapitulation": "Scripture as a whole tells the story of the covenant with Israel, the life, death, and resurrection of Jesus, and the ongoing history of the church as the recapitulation of that life."[35]

By recalling the story of Israel and the story of Jesus, the Christian community recalls and so reconstitutes its own identity as God's people, a people with a rich heritage that gives abiding shape to its present character. In that sense, rehearsing the biblical story becomes an act of re-membering, of constantly putting together and reconstructing Christian identity after the pattern of Israel and Jesus, and so after God. Tradition, then, is nothing less than the way the church has re-membered itself and its collective story with God over the years.[36] For Christians, Jesus is, of course, the pivotal figure in this story.

A Cruciform People

Although the story of Israel is necessary to the story of Jesus, and so to Christians, for Hauerwas the story of Jesus surpasses the story of Israel, since Jesus marks the presence of God's kingdom in a way not previously seen in the story of Israel. This presence is best seen in the character of Jesus' life told by the Gospels, a life anchored in the cross, "the summary of his whole life."[37]

According to Hauerwas's reading of the Gospels, Jesus' identity, and his entire ministry are oriented by the cross. This orientation can best be seen in Mark 8:27–9:1, the story of Peter's confession, which leads directly into the first Passion prediction. Hauerwas cites this passage in full and then comments: "This is obviously not only an important passage for Mark but for the whole New Testament, as it asks the central question, 'Who do men say that I am?' "[38] Hauerwas notes the irony in Peter's confession that Jesus is the Messiah, for Peter appears to give the correct answer, but Peter's ensuing rebuke of Jesus' Passion prediction shows that Peter assumes Jesus will be a powerful Messiah. Jesus' response to Peter ("Get behind me, Satan!"), however, shows that Jesus is not going to be the kind of Messiah Peter expected. Rather, Jesus "insists it is possible, if God's rule is acknowledged and trusted, to serve without power."[39] Again, we see the motif of serving God without coercive power that Hauerwas had developed in relation to Israel.

Jesus' cross also reveals what kind of a world we live in, namely, a world where human beings have usurped God's rule.[40] The cross shows what Christians can expect in this world if they are faithful to God's calling. But the cross is not just a call to self-sacrifice:

> Jesus' cross . . . is not merely a general symbol of the moral significance of self-sacrifice. The cross is not the confirmation of the facile assumption that it is better to give than receive. Rather the cross is Jesus' ultimate dispossession through which God has conquered the powers of this world. The cross is not just a symbol of God's kingdom; it is that kingdom come.[41]

The cross is God's way of defeating opposing powers, but not on their own terms. Jesus demonstrates that God does not use violence against those who use violence in opposing God. Jesus "refused to fight them on their terms,"[42] and in so doing, God brought about the defeat of such violent powers through the cross.

God's people, then, show themselves as God's people inasmuch as they "imitate Jesus' life through taking on the task of being his disciple[s]."[43] Such imitation, such discipleship, essentially involves humble self-renunciation for the sake of and after the manner of Jesus. Discipleship, then, means taking up one's cross and following Jesus:[44] "Thus to be like Jesus is to join him in the journey through which we are trained to be a people capable of claiming citizenship in

God's kingdom of nonviolent love—a love that would overcome the powers of this world, not through coercion and force, but through the power of this one man's death."[45]

But there are limitations to how the cross functions for Christians, to how far Christians can imitate Jesus' self-offering on the cross. Christians cannot and should not seek in an individualistic sense to become like Jesus, for the cruciform life can only be carried out in a communal context. Taking up one's cross requires the nurture and training that only the community can provide. Thus, to be "like Jesus requires that I become part of a community that practices virtues, not that I copy his life point by point."[46] Further, Hauerwas stresses that Christians "are called upon to be *like* Jesus, not to *be* Jesus."[47] Jesus' death on the cross and his resurrection from the dead define and establish how God chooses to relate to humanity. Christians can imitate the cruciform life he initiated, and so participate in it, but they cannot repeat it.

Finally, the cross shows that Jesus' path of nonviolence must also be the path for Christians. This is a recurring theme throughout Hauerwas's writing.[48] As he puts it: "One cannot but feel that those who defend so strongly the use of violence in the service of justice are finally trying to rescue Jesus from the cross."[49] The refusal of Jesus to use violence points to the reality of the peaceable kingdom that he inaugurates. His death on the cross shows that the world has rejected the noncoercive reign of God that Jesus proclaims. But God's raising Jesus from the dead bears witness to God's establishing the kingdom in triumph over the worldly powers of death and so ushers in the eschatological age.[50]

A People Between the Times

Christians live between the times, between the inauguration of God's kingdom in the life, death, and resurrection of Jesus and the final consummation of God's kingdom that Jesus proclaimed. Thus, Christians must constantly learn and re-learn to look at the world from Jesus' eschatological perspective, a world with "a beginning, a continuing drama, and an end."[51] Hauerwas draws repeatedly on the eschatological vision sounded throughout the biblical writings, citing such passages as Isa. 11:6–9 ("the wolf shall dwell with the lamb. . . . the suckling child shall play over the hole of the asp"),[52] as well as various sections of Jesus' Sermon on the Mount (Matt. 5–7).[53] Crucial for Hauerwas is the conviction that such eschatological visions have become fully present in the person of Jesus through his ministry, death, and resurrection. Indeed, the central chapter in his *Peaceable Kingdom* is entitled "Jesus: The Presence of the Peaceable Kingdom."[54] Jesus' life bears witness to what God's kingdom looks like, to how God's kingdom is enacted and made real. That Jesus lived such a life and calls others to such a life shows the real possibility of participating in this peaceable kingdom here and now, that is, between the times.

The Sermon on the Mount, then, is not (contrary to such interpreters as Reinhold Niebuhr) an unattainable individualistic ideal possible only at God's final consummation of history.[55] Rather, Jesus' Sermon on the Mount "challenges our normal assumptions about what is possible, but that is exactly what it is meant to do. We are not to accept the world with its hate and resentments as a given, but to recognize that we live in a new age which makes possible a new way of life."[56] Put simply, God does not call people to approximate love by settling for justice; rather, God calls people to be perfect. Such perfection is attainable because Jesus demonstrated such a life and so inaugurated God's kingdom, in which imitating God's perfection disclosed in Jesus is possible for Christians in the continued presence of God's powerful Spirit. Accordingly, Jesus' life and teachings show

> that God's kingship and power consists not in coercion but in God's willingness to forgive and have mercy on us. God wills nothing less than that men and women should love their enemies and forgive one another; thus we will be perfect as God is perfect. Jesus challenged both the militaristic and ritualistic notions of what God's kingdom required—the former by denying the right of violence even if attacked, and the latter by his steadfast refusal to be separated from those "outside."[57]

Christians *can* bear witness to the presence of God's kingdom, and so call others to it by becoming Jesus' disciples and breaking the cycle of violence through refusing to cooperate with the coercive powers of the world.[58] Jesus is the central eschatological character because only through his life do Christians learn what kind of character they are to have in the present eschatological age. "Thus the Gospels portray Jesus not only offering the possibility of achieving what were heretofore thought to be impossible ethical ideals. He actually proclaims and embodies a way of life that God has made possible here and now."[59]

This eschatological orientation empowers Christians in a communal context to focus more on *what kind* of kingdom Jesus has inaugurated as opposed to *when* this kingdom will be achieved in all its completeness. The proclamation of God's coming kingdom, present and future, "is a claim about *how* God rules and the establishment of that rule through the life, death, and resurrection of Jesus."[60]

The eschatological character of Christian communal existence also highlights the reality that God's kingdom is not to be identified with any human institutions, as if humans on their own could bring about God's kingdom. This is Hauerwas's main criticism of the social gospel movement associated with Walter Rauschenbusch in the early twentieth century and of the temptation liberal Protestantism has faced since then to see social progress as the primary task of the church. According to Hauerwas, "leaving Scripture far behind, Rauschenbusch was able to transform the theocratic image of the Kingdom of God into the democratic ideal of the brotherhood of man,"[61] but this was a false transformation.

In this connection, it is crucial for Hauerwas that Christians are called to be faithful and, ultimately, should not be terribly concerned about whether or not they are being effective. Hauerwas makes this point most clearly in relation to Scripture in his analysis of charity and the Gospel of Luke.[62] His goal in this analysis "is to try to suggest *how* Christians should care for the poor, that is what form our charity should take, and in what sense such a charity is politics."[63] In seeking to address this issue, he then states: "I am going to do a rather extraordinary thing for an ethicist; I am going to let the scripture guide my way," for he contends that "the book of Luke contains important clues about how a politics of charity should be shaped."[64] He points out how Luke is concerned to show the historical success of Christianity especially among the Gentiles,[65] and he also notes Luke's understanding that Jesus is the culmination and fulfillment of God's promise for all humanity that began in Adam (Luke 3:28) and was carried through history in Noah, Abraham, David, Israel, and the prophets.

> This view of history would seem to mean that in a fashion Christians have the key to history—that is, we know its meaning and we know where it is going. . . . Luke's account of history seems, therefore, to support the joining of charity and effectiveness. For the Christ we Christians serve seems to commit us to having a stake in how history comes out. And that seems to give us the warrant necessary to grasp for the means of power offered by this world. It was our destiny to take the reins of the empire from Caesar [with Constantine], the difference being that we will use the power to do good—that is, to be effective.[66]

The problem, however, is that this understanding of history "is a profound misreading of Luke"[67] because Christians are not called, nor are they able, to make history come out right, which is God's task. To be sure, God's activity in Israel and in Christ forms the meaning of history, but the Christian's task is not thereby to force or coerce history to conform to the Christian's understanding of God's kingdom. Rather, the Christian's task is to remember and enact the story of Israel and Christ. "We do not know how God intends to use such obedience, we simply have the confidence he will use it even if it does not appear effective to the world itself."[68]

In other words, Christians are not called to direct history; they are called to be servants of history. God's kingdom will not be established through enforced legislative reform, whether democratic or fascist, but only through making Christ's story our own. Making Christ's story our own means identifying with the weak, with the poor and the sinners. Hauerwas cites various passages throughout Luke's Gospel to support this argument (Luke 5:31–32; 6:20; 12:22–34; 14:33; 16). Luke's emphasis on Jesus' association with the poor shows "*how* God chooses to deal with history, namely through the weak," not through the mighty and powerful.[69] Thus, "charity is not required in order to justify our existence, to rid us of our guilt, but because it is the manner of being most like God. For we are commanded not to be revolutionaries, or to be world-changers, but simply to be perfect."[70]

For Christians to make the story of Jesus their own, then, means that Christians conform their lives, with the support of the Christian community, to the kind of life Jesus lived; in so doing, they participate in the eschatological presence of God's kingdom. "There is no way to remove the eschatology of Christian ethics."[71] There is every chance that, like Jesus, they will experience the poverty and weakness of the cross, but God uses such faithfulness to further God's kingdom, regardless of whether or not such movement becomes clear, regardless of whether or not such faithfulness is effective in the eyes of the world (or of the believer). Thus, concludes Hauerwas, "what charity requires is not the removing of all injustice in the world, but rather meeting the need of the neighbor where we find him," for the story of Jesus "gives us the skills even to be able to see who is our neighbor" (Hauerwas follows this statement with a full citation of the Good Samaritan parable from Luke 10:25–42).[72]

A Worshiping People

A significant aspect of Hauerwas's approach to the Bible involves his conviction that apart from the worshiping community the Bible loses its significance and meaning. This is so because the Bible functions essentially as an extension of the Christian community in that the foundational stories of God's relation to the community have been canonized as Scripture by the community. The Bible is not other than the community of believers; rather, it serves to remind God's people of who they are. In remembering again and again who they are and how they have been called to be with one another in the world, they come together to worship God and to hear the story of their ongoing collective journey with God.

Congregational worship, then, becomes perhaps the most tangible expression of Christian community, for people literally come together in order to express and to renew their identity as God's people. Through singing and prayer, they speak to God, and through Scripture, sermon, and sacraments, God speaks to and empowers them as God's people. Scripture is central in this process insofar as it relates the story of Israel and Jesus that forms and reforms the character and identity of God's people.[73]

Indeed, the formative role of Scripture is best seen in the context of worship, for there Scripture is proclaimed; in worship, Scripture is heard as the people's living story with God, and not as the individually read text out there that relates information about some distant people and what they believed.[74] For Hauerwas, sermons point away from the Bible as written text qua text and toward the Bible as narrative story that shapes communal character. In commenting on one of his own sermons that introduces an essay entitled "The Church as God's New Language," Hauerwas states that the Bible should not be "abstracted from the concrete people who acknowledge the authority of the Bible. Thus, I wrote a sermon in the hopes of reminding us that the emphasis on narrative is unintelligible abstracted from the ecclesial context."[75]

It is this proclaimed character of Scripture through its being read out loud before the gathered community of faith and through its place as the starting point for preaching that makes worship such a crucial context for Hauerwas's understanding of what constitutes the most appropriate use of the Bible. Since the Bible is the people's book, it best functions when the people have gathered together. It is no accident, then, that in Hauerwas's more recent writings, he has given much more attention to sermons as perhaps the most suitable forum for reflecting on what the Bible says to the community of faith.[76]

By emphasizing the role of biblical narrative within the context of communal worship, Hauerwas seeks "to draw our attention to where the story is told, namely in the church; how the story is told, namely in faithfulness to Scripture; and who tells the story, namely the whole church through the office of the preacher."[77] For Hauerwas, to make use of the Bible without attention to its place for the believing community that gathers to worship God is to badly misconstrue and so to misunderstand it. Thus, Hauerwas writes:

> I believe that one of the most promising ways to reclaim the integrity of theological language as a working language for a congregation's life is for seminaries to make liturgy the focus of their life. I do not mean simply that seminaries should have more worship services, though if done well that might be helpful. Rather, I mean that the curriculum of the seminary should be determined by and reflect the liturgical life of the church. For example, why should seminaries continue to teach courses in "Old Testament" and "New Testament" as if those were intelligible theological subjects? Liturgically the Scripture functions not as text but canon. Yet in our classes we treat the Scripture primarily as text, and then as those responsible for the training of ministers we are puzzled why Scripture plays so little part in the life of most Protestant congregations.[78]

This kind of orientation in theological education, argues Hauerwas, would make clearer the connections between the biblical story and the ongoing life of God's people.[79]

Hauerwas also stresses the need for Christian communities to make use of ecumenical lectionaries in their congregational worship. Hearing and preaching from the lectionary demonstrate that the preacher is not self-authorized but is authorized by the community to proclaim the story:

> As pastors, we need to be *clear* about our source of authority. One way to do that is to preach from scripture, specifically, to preach from the ecumenical lectionary. . . . The very act of reading and preaching from scripture is a deeply moral act in our age, a reminder of the source of pastoral authority. When the preacher uses the lectionary, the preacher makes clear that he or she preaches what he or she has been *told* to preach. That is important because it makes clear that the *story* forms us.[80]

Finally, it is appropriate that Hauerwas several times describes himself as "a high-church Mennonite"[81] (though he formally belongs to the United Methodist Church), for his identification with the Mennonite tradition highlights the centrality of a strong self-defined Christian community. And yet his qualifier as being "high church" (which he does not further define) indicates the importance he places on developed liturgical worship, worship in which the Bible has the central function of reminding God's people of their story together with God.

A People Set Apart

For Hauerwas, to say that the Christian community is set apart from the world is to say that Christians are called by God in Christ to be a holy and sanctified people. Although Christians are not to be isolated and withdrawn within the world, they are in the likeness of Christ to be clearly distinguished from the world and the world's values. Thus, "to be formed in Christ, to be sanctified, is to be committed to bringing every element of our character into relation with this dominant orientation."[82]

The motif of Christians as a community set apart permeates Hauerwas's writings, although he makes relatively limited reference to the Bible in developing this theme. The clearest instance of Hauerwas's appeal to the Bible in this regard can be found in his use of and commentary on Phil. 3:20–21 at the beginning of his book *Resident Aliens: Life in the Christian Colony*, coauthored with William Willimon. The book begins with a citation from Phil. 2:5–11 and 3:20–21. This citation is followed by the authors' preface, in which they state: "In his letter to the Philippians, Paul uses an image that appeals to us, that serves as a symbol for the change in mood we describe in this book. . . . Paul reminds them [the Philippians], 'Our commonwealth is in heaven' (3:20). . . . Moffatt more vividly translates this *politeuma* ["commonwealth"] as 'We are a colony of heaven.' "[83] Christian community, then, is a community essentially alien to the present world, hence the title of the book, *Resident Aliens*. In Christ, the old world has ended, although it lingers on, and a new world, embodied primarily in the church, has begun. The church "is a beachhead, an outpost, an island of one culture in the middle of another."[84] As a colony of resident aliens, the Christian community needs to be prepared for battle. In this vein, Hauerwas cites the famous passage from Eph. 6:10–20, in which the author of Ephesians encourages Christians to "put on the whole armor of God" in preparing to defend against the powers opposing God.[85]

In Hauerwas's definition, Christian community is a countercultural minority community if it is truly Christian. This is not to say that it is sectarian, whatever that term means, a charge often leveled against Hauerwas and one to which he strongly objects.[86] But it does mean that Hauerwas is deeply suspicious of any form of Christianity that smacks of Constantinianism, namely, any Christianity that thinks it can use recognized power structures of the world to bring about transformation toward the kingdom of God in a way that does not itself violate the character of God's kingdom as expressed in Jesus' life, death, and resurrection. How can the Christian colony use the dominant culture of the world without at the same time betraying its identity as a community set apart? Thus, Hauerwas revels in Christianity's fall from Constantinian power as evidence of a step in the right direction, toward the regaining of Christianity's true identity.[87]

Finally, Christians are set apart because "they have learned as a forgiven people they must also be able to forgive," and this capability "of accepting forgiveness separates them from the world."[88] This is so because accepting and extending forgiveness mean that Christians no longer participate in the world's illusion that "power and violence rule history."[89] Rather, in Jesus' life, death, and resurrection, Christians have come to know and experience God's forgiving character, which then empowers them to be a community of forgiveness in contrast to the world.

Hauerwas's View of the Authority of Scripture

Before turning directly to Hauerwas's understanding of scriptural authority, it is appropriate to first set his approach to biblical authority in the context of his conviction that Christians need to be wary of two powerful and related movements that have *undermined* the authority of the Bible and the formation of authentic Christian community. According to Hauerwas, both movements are more deceptive and problematic for genuine Christian faith than they are helpful. They have gained too much authority in the Christian tradition and so distort the appropriate authority of the Bible in the Christian community. These movements are Constantinianism and the Enlightenment. According to Hauerwas, both Constantinianism and the Enlightenment have led to the betrayal of true Christian faith and have distorted the true interpretation of the Bible as the church's Scripture.

Put simply, Constantinianism deceived, and still deceives, Christians into thinking that being religious in some generic and diluted sense is what Christian faith is about, or that Christians can fully accommodate to the dominant culture without losing their Christian identity. Constantinianism encourages the formation and perpetuation of a vaguely Christian popular culture and ethos that support the church. But Constantinianism also links Christian faith to political and social structures of power and thereby deceives Christians into thinking that they can use power, even coercive power (violence), in the service of Christian faith, when in fact such cooperation with worldly power structures betrays the noncoercive character of God and so also the character of true Christian faith.[90] The result has been the transformation of the gospel by the world rather than the transformation of the world by the gospel.[91]

The Enlightenment has led Christians astray in that it has encouraged Christians to spend their energy in the apologetic task of making the gospel credible to the world to the degree that Christians have forgotten their primary task of making the world credible to the gospel, namely, of living faithfully in a world revolting against God.[92] The Enlightenment has so emphasized individualism and positivist rationalism that it has led Christians away from the centrality of the community of believers and has misled Christians to trust in the power of human rationality to save rather than to have faith in God's power to save. As a result, this individualistic liberal rationalism has falsely led Christians to believe that they needed to make sense of their faith in terms of the Enlightenment worldview rather than to make sense of the Enlightenment in terms of their faith. In other words, Christians have wrongly molded Jesus to fit the values of rational heroic liberalism rather than molding themselves in faithful community to the likeness of Jesus.[93]

The rhetoric of the Enlightenment promised an adventure that would lead to individual freedom, natural rights that would enable people to fashion their own future unbound by the oppressive claims of tradition and community. But from the beginning it was "an adventure that held the seeds of its own destruction within itself, within its attenuated definition of human nature and its inadequate vision of human destiny. What we got was not self-freedom but self-centeredness, loneliness, superficiality, and harried consumerism. . . . The adventure went sour."[94]

Christianity's cooperation with the Enlightenment has led to the dissolution of vibrant communities of believers, to rootless faith. The values of the Enlightenment have so encouraged Christians to think in isolated individualistic terms that they have forgotten the necessity of community. But genuine Christian faith points in a very different direction, indicated by the Sermon on the Mount:

> The Sermon implies that it is as isolated individuals that we lack the ethical and theological resources to be faithful disciples. The Christian ethical question is not the conventional Enlightenment question, How in the world can ordinary people like us live a heroic life like that? The question is, What sort of community would be required to support an ethic of nonviolence, marital fidelity, forgiveness, and hope such as the one sketched by Jesus in the Sermon on the Mount? . . . The Sermon on the Mount cares nothing for the European Enlightenment's infatuation with the individual self as the most significant ethical unit. For Christians, the church is the most significant ethical unit.[95]

Hauerwas sees the rise of higher biblical criticism (in liberal Protestantism) and fundamentalism in the late nineteenth and early twentieth centuries, both of which remain very much alive at the end of the twentieth century, as in large measure the result of the joining of Constantinian and Enlightenment presuppositions. For Hauerwas, both higher criticism and fundamentalism are Enlightenment ideologies in service to "the fictive agent of the Enlightenment—namely the rational individual—who believes the truth in general and in particular the truth of Christian faith can be known without initiation into a community which requires transformation of self."[96] Thus, according to Hauerwas, higher criticism and fundamentalism are but two sides of the same Constantinian/Enlightenment coin, with higher criticism serving upper-middle-class educated/professional Christians and fundamentalism serving lower-middle-class Christians with less formal education. Both higher criticism and fundamentalism are but attempts to "maintain the influence of Constantinian Christianity— now clothed in the power of Enlightenment rationality— in the interest of continuing Christianity's hegemony over the ethos of our culture—a culture that increasingly learns it can well do without Christian presuppositions."[97]

Similarly, the social gospel movement championed by Walter Rauschenbusch in the early twentieth century was nothing but the attempt of liberal Protestantism to use social structures to help bring about the kingdom of God in the guise of the "brotherhood of man."[98] More to the point of this study, the rise of historical criticism (higher criticism) in approaching the Bible is nothing but the adaptation of Enlightenment philosophy to interpret the Bible, for it reads the Bible as text, not Scripture, torn apart from the community of believers, presuming the possibility and preferability of the solitary individual rationally deducing the objective interpretation of the text (and so isolating *the* meaning of the text) without recourse to the community that authorizes the Bible as Scripture.[99]

I have stressed Hauerwas's distrust of and disdain for Constantinianism and the Enlightenment because his convictions in this regard directly shape his approach to and use of the Bible, and also leave him open to other problems that take the place of the problems discarded with these two movements. (Whether casting out the two demons of Constantinianism and the Enlightenment leads to many more demons taking their place has yet to be seen.)

The basic source presenting Hauerwas's understanding of the authority of Scripture is his essay "The Moral Authority of Scripture: The Politics and Ethics of Remembering," from his 1981 book *A Community of Character*.[100] In this programmatic essay, Hauerwas proposes that discussions or claims about the moral authority of Scripture make no sense without reference to Christian community, for the authority of Scripture is itself authorized by the community.[101] He further argues, as the subtitle to the essay indicates, that in essence "the authority of scripture is a political claim" (p. 53), and biblical interpretation a political act. "It is a process of judgment of a community determining what that community is all about. It is always a question of authority and power."[102] The question of biblical authority is thus always a question of community polity.[103] In order to examine this interrelationship between Scripture and community, it is helpful to look at three aspects: (1) the meaning of authority, (2) the Bible as Scripture and not text, and (3) the limits of biblical authority.

The Meaning of Authority

According to Hauerwas, "the meaning of authority must be grounded in a community's self-understanding, which is embodied in its habits, customs, laws, and traditions" (p. 60). Authority reflects the self-understanding of the community, for the community authorizes that which perpetuates its identity. The community itself is "a group of persons who share a history and whose common set of interpretations about that history provide the basis for common actions" (p. 60). Authority, then, is the behavior of the community to project itself forward based on a shared understanding of its past, or as Hauerwas puts it, "authority is that power of a community that allows for reasoned interpretations of the community's past and future goals" (p. 60). The community evaluates its collective past, its tradition, and decides how best to act in the constant process of redefining and reestablishing itself over time.

Although authority arises from the community, "it is equally true that community must have authority. For authority is that reflection initiated by a community's traditions through which a common goal can be pursued. Authority is, therefore, the means through which a community is able to journey from where it is to where it ought to be" (p. 63). This statement appears to suggest that the community is self-authorizing, but this is not fully true. The community cannot exercise authority apart from its identity as expressed in its tradition and in its formative (authorizing?) origins. Indeed, even though Scripture is a function of the community, the community self-consciously sets up Sscripture in such a way that it critically tests the church's memory and self-understanding.[104]

> By regarding scripture as an authority Christians mean to indicate that they
> find there the traditions through which their community most nearly comes to
> knowing and being faithful to the truth. . . . Scripture is not an authority be-
> cause it sets a standard of orthodoxy . . . but because the traditions of scripture
> provide the means for our community to find new life. (p. 63)

The truthfulness of Scripture is thus crucial to its authority. Ultimately, for Hauerwas, this truthfulness is mediated for the community by God. Scripture does not contain propositional truths about God; rather, it testifies faithfully to the character of God. As Hauerwas puts it, "claims about the authority of scripture make sense only in that the world and the community it creates are in fact true to the character of God" (p. 55).

The community's perception of the truthfulness of its authorizing stories is central both to the community's ongoing task of critically reflecting upon its traditions and to the community's task of authorizing its future direction. "To claim the Bible as authority is the testimony of the church that this book provides the resources necessary for the church to be a community sufficiently truthful so that our conversation with one another and God can continue across generations" (pp. 63–64).[105] Of course, for Hauerwas to stress that the Bible provides the resources necessary for truthfulness is to claim that the Bible is truthful, which raises the question about what it means that the Bible is truthful. In turn, the truthfulness of the Bible is closely related to another dimension of truthfulness, namely, the community's changing perceptions of what counts as truth. As Hauerwas puts it, the community is "set on its way by the language and practices of the tradition, but while on its way it must often subtly reform those practices and language in accordance with its new perception of truth" (p. 63). Thus, the truth itself may not change, but perceptions and appropriations of it do. How does the community's new perception of truth relate to and perhaps affect its understanding of the Bible as the most truthful of resources for its continued life? This is a crucial question, and one to which I will return at the end of this chapter.

The Bible as Scripture and Not Text

One of the concerns Hauerwas has regarding the authority of the Bible for moral reflection in the Christian community revolves around the historical-critical approach to the Bible taken by most twentieth-century biblical scholarship, an approach that has, from Hauerwas's perspective, significantly limited the ability of the church to appropriate the ethical significance of the Bible.[106] The increasing specialization of biblical studies into dozens of separate areas has also led to a fragmented approach to the Bible as a whole, with the result that the Bible has been treated primarily as objectified text and not as communally authoritative Scripture. The problem is that "appeal to scripture is not equivalent to appeal to the text in itself, and it is the latter, rightly or wrongly, which is the subject of most current scholarly effort. . . . However, for Christian ethics the Bible is not just a collection of texts but scripture that makes normative claims on a community" (p. 56).[107]

While historical and sociological reconstruction of the origins of the biblical writings may be important, "it is simply unclear what theological significance such work should have" (p. 56). The discipline of professional biblical studies, then, has partly resulted in treating the Bible as a loose and disparate collection of pieces rather than as a canonical whole authorized by the church. Indeed, Hauerwas states that the

> confusion surrounding the relation of text to scripture has not resulted in ethicists (and theologians) paying too little attention to current scholarly work concerning the Bible; rather their attention is far too uncritical. It has been observed that there is finally no substitute for knowing the text, and it is often unfortunately true that theologians and ethicists alike know the current theories about the development of the text better than the text itself. (p. 56)

What is needed, then, is an approach to the Bible that treats it as Scripture authorized by the Christian community for the Christian community.

To this end, Hauerwas argues for the importance of reading the Bible as canon. To recognize and to approach the stories of the Bible as canonical Scripture means that "we discover our human self more effectively through these stories, and so use them in judging the adequacy of alternative schemes for humankind."[108] But to stress the canonical character of the Bible is not to pretend there are no tensions in Scripture. Rather, the canonization of the inconsistencies in Scripture forces the Christian community to come to terms again and again with the tensions inherent in the Christian story and so in the Christian community, past and present.

> [O]ne reason the church has had to be content with the notion of a canon rather than some more intellectually satisfying summary of the content of scripture is that only through the means of a canon can the church adequately manifest the kind of tension with which it must live. The canon marks off as scripture those texts that are necessary for the life of the church without trying to resolve their obvious diversity and/or even disagreements. (p. 66)

In fact, the subplots and diverse points of view related in the Bible are crucial for qualifying the main story line, "for without them the story itself would be less than truthful" (p. 67). Thus, the canon of Scripture is "not an accomplishment but a task" for the Christian community as it seeks faithfully to remember and to enact these authoritative stories with all of their tensions (p. 68).

In order for canonical Scripture to remain a living resource for the church, the church must avoid two temptations: "either to objectify scripture in a manner that kills its life, or to be willing in principle to accept the validity of any interpretation by way of acknowledging the scripture's variety" (p. 68). To either objectify or completely relativize Scripture means to lose it as the authoritative story on which the church draws for its continuing life.

Another aspect of treating the Bible as canonical scripture involves recognizing that Scripture is always already mediated by church tradition. This is a further reason why the Christian community cannot approach the Bible as mere text, for the Bible is always handed down from one generation of Christians to the next as interpreted and traditioned Scripture. There is no way to approach the Bible apart from how it has been traditioned. Thus, Christian communities should pay attention to how past interpretive communities have appropriated the Bible as canonical Scripture.

If, finally, one asks why the Christian canon contains the writings that it does, Hauerwas answers that "these texts have been accepted as scripture because they and they alone satisfy . . . our craving for a perfect story which we feel to be true" (p. 66). Again, one comes across the rather loose claim that the Bible is true, apparently because the church collectively recognizes it to be "a perfect story" which it "feels to be true." Why should the contemporary church continue to abide by the patristic church's decisions about the formalization of the biblical canon? "We continue to honor that decision made by the ancient church . . . because it is a decision that makes sense" in relation to the character of Christian faith (p. 66). This account of the canon and its distinctive truthfulness raises a serious question about the adequacy of Hauerwas's understanding of the authority of the canon of Scripture, but I will address this question at the end of the chapter.

The Limits of Biblical Authority

Even though the Bible as Scripture provides the most truthful, and so authoritative, resource for Christian community, there are limits to biblical authority. The first limitation, if in fact it should be called a limitation, involves the recognition that—to say it yet once again—for Hauerwas, the Bible has no authority apart from the community of believers. The community authorizes the Bible as Scripture.

Because the community authorizes Scripture, and because Scripture is always already traditioned, a related limitation is that it cannot be the sole authority for the church. Thus, for Hauerwas, the Reformation slogan *sola scriptura* is finally a heresy.[109] It is a heresy because it ironically deceives the church into thinking that Scripture is an authority apart from the church, and that as such Scripture can be approached as an objective set of truths which the church can then mine as text. It is just such an approach, argues Hauerwas, that has led both to fundamentalist literalism and to historicist higher criticism. This approach to Scripture as objectified truth devoid of a tradition of interpretation "sets Scripture as text over the presence of Christ in his church. The doctrine of *sola scriptura* is clearly a heresy that is the seedbed of fundamentalism as well as of higher criticism." [110]

A rather different limitation to biblical authority arises out of Hauerwas's conviction that community authorizes the Bible as Scripture. Because authority is a function of community, the community can also assign different levels of authority to the writings that the community has canonized in Scripture. I think this is the implication, at least, in Hauerwas's statement that "I do not assume that all the moral advice and admonitions found in Scripture have the same significance or should positively be appropriated" (p. 70). Through the process of interpretation and appropriation, the community of believers makes judgments about different layers and levels of biblical authority.

Related to this notion of varying levels of authority is Hauerwas's notable observation that

> one of the remarkable things about Scripture is the inclusion in the text itself of the mistaken directions tradition has taken. Even more importantly, Scripture does not make clear in itself which were the mistakes and which were the successes. Thus it is necessary for each new generation to struggle with and continue the arguments begun in Scripture itself. [111]

Thus, according to Hauerwas, Scripture itself includes the mistaken judgments of past communities of faith. Of course, such mistakes are only seen as such by later communities of faith as they evaluate the understanding and interpretation of Christian faith embedded in Scripture itself. To give an example, Hauerwas is critical of how the Gospel of Luke is so concerned to show that the early Christians were no threat to Rome. Although on one level it is true that Jesus was not a threat to Rome in the sense that the Zealots were, still

> I think that Luke's account of the Gospel can be misleading. . . . [for] in another sense Rome was right to crucify Jesus and his followers, as they were far more subversive than the Zealots. . . . Christianity was far more subversive, because it was constituted by a savior who defeated the powers by revealing their true powerlessness. [112]

Hauerwas believes it is appropriate for the Christian community to critically discuss its authoritative canonical story in deciding how to constitute itself. Although it dare not dismiss its canonical story, the Christian community can change its mind about how much authority it assigns to different parts of that story. Of course, the implicit danger here is that the community will itself make a mistake in its interpretation and appropriation of its authorizing story, but that is part of the process through which the community learns and relearns what it means to be God's people.

There is a significant tension in Hauerwas's work regarding the authority of the Bible. On the one hand, he lifts up the authority of the Bible as Scripture that contains the most truthful accounts of faithful existence. He goes so far as to say that "Scripture is an account of human existence *as told by God*."[113] Hauerwas thus suggests that the Bible should exercise a great deal of authority within the community of believers. But on the other hand, he significantly qualifies and even undercuts the authority of Scripture by making it a function of the community to the degree that he does, and by pointing to past mistakes of the community of believers that have themselves been canonized in Scripture. While Scripture certainly relates the story about the faith community's journey with God, still "God is not the author of Scripture"; rather, "God is the one who Christians believe authorizes a community of interpretation. In this respect, it is God's most fateful political act that he left Jews and Christians to wrestle about what kind of community is required to maintain the existence of these Scriptures."[114] In the end, then, the moral authority of Scripture appears to amount to that authority which the community of believers authorizes Scripture to have in faithfulness to God.

Hauerwas's Hermeneutics

If Hauerwas can be said to employ a particular hermeneutic, namely, a particular theory of interpretation in approaching Scripture, it is narrative. I will discuss Hauerwas's emphasis on narrative and story in four subsections: (1) a communal narrative hermeneutic, (2) the irreducibility of the Christian story, (3) the analogical character of Scripture, and (4) conversing with the saints.

A Communal Narrative Hermeneutic

According to Hauerwas, Scripture is not self-interpreting. There is no "plain sense" of the text that is not already an interpreted sense of the text. Since appropriating Scripture is by definition interpreting Scripture, one needs to be self-conscious about what interpretation entails and how to go about the process of interpretation.[115] One especially needs to be aware that Scripture is primarily the narrative of the people's journey with God and that the context for interpretation is the community of believers.

Already very early on in his writings, Hauerwas appeals to story and narrative as the most fruitful way of approaching the moral life and Scripture's role in shaping that life.[116] But narrative is not an end in itself; rather, it is a crucial tool for exploring theological ethics. Thus, Hauerwas writes:

> I have found the concept of story, or perhaps better, narrative, to be a suggestive way to spell out the substantive content of character. But I also try to use the language of "story" in a carefully controlled sense. I am not trying to do "story theology" or "theology of story," as if this represented some new theological position. Rather I am convinced that narrative is a perennial category for understanding better how the grammar of religious convictions is displayed and how the self is formed by those convictions.[117]

He finds a narrative approach so helpful because he thinks it best suits the nature and task of Christian ethics. As he puts it, "The nature of Christian ethics is determined by the fact that Christian convictions take the form of a story, or perhaps better, a set of stories that constitutes a tradition, which in turn creates and forms a community."[118]

Narrative is not accidental or incidental to Christian identity; rather, the very fact that Christians come to know God through hearing and telling the story of Israel and Jesus indicates that these stories themselves and the process of traditionalizing these stories lie at the heart of Christian faith and practice. "Christian ethics does not begin by emphasizing rules or principles, but by calling our attention to a narrative that tells of God's dealing with creation."[119] It is through the stories of Scripture that Christians construct their identity and the world. Thus, "Jews and Christians believe this [biblical] narrative does nothing less than render the character of God and in so doing renders us to be the kind of people appropriate to that character."[120]

The question then is what a narrative explication of Christian existence shows. For Hauerwas, it reminds Christians of at least three central convictions. First, the biblical narrative "formally displays our existence and that of the world as creatures—as *contingent* beings."[121] Second, narrative highlights and "is the characteristic form of our awareness of ourselves as *historical* beings."[122] And third, "God has revealed himself narratively in the history of Israel and in the life of Jesus," which points to "the essential nature of *narrative as the form of God's salvation*" and thus "is why we rightly attribute to Scripture the truth necessary for our salvation."[123]

The story of Israel and Jesus in Scripture reflects the life of God's people and in turn creates and sustains the community of believers. Like Scripture itself, then, narrative is a function of the community, for the biblical narratives present a community story which is then traditionalized and reappropriated by successive communities. Hauerwas's hermeneutic, like his notion of biblical authority, points directly to the life and role of the Christian community as indispensable to how one goes about interpreting Scripture. Hauerwas asserts that "the emphasis on narrative is unintelligible abstracted from an ecclesial context. Indeed, I suspect the project to develop general hermeneutical theories by some theologians is an attempt to substitute a theory of interpretation for the church."[124] For Hauerwas, church (Christian community) is inseparable from the process of interpretation and in fact is itself a living hermeneutic.

The Irreducibility of the Christian Story

A constant refrain in Hauerwas's discussion of his narrative approach to biblical interpretation is that the story can never be reduced to less than the story. The perpetual temptation to reduce the story to a summary principle or axiom of love or covenant or some other concept must be resisted. For example, to reduce the significance of the biblical narratives to the concept of love is to forget that love is dependent on our prior perceptions of the truth of reality that can finally be approached only through the richness of the language and stories which form what we know. The Christian is thus better advised to resist the temptation to reduce the Gospel to a single formula or summary image for the moral life. Christian ethics and the Christian moral life are as rich and various as the story we hold and the life we must live to be true to it.[125]

The story of the Good Samaritan told by Jesus in Luke 10 cannot be abstracted into a general principle of loving one's neighbor. The story is not an illustration of a general moral principle. Rather, "the story is the moral meaning of the principle. Universal ethical principles become ethically significant only as we learn their meaning in stories."[126] It is the fullness of the story itself that sets the context for understanding the story in the first place. To abstract a principle from the story and make that principle the source of subsequent moral reflection essentially does away with any further need for the story, for then Scripture is treated merely as a source of general principles.[127] Such abstractions are particularly dangerous because they tend to encourage an ahistorical approach to Scripture, namely, an approach that is oblivious to the contexts necessary to understand and make sense of the very Scripture upon which they draw.[128] Thus, "there is no moral point or message that is separable from the story of Jesus as we find it in the Gospels."[129]

Hauerwas is opposed, then, to what he calls a "theology of translation," which assumes that the Christian story found in Scripture is not the real story but that the real story must somehow be abstracted or demythologized (Bultmann) in order to get at the eternal unchanging essence. The problem with this approach is that it

> distorts the nature of Christianity. In Jesus we meet not a presentation of basic ideas about God, world, and humanity, but an invitation to join up, to become part of a movement, a people. By the very act of our modern theological attempts at translation, we have unconsciously distorted the gospel and transformed it into something it never claimed to be—ideas abstracted from Jesus, rather than Jesus with his people.[130]

Hauerwas's emphasis on the irreducibility of the biblical story results in an interesting tension when it comes to relating the unity and diversity of the biblical story/stories. On the one hand, by speaking repeatedly of the *story* of Israel and Jesus in the singular, and by calling Christians to read the Bible as the church's singular Scripture, Hauerwas implicitly stresses the unity of the Bible and so the unified journey of God's people as expressed in relation to Israel and Jesus. And yet, on the other hand, Hauerwas also often refers to the *stories* of Israel and Jesus in their plurality and points to Scripture's diversity as a rich resource for the community of believers:

> The social ethical task of the church, therefore, is to be the kind of community that tells and tells rightly the story of Jesus. But it can never forget that Jesus' story is a many-sided tale. We do not have just one story of Jesus, but four. To learn to tell and live the story truthfully does not mean that we must be able

to reconstruct "what really happened" from the four. Rather it means that we, like the early Christians, must learn that understanding Jesus' life is inseparable from learning how to live our own. And that there are various ways to do this is clear by the diversity of the Gospels.[131]

Scripture's diversity, then, is an important characteristic of the way it functions for Christian community, for this multifaceted quality suggests that there are multiple expressions of faithfulness to God, even different communities of faith that may stand in tension with one another as they seek to enact the story according to how they interpret the story. As Hauerwas has remarked in a different context, there is nothing to suggest that "Christ's love and unity with the church implies that unity is without discord."[132] The existence of diverse communities of interpretation that result from diverse stories in Scripture can be healthy for it forces these communities to reexamine these generative stories in Scripture and so to reconsider whether their interpretations are in accord with the kind of community that the stories engender.

> The remarkable richness of these stories of God requires that a church be a community of discourse and interpretation that endeavors to tell these stories and form its life in accordance with them. . . . the very character of the stories of God requires a people who are willing to have their understanding of the story constantly challenged by what others have discovered in their attempt to live faithful to that tradition.[133]

Still, in the end, Hauerwas envisions the Bible more as a unified *story* than as a mere collection of *stories*, for this collective story has been canonized by the community of believers as Scripture. For Hauerwas, there is a "main story line"[134] modified by a host of stories that make the overarching story more truthful. What unifies the stories as canon is the very community that has made these stories into the scriptural story of the community. Thus, the unity of the Gospels does not depend on harmonizing their different accounts of Jesus' life and their different theologies. Rather, "the unity of the Gospels is based on the unquestioned assumption that the unity of these people [the early Christian community] required the telling of the story of this man who claimed to be nothing less than the Messiah of Israel."[135] Although the story of Israel and Jesus is irreducible, and although there may be no story of stories, there remains a unified story discerned by the community of believers/interpreters, who seek to take into account the various stories within the story.

The Analogical Character of Scripture

In approaching Scripture as the irreducible narrative of God's people, Hauerwas also stresses the analogical character of interpretation. Fundamentally, the stories in Scripture relate, not a revealed morality, but "images and analogies that help us understand and interpret the nature of our existence."[136] By telling parables, for example, Jesus did nothing else than give analogies for understanding the kingdom of God. Scripture, then, provides basic analogies and also invites the Christian community to derive corresponding images as it seeks to enact the Christian story in changing times. The task of the community is to interpret Scripture so that the biblical stories come alive again in the community. The task is never ending, for the context in which the community engages in interpretation is ever changing. Thus, the church must ask again and again what it means to be the people of God in the present situation, what it means to embody the stories of Scripture in this time and place. The church's goal is to "better hear and correspond to the stories of God as we find them in Scripture."[137] Hauerwas calls for the use of lively theological imagination in seeking to form a community that corresponds to the canonical story. Accordingly, "there is perhaps no more serious Christian offense than to fail in imagination, that is, to abandon or forget the [scriptural] resources God has given as the means of calling us to his kingdom."[138]

Conversing with the Saints

One final aspect that Hauerwas assigns a significant place in his approach to biblical interpretation involves the need for the Christian community to converse not only with Scripture but also with the exemplary saints in the Christian tradition about Scripture. This is especially true since the saints most clearly show what it means to embody the story of Scripture in life. "Through the lives of the saints we begin to understand how the images of Scripture are best balanced so that we might tell and live the ongoing story of God's unceasing purpose to bring the world to the peace of the kingdom."[139] Thus, Hauerwas not infrequently draws into his discussion of Scripture what such interpreters as Augustine, Aquinas, Luther, Calvin, and Barth have had to say.[140] To converse with the saints reminds the Christian community that Scripture has already been traditioned, and that to hear Scripture also means to pay attention to how past communities have heard and enacted it.

Hauerwas and the Significance of Scripture for Constructive Christian Ethics

What does a Scripture-shaped community look like in real life? To answer that question, it seems best to present a case used by Hauerwas himself to demonstrate the process of Christian practical reasoning.[141]

The Case of Olin Teague

Olin Teague farms land he inherited from his family that lies midway between Middlebury and Shipshewana, Indiana. He is now in his late fifties. While not wealthy, he makes a modest living raising corn, pigs, and a few milk cows. The latter primarily provides the milk used to make the cheddar cheese his family has made for generations. He has four children, three grown and married, his youngest finishing Goshen College and planning to go to medical school. Olin has promised to help pay her expenses since she is planning to be a medical missionary for the Mennonite Central Committee. Olin is not particularly pious, but he and his family have long been members of the local Mennonite church.

As a way to make extra money to help pay his daughter's medical expenses Olin agreed to let Jim Burkholder, the owner of the Wagon Wheel Cafe in downtown Shipshewana, buy his cheese to sell at his cafe. Because of the large Amish population in the surrounding county, Jim reasoned that tourists would be eager to buy "authentic" farm-made cheese. Olin and Jim agreed on a price for the cheese with the understanding that Jim would pay Olin once a year at the end of the tourist season. At the end of the first year Jim owed Olin $3000. However, Jim told Olin that he could not pay, for even though the cheese had sold well, the cafe had failed to make a profit. He made it clear to Olin that it would be some time before he could pay at all, and perhaps never. Olin was quite upset at this turn of events, but it never crossed his mind to do anything other than talking to Jim about how he might put his finances in order. Olin's daughter, however, had to delay her plans to go to medical school at the University of Indiana. (pp. 74– 75) [142]

One should first observe that Hauerwas supplies the specific context of the story by describing briefly who Olin Teague is (working-class farmer, father, Mennonite) and what has happened to him (he has not been paid what is his due, nor is he likely to be paid in the future). In Hauerwas's discussion that follows this case, he notes that it never crossed Olin Teague's mind to sue Jim Burkholder for the money that was owed, despite the difficult situation in which it left Olin's daughter. The reason he does not sue is simple: he is a Mennonite. Hauerwas locates the background of Olin Teague's Mennonite identity squarely in the story of Israel and the story of Jesus. From the story of Israel, the Mennonite community has been influenced by the notion of the Jubilee year in Leviticus 25, where forgiveness of debt is presented as being part of Israel's character. From the extended story of Jesus related in the whole New Testament, Hauerwas suggests that Mennonite life has been clearly shaped by Paul's comments in 1 Cor. 6:1–11, cited in full by Hauerwas, where Paul chastises the Corinthians for taking one another to civil courts and encourages them rather to suffer the wrong. While historical analysis of 1 Cor. 6:1–11 might be interesting, such historical reconstruction of first-century courts and lawsuits "cannot determine the meaning of the text for the moral guidance of the Christian community—at least as far as Mennonites are concerned" (p. 76). Of more significance is the kind of community necessary to hear and enact what Paul says in this text.

Olin Teague does not sue because he is a Mennonite, and in the Mennonite tradition, one does not sue for damages because to do so would be contrary to the Mennonites' understanding of what it means to be a faithful people, a people shaped by the stories of Scripture. As Hauerwas observes:

> [Paul's] admonition not to take one another to court, therefore, is placed [by the Mennonites] against the background of their being a particular kind of people with a distinct set of virtues. Therefore, unlike most Christians who have tried to turn such passages into a legal regulation so one can start to find

exceptions to it, Mennonites understand the admonition to be but a logical extension of their commitment to be a people of peace. Their reading of this text and the significance they give it are not because they think every command of the Bible should be followed to the letter, but rather reflects their understanding that the fundamental ministry of Christians in the world is reconciliation. (pp. 76–77)

It is because Christians have been called to the ministry of reconciliation, and because such reconciliation is not coercive, that Olin Teague does not consider taking Jim Burkholder to court a valid option for him as a Christian, for it would not be a legitimate form of reconciliation. Hauerwas goes on to point out that Olin Teague's practical reasoning in this case may not even be explicitly self-conscious, and that he "may not even know what I Corinthians 6 says" (p. 81). This simply shows that in a "perfectly straightforward sense Olin's habits as a Mennonite made him know what the practical wisdom of the community required of him" (p. 81). Thus, he did not really "decide" whether or not to sue, because such a decision was never in his range of possibilities as a Mennonite. Rather, what he decided to do—to talk to Jim Burkholder about better arranging his finances—was what was most in keeping with the ministry of reconciliation that had long formed the communal context out of which Olin Teague operated as a Christian.

In this case study, Scripture forms what might be called the subtext or underlying narrative that informs theological ethics. Scripture describes or illustrates the kind of community that most corresponds to the people God has called to the kingdom. It is through being this kind of community that successive generations of Christians enact and embody Scripture, for in this way, Scripture functions with authority, shaping Christian identity and so Christian behavior in the world.

In summary, for Hauerwas, the Bible is true to its purpose when it is approached as Scripture for the community of believers. The Bible presents the authorizing story that has generated the believing community in the first place. In turn, it is the believing community itself that has authorized the stories of Scripture as canon, as rule and measure. Scripture is essentially relational, for its stories bear witness to the character of the relationship between God and humanity, the relationship articulated in the story of Israel and the story of Jesus, God's intended relationship with humanity and with all creation. The community continues to, and must continue to, return to Scripture again and again, in order to check its present identity against its formative identity. Thus, the "church is nothing less than that community where we as individuals continue to test and are tested by the particular way those stories live through us."[143] The church tests its identity by conversing with Scripture and the truthful character of God's people expressed in Scripture. As a result, Scripture has authority, "not because no one knows the truth, but because the truth is a conversation for which Scripture sets the agenda and boundaries."[144] Or, as Hauerwas puts it elsewhere, a "faithful church, determined to live by the truth, allows the Bible to breath again, permits Scripture to blossom within its native habitat. . . . The church is the bridge where Scripture and people meet."[145]

Critical Evaluation

How should Hauerwas's uses of Scripture be evaluated? To begin, I find his constant emphasis on the Bible as the church's communal Scripture a positive and commendable move. In practice, the church does authorize the Bible as Scripture, and the writings of the Bible themselves for the most part are directed to the community of faith. And yet, I see two significant problems in Hauerwas's discussion that need to be resolved. The first has to do with his view that the Reformation credo *sola scriptura* is a heresy because it displaces the community. The second concerns the canon of Scripture authorized by the community.

While Hauerwas is certainly correct that the *sola scriptura* doctrine has resulted in the objectification of Scripture apart from the community, I wonder if Hauerwas himself does not end up with an equally problematic emphasis on the church to the extent that *sola ecclesia* seems to replace *sola scriptura*. For Hauerwas, the community of faith appears as the be-all and end-all of Christian existence, so that there is little to no critical voice that challenges and confronts the church, especially since Hauerwas sees the authority of Scripture as a function of the church itself. I suspect that Hauerwas himself would respond that by definition Scripture does exercise a critical authority over the church by constantly reminding the church of its identity, and that if properly carried out, this critical function of Scripture is sufficient. But still, there is the danger of Scripture's voice being muffled by the *sola ecclesia* position toward which Hauerwas leans, for if history gives any lessons, it teaches that the church can readily deceive itself even in the name of Scripture.

Along the same lines, I wonder if Hauerwas's notion of the church that uses Scripture is not overly idealized and even romantic. Is there a concrete church that in fact corresponds to the type of church that Hauerwas portrays and lifts up? If the church is less than that conceived by Hauerwas, as church history past and present perhaps indicates, then is it sufficient to trust that the community of believers will interpret and so enact the stories of Scripture faithfully, as Hauerwas appears to trust? As separate and as alien as Hauerwas wishes the church to be, in actual practice all but the most radical of Christian communities (from the Catholic Worker movement to some Mennonite churches) struggle constantly to become even but a semblance of the church Hauerwas envisions. If Scripture is authorized by the church, then does it not matter what that real flesh-and-blood church looks like, not only when it is at its best but also when it is at its worst with seeming unawareness?

As for the canon of Scripture, I have serious questions about the rationale Hauerwas gives for why these particular biblical writings were given canonical authority by the church and why they continue to have authority as the church's

Scripture. As noted earlier, Hauerwas asserts that "these texts have been accepted as Scripture because they and they alone satisfy . . . our craving for a perfect story which we feel to be true," and the church continues to abide by the ancient church's decision because "it is a decision that makes sense."[146] What does Hauerwas do with the different canons of Scripture held by different Christian communities, past and present? Is Hauerwas sufficiently attentive to the politics of the canonization of Scripture, itself a dynamic of the politics of interpretation to which Hauerwas calls Christians to be attentive? Is it the case that the biblical canon satisfies our craving for a perfect story, and does the church feel this story to be true?

I must confess that the reasons Hauerwas adduces for the canon of Scripture appear in the end to be but special pleading for the sake of the continuity of the Christian tradition, and not because Scripture is self-evidently a perfect (inspired?) story. Christian tradition itself shows that significant movements within the church (from the Apostolic Fathers to Marcion to Eusebius to Athanasius to Luther to contemporary feminist theology) have found the canon neither to be a perfect story nor to be a decision that makes sense in light of new understandings of the truth of the gospel. Indeed, as Luther moved the Epistle of James to the back of the New Testament because he deemed it unworthy of the canon, and as from time to time it has been suggested that such writings as 2 Peter, 2 and 3 John, and Jude (what a friend has called the "junk mail" of the New Testament) be deleted from the canon, the biblical canon has hardly been considered a perfect story.[147] Even though Hauerwas does acknowledge that the canon is "not an accomplishment but a task,"[148] in that it constantly challenges the church faithfully to recall its authorizing stories, he has not provided a sufficiently convincing argument for his understanding of the canon.

Another problem in Hauerwas's use of Scripture concerns the relationship between the unity and diversity of Scripture. While Hauerwas does a good job of highlighting the diversity of Scripture and of seeing this diversity as a richness which tests the church's memory, at the same time he often speaks of "the story" in the Bible, which appears to presume one particular construal of that story as the authoritative version of that story. And so the question becomes how one (or the church) takes into account different construals of "the story," and in particular how one evaluates and makes decisions about these various construals of "the biblical story." Again, to be fair, Hauerwas does acknowledge the need for communities of faith to be open to and challenged by the readings and interpretations others have made (past and present),[149] but he gives no real rationale for choosing among the range of interpretations.[150] This is particularly important since Hauerwas contends that his construal is truthful to Scripture. How is one to evaluate such truth claims?[151]

Related to the tension between unity and diversity, and also to the issue of canon, is the question of varying levels of authority in Scripture. I noted above Hauerwas's observation that the church assigns different levels of authority to different parts of Scripture. How does the church go about this assessment? Why do some stories have authority and others do not? Surely in part the answer has to do with the church's changing perceptions about the relevance of different parts of Scripture. But how is the church to deal with the authority of conflicting stories? To give an example, one can read the New Testament both as a very anti-Jewish (i.e., non-Christian Jewish) document or as very sympathetic to Judaism. How does one decide which stories to authorize? What does it mean to take Jesus' reference to the Jews as children of the devil (John 8) as authoritative Scripture? If it does not exercise authority, why not? Or is this an example of a wrong turn taken in the early church's life that, while understandable, was unfortunately included in the canon? In other words, what does it mean to appropriate "hard texts" in Scripture for contemporary theological ethics? (Among a host of other passages, one could ask similar questions about the authority of 1 Tim. 2:8–15 for the status of women in the church.)

Finally, there is a problem in Hauerwas's relation of Scriptural authority to other forms of authority for the church. Hauerwas assigns Scripture a primary place of authority in the church since it provides the founding stories that shape and reshape the character and identity of the community of believers. But Scripture is not the sole authority, nor is it *the* primary authority, since only the ongoing presence of Christ's spirit in the church, which is perceived and discerned by the church, can ever be the primary and ultimate authority. Scripture in fact bears witness to this presence by relating stories that speak of and help form the mind of Christ. But what of other related authorities to which the church listens along with Scripture? How is the authority of Scripture related to tradition, to reason, and to experience, through all of which God speaks to the church?

Hauerwas never really fully articulates his understanding of how these complementary authorities function together for the church. Scripture is the basic source for tradition, in that tradition is nothing but the expanded ways in which the stories of Scripture are handed down from one generation to another, so that Scripture and tradition are closely linked. Reason is also related to Scripture; Hauerwas stresses that "rationality is a communal process which involves Scripture and virtues, as well as judgments about particular practices and their implications for other aspects of our lives."[152] And experience is important, for it has authority in that it tests the adaptability of the community's authorities, Scripture included. Indeed, Hauerwas clearly sees Scripture as a truthful narrative, and "an indication of a truthful narrative is one that remains open to challenge from new experience."[153] By definition, Scripture must be traditioned in ways that are responsive to the authority of experience. But beyond these brief indications, Hauerwas does little to develop Scripture's authority as it relates to other aspects of authority within the church.

There is, of course, more that could be said (e.g., regarding what it means to be an eschatological community after twenty centuries of making eschatology less and less central, or regarding Hauerwas's comments on the historical Jesus, or regarding his somewhat caricatured picture of biblical scholarship). So I let these tensions stand and hope that they will lead to an even more reflective and faithful community as it wrestles with its Scriptures.

seven

GUSTAVO GUTIÉRREZ:

Liberating Scriptures of the Poor

*G*ustavo Gutiérrez is widely recognized as the preeminent foundational figure of the Latin American liberation theology movement.[1] The task of theology, to use Gutiérrez's classic definition, is "critical reflection on Christian
praxis in light of the word of God."[2] For Gutiérrez, the Bible is the "word of
God" that provides a fundamental orientation for all Christian action and reflection, and as such the Bible is indispensable for Christians as a source of
revelation about God and humanity.[3]

Given the central place that Gutiérrez assigns to reflection on the Bible, it
is somewhat surprising that so little attention has been directed at Gutiérrez's
use(s) of the Bible. Various treatments of his work make reference to the significance of the Bible, and especially to reading the Bible from the perspective of
the poor, but I have not found any extended analysis of his use(s) of the Bible.[4]
The present chapter is an attempt to address this lacuna.

When we consider how Gutiérrez employs Scripture, it is important to be
aware that his approach to the Bible results from and responds to the traditional
understanding he initially received as a student, namely, pre–Vatican II progressive European Roman Catholicism. Gutiérrez received his formal training at
two of Europe's most prestigious and influential Roman Catholic universities:
the University of Louvain (1951–55), and the Catholic Institute of Lyons (1955–
59).[5] However, this traditional understanding underwent radical transformation
when it came up against Gutiérrez's experiences as a priest in Lima in the early
to late 1960s. After Gutiérrez had returned to Peru as both priest and professor
(at the Pontifical Catholic University of Peru, in Lima), he found that "the
summation of wisdom accumulated on The Theological Grand Tour simply did
not fit the South American reality."[6] And so he began the process of rereading
and revisioning all he had learned, including the Bible, from the perspective of
his situation, the situation of commitment to the poor and the oppressed, the
marginalized, among whom he was working. The experiences of living and
working among the poor compelled Gutiérrez to reappropriate the Scriptures

and the Christian tradition in solidarity with the poor in Latin America. This is the crucial context shaping Gutiérrez's use(s) of the Bible.

Biblical Texts Used by Gutiérrez

General Observations

Much of Gutiérrez's writing can be characterized as reflections on biblical texts and biblical themes. Indeed, I would argue that this is increasingly the case as one traces the development of Gutiérrez's writing. In A *Theology of Liberation* (1971), a section entitled "Biblical Meaning of Poverty" takes up most of the final chapter, "Poverty: Solidarity and Protest."[7] The centrality of biblical reflection for Gutiérrez is also clear when he begins his collection of essays *The Power of the Poor in History* (1979) with a section entitled "Biblical Overview of the Sources of Liberation Theology," in which he presents a powerful criticism of academic biblical study and develops his core understanding of the biblical message. Similarly, biblical motifs permeate Gutiérrez's *We Drink from Our Own Wells* (1983), in which he entitles the first part "How Shall We Sing to the Lord in a Foreign Land?" a clear allusion to Ps. 137:4, and uses such subheadings as "New Wine in Old Bottles" (Matt. 9:17), "A Favorable Time" (2 Cor. 6:2), "Choose Life and You Shall Live" (Deut. 30:19) "Where Are You Staying?" (drawing on John 1:35–42), and "Walking According to the Spirit" (drawing on Rom. 8:4).

Direct reflection on biblical materials is important, although slightly less so, in *The Truth Shall Make You Free* (1986), especially in the section on "The Church of the Beatitudes" (pp. 160–64). In *The God of Life* (1989), Gutiérrez begins by stating that the book is intended "as a reflection on the God of biblical revelation" (p. xiii). The book's introduction includes a section entitled "Thinking the God of the Bible," in which Gutiérrez seeks to provide an orientation for the book as a whole, the goal of which is to go "ever deeper into the content of biblical revelation" (p. xvii). Gutiérrez states, "My desire is that this book may help readers to know more fully the God of biblical revelation and, as a result, to proclaim God as the God of life" (p. xviii). Throughout the book, Gutiérrez touches on various biblical motifs: the Exodus (pp. 3–6), "I Am the Life" (John 14:6; pp. 13–15), the story of Jonah (pp. 37–40), God and mammon (pp. 56–64), "The Last Will Be First" (pp. 110–15), the Beatitudes (pp. 118–28), Philemon (pp. 132–36), a reflection on Job (pp. 145–63), and a reflection on Mary (pp. 164–86), among other discussions of biblical passages and themes. Like his *Theology of Liberation*, not only is *The God of Life* seasoned with hundreds of biblical references, but the biblical texts often form the basis for discussion and reflection. Finally, the entire book *On Job* (1985) is, of course, a theological commentary on the Book of Job, in which Gutiérrez also engages in constant conversation with contemporary biblical scholarship on Job. Thus, Gutiérrez puts reflection on biblical texts at the very heart of his writing, for he sees the Bible as God's liberating word addressed to humanity, and especially to the poor.

Specific Texts

Gutiérrez makes broad use of the biblical canon, ranging widely over both Old and New Testaments, as well as making very limited use of the Old Testament Apocrypha. (I have found 1,687 biblical citations and references, 719 from the Old Testament and 968 from the New Testament.) The most frequent references from the Old Testament are to Second Isaiah (Isa. 40–66) and to the Psalms. Second Isaiah expresses a hopeful vision with which Gutiérrez identifies, and "the present experience of Latin American Christians is one that has been given profound expression in the psalms."[8] The Book of Job is also a very significant witness from the Old Testament, as Gutiérrez has written both an entire book and an extended chapter on Job.[9]

The story of the Exodus (both in the Book of Exodus and elsewhere in the Old Testament, e.g., Deut. 6 and 8) is also quite important for Gutiérrez, because this story identifies God as a liberating God. But the Exodus story is not, I would argue, the crucial biblical story or theme underlying Gutiérrez's liberation theology, a misunderstanding that is often repeated in analyses of Gutiérrez's work.[10] For all the trumpeting of the Exodus as the central story for liberation theology in general, Gutiérrez makes limited use of the Exodus account, often stating clearly that as far as he is concerned, the Exodus account is much less important for liberation theology than generally thought.[11] Indeed, at several places in his writings, Gutiérrez seeks to correct this misunderstanding and to lift up the biblical notions of poverty as being more fundamental. For example, in a discussion with the theological faculty of the Catholic Institute of Lyons, included in *The Truth Shall Make You Free*, Gutiérrez makes the following statement:

> [A]llow me a brief observation with regard to the exodus. The theme of the exodus has been and still is an important one for us, but I think it an overstatement to say that it was the major theme in our theology of liberation. It is important to us because the exodus has been the basic historical experience of the Jewish people and has set its mark on the entire Bible. But I think that we have also treated other themes as important. From the outset, other aspects have been essential in our view—for example, poverty according to the Bible; this is a subject on which greater effort has been spent (including many pages in my own writings) than on the theme of the exodus.[12]

In addition to emphasis on passages from Isaiah, the Psalms, and Exodus, one also finds significant references to the creation story from Genesis; to passages throughout the Old Testament that speak about the poor, the oppressed, and the alien (e.g., Exod. 22–23, Lev. 25 on the year of Jubilee, Deut. 23–24, Amos 5); and to passages that reflect the exile experience (e.g., Jer. 20, 31; Ezek. 36).[13]

From the New Testament, indeed from all of Scripture, the single most important passage for Gutiérrez is clearly Matt. 25:31–46, Matthew's famous story about the judgment of the sheep and the goats.[14] Gutiérrez refers to this passage no fewer than forty-seven times in his writings.[15] Regarding this passage, he writes, "The concrete and definitional character of this passage has long made it play an outstanding role in the spiritual experience of Latin American Christians."[16] This is not surprising, given that the passage identifies ministry to the poor and oppressed with ministry to Christ and that such pastoral ministry, or lack thereof, forms the basis for God's eschatological judgment of humanity. Gutiérrez also uses this story to stress God's call for Christians to be engaged in praxis first and foremost and for such ministry to be centered primarily on "the least" of the world (25:40, 45). Here, among other passages, Gutiérrez finds a locus for "God's preferential option for the poor."[17]

Gutiérrez also uses Matt. 25:31–46 as *the* text to combat claims that Matthew gives a "spiritualized" interpretation of poverty in the Beatitudes of chapter 5, in contrast to Luke's version (Luke 6). As Gutiérrez puts it, the beatitudes of Matthew 5 must be read in light of the whole of Matthew's Gospel, and nothing tells against any notion of spiritualized poverty in Matthew more than the judgment text of Matt. 25:31–46, found alone in Matthew among the four Gospels. The so-called spiritual poverty of Matthew's Beatitudes means nothing else than "to be totally at the disposition of the Lord."[18] On the basis of Matt. 25:31–46, Gutiérrez argues that "no one can deny that the Gospel of Matthew is notably insistent on the need for concrete and 'material' actions toward others and especially toward the poor (see Matt. 25:31–46)."[19] Perhaps Gutiérrez's fullest statement on the relation of Matthew 5 to Matthew 25 is the following:

> The passage on the Beatitudes really ends with v. 16 and shows us the role played by works in the attitudes proper to followers of Jesus. "Blessed are the poor in spirit" and the other Beatitudes mean: Blessed are the disciples, those who practice justice by works of love and life, and who thereby glorify the Father. This approach to the Beatitudes makes it possible to establish a fruitful relationship between the beginning of Matthew 5, where the preaching of Jesus starts, and Matthew 25, where that preaching ends. Blessed are the disciples, because they give food to the hungry and drink to the thirsty, and because they clothe the naked and visit the prisoner; in other words, because by means of concrete actions they give life and thus proclaim the kingdom.[20]

If Matt. 25:31–46 provides Gutiérrez's central vision of Jesus and his ministry, Jesus' inaugural sermon at Nazareth in Luke 4:16–30 is also important, especially the reversal motif that cites Isaiah 61.[21] Overall, Gutiérrez makes the most use of Matthew and Luke, in fairly equal measure. The Gospel of John also figures prominently, if less than Matthew and Luke, especially the Prologue (John 1) and the Last Discourse (John 14–17). The Gospel of Mark receives relatively modest attention, primarily in terms of how Mark portrays discipleship as a "lived response" to Jesus' call, self-surrender to others rather than seeking personal glory.[22]

One interesting observation about Gutiérrez's choice of Gospel texts is that he makes very few references to passages dealing with the Passion and death of Jesus. Indeed, of the over nine hundred references to the New Testament I have been able to identify, Gutiérrez refers to texts from the Passion narratives only thirteen times.[23] I am not completely sure what to make of this observation, for the death of Jesus is not unimportant to Gutiérrez, especially as it expresses the solidarity of Jesus in suffering with all those who are poor and oppressed. Perhaps this deemphasis on the Passion narratives reflects Gutiérrez's reaction to how the death of Jesus has been used in traditional Roman Catholic theology in Latin America to encourage the people to identify with the suffering Jesus in a relatively passive way, in hopes of attaining the resurrected life. Thus, perhaps the lack of reference to the Passion narratives is Gutiérrez's way of moving away from how these texts were used to reinforce the status quo, namely, the oppression of the poor.

Indeed, I would argue that for Gutiérrez the cross is less a symbol of humanity's identifying with the suffering of Jesus and more a symbol of God's identifying with the suffering of humanity in Christ. Thus, a shift takes place in how the Passion of Jesus is envisioned, for it speaks about the degree to which God identifies with the poor and the oppressed rather than giving a tacit endorsement of human suffering with a view to the Resurrection. Gutiérrez clearly moves away from interpretations of the Passion scene with an otherworldly emphasis, where the death of Jesus leads directly to the Resurrection and a focus on the heavenly world; instead, he moves toward a this-worldly affirmation of human existence. The crucial transformation, then, is not the transformation from death to resurrection in the life beyond but the transformation from suffering and oppression to liberation and freedom in this life here and now, which is confirmed by God's raising Jesus from the dead. Let me hasten to add that this vision does not diminish the significance of Jesus' death and resurrection, rather it places more emphasis on the liberating ministry of Jesus here and now (e.g., Luke 4) in eschatological perspective (Matt. 25:31–46) than on otherworldly hopes of resurrection as reward for present sufferings.[24]

Among the writings of Paul, Gutiérrez uses Romans 5–8 extensively, but almost exclusively in his *We Drink from Our Own Wells*, as is the case with most of Gutiérrez's references to the Pauline writings, especially 1 Corinthians and Galatians 5 on freedom.[25] As for the rest of the New Testament, James 2 finds frequent reference, as does 1 John 3.[26]

In conclusion, Gutiérrez has a relatively clear working canon: Matt. 25:31–46 is the guiding and paradigmatic text, amplified by Luke 4:16–30, Isaiah 40–66 (especially Isa. 61 and 65), Exodus 3, the Psalms (especially Pss. 9, 22, 33, 42, and 136), Romans 5–8, Galatians 5, and James 2.

How Gutiérrez Uses Scripture

In describing how Gutiérrez makes use of Scripture, I would call particular attention to four aspects: the role of experience, the themes of creation/salvation and eschatology, poverty in the Bible, and the dialogue between the Bible and the reader.

Experience and the Perspective of the Poor

For Gutiérrez, "all of us approach the Scriptures in the light of our own situation and experience."[27] The questions that we address to Scripture are questions that arise out of our individual and communal experiences. Our readings are always contextual, and our contexts are nothing other than the collective shapes of our experiences. As Gutiérrez puts it in "Expanding the View," the 1988 introduction to the revised edition of his classic A *Theology of Liberation*, "The historical womb from which liberation theology has emerged is the life of the poor and, in particular, of the Christian communities that have arisen within the bosom of the present-day Latin American church. This experience is the setting in which liberation theology tries to read the word of God."[28]

Experience is not neutral. Experience leads us to take stands and advocate positions, whether we acknowledge them or not. The experiences of Gutiérrez and of the poor have led them to consciously take an advocacy stance and commit themselves to finding ways to liberate people from poverty and oppression, as an expression of their understanding of the gospel message. As Gutiérrez puts it in his powerful essay "God's Revelation and Proclamation in History," originally a 1975 address to the summer class in theology offered by the Pontifical Catholic University of Peru:

> For some, the effort to read the Bible may be directed toward simply adapting its message and language to men and women of today. For others, however, it is a matter of reinterpretation. We reinterpret the Bible, from the viewpoint of our own world—from our personal experience as human beings, as believers, and as church. This approach is more radical. It goes more to the roots of what the Bible actually is, more to the essence of God's revelation in history and of God's judgment on it.[29]

Beginning with experience is, from Gutiérrez's perspective, most in keeping with the character of Scripture itself, which is but a record of the experiences of the people of God in their struggles to be faithful to God.[30] This is why all authentic theological reflection by definition "must take as its springboard the experiences and questions of those who hear the word of God, as well as the mental categories that they use in trying to understand their experiences of life."[31]

Experiences, however, are evolving. Experiences change, and we change with them. And so, for Gutiérrez, to say that we begin with experience is to say that we are always beginning afresh from the context of our experiences. For this reason, "a constant dialogue is necessary between the 'old knowing' of Scripture and tradition and the 'new knowing' of the concrete, daily life experiences of the people of God."[32]

Experience shapes one's identity as a believer and one's self-understanding. Gutiérrez expresses this most clearly in his book *On Job*. The wager between

God and Satan is really about Job's experience. Satan wagers that it is only because of Job's pleasant experiences that Job maintains his faith in God, and that if difficult experiences came his way, he would abandon this faith and curse God. Satan wagers that Job's experiences define his faith. In this Satan is actually correct. What Satan does not bargain on, however, is that Job's experiences of unjust suffering will lead him to redefine positively his faith in God and to identify with the poor and the oppressed.

Gutiérrez in fact is led to reflect and to write on Job because of his own experience among the poor and the suffering in Latin America. They are like Job, for they too endure unjust suffering. Perhaps his study of Job will lead to new insights about what it means to maintain faith in the context of oppressive suffering. As Gutiérrez puts it: "The point of view that I myself adopt in this book is important and classic, and, I believe, central to the book [of Job] itself: the question of *how we are to talk about God*. More particularly: how we are to talk about God from within a specific situation—namely, the suffering of the innocent . . . the suffering of the poor—which is to say, the vast majority of the population [in Latin America]."[33]

What separates Job from his friends is his experience. His friends speak from their doctrinal convictions. Job speaks from his experience. This experience leads him to reject the doctrine of retribution which his friends still embrace.[34] Job moves from an ethic of personal reward to an ethic that begins with the needs of one's neighbors.[35] He realizes that he must care for the neighbor for the sake of the neighbor, and not for the sake of some reward he might garner, for this, Job realizes, is how God cares for humanity. And so Job's experience compels him to reformulate his understanding of God and to realize that God's grace, God's gratuitousness, is the ground for life, and that even amid his suffering, God's grace enfolds him. Job's orthopraxis compels him to challenge and to reformulate the brand of orthodoxy he had, until then, embraced along with his friends. Job's experiences, then, lead him to take a prophetic stance on behalf of the poor and to contemplate the unbounded grace of God's love. Thus is Job's faith in God transformed. For Gutiérrez, the Book of Job shows that

> God has a preferential love for the poor not because they are necessarily better than others, morally or religiously, but simply because they are poor and living in an inhuman situation that is contrary to God's will. The ultimate basis for the privileged position of the poor is not in the poor themselves but in God, in the gratuitousness and universality of God's *agapeic love*.[36]

Job illustrates that experiences can often be surprising and unexpected, leading us in unanticipated directions, and challenging deeply held assumptions and presuppositions about life and about God.[37]

Guiding Themes: Creation/Salvation and Eschatology

Gutiérrez sees several guiding themes that recur throughout Scripture and so provide a basic orientation for Christian faith and practice. Two themes stand out: creation/salvation and eschatology. Gutiérrez refers to this tandem throughout his writings, especially in his earlier work.[38] Creation is essentially God's first salvific act, not something prior to salvation. Creation itself commences the process of salvation, a linkage celebrated by the Psalms (see Pss. 74, 93, 95, 135, 136). The coming of Christ is part of the process of salvation but is also an expression of God's new creation. In this connection Gutiérrez appeals particularly to John 1 and to Col. 1:15–20, where Christ is seen as the agent of creation and salvation.[39]

Like creation/salvation, eschatology provides another guiding theme anchored in Scripture. Eschatology points to the consummation of the salvation begun already in creation. For Gutiérrez, "the Bible presents eschatology as the driving force of salvific history radically oriented toward the future. Eschatology is thus not just one more element of Christianity, but the very key to understanding the Christian faith."[40] The eschatological orientation of the biblical writings points us to the transcendent goal of human history, namely, "the full and definitive encounter with the Lord and with other humans."[41] Thus, the eschatological character of Christian existence leads to an emphasis on concrete behavior, on transformative praxis in keeping with the goal and the meaning of human existence.

Nowhere can this connection between eschatology and praxis be more clearly seen than in the parable of the eschatological judgment of the sheep and the goats in Matt. 25:31–46. As Gutiérrez puts it, "The passage is rich in teachings. . . . we wish to emphasize three points: the stress on communion and fellowship as the ultimate meaning of human life; the insistence on a love which is manifested in concrete actions, with 'doing' being favored over simple 'knowing'; and the revelation of the human mediation necessary to reach the Lord."[42]

It is no accident that Gutiérrez devotes an entire chapter in his *Theology of Liberation* to eschatology and politics (chap. 11). The eschatological perspective has "clear and strong implications for the political sphere, for social praxis."[43] Gutiérrez hastens to add that the kingdom of God cannot be equated with any political order, and that a just society is not a necessary precondition for the coming of the kingdom of God, as if God's kingdom were somehow a human achievement. Nonetheless, the enactment of the gospel in human communities "reveals to society itself the aspiration for a just society . . . The Kingdom is realized in a society of fellowship and justice; and, in turn, this realization opens up the promise and hope of complete communion of all persons with God. The political is grafted into the eternal."[44] The gospel message has contemporary political implications for how Christians participate in the eschatological realization of the coming of the kingdom of God. Christians cannot ignore present historical existence in hope of some individualistic future heavenly reward; rather, as Jesus did, they are called to denounce injustices in the present social order and to announce (and to enact) the kind of community to which God calls all people.[45]

As Matt. 25:31–46 points to the culmination of human existence, and so to its meaning, so also is the Exodus experience formative within this eschatological perspective, especially in the prophetic writings, for the Exodus shows "fundamentally the break with the past and the projection toward the future."[46] The Exodus reveals God as the one who is bringing about human liberation, the one who has created human beings for the purpose of liberation. It reveals the identity of God as a God of salvation, and it reveals the true identity of humanity as the people of God engaged in the struggle for liberation and salvation in concrete history.

It is crucial, then, that the eschatological promises not be spiritualized as "pie in the sky," for that is to rob the promises of their core meaning, the redemption of concrete human existence, indeed the redemption of history. "Christ does not 'spiritualize' the eschatological promises: he gives them meaning and fulfillment today (cf. Luke 4:21); but at the same time he opens new perspectives by catapulting history forward, forward towards total reconciliation. . . . Moreover, it is only in the temporal, earthly, historical event that we can open up to the future of complete fulfillment."[47] Nonetheless, the eschatological promises are not to be confused with historical development, for "their liberating effect goes far beyond the foreseeable and opens up new and unsuspected possibilities."[48]

History is the plane on which creation and salvation take place. As God initiated history, and so salvation, with the original creation, so does God in Christ bring about a new creation of humanity, and not just in the abstract but in concrete everyday life.[49] Although Gutiérrez does appeal to Paul's language of new creation (Gal. 6:15, 2 Cor. 5:17), it is striking that he does not pick up on the Adam/Christ typology, so significant for Paul (Rom. 5:12–21, 1 Cor. 15:20–28). Rather, as the Exodus is central to eschatology, so the Exodus experience of Israel provides the link between creation and salvation. "Creation and liberation from Egypt are but one salvific act."[50] We are liberated and re-created as individuals only as we are liberated and recreated within the communal context of the covenant people of God.

Creation/salvation and eschatology, then, tell us of our origins and of our destiny. We have been created for salvation; the goal of existence is salvation. "The lesson to be drawn from these two biblical themes is clear: *salvation embraces the whole man*," namely, from beginning to end, individually and collectively.[51]

The Bible and Poverty

Gutiérrez also uses the Bible as a fundamental source for discerning the meaning(s) of poverty, the primary experiential context out of which he writes. The poor find such affinity with the Bible because in it they find their own story, the story of God's care for those whose lives are rooted in poverty. Already in *A Theology of Liberation*, Gutiérrez devoted the concluding chapter to this motif, "Poverty: Solidarity and Protest." In the chapter's major subsection, the "Biblical Meaning of Poverty" (pp. 165–71), Gutiérrez develops what he sees as the two major lines of thought on how the Bible treats poverty: poverty as a scandalous condition (material poverty) and poverty as "spiritual childhood."

First, poverty is a scandalous material condition. Drawing especially on the prophetic traditions (Amos, Isaiah, Hosea, Micah, Jeremiah), the legal traditions (Exodus and Leviticus), as well as Job and references to New Testament texts in Luke and James, Gutiérrez notes how the Bible quite clearly condemns those responsible for impoverishing other people and how the Bible speaks against material poverty. "The Bible speaks of positive and concrete measures to prevent poverty from becoming established among the People of God."[52]

In particular, Gutiérrez identifies three reasons for the repudiation of poverty: poverty contradicts the meaning of the Mosaic religion (i.e., deliverance from slavery, exploitation, and alienation); poverty contradicts the Genesis mandate for human flourishing on the earth; and human poverty is an offense to God, since human beings are created in God's likeness, so that the impoverishment of human beings and the oppression of the poor contradict God's intentions for humanity. According to Gutiérrez, the Bible teaches that "the existence of poverty represents a sundering both of solidarity among persons and also of communion with God" and is "incompatible with the coming of the Kingdom of God, a Kingdom of love and justice."[53]

Second, poverty means spiritual childhood.[54] As Gutiérrez notes, spiritual poverty, or spiritual childhood, "is not directly or in the first instance an interior detachment from the goods of this world, a spiritual attitude which becomes authentic by incarnating itself in material poverty."[55] Although being "poor in spirit" is often interpreted in this way (e.g., Clement of Alexandria), this approach is misleading and unbiblical.[56] Rather, spiritual poverty "is something more complete and profound. It is above all total availability to the Lord."[57] Drawing again on the prophetic literature and the Psalms, Gutiérrez identifies spiritual childhood as humility before God. It emphasizes an attitude of seeking God and of not relying on oneself (see Zeph. 2:3; Isa. 66:2; Pss. 10:14; 34:9, 20–22; 37:17–18).

Spiritual childhood finds its highest expression in the Beatitudes of Matthew 5. The "poor in spirit" (Matt. 5:1) are those "totally at the disposition of the Lord," those open to the gift of God's transforming love, open as a child.[58] To be "poor in spirit" means to be a disciple, a follower of God. As Gutiérrez writes, " 'Poor in spirit' is a synonym for 'disciple of Christ.' "[59] Spiritual poverty or spiritual childhood, "describes the outlook of the person who accepts the gift of divine filiation and responds to it by building fellowship."[60] Mary is a prime example of someone who exhibits this kind of spiritual childhood, for in Luke's Magnificat she demonstrates a trusting self-surrender to God in conjunction with a commitment to and close association with those who are materially poor.[61] Indeed, this is one of the key features of spiritual childhood, for someone who is truly a disciple of Christ protests with Christ against material poverty and with Christ expresses solidarity with those who are poor. In this way, Gutiérrez closely links the Beatitudes of Matthew 5 with the eschatological judgment of Matthew 25. Thus, the teachings of Jesus "begin with the blessing of the poor

(Matt. 5); they end with the assertion that we meet Christ himself when we go out to the poor with concrete acts (Matt. 25). So the teaching of Jesus is framed in a context that moves *from the poor to the poor.*[62] True discipleship finds reflection in a life committed to the poor.

The Bible and the Reader in Dialogue

A refrain that recurs throughout Gutiérrez's writing is that in the process of reading Scripture, the reader (and primarily the community of readers/hearers) enters into a dialogue with the foundational communities that wrote the Bible and into a dialogue with and about God. The Bible thus functions as a source of individual and community vision (as we read the Bible), and it also functions as a source of questioning and critique (as the Bible also "reads us").[63]

Gutiérrez develops this motif most clearly in *The God of Life*, where he argues that to read the Bible is to initiate a series of dialogues, between faith and faith, between history and history, in nearness and in distance, and between reading and reading. I quote him at length:

> I approach the Scriptures in an attitude of faith. The intention of the books of the Bible is to speak to us of God and to communicate the faith of their authors and of persons, groups, and an entire people. . . . To read the Bible is to begin a dialogue *between faith and faith*, between the believers of the past and the believers of today; a dialogue that is taking place today within the ecclesial community as it pursues its pilgrimage through history. . . . I approach the Scriptures in terms of my own history, in terms of the situation of a people that suffers abuse and injustice but is organizing to defend its right to life and in keeping its hope in God strong. There is thus a dialogue *between history and history*. . . . The Bible is not a book like any other; it is the word of the Lord who, according to Deuteronomy, always speaks to us "today." At the same time, however, we cannot forget that we are dealing with writings that took shape millennia ago, in languages and cultural settings that are not our own. We must therefore make the effort to distance ourselves from them and to acquire knowledge of the cultural, social, and religious context of the texts. . . . The dialogue with the Scriptures will be more fruitful if we are aware that our relationship to the texts of the Bible is one of both *nearness* and *distance*. On the one hand, we will then avoid a facile closeness and even a possible manipulation of the Bible, but at the same time we will be prevented from succumbing to a literalism that pays no heed to human and social circumstances and turns every word into a timeless absolute. . . . But when believers read Scripture, they know that the Scriptures also challenge them. The Bible is not a kind of depository of answers to our concerns; rather it reformulates our questions and sets us on unexpected paths. We can truly say that we read the Bible. But it in turn reads us. . . . The dialogue must therefore also be one of *reading* with *reading*. When the reading of the Bible is done as a community, as a church, it is always an unexpected experience.[64]

Fundamentally, the process of reading the Scriptures initiates a dialogue between experience and experience. On the one hand, the reader brings to the biblical texts his or her own experiences, both as an individual and as one who participates in a community of faith. Each reader, each community, brings various assumptions and questions to Scripture. And yet, on the other hand, the conversation is not one-way, for in approaching the Bible, one finds there other sets of experiences to which the biblical authors give voice. These experiences in turn raise questions for the reader(s), which then give rise to further dialogues between various readers/hearers and reading/hearing communities.[65] As Gutiérrez notes, this reading of the Bible, especially in community, results in yet new and unexpected experiences, which then begins the process all over again. To say that the Bible "reads us" is, for Gutiérrez, a symbolic way of saying "that between us and the Scriptures there is not a one-way street but a circular relationship."[66] Thus, we project ourselves into the experiences reflected in Scripture (our story is like their story), and we allow the experiences in Scripture to be projected onto and to shape our lives here and now (their story becomes our story). And the Spirit of God facilitates this dialogue and this discernment within the community of faith.

Gutiérrez's View of the Authority of Scripture

Authority from Below

Gutiérrez says relatively little explicitly about the authority of Scripture. Indeed, I have been struck by how infrequently Gutiérrez uses the term "authority" in any context. Perhaps this observation is an indication that Gutiérrez sees the language of authority, and especially hierarchical authority, as problematic and open to much misuse. Indeed, Gutiérrez states quite pointedly, "We are called to build the church *from below*, from the poor up, from the exploited classes, the marginalized ethnic group, the despised cultures."[67] His notion of authority is one that moves away from any kind of domination, away from power being imposed by one person or group upon another. In a chapter entitled "Theology from the Underside of History", he asserts that "ultimately the dominator is one who does not really believe in the God of the Bible."[68] Thus, the Bible points away from dominating authority and toward liberating authority.

For Gutiérrez, Scripture repeatedly bears witness to God's preferential option for the poor. Since Scripture shows God as caring especially for the outcast, it authorizes the formation of a particular kind of community, a community that seeks to enact this preferential option out of faithfulness to God. And so the testimony of Scripture is from the poor (Matt. 5) to the poor (Matt. 25). In this way, Scripture recognizes as persons those whom the world treats as nonpersons. Scripture shows how God reverses the injustice and hatred of the world. Just so, Gutiérrez points out, in Luke 16 is poor Lazarus given a name, while the rich man goes nameless.[69] Scripture reflects the faithful testimony primarily of those who bear witness to God from the underside of history, and so Scripture takes on authority most authentically when it is appropriated as it was written, from below.

Authority of Scripture and Authority of the Interpreters

Gutiérrez makes it clear that one cannot speak about the authority of Scripture without at the same time speaking about the authority of those who interpret Scripture. Though Gutiérrez is very aware of academic biblical scholarship and makes significant use of it (especially the work of J. Dupont), he is also very critical of so-called scientific exegesis that, most often unconsciously (yet another problem), essentially disenfranchises those who are poor and "uneducated" and renders them functionally speechless about the very biblical texts that speak to and through them. Thus he is critical of biblical interpretation that does little more than reinforce the status quo, that is, the oppression of the poor, for this often results in authoritative interpretations that point away from the plight of the poor.

> We cannot forget that in reality, the Bible was read and communicated from the dominating sectors and classes. This is what happens to a great deal of the exegesis considered to be scientific. Christianity has been forced to play a role within the reigning ideology which affirms and knits together a society which in reality is divided into classes. . . . the communication of the message with an understanding of the poor and the oppressed and their struggles will have a function of demasking every attempt to use the gospel to justify a situation contrary to "justice and right," as the Bible says.[70]

As he puts it so clearly in his 1975 opening address to the summer session offered by the Department of Theology of the Pontifical Catholic University of Peru:

> [W]e tend to approach the Bible with a certain sense of insecurity. We feel out of our element. We are on unfamiliar ground. . . . We have the idea that serious Bible reading demands historical, philological, theological, and geographical knowledge that most of us do not have. . . . So we look to the specialists, the exegetes, and we depend on their "scientific interpretation of the text" to tell us what the Bible means. And now, alas, we see that not many believers have what it takes to be a scientific exegete. And so now we are more insecure than ever about our contact with the Bible. Exegetes, as someone once said, are members of a very exclusive, expensive club. To become a member of this club you have to have assimilated Western culture—German and Anglo-Saxon culture, actually—because exegesis in the Christian churches of today is so closely tied in with it. (What must an African, an Oriental, a Latin American make of this exegesis, especially on some of the fine points?) I am not suggesting that scientific interpretation is invalid. But we do have to be careful not to exaggerate its importance. We have to remember that its purpose is the proclamation of the good news to the poor.[71]

Ironically, rather than opening Scripture up to the people of God, much professional biblical interpretation has the effect of actually closing people off from Scripture, making it more inaccessible, convincing people that the only authoritative interpretation is the interpretation of the experts. And so one of Gutiérrez's tasks is to walk a fine line between paying attention to what the experts have to say, on the one hand, and yet, on the other hand, paying even more attention to what the people have to say as they gather in the community of faith to reflect on the meanings of Scripture in light of their current situations. Since the authority of Scripture is inseparable from the authority of the interpreters, Gutiérrez seeks to encourage the authority of nonprofessional interpreters who read Scripture in an attempt to hear God's word addressing them today, for both comfort and challenge. And so Gutiérrez can conclude:

> The Bible must be restored to the Christian peoples who believe and hope in the God who reveals himself there. Otherwise all self-styled "scientific" exegesis loses its validity [i.e., authority]. We must reclaim a believing, militant reading of the word of the Lord, and rediscover the popular language needed to communicate it. It will be a reading done from within, and in function of, its proclamation by the people itself.[72]

Challenging Oppressive Authority

If concrete liberation in Christ is to take place here and now—if liberation is corporeal and not just spiritual—then it becomes the task of Christians, both individually and corporately, to call into question structures and expressions of authority that frustrate the liberation of the oppressed. This is precisely what the Bible tells us the prophets did and what Christ did. They protested against and challenged forms of authority that resulted in the dehumanization of people, namely that treated people as nonpersons rather than as persons before God.[73]

Because of this call to protest against oppressive authorities, to name the demons for what they are, Christians should use whatever tools they can (short of violence)[74] to expose the oppressive character of inappropriate authority. To this end, Gutiérrez uses Marxist analysis as a social science tool in order to better describe the situation of the poor, which description then complements, but certainly does not replace, the Christian vision of authentic human communities before God. This full vision then forms the basis for calling into question the legitimacy of economic and political structures (authorities) that necessarily result in the repression of those who are disadvantaged. (Gutiérrez makes it clear that he has some serious differences with various aspects of Marxist theory, especially in his adoption of a theory of dependency over against Marxist critique of this theory.)[75]

But it is not just oppressive political, social, and economic structures of authority that need to be called into question. Ironically, it is also the oppressive ecclesiastical authorities that warrant protest, inasmuch as they do not contribute to the liberation of the community of faith but instead have the regressive effect of leading to the further oppression and depersonalization of the people of God, especially when ecclesiastical authorities have been co-opted by oppressive political, social, and economic authorities. This criticism of ecclesiastical authorities has led, in part, to the establishment and to the flourishing of the "basic ecclesial communities," essentially a church within the church, a church from the bottom up rather than from the top down.[76]

Gutiérrez has at times seen no other way to respond to oppressive ecclesiastical authorities than by being subversive. For example, when some of the more progressive theologians (including Gutiérrez) were excluded from active participation at Puebla, which looked like it might back away significantly from the gains made at Medellín, Gutiérrez and other liberation theologians rented a house nearby and essentially smuggled their own position papers into Puebla through bishops who were friendly to their cause and sought their input.[77] This was a clear case of subverting potentially oppressive ecclesiastical authority structures from within. In the end, Gutiérrez and others friendly to liberation theology succeeded in pushing through at Puebla a reaffirmation of Medellín's central gain, an emphasis on God's preferential option for the poor. For Gutiérrez, this kind of subversive critique of ecclesiastical authority is really no different from the prophetic critique of Amos or Hosea against the oppressive priestly authority of ancient Israel.

Similarly, Gutiérrez has sought to emphasize the places where ecclesiastical authorities have appeared to agree with biblical interpretation from the perspective of liberation theology. So, for example, in commenting on Puebla, Gutiérrez points to how Pope John Paul II affirmed some core values of liberation theology in his choice of a biblical text: "Here the nub is in Christ's identification with the poor as we find it in Matthew 25:31–46, that key text for Puebla and for the pope's addresses in Mexico. It is also a central passage, as we know, for the basic Christian communities."[78]

The role of the Bible as a legitimizing authority for this kind of critique and subversion of oppressive ecclesiastical authority is clear in various statements made by Gutiérrez. For example, in his comments on the Preparatory Document for Puebla in a chapter Gutiérrez subtitled "A Retreat from Commitment" (i.e., a retreat from Medellín), he states that "it is particularly unfortunate that the PD [Preparatory Document] does not say, as was said in simple, clear, and biblical terms at Medellín, that material poverty is *evil*."[79] Thus, Gutiérrez sees Medellín as being more biblical in orientation than Puebla.

Similarly, Gutiérrez's comments on two "instructions" of the Congregation for the Doctrine of the Faith on liberation theology, "Instruction on Certain Aspects of the 'Theology of Liberation' " (*Libertatis Nuntius*, 1984) and "Instruction on Christian Freedom and Liberation" (*Libertatis Conscientia*, 1986), are themselves instructive regarding how he uses the authority of liberation theology's biblical interpretation to critique the authority of official Vatican teachings, which have been relatively repressive in approaching liberation theology. For example, regarding *Libertatis Conscientia* Gutiérrez writes: "The entire process of liberation is directed toward communion. . . . Although *Libertatis Conscientia* has some passages along this line, it does not have any full development of the ideas of communion as the ultimate purpose of liberation; it would have been helped here, had it approached the matter from the viewpoint of the Bible."[80]

Further, the Congregation for the Doctrine of the Faith criticized two particular aspects of Gutiérrez's biblical interpretation when it published in 1983 its

"Ten Observations on the Theology of Gustavo Gutiérrez." First, it charged Gutiérrez with "a selective rereading of the Bible. He emphasizes the theme of Yahweh as the God of the poor as well as the theme of Matthew 25, but does not consider all the dimensions of evangelical poverty." Second, it charged that Gutiérrez "never examines the Beatitudes in their true meaning."[81] Gutiérrez implicitly, but not explicitly, responds to these charges in his 1986 essay "The Truth Shall Make You Free" (chap. 3 in *The Truth Shall Make You Free*), within the context of his comments on the Congregation's two instructions on liberation theology. There, Gutiérrez devotes specific sections to "biblical truth" (pp. 94–95) and "the church of the Beatitudes" (pp. 161–64), where he also deals with Matthew 25 in relation to the Beatitudes of Matthew 5, showing how the "true meaning" of the Beatitudes can only be discovered in light of Christ's charge to Christians in Matthew 25 regarding "the least" of the world.[82]

Gutiérrez envisions the authority of Scripture, then, as authority from below, in keeping with the character of Scripture itself. This authority enlivens the Basic Christian Communities of Latin America as they read and study Scripture together for themselves in light of their experiences and their situations. In turn, this liberating authority leads them to challenge oppressive authority structures wherever they may be (in political, economic, social, and/or ecclesial structures) and to envision new ways of living faithfully as the people of God.

In regard to ecclesial authority, Gutiérrez engages throughout his writings in a fascinating exegesis both of the Bible and of magisterial teachings, often setting one against the other and clearly offering a constructive critique of magisterial teachings in light of his communal reflections on the significance of the Christian vision presented in Scripture.

Gutiérrez's Hermeneutics

"Jesus Christ: Principal Hermeneutic of the Faith"

For Gutiérrez, all biblical interpretation starts and ends with Jesus Christ.[83] The revelation of God in Jesus' life, death, and resurrection in real history as experienced by his earliest followers generated the biblical writings of the early Christians, who believed in him as the fulfillment of prophecy and the substance of the new covenant. And all interpretation and interpreters of Scripture are by definition called back to the person of Jesus, since Scripture bears witness to him. Thus, "Jesus Christ comes forward as the principle, the point of departure, of the interpretation of Scripture."[84]

The historicity of Jesus is an important component of his hermeneutical significance, for what matters is not only *that* he is an expression of God's revelation in history but more *how* and *what* he shows us about God and ourselves. It is crucial for Gutiérrez that Jesus was born as a poor peasant in a rural setting among an oppressed people. There could be no more explicit link between God and the poor. Indeed, "Jesus Christ is precisely *God become poor*."[85] This identification between God and the poor is thus seen both in Jesus' own personal circumstances and in his message: "just as you did it to one of the least of these who are members of my family, you did it to me" (Matt. 25:40). The historicity of those who are poor, then, becomes as significant as the historicity of Jesus, who was poor, of God who has become poor.

This link between God and the poor in the person of Jesus is the interpretive key for all of Gutiérrez's biblical reflections and for his understanding of the "hermeneutical circle." As Gutiérrez puts it:

> The great hermeneutical principle of the faith, and hence the basis and foundation of all theological reasoning, is Jesus Christ. . . . For Jesus is the irruption into history of the one by whom everything was made and everything was saved. . . . This is the basic circle of all hermeneutics: from the human being to God and from God to the human being, from history to faith and from faith to history, from love of our brothers and sisters to the love of the Father and from the love of the Father to the love of our brothers and sisters, from human justice to God's holiness and from God's holiness to human justice, from the poor person to God and from God to the poor person.[86]

In essence, when we look to God, God shows us Jesus, but not an abstract intellectualized Jesus, rather a Jesus born into a concrete historical situation of poverty and oppression. God's actions through Jesus' life, death, and resurrection become the basis of Christian faith, which in turn leads to concrete historical actions of love for one's fellow human beings and love for God as an expression of one's faithful response to the person of Jesus. This love establishes human justice and becomes an expression of God's holiness, which justice/holiness is most clearly seen in relation to those who are poor, among whom is Jesus, who is but God become poor. This hermeneutical circle begins and ends with God's revelation in Christ. But along the way, this revelation and the response it evokes reflect the transformation of human existence so that love and justice for all people, and paradigmatically for the poor, becomes the foundation for a human community of faith renewed by the grace and power of God.

Thus, for Gutiérrez, God's choice to identify with the poor through the incarnation in Jesus Christ forms the foundation for the poor to identify themselves with Jesus Christ and so with God. There is a fundamental closeness between the believer and God in the Christ of Scriptures, and especially between the poor and Christ.

But there is also a significant distance between the believer and the Christ of Scriptures. When he was asked by Jean Delorme, "What biblical hermeneutic do you follow?,"[87] Gutiérrez responded by calling attention to both the closeness and the distance of the biblical text:

> In my writings I try to do theology with a strong biblical basis, but not a work of exegesis in the strict sense. . . . I have always thought it very important to be attentive to the role of challenger that scripture plays when read in the church. . . . From my experience of reading the Bible with groups of the faithful I have learned the need of seeing the text as at once close and distant.

When reading a particular passage in a Christian community, I have often heard someone saying by way of commentary: "That is exactly what happened to me yesterday." . . . This feeling that the word of God is near is doubtless a fine thing, but it does not therefore cease to have its dangers. It is also necessary to see that the text is distant, having been written in another age and another culture; this means that in approaching the text one must take this otherness into account and one must have information about the Bible that is required for putting texts in their context. . . . All this will only bring out more fully the challenging aspect of the Bible.[88]

For Gutiérrez, appropriate interpretation of Scripture emphasizes both God's closeness to and identity with the believer in Christ, and yet at the same time the otherness of God in Christ whose word calls and challenges the believer ever again to renewed understanding and faithfulness. Thus, all authentic readings of Scripture are first and foremost christological.[89]

A Communitarian Hermeneutics

Gutiérrez also argues strongly for reading Scripture within the context of the community of faith. This community has various dimensions. First, it refers primarily to the immediate congregation to which one belongs, in terms of both study groups and communal worship where the word of God is read and proclaimed. Second, it refers to the larger contemporary church in all its diversity. Different readings of Scripture that arise in different settings serve both to corroborate and to challenge the interpretations of each particular community of believers. Third, it refers to the church across time, so that contemporary communities of faith, individually and collectively, benefit from the interpretations of Christian communities in the past, from the tradition of interpretation.

This focus on interpretation within the context of the communities of faith reflects Gutiérrez's emphasis that biblical interpretation is not principally an individual activity, as it has become in most academic settings, but is the task of the entire Christian community. The Bible itself reflects the faith of earlier communities of believers, not isolated individuals, and so it is most appropriate for Christians today to interpret the Bible in the same mode in which it was written, communally.[90]

A Militant Hermeneutics

Another dimension of Gutiérrez's hermeneutics is what he terms a "militant" reading of Scripture.[91] This should not be misconstrued to mean a reading of Scripture that condones violent protest. It is a reading that starts with the struggles of the poor and emphasizes the active commitment of the interpreter to the cause of the poor rather than some supposed "neutral," "objective," and uninvolved reading of Scripture. Essentially, it is another way of expressing the overriding hermeneutic that characterizes liberation theology's reading of Scripture: the preferential option for the poor. As Gutiérrez puts it:

[O]ur reading of the Bible will be a *militant* reading. The great questions about the word of the Lord arise out of Christian practice. It is time to reclaim this militant reading of the word of God in faith. It is time to open the Bible and read it from the perspective of "those who are persecuted in the cause of right" (Matt. 5:10), from the perspective of the condemned human beings of this earth—for, after all, theirs is the kingdom of heaven.[92]

When asked what he meant by a "militant reading" of the Bible, Gutiérrez responded in the following way:

The phrase was a way of emphasizing something I regard as important—namely, the part that our Christian militancy plays in our reading of the Bible. As I said a moment ago, all of us approach the scriptures in the light of our own situation and experience. If persons make a commitment in a perspective springing from faith, this too leaves its mark on their approach; their commitment conditions them as readers, for they want now to see their Christian solidarity and activity in the light of the word. Their reading is made in the context of a committed, active, militant Christian life.[93]

A Historical Hermeneutics

Although the significance of history has come up several times already, it is crucial to recognize that for Gutiérrez the concreteness of history, of real material life, is of paramount significance in all readings of Scripture. There is no such thing as disembodied interpretation. The reader's concrete historical situation has a direct impact on how he or she reads and interprets the Bible and on what she or he finds there. Thus, all interpretation has a dual character: it involves the reading of Scripture, but it also involves the reading of the interpreter. One concrete set of historical experiences interacts with another; the authors of Scripture with the interpreter of Scripture, past communities of faith with present communities of faith, God's real transforming word to others with God's real transforming word to us. As Gutiérrez puts it:

[O]ur reading will be *historical*. God reveals himself in the history of the people that believed and hoped in him—and this leads us to rethink his word from the viewpoint of our own history. But because ours is a true history, crisscrossed by confrontation and conflict, we can enter into it consciously and effectively only by steeping ourselves in the popular struggles for liberation.[94]

Gutiérrez and the Ethics of the Kingdom

For Gutiérrez, the hallmark of Christian identity is in action first and foremost and in words only secondarily. What one *does* matters far more than what one simply *says*, though the two go hand in hand. Scripture points to this emphasis on action, in Gutiérrez's view. It begins with one's first response to the message of the gospel. Gutiérrez cites Acts 2:37–38, the response to Peter's Pentecost sermon: "'What are we to do, my brothers?' Peter answers: 'Repent.' . . . Conversion means a change of behavior, a different approach to life, the beginning of a following of Jesus."[95] Being a Christian means acting and behaving differently. It is no accident, then, that James 2:14 ("What does it profit, my brethren, if a man says he has faith but has not works?") has a significant place in Gutiérrez's writings, though he would certainly not be a proponent of any kind of works-righteousness.[96]

Central to the "ethics of the kingdom,"[97] and thus to Christian life, is the interplay between the kingdom as gift but also as demand. This theme of gift and demand is found throughout Gutiérrez's writings.[98] In a lengthy reflection on the beatitudes, Gutiérrez develops this dual character of Christian existence: God's grace and God's call.[99] The acceptance of God's graciousness is the beginning of all discipleship, and it leads in turn to the development of spiritual childhood in the believer, who lives "fully open to the will of God," seeking creative ways to respond to God's love.[100]

The Matthean Beatitudes find their climax in 5:16, "Let your light so shine before people, that they may see your good works and give glory to your Father who is in heaven." The emphasis is on the good works of the believer, his or her deeds of justice.

> The entire opening section of Matthew 5 is directed toward verse 16, and the evangelist emphasizes the movement by connecting the verse with what has gone before: "Just so"—marked by the identity and visibility of true disciples—their conduct is to shine before others. "Good deeds" refer to concrete behavior that is in accord with God's will; they refer especially to works of mercy, a classical list of which is given in Matthew 25:31–46.[101]

Finally, Gutiérrez appeals to Paul's letter to Philemon in order to invoke another aspect of this active Christian ethic of grace and demand, kingdom and justice. After rehearsing the content and the context of the letter, Gutiérrez points out verse 21, "I write to you, knowing that you will do even more than I say," which he calls "the most important statement in the entire document, a statement that sums up the message of Paul to Philemon and his community," and which he uses as a section heading for his discussion of Philemon:[102]

> Christian love must necessarily and inevitably lead to the elimination of slavery and every other form of oppression, but love must go further than that. The call for gratuitousness is not added on to an already existing Christian life that is built on an almost exclusive basis of duties and rewards; rather it is at the heart of the behavior of a follower of Jesus. It is not an addition but the foundation. In Paul's view, Christians must daily "invent" their life of love and commitment.[103]

This notion of "doing even more than I say" is in keeping with Jesus' Sermon on the Mount, where he tells his followers to do even more than they are asked (Matt. 5:40–41). Works done out of generosity and grace are, then, but extensions of the grace God has already given. Thus, the grace of God necessarily leads the Christian to look to the needs of the other, to the injustices suffered by one's neighbor, and especially to the plight of the oppressed. This is the direction in which Scripture points. And so, "those who claim to find God while being uninterested in their neighbor will not find the God of the Bible. . . . A concern for where the poor are to sleep will make us realize that it is in fact not possible to separate love of God and love of neighbor."[104]

Critical Evaluation

In evaluating Gutiérrez's use of Scripture, perhaps the most obvious place to start is with criticisms that have been made of his work in regard to Scripture. The 1983 statement by the Congregation for the Doctrine of the Faith, "Ten Observations on the Theology of Gustavo Gutiérrez," challenged his "selective rereading of the Bible," especially his focus on Matthew 25, his appeal to the Exodus as a paradigmatic political event, his reading of Mary's Magnificat (Luke 2) in terms of political liberation, and his "failure" to examine the true meaning of the Beatitudes.[105] Similarly, the Congregation for the Doctrine of the Faith's 1984 statement, "Instruction on Certain Aspects of the 'Theology of Liberation,'" criticizes the "new hermeneutic inherent in the 'theologies of liberation,'" which "leads to an essentially political rereading of the scriptures."[106]

How are we to evaluate these criticisms? The core criticism appears to be that Gutiérrez interprets Scripture to have greater political significance than it actually has. The most appropriate response to this charge, I would argue, is simply to point out that all interpretations of Scripture have political significance. The difference is that some readings lead the interpreters to challenge oppressive characteristics of political and social structures, whereas traditional readings may ignore and thereby reinforce such oppressive structures. The disagreement, then, has to do with how active or passive the church's role should be shaping political and social structures. Different modes of biblical interpretation are simply reflections of this disagreement between sectors of traditional church hierarchies and liberationist egalitarian church communities.

One criticism is worth further attention, however, because it figures so prominently in discussions of Gutiérrez's and other liberation theologians' biblical interpretation, namely, the significance of the Exodus story. Although Gutiérrez does downplay the significance of the Exodus story in his response to critics, it is true that this story is important for him.[107] But its importance does not lie in the belief that it can be repeated. Gutiérrez writes:

> [W]hen we remind ourselves of the fact that the exodus of the Jewish people was also a social and political liberation, we are not thereby laying greater emphasis on this aspect than on the proper goal and ultimate meaning of the entire movement. The point of the reminder is rather to indicate the comprehensive character and broad scope of the covenant in the liberating event that was the exodus.
>
> It is because of this comprehensiveness that the event of the exodus can be called paradigmatic for biblical faith. The term "paradigm" is often used in the biblical sciences. The sense is not that the event must be repeated as such

in the history of the Christian community but rather that the deeper meaning of the event—the liberating intervention of God—is permanently valid.[108]

Indeed, I would argue that the greatest problem with appealing to the Exodus story as a political paradigm is not that it has a political dimension but that it necessarily leads to the *conquest* tradition that follows in Joshua. This raises the question of whether or not there can be an Exodus without a subsequent conquest, and if so, what would it look like?[109] Gutiérrez seems to have the same reservations about the Exodus traditions, because he does not use them to advocate any kind of conquest of other people, as this would be but to perpetuate the use of domination as a tool for social change, and in the end all that would really change is who becomes the oppressed and who the oppressor.

Clearly, I disagree with these criticisms of Gutiérrez's biblical interpretation and see them more as misreadings of Gutiérrez. But there is another issue I would raise. Although I am largely sympathetic to Gutiérrez's uses of Scripture, I do think there is a problematic tension between two ways in which he approaches Scripture. On the one hand, Gutiérrez emphasizes over and over again that all biblical interpretation is done from the perspective (experience) of the interpreter, and so his is done in light of the experience of the poor, with the result that poverty becomes the key to his reading of Scripture. Thus, there is a relative subjectivity to biblical interpretation that must be taken into account. On the other hand, however, Gutiérrez tends to use language of an overarching objective interpretation on the basis of which he can evaluate other interpretations as less legitimate. For example, regarding the Preparatory Document (PD) for Puebla, Gutiérrez states, "It is particularly unfortunate that the PD does not say, as was said in simple, clear, and biblical terms at Medellín, that material poverty is *evil*."[110] In commenting on the 1986 Vatican instruction on liberation theology, *Libertatis Conscientia*, Gutiérrez states that "it does not have any full development of the ideas of communion as the ultimate purpose of liberation; it would have been helped here, had it approached the matter from the viewpoint of the Bible."[111] Thus, Gutiérrez appears to think that there is some relatively clear biblical viewpoint, and that he knows what this is. He recognizes it in the Medellín documents, less so in the Puebla documents, and even less so in the various Vatican responses to liberation theology. Essentially, then, Gutiérrez's experience (of God's empowerment from below in the face of oppression from above) seems to be what authorizes his interpretation as being more in keeping with "the meaning" of the Bible than other interpretations.

Another question has to do with how Gutiérrez handles biblical passages that appear to have more of an otherworldly focus than would seem to fit with his general, this-worldly interpretation of the Bible. We have already seen how he approaches interpretations of the Beatitudes that he finds overly spiritualistic. Another test case would be Jesus' classic statement in response to Pilate that "my kingdom is not from this world" (John 18:36), a statement that has often been interpreted popularly to mean that Jesus' kingdom is a heavenly kingdom, not one that is to be established presently in this world. Regarding this passage,

Gutiérrez writes: "Jesus had made the point that 'my kingdom does not belong to this world' (18:36); that is, the power exercised in it is used not to dominate, as was the case with the Roman authorities, but to serve. Jesus is a king who identifies with the least members of society, those whom society scorns." [112] Thus, for Gutiérrez, the passage addresses the kind of power that Jesus uses, not whether Jesus' kingdom is heavenly or earthly. Indeed, Gutiérrez's interpretation suggests that as Jesus used his power to serve and not to dominate (and thus to transform life), so Christians are to assume the task of transforming the world through their service, and not through any attempt to use the oppressive power of the world. It is also interesting that in his interpretation of this passage, Gutiérrez links it directly to his reading of Matt. 25:31–46, which speaks of Jesus coming as the Son of Man, who will sit on his kingly throne in judgment of the world at the Last Day. In that story, Jesus commends those who have used their power in service to the oppressed, and so for Jesus.

Is Gutiérrez blinded to other authentic ways of reading Scripture because of his hermeneutics, his preferential reading for the poor? In the end, I would argue, no. Rather, he welcomes a broad range of readings, trusting that the Spirit of God will lead the community of faith in the process of discernment. Thus, he is interested in the biblical interpretation offered in the context of the basic Christian communities of Latin America, in the exegesis of the official offices of the church (both in past tradition and in present statements), and in what the guild of biblical scholarship has to contribute to a better understanding of Scripture. That kind of openness can only lead to more faithful readings and incarnations of Scripture.

JAMES CONE

Scripture in African American Liberation

James Cone (b. 1938), a longtime professor of theology at Union Theological Seminary in New York, is widely regarded as the most prominent and influential African American theologian of the twentieth century. His groundbreaking writings in black liberation theology in the late 1960s and early 1970s, and beyond, have been foundational for all subsequent work and reflection on theology and ethics from African American perspectives.[1]

James Cone clearly sees himself as a theologian grounded in the Bible. Reflecting on the social and political contexts that shaped the writing of his first book, *Black Theology and Black Power* (1969), contexts of the suffering and oppression of African Americans in such cities as Detroit, Watts, and Newark in the middle to late 1960s, Cone writes:

> What was needed was a new way of looking at theology that must emerge out of the dialectic of black history and culture. Instinctively, I went to the Scriptures as the primary source for this new approach and asked, "What has the biblical message to do with the black power revolution?" My answer is found in my first book, *Black Theology and Black Power.*[2]

Of significance here is that Cone views the Bible as the primary source for theological reflection, and that he characterizes this view as instinctive or natural, a reflection of the prominent role the Bible has played in the African American church tradition in which Cone was reared.[3] Elsewhere, Cone refers to his "assumption that Scripture is the primary source of theological speech."[4] Indeed, for Cone, "that Christian theology must begin with Scripture appears self-evident. Without this basic witness Christianity would be meaningless. This point seems so obvious to me that it is almost impossible to think otherwise."[5]

In reflecting on his task as a theologian, then, it is not surprising that Cone should write:

> The theologian is *before all else* an exegete, simultaneously of Scripture and of existence. To be an exegete of Scripture means that the theologian recognizes the Bible, the witness to God's Word, as the primary source of theological

discourse. To be an exegete of existence means that Scripture is not an abstract word, not merely a rational idea. It is God's Word to those who are oppressed and humiliated in this world. The task of the theologian is to probe the depths of Scripture exegetically for the purpose of relating that message to human existence.[6]

With this vision of Cone's task as a theologian, and the significance he attributes to the Bible, we can turn our attention to the questions guiding this study as a whole.

Biblical Texts Used by Cone

First, reflections on particular biblical passages and themes figure prominently in many of Cone's writings. This is the case far more in his earlier writings (1969–75) than in his more recent work (1976–91).[7] Cone's most significant work in terms of his use of the Bible is *God of the Oppressed* (1975), which alone accounts for about two-thirds of all references to the Bible in Cone's books (229 out of the 370 I have counted). In his writings, Cone considers, for example, "the biblical concept of the righteousness of God," "The biblical view of Revelation," "the character of the New Testament Jesus," "faith and suffering in the Bible," "suffering in the Bible," and "biblical revelation and social existence," in addition to more general treatments of the Bible."[8]

Second, the shape of Cone's working canon of Scripture emerges clearly from the biblical texts he cites. From the Hebrew Bible, Isaiah (31 citations), Exodus (27 citations), the Psalms (16 citations), and Job (16 citations) figure most prominently. Two sections from Isaiah stand out: Isa. 40:1–5, where God comforts an Israel suffering in exile and promises deliverance in a second Exodus, this time from captivity in Babylon to home in Palestine; and Isaiah 53, the famous Suffering Servant passage, which for Cone foreshadows God's redemptive suffering for God's people in Christ.[9]

From the Book of Exodus, with which Cone's work is most often associated, three sections stand out: Exod. 14:11–15, where just before crossing the Red Sea the people complain to Moses that they would have been better off remaining in Egypt and Moses tells them to "stand firm, and see the deliverance that the Lord will accomplish for you today"; Exod. 15:1–3, where Moses sings a song of praise to God for powerfully defeating the Egyptians and delivering the Israelites out of slavery; and, most significantly, Exod. 19:4–6, where God's acts of salvation in the Exodus become the basis for the covenant between God and Israel at Sinai:[10]

> You have seen what I did to the Egyptians, and how I bore you on eagles' wings and brought you to myself. Now therefore, if you obey my voice and keep my covenant, you shall be my treasured possession out of all the peoples. Indeed, the whole earth is mine, but you shall be for me a priestly kingdom and a holy nation.

Cone often refers generically to the Exodus story and he clearly sees it as *the* foundational event/story for Israel's identity. It was through the Exodus that "Israel as a people initially came to know God;" it is the Exodus that is "the most significant revelatory act in the Old Testament," the Exodus that called "Israel into being as the people of the covenant," the Exodus that defines "the meaning of Israel's existence," the Exodus that "was the decisive event in Israel's history, because through it Yahweh revealed himself as the Savior of an oppressed people." The Exodus is for Cone "the great liberation event." Indeed, Cone often simply refers to "the God of the Exodus." It is hard to overstate the significance of the Exodus for Cone.[11]

From the Psalms, Cone cites passages that stress God's deliverance of the poor and the suffering and that show God's righteousness:

> For he delivers the needy when they call,
>   the poor and those who have no helper.
> He has pity on the weak and the needy,
>   and saves the lives of the needy.
> From oppression and violence he redeems their life;
>   and precious is their blood in his sight. (Ps. 72:12–14)[12]

From Job, Cone emphasizes Job's questioning of God's righteousness in the face of innocent suffering. Through God's self-disclosure, Job receives an answer: "because the faithful can experience the reality of divine presence, they can endure suffering and transform it into an event of redemption."[13]

From the New Testament, Cone refers most often to the synoptic Gospels (Matthew, Mark, and Luke). From these Gospels, two passages stand out as the most important for Cone in the entire Bible: Luke 4:18–19 (eleven citations) and Matt. 25:31–46 (eight citations). Luke 4:18–19 is, of course, the proclamation from Isa. 61:1–2 and 58:6 which Jesus reads in the synagogue and pronounces fulfilled:

> The Spirit of the Lord is upon me,
>   because he has anointed me to bring good news to the poor.
> He has sent me to proclaim release to the captives
>   and recovery of sight to the blind,
>   to let the oppressed go free,
> to proclaim the year of the Lord's favor."[14]

For Cone, this and other passages show "the heart of the matter, namely, *Jesus' rejection of any role that would separate him from the poor.*"[15] They show that "Jesus understood his person and work as the inauguration of the new age, which is identical with freedom for the oppressed and health for the sick."[16]

Similarly, Matt. 25:31–46, the Last Judgment parable about how the separation of the sheep and the goats is based on one's attentiveness to the suffering, the poor, and the oppressed, and thus, ultimately, on one's attentiveness to God, figures prominently in Cone's writings. Drawing on this parable, Cone concludes that "God is not necessarily at work in those places where the Word is

truly preached and the sacraments are duly administered (as Reformation theologians defined the Church), but where the naked are clothed, the sick are
visited, and the hungry are fed."[17] Further, according to Cone, "the least in
America are literally and symbolically present in black people."[18]

Along similar lines, Cone gives significant attention to two other passages
that show God valuing the least and the weak in the world: Mark 10:42–45 and
1 Cor. 1:26–28. Mark 10:42–45, where Jesus says that "whoever would be great
among you must be your servant, and whoever would be first among you must
be slave of all," shows that Jesus' "presence in our midst requires that we subordinate our personal interests to the coming liberation for all,"[19] including liberation for the oppressors. Indeed, states Cone, the oppressed must "fight against
the oppressors in order to fight for them. This is what Jesus meant when he
said, 'the Son of man . . . came not to be served but to serve, and to give his
life as a ransom for many' (Mark 10:45 RSV)."[20]

Cone cites 1 Cor. 1:26–28 to show God's preferential option for the weak
and the foolish over against those deemed strong and wise by the world. When
Paul says that "God chose what is foolish in the world to shame the wise; God
chose what is weak in the world to shame the strong" (1 Cor. 1:27), for Cone
this clearly means that "God is found among the poor, the wretched, and the
sick."[21] Further, it shows that black theology appropriately rejects white theology
as heresy and foolishness in God's sight, since it has not originated from among
the poor and the despised of the world.[22]

In general, then, Cone's working canon consists of the following: from the
Torah, the Book of Exodus; from the Prophets, the prophet Isaiah, especially
Second Isaiah; from the Writings, the Psalms and Job; from the New Testament,
the Gospels of Matthew and Luke, especially Matt. 25:31–46 and Luke 4:16–30,
along with selections from Mark and Paul that stress God's election of those the
world deems poor, weak, and foolish.

How Cone Uses Scripture

Telling the Story

First and foremost, Cone uses the Bible as the fundamental source for telling
the story about God and God's people in the world. Telling the story means
showing the connections between Cone's two pillars for theological reflection,
two pillars that have mutually and deeply impacted each other: the Bible and
African American experience. Reflecting on preaching in the black church tradition, for example, Cone writes:

> In the black tradition, preaching as prophecy is essentially telling God's story.
> "Telling the story" is the essence of black preaching. It means proclaiming with
> appropriate rhythm and passion the connection between the Bible and the
> history of black people. What has Scripture to do with our life in white society
> and the struggle to be *somebody* in it? To answer that question, the preacher

must be able to tell God's story so that the people will experience its liberating presence in their midst."[23]

Telling the story means using Scripture as testimony to the identity of God through its narration of what God has done in the past, which then makes apparent what God is doing in the present. This use of Scripture has been called "recital theology" or a "salvation history" approach, focusing as it does on the mighty acts of God.[24] Cone states, for example, that the "Old Testament is a history book. . . . we must think of the Old Testament as the drama of God's mighty acts in history."[25] That the identity of God can be known from what God has done leads to an emphasis on the historicity and this-worldliness of God's actions. God is known in and through the specificity of human contexts and human history.

The mighty acts of God are plainly presented in Scripture. They begin with the Exodus, where God's actions of liberating the Hebrews from slavery in Egypt identify God as one who sides with the weak and the poor, and so a God who acts for the liberation of the oppressed. "Basing ourselves on the exodus and the message of the prophets, we black theologians agreed with our neoorthodox teachers that God is known by God's acts in history and that these acts are identical with the liberation of the weak and the poor."[26] God's mighty acts continued to be expressed in God's covenant with Israel, the gift of the land, the dynamic ministry of the prophets during the monarchy, the "second Exodus" of the Israelites from captivity in Babylon to the return to the Promised Land, and above all in the incarnation in Christ, which reveals "God's self-giving love to oppressed humanity."[27]

By telling the story of God's mighty acts on behalf of God's people, the identity of God and God's people becomes clear. Who is God? Essentially, God is a God of righteousness and justice, and not in the abstract but in concrete human existence. God's righteousness is shown in "the divine decision to vindicate the poor, the needy, and the helpless in society."[28] The story of the Exodus reveals the meaning of God's righteousness, in that God "elected to be the Helper and Saviour to people oppressed and powerless in contrast to the proud and mighty nations."[29] The story of Jesus reveals the righteousness of God as seeking justice for the poor and the oppressed. By contrast, "the rich, the secure, the suburbanite can have no part of God's righteousness because of their trust and dependence on the things of this world."[30]

Above all, God's righteousness means that God identifies with and takes the side of those disenfranchised by the world. As Cone puts it in *Black Theology and Black Power*:

> What, then, is God's Word of righteousness to the poor and the helpless? "I became poor in Christ in order that man may not be poor. I am in the ghetto where rats and disease threaten the very existence of my people, and they can be assured that I have not forgotten my promise to them. *My righteousness will vindicate your suffering!* Remember, I know the meaning of rejection because in Christ I was rejected; the meaning of physical pain because I was crucified;

the meaning of death because I died. But my resurrection in Christ means that alien powers cannot keep you from the full meaning of life's existence as found in Christ." . . . This is God's Word. (p. 46)

God's righteousness shows God as a personal God, a God who seeks right relationships between people and, therefore, social justice, as Israel's prophetic tradition so clearly demonstrates.

God's righteousness is also a necessary complement to God's love. The righteous judgment of God against all oppression is in fact an expression of God's love for the oppressors. The righteousness of God means standing up and saying no to the injustice and inhumanity of oppressors. The righteousness of God means calling people to account for their relationships to the poor and oppressed of the world, with whom God has sided and identified.[31] Love without righteousness is unacceptable. Cone has expressed this bluntly:

> There is no use for a God who loves white oppressors *the same as* oppressed blacks. We have had too much of white love, the love that tells blacks to turn the other cheek and go the second mile. What we need is the divine love as expressed in black power, which is the power of blacks to destroy their oppressors, here and now, by any means at their disposal.[32]

Thus, the Bible is essential because it tells the story of what God has done, which in turn tells us about the identity of God and the character of God's people. But it is crucial for Cone that we not stop there with the recounting of what God has done in the past, for equally important is the concrete direction in which the biblical record points for discerning God's activity in the present situation. As Cone eloquently puts it:

> As long as we blacks located the liberating acts of God for the poor in ancient Hebrew history, that was acceptable biblical exegesis from the viewpoint of white scholars. But when we tried to do systematic theology on the basis of our exegesis, applying God's liberating acts to our contemporary situation in the U.S.A., focusing on the relations between blacks and whites, white scholars vehemently rejected both the procedure and the message. They tried to get around our contemporary application of the biblical message by saying that there were other themes in the Bible besides liberation (which we never denied). Our concern was to locate the dominant theme in scripture and to ask what its message was for the black struggle for freedom today.
>
> We black theologians contended that if God sided with the poor and the weak in biblical times, then why not today? If salvation is a historical event of rescue, a deliverance of slaves from Egypt, why not a black power event today and a deliverance of blacks from white American racial oppression?[33]

The dominant theme that emerges from Scripture, Cone argues, is clear: God's liberation of the poor and the oppressed, in the past, in the present, and as the direction for God's people in the future.

> It seems clear to me that whatever else we may say about Scripture, it is first and foremost a story of Israelite people who believed that Yahweh was involved

in their history. . . . ['I']he import of the biblical message is clear on this point: God's salvation is revealed in the liberation of slaves from socio-political bondage. . . . [T]here are other themes in the Old Testament, and they are important. But their importance is found in their illumination of the central theme of divine liberation.[34]

The story about God and God's people of old related in the Bible serves, then, as the starting point and partner in dialogue for reflecting on the continuing story of God and God's people today. The experiences of God's people recorded in Scripture function as the primary source for reflecting on what it means to be God's people today. One of Cone's favorite examples of such reflection in the black church tradition comes from James Weldon Johnson's *God's Trombones.* Cone writes:

> The texts of the Bible served as starting points for an interpretation consistent with the existence of the folk. James Weldon Johnson speaks of an occasion when a preacher "who after reading a rather cryptic passage took off his spectacles, closed the Bible with a bang and by way of preface said, 'Brothers and sisters, this morning—I intend to explain the unexplainable—find out the undefinable—ponder over the imponderable—and unscrew the inscrutable.' "[35]

Although Scripture is an indispensable source for reflecting on Christian existence, it is not the only indispensable source, for by definition, Scripture is correlated with the experiences of God's people who reflect on and interpret Scripture. Thus, the experience of God's people—and particularly African American people—is equally indispensable for Christian theology. Cone hammers home over and over how both Scripture and African American experience are the two pillars of his theology.[36]

The Dialectic of Scripture and African American Experience

The biblical story only functions appropriately in conjunction with the story of African Americans, who on account of their own long-standing experiences of suffering and oppression so readily identify with the people of God from the biblical story. The biblical story, then, is found not only in the Bible but also in the story of African American people, especially in such traditions as the spirituals, which primarily appropriated the biblical story to tell the African American story, as Cone has so well documented in his study *The Spirituals and the Blues.*

One of Cone's favorite ways of describing this relationship between the biblical story and the African American story is in terms of dialectic, an aspect of his Barthian heritage that has a prominent place in his theological construction, especially in his earlier writings. Standing in dialectic relationship, Scripture and African American experience are reciprocally essential for proper interpretation: Scripture for African American experience, history, and culture; African American experience, history, and culture for Scripture. Cone states this approach in various ways, but most clearly in *God of the Oppressed:*

> [B]ecause we blacks accept his [God's] presence in Jesus as the true definition of our humanity, blackness and divinity are dialectically bound together as one reality. This is the theological meaning of the paradoxical assertion about the primacy of the black experience and Jesus Christ as witnessed in Scripture.[37]

Since the Bible is used not as an artifact but in real life as a living witness to God's activity and character, the interpreter must take into account the social context in which the Bible is read, for this is crucial to how the Bible is then used. This is why Cone emphasizes the dialectical character of black experience and Scripture over and over again as the point of departure for black theology. To have one without the other leads to a distortion of both.[38]

Cone's View of the Authority of Scripture

Biblical Authority as Reliable Witness, Not Infallible Word

Cone's vision of biblical authority derives directly from his understanding of the character of the Bible—namely, that the Bible is a reliable *witness* to God and God's revelation/activity but is not revelation itself. Scripture is a collection of faithful testimony to God's doings in the world. Thus, regarding Scripture as an authoritative source for theological reflection, Cone writes: "There can be no theology of the Christian gospel which does not take into account the biblical witness. It is true that the Bible is not the revelation of God; only Jesus is. But it is an indispensable witness to God's revelation and is thus a primary source for Christian thinking about God."[39] As we have seen, for Cone the central content of the biblical witness is God's solidarity with the poor and the oppressed: "It is indeed the *biblical* witness that says that God is a God of liberation, who speaks to the oppressed and abused, and assures them that divine righteousness will vindicate their suffering."[40]

The Bible is a witness, however, not just to what God has done in the past. Rather, as the people of God, especially the oppressed people of God, reflect on Scripture, they find that Scripture points also to what God is doing in the present. This is crucial for Cone, because it indicates how the Bible functions as a living witness in the African American church tradition, and not as a dead letter written centuries ago. (This stands in contrast to the approach of many white churches which take a relatively antiquarian approach to the Bible which gives tacit approval to the status quo.) Thus, Cone states:

> The God who is present today in our midst is the same God who was revealed in Jesus Christ as witnessed in the scriptures. By reading an account of God's activity in the world as recorded in scripture, it is possible for a community in the twentieth century to experience the contemporary work of God in the world. The meaning of scripture is not to be found in the words of scripture as such but only in its power to point beyond itself to the reality of God's revelation—and in America, that means black liberation. Herein lies the key to the meaning of biblical inspiration. The Bible is inspired: by reading it a commu-

nity can encounter the resurrected Jesus and thus be moved to risk everything for earthly freedom.[41]

The biblical witness thus engenders a conversation between the stories of the faithful who wrote Scripture long ago and the stories of the faithful who read and interpret Scripture here and now. For Cone, the authority of Scripture, then, is its capacity to connect God's liberating activity across time and space and so to connect and empower God's people across changing situations, while at the same time recognizing the specificity and historical concreteness of God's people. As he puts it in *God of the Oppressed:*

> The authority of the Bible for Christology, therefore, does not lie in its objective status as the literal Word of God. Rather, it is found in its power to point to the One whom the people have met in the historical struggle of freedom. Through the reading of Scripture, the people not only hear other stories about Jesus that enable them to move beyond the privateness of their own story; but through faith because of divine grace, they are taken from the present to the past and then thrust back into their contemporary history with divine power to transform the sociopolitical context. . . . Through the experience of moving back and forth between the first and the twentieth centuries, the Bible is transformed from just a report of what the disciples believed about Jesus to black people's personal story of God's will to liberate the oppressed in their contemporary context. (pp. 112–13)

Cone notes that the rise of historical-critical approaches to the Bible has not really shaken the confidence African Americans have placed in the Bible. Unlike most white conservatives, African American Christians have been able to draw a crucial distinction between the reliability of the Bible, on the one hand, and the infallibility of the Bible, on the other. Unlike white fundamentalist and conservative Christians in the nineteenth and twentieth centuries, for whom the infallibility of the Bible has been crucial, African American Christians have focused on the reliability and truthfulness of the biblical story rather than on the infallibility of biblical words. "For this reason there has been no crisis of biblical authority in the black community.[42]

Indeed, Cone regularly blasts those who would defend the doctrine of biblical infallibility:

> [W]e should not conclude that the Bible is an infallible witness. God was not the author of the Bible, nor were its writers mere secretaries. Efforts to prove verbal inspiration of the scriptures result from the failure to see the real meaning of the biblical message: human liberation! Unfortunately, emphasis on verbal infallibility leads to unimportant concerns. While churches are debating whether a whale swallowed Jonah, the state is enacting inhuman laws against the oppressed. It matters little to the oppressed who authored scripture; what is important is whether it can serve as a weapon against oppressors.[43]

> If the basic truth of the gospel is that the Bible is the infallible word of God, then it is inevitable that more emphasis will be placed upon "true" propositions about God than upon God as active in the liberation of the oppressed of the

land. Blacks, struggling for survival, are not interested in abstract truth, "infallible" or otherwise. Truth is concrete.[44]

Cone believes that debates about the infallibility of Scripture essentially function as smoke screens put up by oppressors to avoid dealing directly with the
content of the biblical witness, namely, God's liberating actions on behalf of the
poor and the oppressed and God's call to God's people to be actively engaged
in concrete liberation in this world here and now.

As an essential and reliable witness, if not infallible, the Bible provides
guidance for faithful existence. But Christians are empowered by God's spirit in
freedom to decide what living in faith means here and now. The Bible thus
functions as an important guide but ultimately not in an authoritative and binding manner.

> We *must* make decisions about where God is at work so we can join in the
> fight against evil. But there is no perfect guide for discerning God's movement
> in the world. Contrary to what many conservatives would say, the Bible is not
> a blueprint on this matter. It is a valuable symbol for pointing to God's revela-
> tion in Jesus, but it is not self-interpreting. We are thus placed in an existential
> situation of freedom in which the burden is on us to make decisions without a
> guaranteed ethical guide.[45]

Similarly, the life and ministry of Jesus serves as a crucial guiding witness to
faithful existence but not as the authoritative model to be followed literally in
all times and places. As Cone puts it:

> We cannot use Jesus' behavior in the first century as a *literal* guide for our
> actions in the twentieth century. To do so is to fall into the same trap that
> fundamentalists fall into. It destroys Christian freedom, the freedom to make
> decisions patterned on, but not dictated by, the example of Jesus. Scripture,
> then, does not make decisions for us.[46]

Authority as Authorized by African American Experience

For all the significance Cone assigns to the biblical witness, it is clearly not the
ultimate authority. The ultimate authority is the experience of the oppressed,
which in the context of the United States means the experience of African
Americans. In a section entitled "On Religious Authority" from his first book,
Black Theology and Black Power, Cone writes:

> The discussion of authority must depart from the abstract debate among funda-
> mentalist, liberalist, and neo-orthodox thinkers. . . . Black Theology sees a prior
> authority that unites all black people and transcends these theological differ-
> ences. It is this common experience among black people in America that Black
> Theology elevates as the supreme test of truth. To put it simply, Black Theology
> knows no authority more binding than the experience of oppression itself. This
> alone must be the ultimate authority in religious matters.
>
> Concretely, this means that Black Theology is not prepared to accept any
> doctrine of God, man, Christ, or Scripture which contradicts the black demand
> for freedom now. (p. 120)

The supreme authority is the collective voice of oppressed African Americans, as expressed in African American experience, history, and culture.[47] Since the Bible speaks not on its own but only through the voice of human interpretation, the ultimate measure of the adequacy of any interpretation is the experience of God's oppressed people. Does an interpretation liberate or does it subjugate? As Cone notes, during slavery white masters interpreted the Bible to say only two things: that slaves should obey their masters (Eph. 6:5, Col. 3:22, 1 Cor. 7:21) and that Africans were inferior because of the "curse of Ham" (Gen. 9:18–27).[48] Such interpretations do violence to Scripture because they do violence to oppressed people.

But the experiences of African Americans have led them to see the lie in such biblical interpretations, and instead, African Americans have found liberating voices in Scripture, especially the Exodus story, such passages as Ps. 68:31 ("Let bronze be brought from Egypt; let Ethiopia hasten to stretch out its hands to God"), and the story of Jesus' ministry, death, and resurrection.[49] Such passages have spoken to their experiences of suffering and oppression and have spoken of a God who identifies with them, is on their side, and is seeking their liberation.[50]

Biblical authority, then, becomes a function of the overriding authority of African American experience. When biblical texts and interpretations are experienced by African Americans as liberating, they become authorizing; when biblical texts and interpretations are experienced as enslaving, they are seen as demonic and not authoritative. Cone expresses this well when he states that:

> the black experience requires that Scripture be a source of Black Theology. For it was Scripture that enabled slaves to affirm a view of God that differed radically from that of the slave masters. The slave masters' intention was to present a "Jesus" who would make the slave obedient and docile. Jesus was supposed to make black people better slaves, that is, faithful servants of white masters. But many blacks rejected that view of Jesus not only because it contradicted their African heritage, but because it contradicted the witness of Scripture.[51]

Cone's Hermeneutics

Cone articulates his hermeneutical approach to the Bible in a straightforward manner.[52] After describing the various sources for constructing a black theology of liberation (black experience, history, and culture, revelation, Scripture, and tradition), Cone proceeds to describe the norm of black theology, namely, "the hermeneutical principle which is decisive in specifying how sources are to be used by rating their importance and by distinguishing relevant data from irrelevant."[53] According to Cone, two crucial aspects of a single reality must shape the hermeneutical norm—the liberation of black people and God's revelation of Jesus Christ—for these two features reflect Cone's essential understanding of human beings and God, respectively. Cone states his hermeneutical principle as follows: *"The norm of all God-talk which seeks to be black-talk is the manifestation of Jesus as the black Christ who provides the necessary soul for black libera-*

tion. This is the hermeneutical principle for black theology which guides its interpretation of the meaning of contemporary Christianity."[54] In *God of the Oppressed,* Cone expresses this hermeneutical principle with a focus on biblical interpretation:

> Black Theology's answer to the question of hermeneutics can be stated briefly: *The hermeneutical principle for an exegesis of the Scriptures is the revelation of God in Christ as the Liberator of the oppressed from social oppression and to political struggle, wherein the poor recognize that their fight against poverty and injustice is not only consistent with the gospel but is the gospel of Jesus Christ.* (pp. 81–82)

Three aspects of Cone's hermeneutics deserve special attention, the relation of the historical Jesus with the Christ of Scripture, the notion of Jesus as the black Christ, and, to use the language of Malcolm X, the poison Bible of white mainstream biblical scholarship.

The Historical Jesus and the Biblical Christ

Since Cone stresses Scripture's witness to God's actions in concrete history and the reliability of this witness (not to be confused with literal infallibility), the general historical reliability of the biblical witness becomes important for Cone, especially in regard to its portrait of Jesus. In a section from *A Black Theology of Liberation* entitled "The Historical Jesus and Black Theology," Cone writes:

> Like the theologians of the new quest, black theology also takes seriously the historical Jesus. We want to know who Jesus *was* because we believe that is the only way to assess who he *is.* If we have no historical information about the character and behavior of that particular Galilean in the first century, then it is impossible to determine the mode of his existence now. Without some continuity between the historical Jesus and the kerygmatic Christ, the Christian gospel becomes nothing but the subjective reflections of the early Christian community. . . . The historical Jesus must be taken seriously if we intend to avoid making Jesus into our own images. (Pp. 112–13)

The historical reliability of the general character of Jesus, then, is paramount for Cone. What is this historical character of Jesus? Cone states it directly: "black theology believes that the historical kernel is the manifestation of Jesus as the Oppressed One whose earthly existence was bound up with the oppressed of the land."[55] The notion of historical kernel here is very important, for it avoids two extremes. On the one hand it avoids the error of fundamentalist literalism, for quite clearly Jesus did not say or do many of the things attributed to him in the Gospel accounts. On the other hand, it avoids the error of radical skepticism, which presumes that we have no real access to the historical Jesus.

By avoiding these two extremes, Cone is able to build his constructive theology, which emphasizes concrete historical existence, upon the concrete historical character of Jesus as the oppressed one who identified with and sought the liberation of the oppressed of the land. Thus, for Cone, there is no essential difference between the Jesus of history and the Christ of faith, since, as he argues, the essential kernel of both is the same. For this reason, Cone's starting point is "the assumption that there is no radical distinction between the Jesus of history and the Christ of faith."[56]

The portrait of Jesus in the Gospels, then, is for Cone a reliable characterization of Jesus. What emerges is a picture of Jesus who is in every way aligned with the poor and the oppressed. Jesus is born among the humiliated and abused. His baptism "defines his existence as one with sinners."[57] The public ministry of Jesus shows him standing squarely in the prophetic tradition on the side of the poor and oppressed, both in his teaching and in his healing. And regarding the death and resurrection of Jesus, Cone writes: "His death is the revelation of the freedom of God, taking upon himself the totality of human oppression; his resurrection is the disclosure that God is not defeated by oppression but transforms it into the possibility of freedom."[58]

This historical gist of Jesus' identity and its general historical accuracy as presented in the Bible are absolutely essential to Cone's understanding of Christian faith. "If it can be shown that the New Testament contains no reliable historical information about Jesus of Nazareth or that the kerygma . . . bears no relation to the historical Jesus, then Christian theology is an impossible enterprise."[59] Or as Cone further states, "Unless the biblical story is historically right in its picture of the humanity of Jesus, then there is no reason to believe that he shared our suffering and pain."[60]

Jesus Is Black

The historical character of Jesus as inseparably bound with the poor and the oppressed provides the basis for Cone's identification of Jesus as the black Christ. Essentially, if Jesus historically identified with those who were the poor and oppressed in first-century Palestinian Jewish society, if that is who he *was*, then when we ask who he *is* today, he must by definition be identified with the poor and oppressed in late-twentieth-century America, namely, with African Americans.

> Taking our clue from the historical Jesus who is pictured in the New Testament as the Oppressed One, what else, except blackness, could adequately tell us the meaning of his presence today? Any statement about Jesus today that fails to consider blackness as the *decisive* factor about his person is a denial of the New Testament message.[61]

Put more sharply, Cone states that "whether whites want to hear it or not, *Christ is black, baby,* with all of the features which are so detestable to white society."[62] Unlike Albert Cleage in *The Black Messiah,* however, Cone does not argue that Jesus was literally black, though he hastens to add that Jesus was not white. The literal color of Jesus is ultimately irrelevant. Instead, the significance of the notion of Jesus as the "black Christ" is that "it expresses the *concreteness* of Jesus' continued presence today."[63]

For Cone, "black Christ" is simply a twentieth-century christological title used to express the identity of Jesus, much as Son of David, Lord, Son of God, and Son of Man were christological titles used by first-century Christians who likewise employed various titles to express the identity and significance of Jesus. Indeed, Cone concedes that " 'blackness' as a christological title may not be appropriate in the distant future or even in every human context in our present."[64] But the universality of the title is not the point, rather the particularity of the title is crucial, namely, whether in a specific time and place, in a concrete social and historical setting, the title points to Jesus as God's activity of identifying with and liberating the poor and the oppressed of the land. Thus, in the context of the late twentieth century, "if Christ is not *truly* black, then the historical Jesus lied. . . . if Christ is not black, the gospel is not good news to the oppressed."[65]

This emphasis on the particularity of God is crucial for Cone, who articulates God's particularity most clearly when he argues that God is not color-blind. To suggest that God is color-blind is to suggest that God is concerned neither with the concreteness of human existence nor with human oppression that arises precisely from the particularity of race. If God has chosen the oppressed, then God has not chosen, and indeed has rejected, oppressors. To put it succinctly, God takes sides.

> In a racist society, God is never color-blind. To say God is color-blind is analogous to saying that God is blind to justice and injustice, to right and wrong, to good and evil. . . . In the New Testament, Jesus is not for *all*, but for the oppressed, the poor and unwanted of society, and against oppressors. . . . the God of the oppressed takes sides with the black community. God is not color-blind in the black-white struggle, but has made an unqualified identification with blacks.[66]

Thus, to talk about Jesus as black is simply to translate the identity of Jesus in the first century, who he *was*, into the identity of Jesus in the twentieth century, who he *is* today.

The only appropriate response to Jesus' blackness, according to Cone, is for followers of Jesus to identify with his blackness just as Jesus has identified with the poor and the disenfranchised of the land. In particular, this means that whites must shed their whiteness and become black, no easy task. "To be black means that your heart, your soul, your mind, and your body are where the dispossessed are. . . . Therefore, being reconciled to God does not mean that one's skin is physically black. It essentially depends on the color of your heart, soul, and mind."[67]

The Poison Bible

In his most recent book, *Martin and Malcolm and America*, Cone describes Malcolm X's critique of Christianity as white and the Christian Bible as a "poison book."[68] This image of a poison Bible is a powerful one for describing an important aspect of Cone's hermeneutics, namely, his critique of how whites have used the Bible to enslave and to oppress African Americans, in essence to poison and to kill them. During the time of slavery, the Bible became a poison book when it was used to justify slavery. After slavery, the Bible continued to be used by whites to offer pie-in-the-sky theology to African Americans and so falsely justified the active oppression of African Americans and the ignoring of their plight as the disenfranchised of the land. Such interpretations of the Bible offered a heavenly feast in some afterlife by and by at the price of serving meager meals laced with deadly poison day after day in the here and now.

A major contributor to this poisoning of the Bible has been the academic guild of so-called professional biblical scholars, until recently an almost exclusively white male club. Under the guise of "objective scholarship," biblical scholars have generally taken a distinctively antiquarian approach to the Bible, emphasizing what it meant a long time ago but saying almost nothing about the significance of the biblical witness for constructing theology today. As Cone put it in his first book, *Black Theology and Black Power,* "The scholarly demand for this kind of 'objectivity' has come to mean being uninvolved or not taking sides."[69] Indeed, when challenged by the rise of black liberation theology, the initial response of most white scholars was to take a rather literalist approach to the Bible, calling for African Americans to be nonviolent and to "turn the other cheek," which became simply another way of poisoning the words of Jesus in an attempt to maintain white privilege at the expense of continued oppression of African Americans.

One of the main ways that white biblical scholars have poisoned the Bible is through the construction of an academic guild sitting on a white hill, a guild emphasizing ideas and concepts to be exchanged at scholarly meetings rather than a consideration of concrete social conditions of oppression and poverty.[70] By separating the Bible from social realities and from the communities of faith, white biblical scholars have perpetuated an ideology that itself perpetuates the status quo, namely, white privilege purchased at the expense of African Americans.

Cone asserts that white scholars have also poisoned the Bible by masking and shrouding its essential message of social and political liberation of the oppressed. For example, regarding Mark 1:14–15, the opening proclamation of Jesus in Mark ("the kingdom of God is at hand; repent and believe in the Gospel"), Cone writes: "New Testament scholars have spent many hours debating the meaning of this passage, which sometimes gives the average person the impression that there is a hidden meaning discernible only by seminary graduates. But the meaning is clear enough for those who are prepared for a radical decision about their movement in the world."[71]

By emphasizing the obscurity of the Bible and the difficulty of understanding it, and so ensuring the security of their/our/my own jobs, white biblical scholars have poisoned the liberating witness of Scripture, according to Cone. Cone puts it sharply, but, I believe, accurately, when he writes: "If white biblical exegetes think that the God of Jesus gave them a hermeneutical privilege in

biblical interpretation, then they have not only misread scripture but have substituted their scientific knowledge about the Bible for a genuine encounter with
biblical faith."[72] In short, white biblical scholars have as a matter of course
missed the forest for the trees, have studied the grammar and historical setting
but have missed the message, have written learned commentaries on Paul's
statement in 1 Cor. 1:26, that God has chosen the weak and the foolish of the
world rather than the strong and the wise, but have not heard, listened to, or
digested what Paul is saying. As Cone writes, most white biblical scholars in
essence "continue as in a vacuum, writing footnotes on the Aramaic substratum
of Mark's Gospel" and the like.[73] In short, for Cone such biblical scholarship
by and large is garbage.[74]

Further, white biblical scholars have often poisoned the Bible by spiritualiz-
ing the biblical message so that it has no real significance for social existence.
For example, regarding Jesus' Sermon on the Mount, white biblical scholars
have generally interpreted Matthew's "poor in spirit" as a reference to one's
internal disposition alone, with no regard either for Luke's version or for what
else Matthew has to say regarding poverty, especially in Matt. 25:31–46, the parable of the sheep and the goats. As Cone states, "It is this kind of false interpretation that leads to the oppression of the poor. As long as oppressors can be sure
that the gospel does not threaten their social, economic, and political security,
they can enslave others in the name of Jesus Christ."[75]

Cone and the Significance of Scripture for Ethics/Praxis

Cone's hermeneutics yields a relatively clear ethic: to identify with the poor and
the oppressed and to seek their liberation in concrete terms. That is what Scripture is all about for Cone. The Christian tradition has gotten off track because
it has separated its theology from its ethics. As he puts it in a section entitled
"The Interdependence of Theology and Ethics," from *God of the Oppressed*:

> Theologians of the Christian Church have not interpreted Christian ethics as
> an act for the liberation of the oppressed because their views of divine revela-
> tion were defined by philosophy and other cultural values rather than by the
> biblical theme of God as the Liberator of the oppressed. If American theolo-
> gians and ethicists had read the Scripture through the eyes of black slaves and
> their preachers, then they would have created a different set of ethical theories
> of the "Good." For it is impossible truly to hear the biblical story as told in the
> songs and sermons of black people without also seeing God as the divine power
> in the lives of the oppressed, moving them toward the fullness of their human-
> ity. (pp. 199–200)[76]

Cone offers a wholesale indictment of the most prominent Christian ethicists of the twentieth century, from Reinhold Niebuhr to Paul Ramsey to James
Gustafson, for their failure to hear the biblical witness and to see its implications
for Christian identity and action. When Niebuhr says that the founding fathers

of the United States must not be considered immoral just because they were slaveholders, Cone responds: "What else can this ethical judgment mean than that Niebuhr derived his ethics from white culture and not biblical revelation?"[77] For Cone, the underlying cause of problems in contemporary theology "is not its separation from ethics but its separation from the Scripture and its claim that God is the Liberator of the poor."[78] The problem is that ethicists are biblically illiterate, a situation that most biblical scholars have, ironically, only made worse.

Cone saves his sharpest critique, however, for Preston Williams, an African American ethicist who wrote an article entitled "James Cone and the Problem of a Black Ethic."[79] Cone finds it especially tragic that Williams has also failed to ground his ethical analysis in the biblical story of divine liberation of the oppressed, for in so doing, Williams has bought into the values of white oppressive culture. When Williams calls for more by way of rational ethical discourse from Cone, Cone responds that Williams has mistakenly relied upon white theological irrationality, for when the oppressor defines the meaning of rational discourse for the oppressed, then what is it but irrationality for the oppressed to buy into such discourse? Cone writes:

> Unlike Preston Williams, who begins with white rationality and American constitutional principles, I contend that the black Christian ethic must start with Scripture and the black experience. We must read each in the light of the other, and then ask, "What am I to do?" We cannot afford to let white people interpret the meaning of Scripture for us. Inevitably they will interpret the biblical story according to their racial interests. We black people must read the Bible in the light of our story to survive and God's promise to set the captives free. With the Bible in one hand and High John the Conqueror in the other, we must investigate the ethical trust of our lives. [High John the Conqueror is a trickster-hero in African American folklore, especially during and immediatley after nineteenth-century slavery.] . . . James Gustafson and other white ethicists cannot help us, for they are part of the reason that we are faced with the problem. They would have us believe that black people's ethical dilemmas are similar to those of whites. But experientially, we know that that is not the case."[80]

In moving beyond Williams toward defining a "black ethic of liberation," Cone writes: "the answer to the ethical question 'What am I to do?' can be stated simply: be a liberator of Christ, because that is what you are!"[81] But being such a liberator means first locating oneself within the community of the oppressed, as Jesus had done, for the criteria of ethical judgment can only be worked out in the communal context of the poor and the oppressed.[82]

The difference between Christian and non-Christian ethics is not necessarily to be found in particular actions but in the source from which actions arise. "For Christians, Jesus is the source for what we do . . . Jesus is the criterion of our ethical judgment."[83] It is not that we ask what Jesus would do today if he were here; rather, it is asking what is Jesus doing today, for he is here in the community of faith. Cone writes:

> We must carve out the answer for every new situation *in dialogue* with Scripture and tradition, as well as with other victims in our social existence. But even this dialogue does not grant the certainty of the truth of our answer. The only certainty we are permitted to know is that the Scripture claims that Jesus will be with us in our struggles.[84]

Crucial for Cone, however, is that the oppressor is not in a position to decide for the oppressed what constitutes appropriate Christian behavior. In looking at the history of African Americans, especially during the time of slavery, Cone articulates various components of black ethics that have developed out of the situation of oppression, for example, the distinction between stealing and taking and the theme of deception in the face of white masters. In short, an appropriate ethic arises out of the concrete struggle for freedom.[85]

Thus, Jesus is the primary source for developing an African American ethic of liberation, but only in dialogue with the actual existence and experience of African Americans in community. What Jesus did is important but is not to be mindlessly imitated today. Rather, "we must regard his past activity as a *pointer* to what he is doing now. His actions were not as much examples as *signs* of God's eschatological future and the divine will to liberate all people from slavery and oppression."[86]

Critical Evaluation

In this evaluative section, I will raise three questions regarding Cone's biblical interpretation, followed by some questions about my own ideological approach to the Bible.

My first question has to do with the Exodus traditions and their centrality to Cone's and most African American biblical interpretation. Clearly, the Exodus event is seen as paradigmatic for our understanding of who God is, how God acts, and who we are as followers of God. God is a God who liberates the poor and the oppressed in concrete history and who calls us to be similarly involved. My question stems from the biblical story that follows upon the Exodus, namely, the narratives about the conquest of the land of Canaan. Cone says very little in his writings about the conquest tradition, but clearly in the biblical story there is no Exodus from the land of Egypt without the conquest of the land of Canaan. Indeed, since the Exodus from Egypt necessitates that the Israelites go someplace, the conquest tradition seems inevitable. But what about the Canaanites? Why are they dispossessed of their land? How does African American liberation theology deal with this dilemma of attaining a promised land and freedom at the expense of other peoples, in particular the Canaanite peasants? Would it not make more sense for the Israelites to get land from their oppressors, the Egyptians? Regarding the Canaanites, Cone writes that "Yahweh sides with Israel against the Canaanites in the occupancy of Palestine," but he does not articulate why this is so.[87] Is it possible to have a theology of the

Exodus grounded in a historical event, which is important to Cone, without by necessity also having a theology of conquest also grounded in concrete historical events?

Perhaps an answer is found in the work of such biblical scholars as Norman Gottwald, who argues that the most likely interpretation of the conquest narratives is the "social revolution model," in which disenfranchised Canaanites join the loosely confederated Israelites in a series of revolts against Canaanite hierarchical overlords, even though on the surface the biblical tradition presents the situation in rather monolithic terms as Israelites versus Canaanites.[88] Such a social revolution model of the conquest would fit well with Cone's general reading of the Exodus story as God's liberation of an oppressed people. Still, Gottwald's work is relatively recent and does not account for how Cone would address the issue of the conquest in terms of his books *Black Theology and Black Power*, *A Black Theology of Liberation*, or *God of the Oppressed*, published in 1969, 1970, and 1975, respectively.

In private correspondence, Cone has called attention to an article by one of his former students, Robert Allen Warrior, a Native American, who pointed to similar problems with the use of the Exodus traditions in a 1989 essay "Canaanites, Cowboys, and Indians: Deliverance, Conquest, and Liberation Theology Today."[89] Warrior argues that even if not historically accurate, the biblical narrative presents the conquest tradition as the necessary conclusion of the Exodus story. "Yahweh the deliverer became Yahweh the conqueror. . . . it is the Canaanite side of the story that has been overlooked by those seeking to articulate theologies of liberation. Especially ignored are those parts of the story that describe Yahweh's command to mercilessly annihilate the indigenous population" (p. 262). Warrior suggests that any truly liberative constructive use of the Exodus-conquest tradition must make the Canaanites "the center of Christian theological reflection and political action" (p. 264). In this way, the traditional values inherent in the conquest tradition will be called into question, and people will not be blind to the move too readily made from God the deliverer to God the conqueror. Warrior states that "perhaps, if they are true to their struggle, people will be able to achieve what Yahweh's chosen people in the past have not: a society of people delivered from oppression who are not so afraid of becoming victims again that they become oppressors themselves" (p. 264).

Reflecting on this essay and possible problems with constructive use of the Exodus traditions, Cone writes:

> I do not believe that there are any sacred documents which are free of ambiguity. They should never be used in a literal sense, without regard to the religio-cultural and socio-political contexts. The Exodus is a powerful, liberating story when seen through the eyes of black slaves and many poor blacks in the 20th century, especially during the civil rights and black power movements during the 1960s. But through the eyes of Native Americans whose land was confiscated by white Europeans [who] justified it by calling themselves the "new Israel," the Exodus story becomes depressive and even demonic. There is no sacred writing free of possible misuse. The next time I write about the Exodus,

I will explore these issues. I do not think that Gottwald's work provides a satis-
factory answer. It is another scientific response—interesting but not liberating
for my people.[90]

My second question has to do with Cone's depiction of Jesus. When Cone
tells the story of Jesus, he focuses on the prophetic image of Jesus presented, for
example, in Luke 4:16–30, where Jesus clearly proclaims God's inclusion of
those who have been excluded and cast out by the dominant society and culture. Strikingly absent from Cone's depiction of Jesus is any significant reliance
on the Gospel of John, which has been used throughout Christian history to
present a rather heavenly and detached portrait of Jesus and to advocate similar
detachment in relation to the concrete world in which we live. Would Cone
see the Johannine Jesus as a betrayal of the Jesus of the synoptic Gospels? What
does it mean to treat the Gospel of John, or other biblical texts that might
subvert Cone's interpretation, as part of Christian Scripture?[91]

A third question is related to this. Cone emphasizes the historical character
of Jesus as one who identified with the poor and the oppressed in the land and
sought their liberation. The general historical accuracy of this vision is crucial
to Cone. How does Cone deal with new interpretations of the historical Jesus
emerging in contemporary biblical scholarship, especially images of Jesus as a
cynic or sage who was a troublemaker but did not have a holistic vision of the
coming kingdom of God? My hunch is that Cone would simply dismiss such
historical reconstructions as reflections of white male university professors proj-
ecting their own idealized selves into their reconstructions of the historical Jesus.
Still, what does it mean to talk credibly about the historical Jesus as presented
in Scripture in relation to the concrete historical Jesus that biblical scholars seek
to reconstruct with critical methods? In response to this question, Cone has
written:

> The historical Jesus issue as debated by critical biblical scholarship does not
> affect the way blacks and other poor people talk about Jesus. The Jesus of the
> black experience and of black liberation theology is not dependent on what
> white biblical scholars say. . . . What white biblical scholars say is too much
> determined by an academic guild that is oppressive to blacks.[92]

Finally, it would be dishonest of me as an author if at this point I did not
raise some questions I have been asking of myself (and my guild) as a result of
reading and reflecting on Cone's uses of the Bible. For me, the essential question revolves around my identity as a white male Christian biblical scholar who
is largely sympathetic to Cone's biblical interpretation and his challenge to the
white academy. It is perhaps a question about repentance and conversion. Simply put, if my own privilege and status as an educated and upper middle class
white academic has been purchased by my parents and grandparents at the
expense of oppression of African Americans, then what am I to do? What does
it mean for me as the son of an Egyptian or Virginian slaveholder to embrace
the liberation of those whom my forebearers enslaved and oppressed?

In part, I know that it means seeking to listen to and to understand as best

I can what African Americans are saying, whether expressed in the writings of James Cone, in the riots of Los Angeles, or in the voices of African American colleagues and students where I teach. In part, I know that it means challenging my white suburban Presbyterian church where I regularly preach to reflect on and to act in ways that are faithful to a God who in the Exodus and in Jesus has chosen the poor and the oppressed. But I would be lying if I said I had much confidence beyond these things about what it means in concrete terms for white male Christian biblical scholars to be engaged in the process of God's liberating activity among African American communities (or Asian American or Latin American communities). Perhaps to raise this question sounds like the whining of a naive liberal Protestant Christian at the end of the twentieth century. Nonetheless, it should not go unsaid that an encounter with Cone's use of the Bible compels a great deal of soul-searching among white male members of the establishment guild of traditional biblical scholarship.[93]

nine

ROSEMARY RADFORD RUETHER

Scripture in Feminist Perspective

*R*osemary Radford Ruether (b. 1936) is one of the foremost contemporary feminist theologians. With some twenty-five books and over four-hundred articles to her name, she is certainly one of the most prolific. And although she is most widely known for her work in feminist theology, it should not be forgotten that her writings cover a much broader range of subjects, all of which she sees as closely interrelated, including Jewish-Christian relations, race and class relations, environmental ethics, contemporary Palestinian-Israeli relations, and various issues in contemporary Roman Catholicism.

Ruether's professional training was in historical theology, with an emphasis on classics and patristic theology. After she received her Ph.D. from Claremont Graduate School in 1965 (her dissertation was "Gregory Naziansus: Rhetor and Philosopher"), she taught church history, among other things, at Howard Divinity School, a primarily African American seminary in Washington, D.C. During the mid-1960s she participated actively in the Civil Rights movement. In 1976 she moved to Garrett Evangelical Theological Seminary in Evanston, Illinois (outside Chicago), where she became the Georgia Harkness Professor of Applied Theology, and where she still teaches today. She grew up and remains a Roman Catholic, though she engages in constant critique of the church.

I relate this brief account of her personal history because Ruether herself sees clear relationships between one's personal story, the work one chooses to do, and how one goes about doing it.[1] As we will see, her own experiences also have a significant bearing upon how she makes use of the Bible in constructing her theology.

Ruether's first exposure to the Bible was, not surprisingly, growing up in church, where she would hear the various lectionary readings. But as was the case for most Roman Catholics growing up during the 1930s, 1940s, and 1950s, this exposure to the Bible made little impression. She first actually read and studied the Bible in the context of college and graduate school, so that she "learned the Bible through the medium of historical criticism."[2] Thus, from the start she has seen the Bible very much as a product of human history, the record of various human experiences seeking to articulate visions of faithfulness to God, with some of these visions doing a more credible job than others.

Biblical Texts Used by Ruether

From the Hebrew Bible (357 references counted), Ruether makes significant reference to four groups of texts: (1) the creation and "fall" stories from Genesis 1–3, (2) the traditions about Jubilee legislation in Leviticus 25, (3) various traditions from the wisdom writings (especially Prov. 8 and Wisd. of Sol. 6–8), and (4) the prophetic writings (especially Isa. 24, 61, and 65; Amos 5; and the traditions about Israel as the faithless bride of God from Hosea 2).[3] Ruether appeals in a positive way most extensively to the prophetic writings, and to Isaiah in particular.

From the New Testament (506 references counted), one can identify five groups of texts from which Ruether draws: (1) traditions about Mary, the mother of Jesus, particularly from the birth narratives of Matthew and Luke; (2) traditions which show the subordination of women to men, particularly from 1 Corinthians 11, Ephesians 5, and 1 Timothy 2; (3) traditions which Ruether sees as presenting more of an egalitarian view of women, especially Gal. 3:28, the Joel prophecy in Acts 2, and the Mary and Martha story from Luke 10:38–42; (4) traditions which Ruether sees as articulating Jesus' positive vision of the kingdom, especially from Jesus' inaugural sermon in Nazareth from Luke 4; and (5) traditions which can be classified as antiestablishment or antihierarchalist sayings of Jesus, especially Jesus' indictment of religious authorities from Matthew 23, sayings that stress servanthood rather than lordship from Matt. 20:25–28, and Paul's hymn to Christ from Philippians 2 (though only the first part of the hymn, which stresses emptying, and not the second part of the hymn, which stresses God's exaltation of Christ).

Ruether has a strong preference for the synoptic Gospels over the Gospel of John, and among the synoptic Gospels, she refers the most to Luke, with Matthew a close second and with Mark receiving very little attention. Notably absent from Ruether's New Testament usage is any significant reference to the Passion or resurrection stories of Jesus.

One way to get a feel for what Ruether considers to be the basic story of the Bible is by looking at a little forty-eight-page booklet she wrote in 1968 entitled *Communion Is Life Together*. This book was written for use in catechism leading up to first communion in the Roman Catholic tradition (imprimatur and all!), which means that this book is addressed to seven- and eight-year old children.

In the book, Ruether retells the story of the Bible in a relatively conventional, yet intriguing way. She begins, quite naturally, with the creation story from Genesis, then moves on to God's covenant with Abraham, then relates the story of the Exodus from Egypt, stressing how God saves the people. She then tells the golden calf story, stressing the disobedience of God's people. Only after this does she relate the "fall" story of Adam and Eve along with Cain's murder of Abel as two other stories that illustrate human unfaithfulness to God. The next section of the book presents the prophets, who "showed the people their sins and called them back to the covenant with God" (p. 28). Here, she refers to Micah and tells the story of the prophet Elijah and how he dealt with Ahab in connection with Naboth's vineyard. Thus, Ruether stresses the social dimensions of the prophetic traditions.

She then turns to the story of Jesus, and in the process she relates the Lord's Prayer, the Great Commandment, and the parable of the Good Samaritan. She then briefly tells the story of Jesus' death and resurrection, turning finally to address the establishment of God's kingdom, where she again picks up on renewal themes from the prophetic literature (Joel, Jer. 31, and Isa. 65). Ruether draws the book to a close first by referring again to human sinfulness (highlighting anti-Semitism, slavery, warfare, and the abuse of the poor by the wealthy) and second by making another appeal to the prophetic character of authentic Christian existence. She concludes:

> God has not changed. He still loves the people of the world.
>
> He is still waiting for them to turn and hear his word. He is still working to bring them into that good land which he promised them from the beginning. God is still sending his prophets to show the people their sin and call them back to his ways.
>
> Whenever a man stands up against the crowd and says, "You are thieves and murderers. You do not love your brothers. The world is ugly and sad because you do not love your brothers," that man is God's prophet. We must learn to hear God's prophets. We must learn to follow God's word. (p. 47)

This little first communion catechism is instructive about Ruether's vision of the biblical story. She considers the creation good and not fallen in any ultimate sense. Indeed, she tells the story of the disobedience of Adam and Eve as simply another illustration of human sinfulness alongside the golden calf story. God's response to human disobedience, and especially societal sin, is to send the prophets, who convict the people and call them back to covenant faithfulness. (It is interesting that Ruether essentially leaves out all of Israel's monarchy traditions.) Jesus was another prophet of God, who as God's son had a special authority. And although the people killed him, God raised him from the dead.[4]

To be sure, Ruether's approach to the Bible has developed in some significant ways since 1968, especially in terms of her feminist critique. Nonetheless, her book on first communion does present clearly several themes that have guided her constructive use of the Bible: creation, covenant, exodus, disobedience, and the voice of God's prophets.

How Ruether Uses Scripture

What Is the Bible?

In order to get some handles on Ruether's use of the Bible, it is helpful first to have some sense of how Ruether envisions the character of the Bible. In commenting on her preference for what she calls a biblical worldview over the worldview of classical humanism (though she is quick to add that this is not an exclusive preference), Ruether writes:

> If I feel relatively less betrayed by the biblical world, it is because I happened upon it with a more realistic approach to what it is. I never assumed that it dropped out of heaven undefiled by historical gestation. Rather, I understand it as a product of a human quest for meaning that moved through many different stages and contexts. It is certainly not all of a piece, and it is incomprehensible to me why anyone would expect it to be. It is shaped by, dependent on, and yet responding to, the religious world around it.[5]

Thus, for Ruether, the Bible is first and foremost a collection of historically conditioned writings in which various Jews and Christians have spoken human words about God. As she puts it in her first book, *The Church Against Itself*: "Scripture, along with all other expressions of church tradition, occupies the category of human words about God's Word. They attempt to express God's Word within their finite cultural contexts, but they remain finite and historical" (p. 226).

Since the Bible presents human words about God that are necessarily historically conditioned, and since those who read the Bible also operate in specific and limited historical contexts, all uses of the biblical traditions are by definition finite. Any interpreter who uses the Bible thus must seek to gain relative clarity both about the sociohistorical circumstances of the biblical traditions being utilized and about the sociohistorical circumstances of the contemporary setting in which such biblical traditions are being used. For Ruether, then, all use of the Bible, and indeed Christian existence itself, is by definition dialectical, a conversation between people who sought to speak about God in a past historical setting and people who seek to speak about God in the present historical setting. The process of the conversation may, for Ruether, lead to hearing God's word in the midst of all the human words about God.[6]

One Bible, Two Religions

In a 1982 article for the *Journal for the Study of the Old Testament*, entitled "Feminism and Patriarchal Religion: Principles of Ideological Critique of the Bible," Ruether articulates a twofold approach to the Bible:

> Let us begin by saying that there are two religions within the biblical texts. One religion provides what might be called the "sacred canopy" for the existing

social order. . . . Running as a central thread of biblical religion in both testaments, however, is the denunciation of the religion of the sacred canopy. The Word of God comes as a judgment against this religion. It is denounced as idolatry and apostasy.[7]

For Ruether, what one finds in the Bible is the religion of the sacred canopy, the status quo, along with the religion of the prophetic critique of the status quo. The first must be identified for what it is and denounced; the second must be lifted up and transformed ever anew in the face of new situations and new experiences—it requires "constant discernment in changing contexts."[8] The Bible, then, contains both destructive and constructive traditions.

DESTRUCTIVE BIBLICAL TRADITIONS AND THE SACRED CANOPY

According to Ruether, the single most pernicious, pervasive, and destructive biblical tradition is the sacralization of patriarchy. Essentially, patriarchy refers to the elevation and consequent domination of men and the concomitant subordination and dehumanization of women, all backed up with divine warrant. In the Hebrew scriptures patriarchy finds expression particularly in the legal codes as divine revelation. The list of such patriarchal and androcentric laws is a long one and has been well documented in various studies.[9] In general, the laws present women as less valuable than men and only give women status in relation to men, primarily husbands and fathers.

The creation and fall stories from Genesis 1–3 also give prime evidence of the sacralization of male dominion and female subordination. As Ruether points out in several places, Genesis 1–3 shows man as first in creation and second in sin, whereas woman is second in creation and first in sin.[10] The Genesis story has reversed the normal pattern of birth by having the man Adam give birth to the woman Eve. And responsibility for human rebellion against God is squarely placed upon the woman, who was both deceived and became the agent of the deceiver. The ensuing curse, that the woman would cleave to her husband and be subordinate to him, came eventually to be seen, not as a curse, but as the divine order of creation. This is clearly the case in the notorious passage from 1 Tim. 2:13–14; "For Adam was formed first, then Eve; and Adam was not deceived, but the woman was deceived and became a transgressor."

In the New Testament, the sacralization of patriarchy can be seen in the relatively later writings, especially in the deutero-Pauline traditions of Ephesians 5 and the pastoral Epistles. As Ruether puts it: "In the New Testament there is a shift from patriarchy as positive divine law to patriarchy as natural law. Male leadership is regarded as the order of nature."[11] The lordship of Christ over man is mirrored in the lordship of man over woman. Woman has no direct access to God; rather, the man is head of his wife and so mediates the woman's relationship with Christ, who in turn mediates human relationships with God.

The household codes reflected in Ephesians, Colossians, the pastoral Epistles, and 1 Peter are particularly effective in giving God's blessing upon the traditional patriarchal social order. But already in 1 Corinthians 11, Ruether sees an early tendency in Paul himself to buy into the natural-law hierarchical subordination of woman to man, despite other traditions in Paul that stand in tension with this patriarchal expression. Regarding the biblical materials, Ruether concludes: "Divine patriarchy is seen as the original source and sanction for the social patterns of patriarchy, instead of recognizing that it is the social patterns of patriarchy that are the models for the religious ones, i.e., that the religious imagery is an ideological projection of the patriarchal social order." [12]

CONSTRUCTIVE BIBLICAL TRADITIONS AND PROPHETIC CRITIQUE

Ruether believes that all the biblical traditions have been mediated through patriarchal ideology, and so one should expect to find in the Bible nothing other than divine sanctions of patriarchy. And yet, there is a prophetic counterculture, so to speak, that directly challenges the dualistic and hierarchical presuppositions of patriarchal religion. This prophetic critique provides traditions with which to debunk and denounce appropriations of biblical patriarchalism and to construct new visions of authentic and redeemed human communities that truly express God's purposes for human existence. Indeed, as Ruether states, to neglect this prophetic critique is "to miss the essential dynamism and conflict of biblical religion and the dialectic of its own internal self-critique and development. . . . the core dynamic of creative insight in biblical religion occurs precisely in the confrontation between the religion of the sacred canopy and prophetic faith." [13] The prophetic critique is so valuable to Ruether because it is not concerned with the self-justification of the status quo; rather, its express purpose is the internal *self*-critique of the status quo, to call into question and to challenge the divinizing and the perpetuating of all human values in one's own tradition in light of renewed understandings of what it means to be faithful here and now.

In her landmark 1983 book, *Sexism and God-Talk,* Ruether identifies four themes from her reading of the Bible that are "essential to the prophetic-liberating tradition of Biblical faith":

> (1) God's defense and vindication of the oppressed; (2) the critique of the dominant systems of power and their powerholders; (3) the vision of a new age to come in which the present system of injustice is overcome and God's intended reign of peace and justice is installed in history; and (4) finally, the critique of ideology, or of religion, since ideology in this context is primarily religious. Prophetic faith denounces religious ideologies and systems that function to justify and sanctify the dominant, unjust social order. These traditions are central to the Prophets and to the mission of Jesus. (p. 24)

As Ruether herself readily acknowledges, her description of this biblical prophetic norm is closely aligned with similar notions in Latin American liberation theology, especially with the "preferential option for the poor" so clearly articulated at Medellín. [14]

From the Hebrew Scriptures Ruether draws primarily from Isaiah, Amos, and Jeremiah for critical prophetic voices that speak on behalf of the oppressed and severely criticize the dominant powers of society who are responsible for societal injustices. For example, Ruether cites Isa. 10:1–2, which declares "woe to those who decree iniquitous decrees, and the writers who keep on writing oppression, to turn aside the needy from justice, and to rob the poor."[15] She also appeals to the famous indictment from Amos 8:4–6, which attacks those "who trample upon the needy and bring the poor of the land to an end, . . . [and who] buy the poor for silver and the needy for a pair of sandals."[16]

Similarly, Ruether makes significant use of Isa. 61:1–2 and its New Testament citation by Jesus in Luke 4:18–19: "The spirit of the Lord is upon me, because he has anointed me to preach good news to the poor. He has sent me to proclaim release to the captives, the recovering of sight to the blind."[17] Another New Testament passage that figures prominently in Ruether's vision of prophetic texts that lift up the oppressed and critique the powers of domination is the Magnificat of Mary from Luke 1:47–55: "My spirit rejoices in God my savior, for he has regarded the low estate of his handmaiden. . . . He has scattered the proud in the imagination of their heart, he has put down the mighty from their thrones, and exalted those of low degree; he has filled the hungry with good things, and the rich he has sent empty away" (Luke 1:48, 51–53).[18]

For Ruether, the vision of a new age in which injustice is overcome and God's reign is realized in history also finds expression in these prophetic texts, as well as in the rather striking passage from Jer. 31:22, where the prophet announces that "the Lord has created a new thing on the earth: a woman protects a man" (RSV).[19]

But it is the use of prophetic biblical traditions to critique the ideology of the status quo, and especially religious ideology, that stands out most prominently in Ruether's writings. Again, from the Hebrew Scriptures she utilizes Isaiah, Amos, and Jeremiah most often. For example, she frequently cites the famous denunciation from Amos 5:21–24: "I hate, I despise your feasts, and I take no delight in your solemn assemblies. . . . Take away from me the noise of your songs, to the melody of your harps I will not listen; but let justice roll down like waters and righteousness like an ever-flowing stream."[20] Similarly, she draws attention to Jer. 7:4–11, in which the prophet attacks the hypocrisy of the people's worship.[21]

From the New Testament, Ruether appeals repeatedly to Jesus' critique of the Pharisees and the priests, the established religious leaders of his day. The basic text here is Matt. 23:23: "Woe to you, scribes and Pharisees, hypocrites! For you tithe mint and cummin, and have neglected the weightier matters of the law: justice, and mercy and faith."[22] While Ruether is quick to point out how Matthew 23 has been wrongly used to justify Christian anti-Judaism, she sees it nevertheless as an important prophetic indictment of a religious ideology that has forgotten its true purpose.

Another significant aspect of Jesus' critique of the religious ideology of his day was his reinterpretation of messianism away from triumphalism and revenge theology to a radically new religious vision of servanthood. Here, Ruether draws especially on Matt. 20:17–28, where Jesus says that whoever would be great must be a servant. Thus does Jesus renounce domination as a false power relationship.[23] As Ruether puts it:

> People will no longer model political, social or familial relations, *or relations to God*, after that sort of power which reduces others to servility, but rather after that kind of power that empowers others and brings all to mutuality and mutual enhancement. This is the true relation of redemptive divine power to creation which Jesus tried to model in his interpretation of messianic servanthood.[24]

It is important to note that in her initial presentation of the biblical prophetic norm, Ruether does not explicitly mention women. But women are clearly implicit here, since it is largely women who have been victims of oppression, women who have been powerless, and women who have been excluded by patriarchal ideology. Ruether is not content to leave the connection between women and the prophetic tradition only implicit. Rather, she explicitly addresses the need to develop a feminist radicalizing of the prophetic tradition, for the prophets were not concerned in any significant way with the victimization and exclusion of women per se. Thus, Ruether states that "feminism goes beyond the letter of the prophetic message to apply the prophetic-liberating principle *to women*. Feminist theology makes explicit what was overlooked in male advocacy of the poor and the oppressed: that liberation must start with the oppressed of the oppressed, namely, *women* of the oppressed."[25]

In using the biblical traditions, then, Ruether argues that we must always be aware that the Bible presents two traditions that stand in tension, the religion of the status quo and the religion of prophetic critique. The biblical traditions associated with the status quo cannot be used in any significant way because they image God in the likeness of human and particularly patriarchal injustices, emphasizing domination, hierarchy, and dualism. Such traditions and images call for radical critique. The biblical traditions associated with the internal prophetic critique of religious ideology are the only traditions that can be used positively in the construction of faithful visions of human existence that hear the word of God and so seek to transform humanity into the image of God.

Significantly, Ruether does not conceive of the religion of the sacred canopy and the religion of prophetic critique in static dualistic terms, for neither finds expression in anything like a pure form. Rather, the religion of the sacred canopy can and most often does include some aspects of prophetic critique, just as the religion of prophetic critique can and most often does include dimensions of the status quo. Thus, for example, in the prophetic writings of the Hebrew Bible one finds that "the spokesman for the transcendent stands simultaneously within the social covenant and over against the ruling structures of king and temple priesthood."[26] The dynamic relationship between the religion of the sacred canopy and the religion of prophetic critique, then, is an ever-evolving dialectic with ebbs and flows, sometimes reflecting greater faithfulness to God and sometimes sacrificing authentic faithfulness to the gods of the status quo.[27]

Constructing and Renewing Prophetic Religion

Having identified the prophetic principle as the usable and evolving core of authentic biblical religion, Ruether utilizes several traditions from the Hebrew Bible and from the New Testament writings in a constructive effort to describe a renewable and liberating prophetic Christian faith.

TRADITIONS FROM THE HEBREW BIBLE

Three traditions from the Hebrew writings recur in Ruether's work: covenant, Exodus, and Jubilee.

COVENANT   The tradition of biblical covenant is a significant motif throughout Ruether's writings. Already in her 1968 booklet *Communion Is Life Together,* she stressed the importance of God's covenant with Abraham.[28] Ruether's notion of biblical covenant emphasizes reciprocity and partnership, mutual agreement to a mutual commitment. But, of course, the people regularly broke their part of the covenant agreement. The prophets then stepped in, for they "showed the people their sins and called them back to the covenant with God."[29]

Ten years later, Ruether coauthored a book with Wolfgang Roth entitled *The Liberating Bond: Covenants—Biblical and Contemporary.*[30] She uses the notion of covenanted communities as a positive ideal. Indeed, the "strength of the covenantal idea of the Church lies in its stress on active faith and commitment of each member."[31] The weakness of such covenanted communities, however, is that they find it difficult to sustain themselves historically, for they stand in need of continual renewal amid changing circumstances, new circumstances that are significantly different from those that provided the reasons for the communities' formation in the first place. To speak of covenant, then, is always to bear in mind how covenants get broken and renewed. Ruether is aware of how covenant communities, from ancient Israel forward, can exploit their covenant with God by seeing it as a birthright rather than as a commitment that stands in need of constant renewal. Nonetheless, according to Ruether, the "covenant is one of the great illuminating paradigms of existence that comes from scriptural revelation. It illuminates life with God and each other. It is valid for whoever adopts it and seeks to live truthfully out of its mandate."[32]

Ruether's notion of covenant comes to fruition for women in the creation of Women-Church communities. In her 1985 book *Women-Church,* Ruether includes a section on "covenanting," which addresses "foundational covenanting" and "covenanting celebration."[33] The foundational covenanting involves a group of people (especially women) who desire to "form an exodus community from patriarchy."[34] The group should discuss in detail what kind of community they wish to form, how their group will or will not be related to the historical church institution, and what kind of lifestyle commitments they wish to make in common.[35]

After deciding what kind of covenant community this particular group of Women-Church will be, it is then appropriate for the covenanting community to have a celebration in which they create a "Book of the Covenant." This book would contain the basic credal statements and theological visions of the community. The celebration might begin with a renewal of baptism and include a communal recitation of the credal statement. The members would then enter their names in the Book of the Covenant. Ruether stresses that community covenants should last for specific periods of time, such as a year, so that "periodically the community will renegotiate its covenant."[36] New decisions made during the time of recovenanting would then be entered into the community's Book of the Covenant. Ruether also includes various other covenant celebrations that might take place in the community (e.g., covenant celebrations for creating new families, covenant celebrations for heterosexual couples, and covenant celebrations for lesbian couples).[37]

One final aspect of biblical covenant that Ruether develops involves ecological covenanting, especially as it is articulated in a section entitled "Healing the World" in her 1992 book *Gaia and God*.[38] The covenant tradition "shapes our relation to nature and each other in terms of law and ethical responsibility."[39] Indeed, the Hebrew creation story with its emphasis on God's resting on the seventh day provides a basic vision for a covenant between humanity and nature that leads to the restoration and reciprocal renewal of both. The biblical perspective on nature, according to Ruether, has been overly distorted as being a "dominion theology" that legitimizes human destruction of the natural world. A more appropriate interpretation of the biblical traditions shows a tradition with "keen awareness of the limits of human power" and a concern for the renewal of the natural world.[40] Indeed, as Ruether states:

> Hebrew thought knit the covenantal relation of God to Israel in a close relation to the gift of the "land." . . . The gift of the land is not a possession that can be held apart from relation to God. If Israel "pollutes" the land with iniquity, "the land will vomit you out for defiling it, as it vomited out the nation that was before you" (Leviticus 18:28).
>
> One of the major fruits of this Hebraic understanding of the covenantal relationship between justice and prosperity in the land is found in sabbatical legislation.[41]

Giving the land and animals rest every seventh day is a tradition from the Hebraic covenant that provides a constructive vision for sustainable existence, both for humans and for the natural world (with the realization that humans are part of the natural world!). This Sabbath tradition and its culmination in the Jubilee tradition, to which we will turn below, create a "covenantal vision of the relation of humans to other life forms" that "acknowledges the special place of humans in this relationship as caretakers, caretakers who did not create and do not absolutely own the rest of life, but who are ultimately accountable for its welfare to the true source of life, God."[42]

EXODUS   Ruether uses the story of the Exodus from Egypt as a model of liberation that can be appropriated by women (and men) today who seek to be liberated from the Pharaoh of patriarchy that enslaves and suffocates the living Spirit in the church. By way of commenting on part of a sermon text that she wrote, Ruether states: "The ancient vision of Church as an exodus community is reworked here, not only to include women but to name patriarchy as the key symbol of the system of 'rape, genocide, and war' that oppresses women, children, and the earth. Men too are called upon to identify with this exodus community and to flee from the idol of patriarchy."[43]

Ruether's vision of Women-Church closely resembles the base ecclesial communities prominent in Latin American liberation theology. Indeed, Ruether even calls these Women-Church communities "feminist base communities."[44] The purpose of such feminist Exodus communities is to provide free space in which new possibilities of authentic Christian community can be envisioned and enfleshed, which in turn can be communicated to the traditional institutional church in the hope of transforming it into a more liberating community. As she states in *Women-Church*, "We must think of Women-Church as a feminist counterculture to the *ecclesia* of patriarchy that must continue for the foreseeable future as an exodus both within and on the edges of existing church institutions."[45]

JUBILEE   The Jubilee tradition from Leviticus 25 provides Ruether with a powerful vision of redemptive living in the here and now. To a degree, the Jubilee tradition is simply a feature of the renewal of covenant faithfulness. It epitomizes what covenant community is all about. Indeed, the "Jubilee teaches that there are certain basic elements that make for life as God intended it on earth. Everyone has their own vine and fig tree. No one is enslaved to another. The land and animals are not overworked."[46] For Ruether, the Jubilee tradition presents a more appropriate model of messianic redemption than the "eschatological endpoint of history does."[47]

It is no accident, therefore, that in a chapter entitled "The New Earth: Visions of Redeemed Society and Nature," in her book *WomanGuides*, what she calls "the Biblical vision" includes three texts: the Jubilee laws from Leviticus 25 (25:10–14, 17, 23–28, 39–42), Isaiah's vision of the messianic age (Isa. 2:1–4, 11:6–9, 40:3–5, 65:17–25), and Jesus' proclamation of good news to the poor (Luke 4:14–21).[48] The Jubilee tradition, which Ruether sees clearly reflected in Jesus' own proclamation from Luke 4,[49] thus functions as a prophetic critique of status quo injustices.

While Ruether recognizes that the Jubilee legislation allows Jews to retain Gentile slaves through the Jubilee year (Lev. 25:44–46), she would no doubt reject this tradition as a betrayal of the Jubilee vision.[50] Similarly, though Ruether acknowledges that it is doubtful whether the Jubilee laws were actually ever fully enacted, the tradition reflects

> a time of periodic righting of unjust relations, undoing the enslavements of human to humans, the losses and confiscations of land, that have created classes of rich and poor in Israel. . . . Their importance . . . lies in providing a model of redemptive eco-justice. Unlike apocalyptic models of redemption, the Jubilee vision does not promise a "once-for-all" destruction of evil. Humans

will drift into unjust relations between each other, they will overwork animals and exploit land. But this drift is not to be allowed to establish itself as a permanent "order." Rather, it is to be recognized as a disorder that must be corrected periodically, so that human society regains its right eco-social relationships and starts afresh.[51]

In this sense, the Jubilee laws are an expression of the prophetic call to covenant faithfulness as it was originally intended by God.

In Ruether's use of all three of these traditions from the Hebrew Bible (covenant, Exodus, and Jubilee), she appropriates these traditions for motifs that she believes can be liberating for faith communities but does not take over any of the themes literally. She is interested in the general motif of covenant as a reciprocal agreement of caring and not in the details of the Abrahamic, Mosaic, and certainly not the Davidic covenants.[52] She uses the Exodus theme as a vision of liberation from oppression: the Hebrews from slavery in Egypt and women (and men) of today from the oppression of patriarchy. She has no use for the Exodus that leads to conquest of another people's land. Similarly, the Jubilee tradition provides a model for restoring right relationships between people and between people and nature on a regular basis, recognizing that because people regularly fall away from the mutual caring intended by God, they need to regularly recommit themselves to such caring as reflected in genuine covenant faithfulness.

TRADITIONS FROM THE NEW TESTAMENT

FROM MARY (MOTHER OF JESUS) . . . One way in which Ruether further develops a constructive vision of prophetic religion, particularly in relation to women, is through her use of the biblical traditions about Mary the mother of Jesus and Mary Magdalene.

In several places throughout her writings, Ruether addresses the figure of Mary the mother of Jesus and the developments of Mariological doctrine throughout church history.[53] Not surprisingly, Ruether rejects most aspects of official Mariological doctrine in the church as simply co-optations of Mary in patriarchal theology. Such doctrines include the perpetual virginity of Mary, her divine maternity, her bodily assumption into heaven, and her immaculate conception.[54] As Ruether notes, the Mary of official church teachings has been Mary the docile and obedient virgin, who in turn has become a patriarchal model that the androcentric church has extolled as embodying (or disembodying) the highest calling for women, namely, to be virgin, mother, and wife (and preferably all three).[55]

There is, for Ruether, an authentic Mariology, which focuses on Mary as representative of pure humanity, humanity in its original goodness and anticipation of the eschatological humanity. In this sense Mary is

> the concrete realization of the possibility of the final glorification of the human community and the creation in that new heaven and new earth when all reality is reconciled with God. In this sense Mary is the *persona ecclesiae,* the new

Israel, the hope of humankind. This is the authentic message of Mariology which is obscured under the false naturalism of nominalism and the antisexuality of the development of the doctrine of the immaculate conception.[56]

In this way, Mary represents neither divine nor human femininity; rather, she represents in concrete terms the "original wholeness of humanity destroyed by sin."[57]

The most useful biblical traditions about Mary come from Luke's Gospel, where in the infancy narrative, Mary appears as an independent and active agent who freely chooses to cooperate with God, rather than as the passive receptacle of Matthew's birth narrative. Indeed, in a section entitled "Liberation Mariology" from *Sexism and God-Talk*, Ruether stresses how "Lucan Mariology suggests a real co-creatorship between God and humanity," which is an authentic insight of genuine prophetic religion and which finds profound expression in Mary's Magnificat.[58]

It is significant, however, that in her book *WomanGuides*, Ruether discusses the Magnificat in the chapter "Redemptive Community," with "Mary as liberated Israel, representative of the oppressed," whereas in the following chapter, "Foremothers of WomanChurch," Mary the mother of Jesus is absent. Instead, one finds there Mary Magdalene, "apostle to the apostles" (John 20:1–18), in the company of other "foremothers": Miriam, Deborah, Huldah, Thecla, Perpetua and Felicitas, and Maximilla and Priscilla.[59] Ruether concludes her chapter on Mariology in *New Woman/New Earth* with the following statement:

> [T]he Mary whom we should venerate may not be Mother Mary, the woman who represents the patriarchal view that woman's only claim to fame is the capacity to have babies, the relationship which Jesus himself rejected. The Mary who represents the Church, the liberated humanity, may, rather, be the repressed and defamed Mary of the Christian tradition, Mary Magdalene, friend and disciple of Jesus, the first witness of the resurrection, the revealer of the Christian Good News. Blessed is the womb that bore thee, the paps that gave thee suck? Nay, rather, blessed is she who heard the Word of God and kept it (cf. Luke 11:27–28). (p. 59)

JESUS THE ICONOCLASTIC TEACHER/HEALER   Ruether's emphasis on concrete historical existence leads her to stress the historicity of Jesus as something necessarily separable from the exalted Christ of Christian dogma. Indeed, she states, because "the centre of Christian theology is not an idea, but a person, a historical person, Jesus of Nazareth, what we can know about who this person was and what he did is of vital importance."[60] Thus, already in her 1967 book, *The Church Against Itself*, Ruether includes a separate chapter entitled "The Jesus of History and the Christ of Faith." She surveys the various quests for the historical Jesus and seems sympathetic with what has been called the "new quest" for the historical Jesus, which seeks "to recover the historical Jesus in the only way possible through the sources; namely, to recover Jesus' historical action as kerygmatic encounter with our own present existence."[61] Thus, for Ruether, one should not jump too quickly from Jesus to Christ, for in so doing, one may actually miss seeing Jesus for who he was (and is).[62]

Who was Jesus? Essentially, Ruether sees Jesus as an iconoclastic and prophetic teacher/healer.[63] Ruether locates Jesus squarely within the critical prophetic tradition of the Hebrew Bible. Indeed, she goes so far as to state that the "Hebrew prophetic critique of religion reaches a climax in the ministry of Jesus."[64] His ministry can be characterized as "a climax" because he actively rejected popular attempts to cast him in the role of a kingly and triumphant (Davidic) Messiah, even though church tradition succeeded in doing so fairly soon after his death. Instead, the core of his messianic activity was opposition to all systems of domination, especially that of religious hierarchy, not in order to reverse the patterns of domination, so that the formerly poor became oppressors of the formerly rich, but to overcome "the whole structure that sets people in oppressive relationships to one another."[65]

An example of Jesus' transformation of systems of domination can be seen in Ruether's "The Kenosis of the Father: A Feminist Midrash on the Gospel in Three Acts," which begins her book *Sexism and God-Talk*, with act 2 entitled "The Iconoclastic Teacher." She offers here a close paraphrasing of Matt. 20:25–28, which shows Jesus as strongly opposed to the theology of glory and revenge articulated by the sons of Zebedee in their request to sit beside Jesus in the kingdom:

> Jesus shook his head with that look of profound sorrow he often had when they spoke to him of their expectations. "No," he insisted, "we must have a different view of the world to come. It must not be a world where one ruler replaces another, but a world where rulers and ruled are no more. Don't you see how much your ideas of power resemble those of the Gentiles? They have rulers who lord it over them; their great men exercise authority over them. But it shall not be so among you. Whoever wishes to be great among you must be as a servant, and whoever would be first must be first in helping others. The Messiah, the One who is to come for which you look, will not come as king, but as servant of all. He will not come to be served, but to serve, and to give his life as ransom for many." (p. 5)[66]

This "annoying message," as she calls it (p. 5), was the hallmark of Jesus' prophetic critique of the status quo powers, including the Jewish religious powers of the day. Jesus' call was for mutual servanthood, not competitive lordship.

A prime example of his iconoclastic message and practice, according to Ruether, is his treatment of women, for he treated women as equals. Here Ruether appeals most forcefully to the story of Mary and Martha in Luke 10:38–42. The simple point of this story is that Jesus "supported their [women's] right to be members of the fellowship of disciples gathered around him, instead of staying in the kitchen and preparing the food, like proper women of Israel."[67] Regarding this passage, Ruether makes the further crucial observation that

> although Jesus held up the image of service to overthrow a ruling-class concept of hierarchical power for men, he does not use this image of service to reinforce

the image of women as servants. On the contrary, the one person whom he rebukes for being "much occupied with serving" is a woman, Martha. . . . "Mary has chosen the better part which shall not be taken from her" (Luke 10:38–42). The principles of Christian community are founded upon a role transformation between men and women, rulers and ruled. The ministry of the Church is not to be modeled on hierarchies of lordship, but on the *diakonia* of women and servants, while women are freed from exclusive identification with the service role and called to join the circle of disciples as equal members.[68]

This is why Jesus commended Mary for listening to his teaching as a disciple, rather than rebuking her for stepping out of her expected servile role. In this story, Mary exemplifies through her actions the kind of iconoclastic message Jesus was teaching. The irony, of course, is that it was not the other, male disciples who asked Jesus to put Mary in her place (i.e., back in the kitchen) but her own sister Martha whose very request for Jesus to rebuke Mary shows that she did not understand the social impact of Jesus' teaching and praxis. Rather, even as a "victim" of patriarchal domination, she bought into the system and expected her sister Mary to toe the same line. Jesus, however, had a different vision, one of equality between women and men.

Along with Jesus' rejection of Davidic messianism and his iconoclastic inclusion of women as equals, Ruether emphasizes that the historical Jesus was not an apocalyptic eschatological preacher. Rather, "Jesus's vision of the kingdom was essentially this-worldly, social and political, and not eschatological. . . . his sayings suggest that his view of the kingdom remains primarily in the prophetic tradition, a vision of a this-worldly era of peace and justice."[69] As evidence of this characterization, Ruether points to Jesus' teaching of the Lord's Prayer, which she considers the saying of Jesus "that most probably comes down to us close to its original form."[70] According to Ruether, the petition "thy kingdom come, thy will be done, on earth as it is in heaven" (Matt. 6:10), is a request that God's dwelling place be established on earth. The kingdom "is defined quite simply as 'God's will done on earth,'" which means "the fulfillment of people's basic human physical and social needs: daily bread, remission of debts [the wronging of others and financial indebtedness], avoidance of the temptations that lead us to oppress one another."[71]

Thus, for Ruether, Jesus' vision of the kingdom is not pie in the heavenly sky, nor is it the sudden apocalyptic inbreaking of God's coming with an army of angels to force the kingdom, but rather, it is primarily a this-worldly undoing of the roots of oppression. Jesus saw these roots as being "the love of prestige, power and wealth that causes people to seek domination and to lord it over each other."[72] Only with the overcoming of "this fundamental lust for domination" can a new community emerge after the pattern set by Jesus' own praxis, one of reciprocal service.[73]

Because Ruether does not consider Jesus' message fundamentally apocalyptic or eschatological, she goes on to argue that "we cannot speak of Jesus as having 'fulfilled' the hopes of Israel," since these hopes were for a Davidic messiah who would usher in God's apocalyptic kingdom and with it the defeat of

Israel's enemies.[74] But such a kingdom did not come in any final or unambiguous form. And so faith in Jesus as the Christ must be reformulated in two ways. First, "Christians must formulate the faith in Jesus as the Christ in terms that are proleptic and anticipatory rather than final and fulfilled. . . . Second, we must see Christology, not only as proleptic, but also as paradigmatic."[75] Jesus announced a new vision of messianic hope, and in his ministry he even gave signs of its presence, but he died before it was fulfilled in any real sense.[76]

Jesus' life is also paradigmatic, but this means that his life is also relative to a particular people in a particular time in a particular place; that is, even Jesus' life must be seen in a radically historical context. The model of Jesus may be as full a paradigm for authentic humanity as we can find, but nonetheless "this model must be seen as partial and fragmentary, disclosing from the perspective of one person, circumscribed in time, culture, and gender, something of the fullness we seek."[77] Thus, Jesus' praxis is paradigmatic but not exhaustive, since his own historicity does not exhaust the concrete historicity of all human beings, especially women. This does not mean that feminist theology cannot affirm the historical Jesus as a "positive model of redemptive humanity," but it does mean that "we need other clues and models as well, models drawn from women's experience, from many times and cultures."[78]

While Jesus may be a starting point for revisioning authentic human existence before God and between one another, especially as he exemplifies the prophetic and redemptive activity of God in the present and the future, even he is not the final word. To "encapsulate Jesus himself as God's 'last word' and 'once-for-all' disclosure of God, located in a remote past and institutionalized in a cast of Christian teachers, is to repudiate the spirit of Jesus and to recapitulate the position against which he himself protests."[79] Thus, Jesus is an essential starting point, especially the Jesus of the synoptic Gospels in contrast to the Jesus of later orthodoxy, but he is not everything. Even so, Ruether is quick to point out that this prophetic iconoclastic Jesus is "remarkably compatible with feminism," because Jesus' critique of religious and social hierarchy is quite parallel to feminist critique of patriarchy and all that goes with it.[80]

Although Ruether is concerned to provide some limits to the significance of Jesus, primarily limits of his own historicity in relation to the limits of our own historicity, she does, nevertheless, characterize him as presenting a liberating image both of God's self-emptying and of human relationality. It seems fitting, then, that since Ruether thinks it important to begin with Jesus and the vision of human existence he models, she paraphrases and models Jesus' parting words from the Gospel of Luke ("Father, into your hands I commend my spirit," Luke 23:46) as she meditates on what parting words might be appropriate before our own death: "Our final gesture, as we surrender ourself into the Matrix of life, then can become a prayer of ultimate trust: 'Mother, into your hands I commend my spirit. Use me as you will in your infinite creativity.' "[81]

PAUL AND KENOTIC CHRISTOLOGY   When it comes to Paul, Ruether clearly has mixed feelings. Her ambivalence can be summed up in her observation that Paul "was a theological radical, but, at least provisionally, a social conserva-

tive." [82] His radical theology can best be seen (and appropriated) in two traditions that most scholars agree Paul adopted from Christian traditions before him,
namely, the hymn to Christ from Phil. 2:5–11 and the baptismal formula from
Gal. 3:28. Ruether uses these traditions in important ways in constructing her
theological vision.

For Ruether, the most useful image from Paul comes from the hymn to
Christ in Phil. 2:5–11. Indeed, as noted in connection with her portrait of Jesus,
Ruether stresses Jesus' identity as servant rather than lord. This can be seen
nowhere more clearly than in the hymn to Christ, which forms the core of
Ruether's "The Kenosis of the Father: A Feminist Midrash on the Gospel in
Three Acts," of which act 1 is entitled "The Kenosis of the Father." This particular act ends with God the bellowing Father coming to the following startling
realization (with the help of the Queen of Heaven [not Mary!], the Mother of
all gods and humans, the Creatrix of all things):

> "Perhaps this hierarchy of earth and heaven is a facade, a delusion, concealing
> other realities that we dare not know. The rebelliousness that I experience
> among my Sons, the rebelliousness that the kings of the earth experience
> among their menservants and, even worse, their maidservants, point to this
> other reality. Perhaps it is She! There is another power outside Our rule that
> still eludes Us!"
>
> "In former times I have known other ways of being God," God the Father
> reflected. 'To put the mighty down from their thrones, to vindicate the op-
> pressed and release the captives from their prisons. I must call to mind these
> ways of being God again, even extend them to others, to slaves, to Gentiles,
> perhaps even to women." A bolt of light flashed from one end of the skies to
> the other, rending the closed fabric of the universe and opening a crack
> through which poured a beam of light from beyond. Like a shooting star this
> light flew to earth. An echo arose from the comet like a whisper through the
> heavens: "Being in the form of God, he did not count equality with God a
> thing to be prized, but emptied himself and became a servant" [Phil. 2:6–7]. [83]

This *kenosis,* or self-emptying, of God the Father is the liberating Word of God
and so "manifests the *kenosis of patriarchy.*" [84] This self-emptying of the mighty
thus becomes the paradigm for how humanity should deal with power; it should
be used on behalf of those in need, as Christ was emptied out in his service to
the poor and the suffering. But such self-emptying is not once for all but is an
ongoing process of transformation. [85]

One interesting facet of Ruether's use of the hymn to Christ from Philippians 2 is that she really only appeals to the process of *kenosis,* to the self-emptying
of the powerful that is the subject of the first half of the hymn (2:5–8). She does
not make constructive use of the second half of the hymn, which highlights
God's exaltation of this Jesus who poured himself out on the cross. Perhaps the
exaltation language smacks too much of the triumphalism that is negated in
the first half of the hymn. Perhaps Ruether finds this transition from *kenosis* to
glorification dangerous, in that it makes self-emptying the means to a more
glorious end rather than focusing on the process of using power in service to

those in need, as Jesus did. Thus, though Ruether does not specifically say as much, perhaps the second half of the hymn can too easily be used to undermine the first half of the hymn, when all the second half of the hymn really expresses is that God is faithful to those who pour themselves out on behalf of others.

As for the famous baptismal formula from Gal. 3:28 ("There is no longer Jew or Greek, there is no longer slave or free, there is no longer male and female; for all of you are one in Christ Jesus"), Ruether refers to this passage often but primarily to show the clear understanding at least in some quarters of earliest Christianity that Jesus' teachings and praxis were perceived to have profound implications for male/female relationships, indeed for all hierarchical relationships.[86] The significance of the understanding was that God sought the elimination of systems of domination and hierarchy, of one person or class lording it over another, because of their destructive and dehumanizing impact. Jesus also showed that God sought the undermining of all attempts to justify such patterns of domination.

While Paul could affirm this theological vision in principle, and even to a degree in practice, given the prominence of various women in the churches with which he was associated, he had trouble realizing the full significance of this vision in the face of the social values of hierarchy and domination which confronted him on a daily basis in first-century Greco-Roman society. Thus, one must be wary of Paul's social conservatism, which was reinforced by his apocalyptic eschatological expectations about the return of Christ in power and the coming end of the age. His social conservatism finds expression especially in such passages as 1 Cor. 11:3, which articulates a hierarchical vision of man over woman; in Romans 5–7, where Paul expounds his dualistic, flesh-versus-spirit vision of life; and in the deutero-Pauline traditions, especially the hierarchical understanding of the church as the body under Christ's head, analogous to the relation of husband as head and woman as body, in Ephesians 5; and the social conservatism of the household codes, with their clear subordination of women in Colossians and in 1 Timothy.

The fundamental problem with Paul, according to Ruether, is his eschatological dualism, which leads to the dualism of body and spirit. Since Paul expects the end to come soon, he counsels being prepared and being concerned with the transformation of oneself in the context of the Christian community rather than with God's transformation of all human relations and their societal structures. For Paul, the dominating powers of the present age are soon to pass, with the coming of Christ on the clouds in glory (1 Thess. 4). Thus, one's current transformation in Christ is but a foreshadowing of a greater transformation that awaits the Christian, the spiritual body of the resurrected life. And for Ruether, this otherworldliness of Paul moves in the wrong direction. "The problem in Paul's thought lies in the extent to which he identifies this evil condition with natural or created life, and thus sees redeemed life as something fundamentally transcendent to our original, created potential."[87]

One place where Ruether spells out her understanding of Paul most clearly, especially in relation to women, is in an article comparing Paul's thought with that of Sarah Grimké (the nineteenth-century American abolitionist). Paul and Grimké represent two different paradigms of women's equality in Christ. "Each paradigm relates nature, society and eschatology in different ways and comes up with radically different conclusions about the social implications of women's place in both nature and in the new Christian order."[88] Though Paul can articulate a vision of the radical equality between men and women within the churches, expressed most clearly in such passages as Gal. 3:28 and Phil. 4:3, from Ruether's perspective "Paul draws the line where these changed roles in and for the church suggest a dissolution of male hierarchy in the family."[89]

Even if one dismisses from consideration the deutero-Pauline Epistles of Ephesians, Colossians, 1 Timothy, and Titus, as well as the possible interpolation of 1 Cor. 14:34, there are still at least two passages that show the limitations of Paul's approach: 1 Cor. 7:17–40 and 1 Cor. 11:2–16. In 1 Cor. 7:17–40, Paul equates slavery and marriage with the passing form of the present world. But, as Ruether notes, as passing forms they cannot be altered. For Paul, "eschatology gives the Christian no mandate to change slavery or sexism as worldly institutions."[90] Until the powers of the external world are dissolved by Christ's return, we simply must endure these fixed, though transient, forms of servitude.

Similarly, Paul's arguments in 1 Cor. 11:2–16 for the veiling of women in the assembly are grounded in a view of women's subordination to men, both in the created order and in social custom. Such subordination language clearly undercuts the theology of women's equality with men in Christ. Ruether acknowledges Paul's own apparent unease with his justifications for the subordination of women, and she notes Paul does try to preserve mutual interdependence between men and women in the created order, but ultimately in the context of the subordination of women to men. When all is said and done, Paul sticks to his requirement that women wear a veil when prophesying, and so he "brings together in sharp relief the contradiction between women's eschatological equality and their continued subordination in what Paul assumes to be the 'order of nature.'"[91] Equality stops when it changes social roles. And so Paul sets the stage for the continued subordination of women in the church for centuries to follow, with new justifications and rationalizations cropping up along the way.

For Ruether, Sarah Grimké provides a preferable alternative paradigm to that of Paul, for Grimké was a woman who advanced theological rationales for ending slavery (and women's subordination) here and now, rather than leaving it to some eschatological by and by.[92] She insisted that equality in Christ has social and not just spiritual implications. The eschatological future now becomes the eschatological present, for life in Christ means the restoration of God's created order, the redemption of life in the present. As Ruether points out, Sarah Grimké and her sister, Angelina Grimké, were among the first to note the similarity and to develop parallel arguments for the rights of both slaves and women.[93]

Obviously, Ruether prefers Grimké's line of reasoning to Paul's. And so from Paul she adopts his language of *kenosis* and his occasional affirmations of equality of men and women in the churches. But she eschews his social conservatism, which was at least partly based on his future eschatology, and sides with Grimké's emphasis on wholesale transformation and renewal of human relationships in Christ here and now.

. . . TO MARY (MAGDALENE)   The prominence of Mary Magdalene for Ruether can be seen most clearly in her book *Sexism and God-Talk*, with its playful beginning, "The Kenosis of the Father: A Feminist Midrash on the Gospel in Three Acts." After act 1 ("The Kenosis of the Father") and act 2 ("The Iconoclastic Teacher"), act 3 is entitled "Mary Magdalene's Witness." (Already in act 2 Ruether remarks that there was "a closeness between these two [Jesus and Mary Magdalene] that was annoying to the men" [p.6]) In act 3, Mary Magdalene sits by the tomb of Jesus after his death and burial. The disciples have scattered. Jesus then appears to her and tells her that he is risen. As the image of Jesus fades, Mary sees "a taller and more majestic image, regal and yet somehow familiar, a woman like herself," who addresses Mary: "You, Mary, . . . are now the continuing presence of Christ. Do not look backward to him, but forward. He has gone ahead into your new future. It is for you to continue the redemption of the world." (p. 8).

With this vision, Mary Magdalene realizes why Jesus had to die, namely, to teach his followers that they must abandon the longing for power and revenge. Mary then thinks what is so crucial to Ruether's understanding of Christian faith: "We must make our selves and our relationships with each other anew. This is the beginning of the new world. Only when we are no longer slaves, but also no longer desire to be masters and to make our former masters into slaves, can we lay the foundation for the world to come" (p. 9). Mary goes to Peter and the (male) disciples and tells them of her experience of the risen Jesus, and she tries to communicate to them this new understanding she has come to have about his ministry and death, but they cannot believe that Jesus would appear first to a woman and not to them. Peter then picks up on her testimony that Jesus has risen but ignores the rest of what she has said. Peter tells the disciples that their hopes of a powerful messianic king are not shattered but only postponed for a short time. Jesus will return from heaven with an army of angels. In the meantime, the men must take charge, lest they look too foolish and weak.

Mary slips away from the founding of the (male) church. And as she looks toward the sky, she wonders about what Peter has said. What is she to make of God's silence when Jesus cried out from the cross? What is she to make of Peter's trust in the coming of an avenging God? And so, Ruether has her think:

> Perhaps it is this very idea of God as a great king, ruling over nations as His servants, that has been done away with by Jesus' death on the cross. With Jesus' death, God, the heavenly Ruler, has left the heavens and has been poured out upon the earth with his blood. A new God is being born in our hearts to teach us to level the heavens and exalt the earth and create a new world without masters and slaves, rulers and subjects." (pp. 10–11)

But Mary realizes that her message will not easily be received by Peter and the others, who even now were busy filling the throne that Jesus had just emptied on the cross. She can only hope that others will catch a glimpse of the true vision she has had and so continue to create the world that Jesus had begun, a world to which she would remain a faithful witness.

As Ruether relates this story about Mary Magdalene, it is clear that for her Mary Magdalene represents what it means to be a faithful disciple. Mary Magdalene was at the cross of Jesus. Mary Magdalene was at the tomb of Jesus. Mary Magdalene was witness to the risen Jesus. Mary Magdalene became apostle to the apostles. As Ruether puts it in her book on Mary the mother of Jesus, *Mary—The Feminine Face of the Church*, Mary Magdalene is "an unconventional woman" who challenges the model for women articulated by the later official church tradition, a tradition that suppresses the role of Mary Magdalene and groundlessly aligns her with the nameless prostitute of Luke 7:36–50. For Ruether, she represents a positive "role model for women that later church leaders probably preferred to neglect!" (p. 40).

By contrast, Mary the mother of Jesus represents "a conventional woman," a woman who even against the teaching of Jesus and the testimony of the earliest church (Mark 3:31–35; Matt. 12:46–50; Luke 8:19–21, 11:27–28) comes to represent the faithful woman at Jesus' side. As Ruether puts it,

> By replacing Mary Magdalene with Mary, the mother, as the "woman who loved him," the church replaced a dangerously unconventional role model with a conventional role model and relationship. . . . It is the woman disciple, Mary Magdalene, who puts to shame not only the family but also the male disciples by her faith and her steadfastness at the final time of crisis. These facts must make us put a question mark beside the tradition of Mary, Jesus' mother, as the woman who best represents "the church." (p. 41)[94]

Ruether's View of the Authority of Scripture

Women's Experience as Normative

Given Ruether's understanding of the character of Scripture as "human words about God's word," it comes as no surprise that Ruether does not locate any final authority within the objective text of Scripture.[95] Rather, we must see that Scripture itself is merely a reflection of human experiences, experiences of people seeking to hear and to enact God's word.[96] "Codified tradition both reaches back to roots in experience and is constantly renewed or discarded through the test of experience."[97] Thus, Scripture has authority only when the experiences it relates of God's Spirit and God's word resonate with the contemporary reader's experiences of God's Spirit and God's word, especially in the context of the community of believers. As Ruether puts it, the human words about God's word in Scripture attempt to express God's Word within their finite cultural contexts, but they remain finite and historical. Their authority is relativised in relation to the divine Word which is manifest in them, but not exhaustively manifest in them. This inner or divine Word finds its primary communication in the living personal relationship of man to God. This is revelation, this is the "inner word"; and all "outer words," whether of scripture, tradition, theology, or law, are as tracks left in the sand by the passing of the living personal relationship of the community with God.[98]

Thus, human experience tests Scripture's various human words about God's word, and we find Scripture's words "are either authenticated or not through their ability to illuminate and interpret our experience. . . . If a symbol does not speak authentically to experience, it becomes dead or must be altered to provide a new meaning."[99]

Human experience, then, provides the ultimate norm of whether Scripture speaks with authority or not, of how Scripture is normative or not in changing contexts. For Ruether, this has always been the case, whether acknowledged or not, though completely skewed in an androcentric direction. What is new in her approach, then, is not its use of experience as normative "but rather in its use of *women's* experience. . . . The use of women's experience in feminist theology, therefore, explodes as a critical force, exposing classical theology, including its codified traditions, as based on *male* experience rather than on universal human experience."[100] Of course, this statement begs the question of what counts as "universal human experience," especially since all experience is, as Ruether is quick to show, particular and limited by specific historical situations. But I will return to this question at the end of the chapter.

Finally, Ruether points out that feminist theology does not rise out of generic women's experience, as if there were such a thing, but from feminist women's experience in particular:

> I suggest that feminism starts not with scripture or tradition but with the feminist experience of women affirming themselves as autonomous persons, not only in legal and political relations, but also in sexual relations. It is often said that feminist hermeneutics starts with "experience," but what is left unsaid in this formula is that the experience that is assumed here is feminist experience. By feminist experience is meant a consciousness-raising experience in which women shake off their indoctrination into feeling themselves dependent and inferior and claim themselves as fully capable of self-determination.[101]

An Open Canon

When starting with women's experience, it is crucial to understand that many (most) women have experienced (male) appeals to biblical authority as dehumanizing and oppressive, for the Bible has been used as a weapon against the inclusion of women and against seeing women as fully human moral agents time and again. The very development of the New Testament canon, for example, shows an increasing emphasis upon the subordination of women both in the church and in the home (e.g., 1 Timothy, Ephesians),[102] as Christianity adopted and lightly baptized the traditional patriarchal household codes of Greco-Roman society as part of its bid for greater respectability and acceptance in the Greco-Roman world of the first few centuries C.E. What began as an egalitarian and countercultural vision of redeemed human communities in the ministry of Jesus devolved into the continued sacralization of patriarchy and dominating hierarchies in the development of early Christianity. According to Ruether, then, what was canonized in the New Testament in large part reflects exactly the kind of traditions against which Jesus spoke. If this is the case, "then the authority of the official canonical framework is overturned. . . . In the New Testament a suppressed tradition must be brought to the surface to criticize and refute the dominant hermeneutical line established by those who shaped the written canon."[103]

But Ruether's notion is still more radical. Not only must Christians today recover the more authentic and often buried traditions of the liberating and egalitarian message and praxis of Jesus and earliest Christianity, but Christians today must not be content simply with a past collection of writings, for in principle we must never close the canon. This is because implicit in the Jesus movement

> is a challenge to religious authority embodied in past revelation and institutionalized in the hands of a privileged group of interpreters. Jesus declares that God has not just spoken in the past but is speaking *now*. Prophecy is not canonized in past texts; the Spirit of God speaks today. . . . Jesus frees religious experience from the fossilization of past traditions.[104]

Jesus was not content merely to repeat and slightly reinterpret codified texts from the past. Rather, he directly challenged traditions, even time-honored traditions, that were not in keeping with his understanding of God's word as it was breaking into the world through him. And so he can say, "You have heard it said of old . . . , but I say to you" (Matt. 5).

Thus, for Ruether, we are not bound and should not bind ourselves exclusively to the canonized Scriptures. Rather, just as Jesus criticized some of the central aspects embedded in the Scriptures that he inherited, so are Christians today to be engaged in critical reading of the Scriptures that we have inherited. To do otherwise is to risk missing the Spirit of God as it speaks today, both through and against the canonical writings of Scripture. As Jesus did, "so feminism, too, recognizing that patriarchal texts deform the liberating spirit for women, rejects a theology confined to commentary on past texts."[105] It is no accident, then, that in her book *WomanGuides*, Ruether is rather self-consciously seeking to offer readings toward a new working canon, for feminist theology "must create a new textual base, a new canon" (p. ix).[106]

> Feminist theology cannot be done from the existing base of the Christian Bible. The Old and New Testaments have been shaped in their formation, their transmission, and, finally, their canonization to sacralize patriarchy. They may pre-

serve, between the lines, memories of women's experience. But in their present form and intention they are designed to erase women's existence as subjects and to mention women only as objects of male definition. In these texts the norm for women is absence and silence. . . . Thus the doing of feminist theology demands a new collection of texts to make women's experience visible. (pp. ix–x)

How does one select new texts for a working canon? There is no magic formula; rather, one primarily discovers that a text speaks to and reflects one's experience, in both individual and communal contexts. One discerns God's Spirit, God's word, speaking in and through a text. Nor are we bound exclusively to past texts, for "we are also free to generate new stories from our own experience that may, through community use, become more than personal or individual" (p. 247).

Such a process has its dangers, of course, for people are not likely to choose texts that are challenging, with the result that even new working canons will probably tend to sacralize the particular experiences and understandings of those choosing the texts. It is up to others in the community (men and women), then, to criticize the sacralization of texts and experiences that are dehumanizing and demeaning. This does not mean that one should necessarily literally throw out such texts. Indeed, Ruether suggests that "Women-Church could also study texts that consciously intend to repress women, such as the story of Eve or I Timothy's dictum that women should keep silence" (p. 136). The purpose of such study would not be to give these texts any authority but to seek evidence of the liberating communities against which such texts speak.

Exorcism of Patriarchal Texts

How then does one deal with oppressive patriarchal biblical traditions to which an androcentric church has appealed to keep women in subordinate roles? One of the most remarkable sections concerning Scripture in Ruether's writings is a liturgy[107] she includes in her book *Women-Church*, in a chapter entitled "Creating Women-Church." She comments:

Since patriarchal texts have exercised such coercive influence on our lives, although perhaps more so among Protestants who give primary authority to Scripture, it is useful as one Women-Church ritual to exorcise patriarchal texts and thus to break their oppressive power over their lives. This does not mean that one would never study biblical texts again, but rather that one can study them in the full freedom of the Spirit, taking the goal of liberation from patriarchy as our norm. (p. 136)

Ruether then relates a sample exorcism rite, which has been used in various feminist liturgies. Ruether gives the following guidelines on the setting and the procedure: "A small table with a bell, a candle, and the Bible are assembled in the center of the group. A series of texts with clearly oppressive intentions are read. After each reading, the bell is rung as the reader raises up the book. The community cries out in unison, 'Out, demons, out!' " (p. 137). She then provides a list of "suggested texts in need of exorcism." They include Lev. 12:1–5 (unclean-liness of women after childbirth); Exod. 19:1, 7–9, 14–15 (shunning of women during giving of the Law at Sinai); Judges 19 (rape, torture, and dismemberment of the concubine); Eph. 5:21–23 (male headship over women compared to the relation of Christ and the church); 1 Tim. 2:11–15 (women to keep silent in church and to be saved by bearing children because they are second in creation and first in sin); 1 Pet. 2:18–20 (slaves exhorted to accept unjust suffering from their masters as a way of sharing in Christ's crucifixion). Interestingly, Ruether includes no sayings of Jesus among these texts, indeed no Gospel traditions at all, and only includes Old Testament and deutero-Pauline materials, though we might suspect that some of Paul's own statements might be appropriate for exorcism from the perspective of Women-Church (e.g., 1 Cor. 11:2–16).

At the end of the exorcism rite, "someone says, 'These texts and all oppressive texts have lost their power over our lives. We no longer need to apologize for them or try to interpret them as words of truth, but we cast out their oppressive message as expressions of evil and justifications of evil' " (p. 137). And so ends this particular liturgy.

Immediately following the rite of exorcism of patriarchal texts, Ruether includes a "Litany of Disaffiliation from Patriarchal Theology," which includes the rejection of various statements from such church figures as Tertullian, Augustine, Aquinas, Luther, Barth, and the 1976 Vatican Declaration on Women's Ordination. After each reading of a patriarchal passage from the authors, those assembled say, "From the evil power of this tradition, O Holy Wisdom, deliver us" (pp. 139–40). Thus, all patriarchal traditions, biblical or from church tradition, are lifted up for critique and rejection.

Scripture: One Foundation Among Several

Finally, for Ruether Scripture cannot stand alone as a foundational source for theological reflection and construction (and in practice it has never really stood alone). Rather, Scripture provides one source among several upon which Christians, and Women-Church in particular, can and should draw. In *Sexism and God-Talk*, Ruether identifies five sources of "usable tradition": (1) Scripture, (2) marginalized or "heretical" Christian traditions (especially radical Christian groups such as Gnostics, Montanists, Quakers, and Shakers), (3) the central theological traditions of dominant/classical Christian theology (from orthodox, Catholic, and Protestant traditions), (4) non-Christian Near Eastern and Greco-Roman religious and philosophical traditions (which have given shape to many aspects of Christianity), and (5) critical post-Christian worldviews (liberalism, romanticism, Marxism) (pp. 21–22).

All these traditions are used in conjunction with the others, and each of them presents significant critiques of the others. The result is that one has access to a dynamic collection of traditions where one tradition can act as a check or a corrective on another tradition. Most important, however, none of these traditions are taken over completely, but all are used in keeping with feminist critical principles, namely, in light of feminist hermeneutics.

Ruether's Hermeneutics

Correlating Critical Principles of Feminism and the Bible

In her book *Sexism and God-Talk*, Ruether articulates what she calls "the critical principle of feminist theology."[108] Simply put, the critical principle is that women are and should be treated as fully human, as individual moral agents in their own right. The critical principle is

> the promotion of the full humanity of women. Whatever denies, diminishes, or distorts the full humanity of women is, therefore, appraised as not redemptive. Theologically speaking, whatever diminishes or denies the full humanity of women must be presumed not to reflect the divine or an authentic relation to the divine. . . . This negative principle also implies the positive principle: what does promote the full humanity of women is of the Holy, it does reflect true relation to the divine. . . . But the meaning of this positive principle—namely, the full humanity of women—is not fully known. It has not existed in history. What we have known is the negative principle of the denigration and marginalization of women's humanity. (pp. 18–19)

When this critical principle is applied to Scripture, those traditions that promote the full humanity of women are expressions of the divine and so are authentic and authoritative traditions. But even these positive traditions were formulated in highly androcentric contexts, and therefore, they must be recontextualized to reflect liberation from patriarchy.[109]

For Ruether, the primary biblical texts that pass the basic test of feminist theology's critical principle can be characterized as "the prophetic-liberating tradition," a tradition examined above.[110] Ruether sees this prophetic tradition not simply as one among many themes in the Bible but as a "tradition that can be fairly claimed, on the basis of generally accepted Biblical scholarship, to be *the central tradition*, the tradition by which Biblical faith constantly criticizes and renews itself and its own vision."[111]

The primary reason she values the prophetic tradition above all others is that it is self-consciously self-critical of the larger dominant tradition in which it stands. Thus, the prophets often spoke on behalf of God against the very institutions (temple, cult, king) that presented themselves as representing God to the people, and the people to God. Prophetic critique, then, is the internal critical principle of biblical faith itself that is ever being renewed through its application to new situations.[112]

The question, then, is how one constructively links the critical principle of biblical faith (the prophetic tradition) with the critical principle of feminist theology (the full humanity of women). Ruether makes this link through what she terms "the feminist radicalizing of the prophetic tradition." [113] Essentially, feminist theology is nothing but a new and long overdue expression of the prophetic tradition, with patriarchy and androcentrism as the sacralized targets in need of sharp and prolonged critique, even if Scripture itself forms part of the target. [114]

When reading Scripture, we must be honest about when its traditions reflect the dehumanization of women, and such texts must then be subjected to the liberating norm of the prophetic tradition, critiqued, and rendered powerless. As Ruether points out:

> The answer of Christian tradition to the vital issues of our times, then, turns out to be double edged. On the one hand, we must confront the fact that scripture and theology have contributed to these very evils that trouble us. They have functioned as sanctions of evil. Yet we discover within the prophetic tradition and the gospels essential resources to unmask these very failures of religion. [115]

Feminist biblical interpretation, then, is a necessary extension of the long established hermeneutical tradition of prophetic critique, and as such it continues the process of the very hermeneutic internal to Scripture itself, "whereby the text is reinterpreted in the context of new communities of critical consciousness." [116]

The Hermeneutical Circle

Another dimension central to Ruether's hermeneutic is the plain acknowledgment that when we read the Bible, we do so with our own questions, concerns, and presuppositions in mind. [117] Thus, we are necessarily engaged in a hermeneutical circle, a dialogue (sometimes monologue) between Scripture and contemporary concerns. "We must be questioned by but also be prepared to question scripture." [118] It is safe to say, however, that Ruether finds the Bible so overtly androcentric and patriarchal that more often than not we find ourselves in the position of questioning and challenging Scripture rather than the reverse. But engaging in critique of Scripture in this way is both rooted in and simply an expression of "the self-criticism that goes on in and is basic to biblical faith itself." [119]

Thus, one cannot and should not escape the hermeneutical circle that moves from experience to experience, from the experience reflected in the various biblical writings to the experience of the contemporary reader/believer who identifies with the tradition generated by the foundational experiences of the biblical writings. [120] One is never finished, either individually or communally, with reappropriating and resignifying the central themes of Scripture in new and changing times. Such is the dynamic character of prophetic critique. Such is the perpetual call of God.

How does one test the new meanings given to Scripture in light of feminist prophetic critique? The authenticity or validity of a new interpretation enters into the same hermeneutical circle that generated it in the first place. A new interpretation will be experienced as either liberating or enslaving (or, of course, somewhere in between). If it is liberating and so promotes the full humanity of women, without at the same time dehumanizing others, it will legitimately be affirmed by the authorizing community as a genuine interpretation, for it leads to practices of mutuality and reciprocity and to advocacy on behalf of the disenfranchised rather than to practices of oppressive hierarchical domination. Essentially, if it is authentic, it will be experienced as such. And so the cycle of interpretation and reinterpretation in light of human (female and male) experience will continue.

Ruether and the Significance of Scripture for Ethics

What is the practical impact of Ruether's approach to and use of Scripture? Her approach allows her to use parts of Christian tradition in constructing a liberating theological vision. It allows her to be honest about the relationship, often conflicted, between the "tradition" of her own experiences as a woman and the tradition of patriarchal, androcentric, American Roman Catholicism, along with its authorizing Scriptures, a tradition into which she was born and within which she grew up.

Her approach to Scripture means that she is not bound by traditions she finds oppressive and that she does not have to hypocritically finesse such traditions (as much of Christian tradition does) but can call them by name, identify them as demonic, reject their authority, and move on to liberating traditions. As a historian, she can understand how and why patriarchal traditions developed as they did, but such understanding does not mean that one is powerless to comment on the problems with the traditions. She feels free, then, to look at the entire biblical canon with noncanonical eyes and so to discern the themes and texts which feed and nurture a vision of human community that she can live with and see as coming from God and authenticated by experience.

When she takes over the themes of covenant, Exodus, and Jubilee from the Hebrew Bible, she does so because these traditions help to establish and to renew human communities in which people live in authentic and loving relationships with God, with one another, with the created world, and with themselves. She encourages people to enter into mutual covenants where all parties to the covenant are equals, where reciprocal care is demonstrated.

She encourages people to "exodus" from exploitive and oppressive situations, relationships, and communities, and to do so as an act to which God calls them. Thus, battered women should leave relationships of physical and psychological abuse and enter into new relationships that provide sanctuary and healing, relationships that lead to a new and liberating place.

On a regular basis, communities of people should look again at their communities and should undo oppressive relationships that have developed, whether economic, social, or religious in character. Covenanted communities should be aware of the human propensity to acquire dominating power and should develop structures to hold such propensities in check. The Jubilee traditions remind us, as they reminded the Israelites, that both in principle and in practice just and righteous relationships mean the empowering of the powerless, even when this means rendering the powerful less powerful.

The usable traditions from the New Testament help to articulate a vision that Ruether closely identifies with the historical Jesus. As Jesus criticized and rejected the hierarchical domination of religious and social elites over the people, so does Ruether encourage a similar criticism and rejection of ecclesiastical structures that create a great divide between clergy and laity (Ruether also challenges the hierarchalism of the academic world). The status quo calls for constant prophetic critique.

As Jesus renounced triumphalism and, from her perspective, a theology of apocalyptic revenge, so does Ruether encourage the renunciation of power over others as well as the rejection of a theology that makes permanent enemies of those who have been oppressors. This is one reason why Ruether is ultimately uncomfortable with the approach of Mary Daly, for Ruether sees Daly's theology as simply replacing patriarchy with matriarchy, replacing one oppressive system with another.

As Jesus identified with the poor and the outcast, so does Ruether encourage Christians today to identify with the poor and the outcast of today's world; she especially lifts up the poorest of the poor, women. In this regard, Ruether finds Paul's kenotic Christology a helpful model. When the powerful empty themselves of power in service to those who are powerless, then does reconciliation and renewed community take place.

Finally, Ruether's use of the traditions about Mary the mother of Jesus and about Mary Magdalene has a rather direct and pragmatic consequence. Humanity is not ultimately in a hopeless situation, forever and irreversibly doomed by sin; rather, as illustrated by Mary the mother of Jesus, we have reason to be hopeful that the full humanity of all people can be envisioned ever anew, for God seeks the restoration of authentic human relationships. As Mary actively and independently chose to cooperate with God's redemption of humanity, so Ruether suggests that people today have the same capacity and the same choice.

And as Mary Magdalene broke out of the conventional patriarchal repression that had long bound women in powerless servitude to men and male culture, so Ruether challenges women (and men) today to iconoclastically break the status quo conventions of repression which continue to bind people in powerless servitude. Ruether also sees Mary Magdalene as one who challenged the early church's deformation of Jesus' prophetic message and praxis into a new patriarchal and hierarchical status quo. Therefore, she is a model for debunking and challenging the processes by which the dynamic and liberating ministry of Jesus is deformed into a fossilized religion which merely sacralizes the past rather than giving birth to new expressions of a liberating community of equals.

Critical Evaluation

Ruether's approach to and use of Scripture have been criticized on several fronts, from traditional to more radical forms of Christianity. From the more traditional side, for example, Elizabeth Achtemeier accuses Ruether and other feminists of uncritically accepting all lifestyles. Referring to Ruether's book *Women-Church*, Achtemeier writes: "Thus, Ruether has written liturgies brimming over with acceptance—of extra-marital sex, of lesbian 'marriage,' of any divorce or abortion, even of female narcissistic examination of their bodies and menstrual blood. Anything is acceptable if one has no standard of judgment."[121] It is incorrect to say that Ruether has no standard of judgment. Ruether's standard is simply rather different from the one Achtemeier finds appropriate. To put it strongly, Achtemeier's critique comes across as a rather prudish endorsement of patriarchal values that ignores the standard of judgment that Ruether articulates (reciprocity, mutuality, full humanity).[122]

Most significant, however, are the critiques that other feminists have offered of Ruether's work. Elisabeth Schüssler Fiorenza, for example, has criticized Ruether for taking a neo-orthodox approach to the Bible that idealizes the prophetic tradition and fails to see the androcentric elements of the traditions themselves:

> In the last analysis, reduction of the Bible to the prophetic-messianic tradition on the one hand and the concomitant reduction of this tradition to an abstract dehistoricized critical key on the other hand indicates that Ruether's hermeneutical proposal is more neo-orthodox than she perceives it to be. It serves more to rescue biblical religion from its feminist critics than to develop a feminist historical hermeneutics that could incorporate . . . [a] feminist spiritual quest for women's power.[123]

Ruether does refer to the prophetic tradition in a collective sense, rarely differentiating the various prophetic writings from one another in terms of social and historical location, so it is possible to see why Schüssler Fiorenza characterizes Ruether's appeal to the prophetic tradition as overly idealized. And yet, Ruether regularly emphasizes the centrality of historical concreteness and recognizes that even the prophetic traditions can perpetuate androcentric values.[124]

In her own review of Schüssler Fiorenza's *In Memory of Her*, Ruether responds directly to Schüssler Fiorenza's critique of her own work:

> First of all, I do not subscribe to a timeless essence versus historical accidents model of truth. Rather what I have tried to describe is a certain liberating "dynamic" which is expressed in the prophetic messianic tradition, and also, in secular form, in modern liberation movements, which have unacknowledged roots in biblical faith.[125]

Indeed, Ruether sees Schüssler Fiorenza's own approach to Scripture as being fairly similar to her own: "[D]oes not Fiorenza have a fairly similar 'prophetic-liberating norm' by which she judges what is truth and falsehood, good and bad, in early Christian texts, once it is clear that what we are both talking about is not 'timeless truth,' but community-based experience in historical social contexts?"[126]

Carol Christ is also critical of Ruether's use of the prophetic tradition as normative. Her central critique is that "even the traditions Ruether cites as liberating are themselves part of an oppressive patriarchal theology and not themselves adequate models for feminist theology and spirituality."[127] Like Schüssler Fiorenza, Christ argues that Ruether has idealized the prophetic-messianic tradition to the point of ignoring significantly patriarchal and destructive aspects of the tradition. For example, whereas Ruether claims that "the Bible for the most part, is not written from the standpoint of world power, but from the standpoint of people who take the side of the disadvantaged,"[128] Christ is not convinced that the evidence is so straightforward or simple. Christ points out that much of the Bible, and even the prophetic traditions, in fact reflect "a relatively comfortable, urban (and it should be added misogynist) priestly class. . . . Though I too find some of the ethical injunctions of the prophets inspiring, I find them embedded in a patriarchal 'Yahweh alone' theology, which I find problematic."[129] Christ finds the prophetic traditions laced with a vindictive and intolerant approach to other religious traditions.

Again, although one can understand Christ's reading of Ruether in this regard, in later writings (1983) Ruether does state that we must be wary of "revenge theology," and she warns about the danger of "the deformation of prophetic themes into ideology." Ruether states: "It is important to see that the prophetic-liberating tradition is not and cannot be made into a static set of 'ideas.' Rather it is a plumb line of truth and untruth, justice and injustice, that has to be constantly adapted to changing social contexts and circumstances."[130]

Finally, along similar lines as Christ and Schüssler Fiorenza, Rebecca Chopp criticizes Ruether's use of the prophetic tradition:

> [W]e can see the limitation of Ruether's methodological construction in the prophetic-liberating tradition of biblical faith, a molding of Christian theology into an ideology critique that successfully raises consciousness, but is, itself, problematic due to its failure of historical accuracy and its inability to identify already existing practices of subversion and transformation. . . . Is such a thing as the prophetic-liberating tradition not an abstract formulation of Christianity, a formulation that prevents a thick description of Christian practices showing the relation of power, language, institutions, and subjectivity?[131]

Essentially, then, two criticisms stand out in these various responses to Ruether's use of prophetic traditions. First, although Ruether warns against the danger of ideology, she herself seems to construct just such an ideology with the use of "the prophetic principle." Second, although throughout her work Ruether emphasizes the need to deal with concrete history, and not abstract themes, she herself does not deal with the prophetic traditions in a sufficiently historical manner. Is her own historical reconstruction overly positivist and is it sufficiently critical? These two problems threaten to undermine her use of the Bible at its very heart.

I would agree that these are problems in Ruether's use of the Bible, though Ruether does seem to be aware of how the cutting edge of prophetic critique can be dulled into a rather flat ideology. I would pose the question, however, from another side. First, when Ruether lifts up internal prophetic critique as a dynamic constructive model, it begs the question: who critiques the prophets? Other prophets? The community? How does one discern which prophets speak on behalf of God? Ruether does lay down some guidelines, namely, that authentic prophetic voices speak on behalf of the poor and the oppressed and against dominating patriarchal hierarchies. But are these sufficient? When the prophetic message of Jeremiah conflicts with the prophetic message of Hananiah (Jer. 27–28), to whom should we listen? In counseling to surrender to the Babylonians, could not Jeremiah be interpreted as giving in to the powerful empire and Hananiah as speaking up for the poor, oppressed vassal remnant of Judah? Does not Jeremiah say that it is better to live even in an oppressive situation than to protest enslavement and risk death? Or would Ruether align herself against the biblical tradition in this instance and side with Hananiah, who counseled hope in deliverance from the Babylonians? So who critiques the prophets? When does prophetic critique become inverted so that it too functions as yet another expression of the status quo? Is a prophet only iconoclastic, or can a prophet also offer words of healing? (Or is iconoclasm the first step toward healing?) Is prophetic critique of prophetic critique ever appropriate?

Second, Ruether asserts that the prophetic-liberating tradition "can be fairly claimed, on the basis of generally accepted Biblical scholarship, to be the central tradition" of the Bible.[132] And we must ask, is that really the case? Is it the case that the prophetic tradition is the most central, and even if it is, do most biblical scholars (to whom she makes a surprising and perhaps unnecessary appeal in this regard) construe the prophetic tradition as Ruether has done? And does not Ruether's appeal to the prophetic tradition as "the central tradition" lend credence to the claim that she is constructing an abstract ideal out of a recurring theme? If one is looking for a central tradition, why not choose covenant (as Paul Ramsey has done)? Or why not creation and salvation (so important for Gutiérrez)? And so again, we must ask if Ruether has sufficiently taken into account the problems of claiming the prophetic tradition as the core biblical principle.

A third problem has to do with Ruether's characterization of Jesus. As she herself comments, in agreement with Schweitzer's analysis before her, interpreters tend to portray Jesus after their own image. And so we must ask, has Ruether constructed an iconoclastic Jesus after her own iconoclastic self? Is she overly confident about her ability to locate the historical Jesus stripped of the doctrinal accretions that have shaped his image already in the earliest layers of the New Testament? I imagine that if Ruether were convinced that in fact Jesus was the wild-eyed apocalyptic preacher that Schweitzer and others claimed he was,

Ruether would simply reject this aspect of the historical Jesus as being useless tradition and reiterate the traditions from and about Jesus that were usable.

In conclusion, although there are problems with Ruether's use of Scripture, in the end I find her approach to the Bible both challenging and refreshing. Ruether forces one to think through how and why the Bible is used as it is in the church. She does try to recover from all too often fossilized texts and fossilized interpretations of the texts a living and enlivening tradition that enables us to hear the Word of God anew.

ten

CONCLUSION

*I*t is difficult to draw neat conclusions at the end of this study. The temptation is to look back on the uses and construals of Scripture by the different authors surveyed and to derive various "lessons" from their respective uses of Scripture. I intend to resist this temptation, however, as much as possible. One of my goals in this book has been to provide thickly descriptive analyses of how Scripture has been used and interpreted in the theology and ethics of some of the most prominent and influential Christian theologians of the twentieth century. I therefore want to avoid reductionistic characterizations, and I am concerned that deriving certain lessons from this undertaking might undercut the larger purpose of the project.

I am convinced that we need to pay more attention to the actual practices of biblical interpretation as these are carried out in constructive theology and ethics. To this end, I have concentrated on concrete and specific uses of discrete biblical materials. I certainly hope that this study contributes to a better understanding of the constructive work of the eight figures that have been the subject of the study. Beyond this, however, I hope that this study points to some of the larger questions and issues associated with appeals to the Bible in theology and ethics. By way of summary, I will use one focal passage (the Sermon on the Mount) to provide a brief comparative overview of the various approaches to Scripture presented above.

The Sermon on the Mount

One place where different ways of relating Scripture to Christian ethics can be readily seen is in the various appropriations of the Sermon on the Mount in the constructive theology and ethics of the eight figures examined in this book. The Sermon on the Mount from Matthew 5–7 is arguably the most significant block of teaching material attributed to Jesus in the Gospel traditions, especially from the vantage of theological ethics. A comparative summary of how the different authors have made use of the Sermon on the Mount will highlight some aspects of their biblical interpretation as a whole.[1]

As we saw, Reinhold Niebuhr makes extensive use of the Sermon on the Mount in his writings. For Niebuhr, the ethic of Jesus expressed in the Sermon on the Mount is an impossible ethical ideal of love. As he puts it in his *An Interpretation of Christian Ethics*, "Christ is thus the revelation of the very impossible possibility which the Sermon on the Mount elaborates in ethical terms" (p. 73).

Two proximate "pinnacles of love" lie at the heart of the ideal love ethic Jesus embodies in his life and articulates in the Sermon on the Mount: sacrificial love and forgiving love.[2] The sacrificial love of Jesus is most clearly and ultimately seen in Jesus's acceptance of death on the cross for others. While Jesus' death was for humanity as a whole, individual Christians can practice sacrificial love only in relation to other individuals. Forgiving love involves one individual's bearing with the sins and shortcomings of another individual. Both expressions of love in the life of the Christian are but approximate expressions of the full ideal embodied in Jesus, but these approximations are as close as Christians can reasonably get within historical existence. Nonetheless, the ethical ideals advanced by Jesus in the Sermon on the Mount are absolutely indispensable for expressing individual Christian ethical responsibilities in the world in relation to God and neighbor.

H. Richard Niebuhr sees in the Sermon on the Mount more than simply implications for relations between individuals or between the single believer and God. In his essay "Biblical Ethics" from his sourcebook of Christian ethics, he devotes a section to the Sermon on the Mount. For Niebuhr, the Sermon reveals Jesus' fundamental conviction that God rules in the present, in the here and now, not merely that God *will* rule sometime in the future.

The present rule of God expressed in the Sermon on the Mount shows three distinctive aspects of Jesus' view of God and his consequent ethics. First, Jesus addresses the poor directly rather than addressing the powerful and influential in the community. Jesus adopts the viewpoint of the poor and the oppressed themselves. Second, Jesus envisions one's enemy as among those to be counted as neighbor in the eyes of God. And third, and most important, Jesus emphasizes the type of attitude one should have toward one's neighbor. Here, Niebuhr clearly has in mind the "New Law" Jesus gives in the antitheses of the Sermon on the Mount. For H. Richard Niebuhr, then, Jesus' teachings in the Sermon on the Mount are not merely ideal but actual and practical ethics to be embodied by the community of Christian believers as they seek to show the presence of God's kingdom here and now.

The Roman Catholic moral theologian Bernard Häring also makes significant use of the Sermon on the Mount. Of particular relevance is his 1967 essay "The Normative Value of the Sermon on the Mount." Häring emphasizes the Sermon as new normative covenant law set over against the old covenant Mosaic law. In this new law, Häring sees Christ stressing the inner law written on the heart. The specific ideals and goals of this inner law find expression in the Sermon on the Mount.

God's revelation of the law to Moses on Sinai took place at a distance from the people of Israel, but God's revelation of the new law through Jesus took place in close proximity to the disciples and crowds of people. For Häring, one of the most important aspects of the Sermon on the Mount is the way in which it shows the closeness of Jesus to the people, in contrast to the distance of God from the Israelites of old. The combination of Jesus' authority and his closeness stands out. Authority does not come from Jesus' lording over the disciples but from his approaching them as a compassionate servant. (Here the Jesus of John's Gospel functions as an important interpretive lens for Häring's reading of the Sermon on the Mount.)

The central message of the Sermon on the Mount is found in Matt. 5:43–48: "Love your enemies and pray for your persecutors; only so can you be children of your heavenly Father, who makes his sun rise on good and bad alike. . . . [Y]ou must therefore be all goodness [perfect], just as your heavenly Father is all good."[3] The new covenant in Christ demonstrates the closeness and loving compassion of God in relation to God's people.

The Sermon preserves a set of minimal moral limits and shows a new approach to the law. But it goes far beyond this, for it points toward the complete inner renewal and transformation of the believer as the goal of Jesus' teachings in the Sermon. The goal commandment of perfection is at the very heart of the Sermon on the Mount.

Paul Ramsey's approach to the Sermon on the Mount, seen most clearly in his book *Basic Christian Ethics*, is distinguished by an overall suspicion of Matthew's Gospel. As we have seen, for Ramsey Matthew's Gospel says more about "the rebirth of legalism within early Christianity than it does about Jesus" (*BCE*, p. 64). Nevertheless, Ramsey makes significant use of the material in Matthew 5–7. In the process, however, he highlights the apocalyptic and eschatological character of Jesus' understanding of covenant righteousness and obedience. Some of Jesus' teachings in the Sermon on the Mount are eschatological teachings stressing urgency that can be stated in noneschatological terms *without* changing their essential meanings (e.g., do not be angry, do not lust, be singleminded). General ethical principles can be discerned from those teachings of Jesus which do not have an essentially apocalyptic eschatological character.

Some of Jesus' teachings, however, are more essentially apocalyptic and eschatological and so cannot be translated into noneschatological terms (e.g., nonresisting love, unlimited forgiveness, unconditional giving to every need). Here "the radical content of Jesus' strenuous sayings depends . . . on his apocalyptic expectation" (*BCE*, p. 35). Since we no longer share the apocalyptic eschatology of Jesus, this strenuous ethic must be limited to its appropriate sphere of relations between individuals on a one-to-one basis. In a noneschatological setting, a vigorous eschatological ethic is neither possible nor prudential beyond one-on-one relationships. This is reminiscent of the approach taken by Reinhold Niebuhr.

Stanley Hauerwas presents a significant contrast and challenge to the positions of Reinhold Niebuhr and Paul Ramsey. According to Hauerwas, Christians live "between the times" and must learn to look at the world precisely from

Jesus' eschatological perspective. The Sermon on the Mount, then, is not an unattainable individualistic ideal possible only at God's final consummation of history. Rather, Jesus' Sermon on the Mount "challenges our normal assumptions about what is possible, but that is exactly what it is meant to do. We are not to accept the world with its hate and resentments as a given, but to recognize that we live in a new age which makes possible a new way of life."[4]

In the Sermon on the Mount, God does not call people to approximate love by settling for justice; rather, God calls people to be perfect. Such perfection is attainable because Jesus demonstrated such a life and so inaugurated God's kingdom, in which imitating God's perfection disclosed in Jesus is possible for Christians in the continued presence of God's powerful Spirit. "Thus the Gospels portray Jesus not only offering the possibility of achieving what were heretofore thought to be impossible ethical ideals. He actually proclaims and embodies a way of life that God has made possible here and now."[5]

Gustavo Gutiérrez makes significant use of the Sermon on the Mount, but only in light of Matt. 25:31–46, the heart of Gutiérrez's canon within the canon. Here, among other passages, Gutiérrez finds a locus for "God's preferential option for the poor." As we have seen, Gutiérrez uses Matt. 25:31–46 to combat claims that Matthew gives a "spiritualized" interpretation of poverty in the Beatitudes of Matthew 5. The so-called spiritual poverty of Matthew's Beatitudes means "to be totally at the disposition of the Lord."[6] The teachings of Jesus "begin with the blessing of the poor (Matt. 5); they end with the assertion that we meet Christ himself when we go out to the poor with concrete acts (Matt. 25). So the teaching of Jesus is framed in a context that moves *from the poor to the poor.*"[7]

James Cone makes only a handful of references to the Sermon on the Mount in all of his writings, and when he does, he has mostly critical comments to make about traditional uses of it in relation to African Americans. For example, in his classic book *A Black Theology of Liberation*, Cone writes:

> There is no use for a God who loves white oppressors *the same as* oppressed blacks. We have had too much of white love, the love that tells blacks to turn the other cheek and go the second mile. What we need is the divine love as expressed in black power, which is the power of blacks to destroy their oppressors, here and now, by any means at their disposal. (p. 70)

In short, the Sermon on the Mount has traditionally been used in such a way as to poison the Bible for African Americans. Here, as we have seen, Cone appropriates language from Malcolm X, who criticized Christianity as white and the Christian Bible as a "poison book."

A major contributor to this poisoning of the Bible, according to Cone, has been the academic guild of so-called professional biblical scholars. Under the guise of "objective scholarship," biblical scholars have emphasized what the Bible may have meant a long time ago and have given little or no attention to the significance of the biblical witness for constructing a liberating theology for today. "The scholarly demand for this kind of 'objectivity' has come to mean being uninvolved or not taking sides."[8] Most white scholars have responded to black liberation theology with a literal appeal to the Bible and a call for African Americans to be nonviolent and to "turn the other cheek," which has become simply another way of poisoning the words of Jesus in an attempt to maintain white privilege. For these reasons, Cone makes little constructive use of the Sermon on the Mount because it has such a long history of being spiritualized in support of an accommodationist approach where African Americans make all the sacrifices that it has ceased to have a liberating function for African Americans in relation to white oppression. Therefore, it has lost much of its authority.

Finally, Rosemary Radford Ruether makes virtually no use of the Sermon on the Mount.[9] In the context of discussing "Mariology as symbolic ecclesiology" in *Sexism and God-Talk*, Ruether does refer favorably to Luke's version of the Beatitudes (6:20–25) in contrast to Matthew's: "Luke does not minimize the socioeconomic dimension of redemption, as does Matthew with his spiritualization of the Beatitudes; in fact he emphasizes it by adding the negative judgmental side of God's redemption as judgment on the rich" (p. 156). Thus, argues Ruether, "social iconoclasm plays a key role in Luke's understanding of God's redemptive work" (p. 156). Here, Ruether discounts Matthew's version of the Beatitudes as overly spiritualized and hence minimizing the socioeconomic impact of God's redemption.

Perhaps another reason for Ruether's relative disinterest in the Sermon on the Mount is because there is little in it that resonates directly with feminist experience, either positively or negatively. It may also be that Ruether is uncomfortable with lifting up meekness, mourning, and poverty of spirit as dispositions that fit well with a critical feminist awareness and suspicion of patriarchy, which has all too often coerced women into positions of meekness, mourning, and poverty (spiritual and otherwise). Thus, Ruether sees in Luke's version of the Beatitudes the liberating and iconoclastic Word of God, while in Matthew's Beatitudes, it appears that she sees, contrary to Gutiérrez, only spiritualization and domestication of the radical transforming Word of God.

In surveying these various approaches to the Sermon on the Mount, we find three general interpretations. First, in the writings of Reinhold Niebuhr, Paul Ramsey, and Bernard Häring, we encounter an understanding of the Sermon in ideal terms. Jesus does not really offer here a prudential ethic. Rather, he offers an ideal or goal toward which Christians can and should strive, but an ideal that is not attainable in concrete human existence. Still, the goal is necessary for providing an orientation for Christian behavior in the world. This approach is the most traditional and conservative interpretation of the Sermon on the Mount.

Second, in the writings of H. Richard Niebuhr, Stanley Hauerwas, and Gustavo Gutiérrez, we find an understanding of the Sermon as presenting a practical, prudential, and realizable—if radical—ethic for Christian existence in the world. Jesus lived out this radical ethic of love, especially love of enemy, and so provides not just an ideal but an example for Christians in real life. Particularly noteworthy is Gutiérrez's linkage between Matthew 5 and Matthew 25 and his consequent emphasis on God's preferential option for the poor.[10]

Third, in the writings of James Cone and Rosemary Ruether we find in many ways a cautionary warning about too quickly embracing the Sermon on the Mount. African Americans and women have long experienced oppression at the hands of white men, and so they should be suspicious of exhortations from traditional oppressors to turn the other cheek or to trust in some heavenly reward for a humble and servile life here and now. Cone and Ruether see a much more iconoclastic gospel (to use Ruether's term) that sharply calls into question any attempt to undercut God's empowerment of oppressed peoples with an appeal to the traditional gospel of the status quo.

Patterns

An overview of interpretations of the Sermon on the Mount highlights some of the differences between the various authors surveyed. Amid the differences, are there also patterns that emerge from the disparate uses of Scripture that we have encountered? I would highlight a few patterns that are not terribly surprising but are worth noting nonetheless. First, it is apparent that the professional and academic social contexts out of which people come significantly affect their approach to the Bible. This can be seen, for example, in Reinhold Niebuhr's essentially liberal Protestant interpretation of the Bible; in Bernard Häring's intentional move away from negative moral prohibition so dominant in pre–Vatican II moral theology to a more positive appreciation of the goal commandments of Jesus; in Paul Ramsey's adoption of covenant theology, so much in vogue in the 1950s, as the centerpiece of his biblical interpretation; and in Rosemary Ruether's strong skepticism regarding the biblical material inculcated by historical-critical readings of the Bible. I have not encountered much significant change in approach to the Bible over time in the respective writings of the various authors examined (and this despite customary references, e.g., to the "early" Niebuhr or to the "later" Ramsey).

Second, and perhaps I am especially aware of this as a biblical scholar, the appeals to the Bible by theologians and ethicists show relatively little interaction with the professional guild of biblical scholarship, though there are significant exceptions to this generalization. The separation between biblical studies and theology/ethics has, of course, long been a problem in theological education and theological discourse in general. The lack of critical integration between biblical scholarship and theology/ethics has resulted in the seeming irrelevance of much academic (and antiquarian) biblical scholarship, on the one hand, and in the seeming groundlessness of many appropriations of the Bible for theology and ethics, on the other hand. (In the writings of many theologians and ethicists, one not infrequently finds little to no awareness of or attention to the concrete historical and social contexts out of which the biblical documents arose.)

My own conviction is that paying more attention to the ethics of interpretation, from the perspectives of both theological ethicists and biblical scholars, will serve as an integrating force between biblical scholarship and theological ethics.[11] Critical reflection and consciousness of the constituency one is addressing and serving are of paramount importance in the ethics of biblical interpretation. This perspective is certainly not new, but it is crucial to restate it.

In the closing comments of her presidential address to the Society of Biblical Literature, the main academic guild of biblical scholars in North America, Elisabeth Schüssler Fiorenza advocated the following:

> In short, if the Society [of Biblical Literature] were to engage in a disciplined reflection on the public dimensions and ethical implications of our scholarly work, it would constitute a responsible scholarly citizenship that could be a significant participant in the global discourse seeking justice and well-being for all. The implications of such a repositioning of the task and aim of biblical scholarship would be far-reaching and invigorating.[12]

The ethics of reading and interpreting must be taken into account in the process of interpreting and appropriating the Bible anew, by biblical scholars and theologians alike. Indeed, in addition to the renewed public role of biblical interpretation to which Schüssler Fiorenza calls attention, I would also stress the need for a renewed awareness of the ecclesiastical dimensions and implications of biblical interpretation. Theologians and ethicists are perhaps more practiced in their discourse at identifying the communities they seek to shape. Biblical scholars need to be much more self-conscious and forthright about the significance of their work for constructive theological ethics.[13] Of course, there is a significant role for descriptive work here as well, as I hope this book demonstrates.

Third, the issue of unity and diversity in the biblical materials is one that finds too little constructive attention in the writings of the various authors examined. Although most of the authors are perfectly aware of the great diversity represented in the biblical writings (reflected, e.g., in the various typologies developed in H. Richard Niebuhr's *Christ and Culture*) and have made some observations about the rich variety of theological visions in Scripture, they tend to stress the unity of the biblical witness notwithstanding. Perhaps this should be expected from theologians who are, after all, attempting to build holistic constructive visions of Christian faith and practice. Nevertheless, perhaps it is the role of biblical scholars to cry out, "Not so fast!" in calling attention once again to the great diversity (sometimes contradictory diversity) of theological and ethical visions articulated by the different biblical writers.[14] The ethics of biblical interpretation, in my view, means being honest about which biblical visions one chooses and why these are seen as being the most appropriate ones to emphasize. The liberation theologians have, from my perspective, done a better job of this than most.

Appeals are often made to the need to use the whole of Scripture in arriving at the most appropriate theological and ethical formulations for Christian faith and practice. While it is important to be aware of the whole of Scripture in this regard, more attention needs to be given to the articulation of criteria for authorizing one set of canonical contours as opposed to another. The relation of unity and diversity is certainly not something that can be "solved," however, for the very character of the question propels a continual conversation between rival understandings of the gospel (and the Gospels) in changing times and places.

Thus, the issue of unity and diversity for Scripture and ethics in our day is in principle no different than it was for the authors of our Scriptures in their day. What has God shown in these writings? What does it mean to interpret them faithfully? How and why do we make the interpretive decisions that we do?

Conversing with Scripture

There is a hermeneutical circle in approaching the Bible for constructive theology and ethics. We come to these foundational Scriptures out of specific contexts, particular theological traditions, particular personal and communal experiences, all of which profoundly shape which biblical texts we choose to read, which texts we listen to, how we read and hear, what we discern when we read, the implications for faith and practice that we derive from our interpretations. In turn, to larger and lesser degrees, we find our worlds affected and shaped by the very Scriptures we seek to understand. The faith expressions of the various formative communities that wrote and rewrote the biblical materials help us to interpret our lives and our faith commitments in the contexts of the communities to which we belong.

We read and interpret the biblical writings because these writings have fashioned the various traditional appropriations of Christian faith in which we stand and move. In turn, we further shape and mold the interpretive tradition based on our understandings and experiences of what it means to be faithful. As Christians, we believe that God is at work in this process, prodding and leading and pulling us along, even if we are not in agreement with one another about the directions in which God is calling us.

Each of the authors examined in this book has a powerful vision of what it is that God has done and is doing in our midst. Each has brought to Scripture commitments forged through years of active reflection and Christian practice. Each has articulated a coherent and constructive holistic vision of what it means to be a Christian in the world and to live faithfully with one another before God. Each has actively worked Scripture into the soil that nurtures his or her understanding of a living faith. Despite the family resemblance of these expressions, we have seen significant differences among these influential theologians.

In reading and in writing about these authors, I have often found myself both resonating with and reacting against their respective understandings of Christian life, especially as they have appealed to the foundational Scriptures of the church in the process. As I indicated in the Introduction, I also, of course, come to these authors and their interpretations of the Bible out of my own specific set of contexts. Still, I hope that this book has portrayed fairly and accurately the various approaches to and uses of the Bible adopted by these eight authors. I hope that these portraits of uses of the Bible in the twentieth century will stimulate further engaged and vigorous conversation about what it means to interpret faithfully the Christian Scriptures for Christian life and community in the present and as we move into the twenty-first century.

NOTES

Chapter One

1. Among the more recent studies, see, e.g., J. I. H. McDonald, *Biblical Interpretation and Christian Ethics* (Cambridge: Cambridge University Press, 1993); C. F. Sleeper, *The Bible and the Moral Life* (Louisville: Westminster Press/John Knox Press, 1992); S. E. Fowl and L. G. Jones, *Reading in Communion: Scripture and Ethics in Christian Life* (Grand Rapids: Eerdmans, 1991); B. Birch, *Let Justice Roll Down: The Old Testament, Ethics, and Christian Life* (Louisville: Westminster Press/John Knox Press, 1991); R. B. Hays, "Scripture-Shaped Community: The Problem of Method in New Testament Ethics," *Interpretation* 44 (1990); 42–55; B. Birch and L. Rasmussen, *Bible and Ethics in the Christian Life*, rev. and exp. ed. (Minneapolis: Augsburg, 1989); M. Cartwright, "The Practice and Performance of Scripture: Grounding Christian Ethics in a Communal Hermeneutic," *The Annual of the Society of Christian Ethics, 1988*, ed. D. M. Yeager (Washington, D.C.: Georgetown University Press, 1988), pp. 31–53; S. C. Mott, "The Use of the New Testament for Social Ethics," *Journal of Religious Ethics* 15 (1987): 225–60; R. J. Daly et al., *Christian Biblical Ethics: From Biblical Revelation to Contemporary Praxis, Method and Content* (New York and Ramsey: Paulist Press, 1984); A. Verhey, *The Great Reversal: Ethics and the New Testament* (Grand Rapids: Eerdmans, 1984); the various essays collected in C. E. Curran and R. A. McCormick, eds., *Readings in Moral Theology, No. 4; The Use of Scripture in Moral Theology* (New York and Ramsey: Paulist Press, 1984); and T. Ogletree, *The Use of the Bible in Christian Ethics* (Philadelphia: Fortress Press, 1983).

2. Among the most significant studies in this regard, see especially McDonald, *Biblical Interpretation and Christian Ethics*; W. C. Spohn, *What Are They Saying About Scripture and Ethics?* (New York and Ramsey: Paulist Press, 1984); A. Verhey, "The Use of Scripture in Ethics," *Religious Studies Review* 4 (1978): 28–39; D. H. Kelsey, *The Uses of Scripture in Recent Theology* (Philadelphia: Fortress Press, 1975); J. Gustafson, "The Changing Use of the Bible in Christian Ethics," in Curran and McCormick, *Readings in Moral Theology*, pp. 133–50; J. Gustafson, "The Place of Scripture in Christian Ethics: A Methodological Study," *Interpretation* 24 (1970): 430–55; and E. L. Long, "The Use of the Bible in Christian Ethics: A Look at Basic Options," *Interpretation* 19 (1965) 149–62. Perhaps the relative lack of work in this area should not come as a big surprise, given that biblical scholars are generally not very well equipped to do critical analysis in the

field of theological ethics, and similarly, theological ethicists often do not feel sufficiently qualified to address issues of biblical interpretation, particularly when it comes to detailed exegetical analysis.

3. See, e.g., Birch, *Let Justice Roll Down*; Verhey, *Great Reversal*; Ogletree, *Use of the Bible in Christian Ethics*; J. Hempel, *Das Ethos des Alten Testaments* (Berlin: Alfred Töpelmann, 1964); W. Janzen, *Old Testament Ethics* (Louisville: Westminster/John Knox Press, 1994); J. L. Crenshaw and J. T. Willis, eds., *Essays in Old Testament Ethics* (New York: KTAV, 1974); W. Kaiser, *Toward Old Testament Ethics* (Grand Rapids: Zondervan, 1983); C. H. Dodd, "The Ethics of the New Testament," in *Moral Principles of Action*, ed. R. N. Anshen (New York: Harper & Row, 1952), pp. 543–58; R. Schnackenburg, *The Moral Teaching of the New Testament* (New York: Herder & Herder, 1965); V. Furnish, *Theology and Ethics in Paul* (Nashville: Abingdon Press, 1968); J. L. Houlden, *Ethics and the New Testament* (Baltimore: Penguin Books, 1973); E. Osborn, *Ethical Patterns in Early Church Thought* (New York and Cambridge: Cambridge University Press, 1976); W. Schrage, *The Ethics of the New Testament* (Philadelphia: Fortress Press, 1987); W. Marxsen, *New Testament Foundations for Christian Ethics* (Minneapolis: Fortress Press, 1993); W. Meeks, *The Origins of Christian Morality: The First Two Centuries* (New Haven: Yale University Press, 1993).

4. In his work *The Uses of Scripture in Recent Theology*, David Kelsey poses four guiding questions:

1. What aspect(s) of scripture is (are) taken to be authoritative?
2. What is it about this aspect of scripture that makes it authoritative?
3. What sort of logical force is ascribed to the scripture to which appeal is made?
4. How is the scripture that is cited brought to bear on theological proposals so as to authorize them? (pp. 2–3)

See also the "core set of questions" posed by Birch and Rasmussen:

• What kind of authority for Christian morality is the Bible?
• At what points and for what purposes in the moral life might biblical materials play an appropriate and influential role?
• How should different kinds of biblical materials function in the moral life? How are they made available and properly used?
• What comprises "the moral life" and what are the basic categories, elements, and tasks of Christian ethics? At what critical points does Christian ethics draw upon biblical materials, for what purposes?
• What are the roles of the faith community in the moral life? Specifically, what are the manifold uses of Scripture in the church for fashioning moral character and conduct? (*Bible and Ethics in the Christian Life*, p. 10):

Finally, in his essay "The Use of Scripture in Ethics," Allen Verhey identifies "four critical questions" for assessing uses of Scripture in ethics:

1. What are these writings (the Bible)?
2. What question is appropriate (of the biblical texts)?
3. What does one understand when one understands these writings (the Bible)?
4. What is the relevance of other sources?

5. Two doctoral dissertations have been written on Rauschenbusch's uses of Scripture: A. Verhey, "The Use of Scripture in Moral Discourse: A Case Study of Walter Rauschenbusch" (Ph.D. diss., Yale University, 1975); and W. F. McInery, "Scripture and

Christian Ethics: An Evaluative Analysis of the Uses of Scripture in the Works of Walter Rauschenbusch" (Ph.D. diss., Marquette University, 1983). As significant as J. Gustafson's essays on Scripture and ethics have been, Gustafson himself deliberately makes very little direct use of Scripture in his own constructive ethics (*Ethics from a Theoocentric Perspective* [Chicago: University of Chicago Press, 1981], vol. 1). The same is true for Beverly Harrison's writings.

6. David Kelsey's significant work *Uses of Scripture in Recent Theology*, e.g., considers the writings of seven Protestant theologians (primarily between the 1920s and the 1960s): K. Barth, H.-W. Bartsch, R. Bultmann, L. S. Thornton, P. Tillich, B. B. Warfield, and G. E. Wright. Of these, Bultmann and Wright are perhaps better known for their work in biblical studies, as both wrote much in the way of "biblical theology." Of the seven theologians, all Protestant men, examined by Kelsey, two are from the United States (Warfield and Wright) and the rest are European (German, Swiss, and British).

Of the eight theologians/ethicists considered in this book, five are Protestant (R. Niebuhr, H. R. Niebuhr, P. Ramsey, S. Hauerwas, and J. Cone) and three are Roman Catholic (B. Häring, G. Gutiérrez, and R. Ruether). All but two are from the United States (B. Häring is German and G. Gutiérrez is Peruvian). All but Gutiérrez and Cone are Caucasians of European descent (Gutiérrez is of Latin American and Indian American descent; Cone is of African American descent). R. Ruether is the only woman here.

7. Other scholars have suggested various types of construals of Scripture for theological ethics. See, e.g., W. C. Spohn's *What Are They Saying About Scripture and Ethics?*, where he develops six general types: (1) the command of God, (2) Scripture as moral reminder, (3) call to liberation, (4) response to revelation, (5) call to discipleship, and (6) Scripture as the basis for responding love.

8. For those interested in the history of research, such as it is, into uses of Scripture in ethics, see especially M. C. Cartwright, "Practices, Politics, and Performance: Toward a Communal Hermeneutic for Christian Ethics" (Ph.D. diss., Duke University, 1988), pp. 1–146. Among other things, Cartwright surveys the studies of E. L. Long, J. M. Gustafson, F. Sleeper, A. Verhey, and B. Birch and L. Rasmussen.

Chapter Two

1. The first major collection of essays on Niebuhr was C. W. Kegley and R. W. Bretall, eds., *Reinhold Niebuhr: His Religious, Social, and Political Thought* (New York: Macmillan, 1956). For the most recent studies on Niebuhr, see esp. G. Gaudin and D. J. Hall, eds., *Reinhold Niebuhr (1892–1971): A Centenary Appraisal* (Atlanta: Scholars Press, 1994); R. Harries, ed., *Reinhold Niebuhr and the Issues of Our Time* (Grand Rapids: Eerdmans, 1986); J. R. Neuhaus, ed., *Reinhold Niebuhr Today* (Grand Rapids: Eerdmans, 1989); L. Rasmussen, ed., *Reinhold Niebuhr: Theologian of Public Life* (London:Collins, 1989); R. W. Fox, *Reinhold Niebuhr: A Biography* (New York: Pantheon, 1985); J. W. Cooper, *The Theology of Freedom: The Legacy of Jacques Maritain and Reinhold Niebuhr* (Macon, Ga.: Mercer University Press, 1985); C. C. Brown, *Niebuhr and His Age: Reinhold Niebuhr's Prophetic Role in the Twentieth Century* (Philadelphia: Trinity Press International, 1992); and, with significant analyses of Niebuhr's political realism, D. Meyer, *The Protestant Search for Political Realism, 1919–1941* (Middletown, Conn: Wesleyan University Press, 1988); D. P. McCann, *Christian Realism and Liberation Theology: Practical Theologies in Creative Conflict* (Maryknoll, N.Y.: Orbis Books, 1981); and R. Stone, ed., *Faith and Politics: A commentary on Religious, Social, and Political Thought in a Technological Age* (New York: George Braziller, 1968). See also the extensive bibliography of

writings by and about Reinhold Niebuhr compiled by D. B. Robertson, *Reinhold Nie-buhr's Works: A Bibliography* (Boston: G. K. Hall, 1979).

2. Regarding Niebuhr, Paul Tillich remarks: "He is basically a Biblicist, not in the bad sense, but in the sense that all his writings continuously refer to the Biblical founda-tions of the Christian faith" ("Sin and Grace in the Theology of Reinhold Niebuhr," in *Reinhold Niebuhr: A Prophetic Voice in Our Time*, ed. H. R. Landon [Greenwich, Conn: Seabury Press, 1962], p. 33).

3. When one turns to secondary literature on Niebuhr's use of Scripture, there is surprisingly little to be found. In what is still one of the most important collections of essays on Niebuhr's thought (Kegley and Bretall's *Reinhold Niebuhr*), there is no discus-sion of his use of Scripture. In his very significant book *The Politics of Jesus* (Grand Rapids: Eerdmans, 1972), J. H. Yoder offers a short but important critique of Niebuhr's use of Scripture (pp. 16, 110–13). Richard Hays also briefly examines Niebuhr's use of Scripture in relation to his treatment of war and violence in his *Community, Cross, New Creation: New Testament Ethics* (New York: HarperCollins, 1996). D. P. McCann has written a brief analysis of Niebuhr's essay "Biblical Rhetoric of Irony" in "The Christian Element in Christian Realism," in *The Bible in American Law, Politics, and Political Rhetoric*, ed. J. T. Johnson (Philadelphia Fortress Press; Chico, Calif.: Scholars Press, 1985), pp. 153–72. See also another pertinent essay by McCann, "Hermeneutics and Eth-ics: The Example of Reinhold Niebuhr," *Journal of Religious Ethics* 8, no. 1 (1980): 27–53. But beyond this, one finds only an occasional passing comment on Niebuhr's use of Scripture. See, e.g., E. L. Long, "The Use of the Bible in Christian Ethics: A Look at Basic Options," *Interpretation* 19 (1965): 149–62 (esp. pp. 157–58; R. B. Hays, "Scripture-Shaped Community: The Problem of Method in New Testament Ethics," *Interpretation* 44 (1990): 42–55 (esp. p. 50); C. E. Curran and R. A. McCormick, eds., *Readings in Moral Theology, No. 4: The Use of Scripture in Moral Theology* (New York and Ramsey: Paulist Press, 1984), pp. 3, 139, 141, 181; M. Cartwright, "The Practice and Performance of Scripture: Grounding Christian Ethics in a Communal Hermeneutic," in *The Annual of the Society of Christian Ethics, 1988*, ed. D. M. Yeager (Washington, D.C.: George-town University Press, 1988), pp. 31–53; S. C. Mott, "The Use of the New Testament for Social Ethics," *Journal of Religious Ethics* 15 (1987): 225–60.

4. M. G. Cartwright, "Practices, Politics, and Performance: Toward a Communal Hermeneutic for Christian Ethics" (Ph.D. Diss., Duke University, 1988), p. 32.

5. Niebuhr wrote 21 books, contributed chapters to 126 more books, and wrote over 2,600 articles (see Rasmussen, ed., *Reinhold Niebuhr*, p. ix).

6. Indeed, as J. Gustafson has observed, even in the realm of theological ethics "Niebuhr was not methodologically self-conscious in the way that many more recent theologians have become" ("Theology in the Service of Ethics: An Interpretation of Rein-hold Niebuhr's Theological Ethics," in *Reinhold Niebuhr and the Issues of Our Time*, ed. Harries, p. 30).

7. See Niebuhr's own opening statement in his "Intellectual Autobiography," where he observes: "It is somewhat embarrassing to be made the subject of a study which assumes theology as the primary interest. I cannot and do not claim to be a theologian" (Kegley and Bretall, eds., *Reinhold Niebuhr*, p. 3). See also the introductory essay by Rasmussen in his edited volume *Reinhold Niebuhr*: "Theological method and careful definition of categories evidently belonged to the 'fine points of pure theology' for which he had little time. As a result he was not very precise about the framing of his own thought. In this respect he was not a professional theologian, and was occasionally chided for it. Paul Tillich once scolded him affectionately at a symposium held in his honor: 'Reinie never tells us how he knows; he just starts knowing!' " (p. 17; see also p. 2).

8. R. Niebuhr, *Justice and Mercy*, ed. U. M. Niebuhr (New York: Harper & Row, 1974), p. 4.

9. See the original preface to volume 2 of Niebuhr's *The Nature and Destiny of Man* (New York: Charles Scribner's Sons, 1943), p. v.

10. As Rasmussen notes, "Niebuhr was at his very best in his ability to render a theological interpretation of events as a basis for common action for a wide audience. But precisely because of the audience's diverse beliefs, Niebuhr often cast his case in ways which left his Christian presuppositions and convictions unspoken" (*Reinhold Niebuhr*, p. 3).

11. R. Niebuhr, "The Conflict Between Nations and Nations and Between Nations and God," in *Love and Justice: Selections from the Shorter Writings of Reinhold Niebuhr*, ed. D. B. Robertson (Gloucester, Mass.: Peter Smith, 1976), pp. 161–62.

12. This essay can be found in *How My Mind Has Changed*, ed. H. E. Fey (New York: Meridian Books, 1961), pp. 116–32 (quotation from p. 117). In the same essay he also defines what he sees as some of the enduring values of the liberal tradition: "freedom to subject all historical and dogmatic statements to rigorous inquiry, and the spirit of toleration in dealing with one's opponents" (p. 117). See also Niebuhr's "Intellectual Autobiography," where he states: "My early writings were all characterized by a critical attitude toward the 'liberal' world view, whether expressed in secular or in Christian terms. . . . I note to my embarrassment that my criticisms could not have been very thoroughgoing because they revealed so many vestigial remnants of the culture which I ostensibly criticized" (Kegley and Bretall, eds., *Reinhold Niebuhr*, pp. 7–8). On Niebuhr's indebtedness to the liberal tradition, as well as his criticism of it, see Rasmussen, ed., *Reinhold Niebuhr*, pp. 21–26.

13. Niebuhr makes constant reference to "prophetic religion" throughout his writings. See, e.g., *Nature and Destiny of Man*, 1:137–42, 214–16, 223–27; 2:18–20, 23–34, 38–53; *An Interpretation of Christian Ethics* (1935; reprint, New York: Crossroad and Seabury Press, 1979), pp. 18, 19, 22, 44, 61, 62, 69, 94, 146 (page citations are to the reprint edition).

14. R. Niebuhr, *Nature and Destiny of Man*, 2:25.

15. R. Niebuhr, *Interpretation of Christian Ethics*, p. 63.

16. See, e.g., Niebuhr's discussion of "prophetic messianism" in *Nature and Destiny of Man*, 2:23–24.

17. See, e.g., Niebuhr's essays collected in *Faith and Politics*; ed. Stone.

18. R. Niebuhr, *Interpretation of Christian Ethics*, p. 22. As Larry Rasmussen has observed, "For Niebuhr Jesus embodied and revealed a spiritual and moral ideal of an absolute and transcendent nature, the very nature of God and God's love" (*Reinhold Niebuhr*, p. 21).

19. See, e.g., R. Niebuhr's sermon "We See Through a Glass Darkly" (*Justice and Mercy*, pp. 35–37), where he develops his interpretation of these two kinds of love, as well as his "Love and Law in Protestantism and Catholicism" (in *The Essential Reinhold Niebuhr*, ed. R. M. Brown [New Haven: Yale University Press, 1986], pp. 142–59). In this latter article Niebuhr again presents love as universal and love as standing in the place of the other. In *Nature and Destiny of Man*, Niebuhr also discusses love, mostly in the second volume, where he considers love as mutual, sacrificial, and suffering. In addition, see the final essay in *Interpretation of Christian Ethics*, which is entitled "Love as Forgiveness."

20. The classic articulation of this position is Niebuhr's essay "The Relevance of an Impossible Ethical Ideal," from *Interpretation of Christian Ethics* (pp. 62–83). He begins the essay by conflating his two constructs of prophetic religion and the love ethic of Jesus into a single term, "Prophetic Christianity." On Niebuhr's notion of love, see also the

introductory comments of R. M. Brown, who states that for Niebuhr, "love is the ultimate norm for all human activity, hovering over every situation as a possibility of achievement, and yet impossible in the sense that it can never be fully achieved in any human situation. Rather than destroying the relevance of love, such a recognition establishes it even more fully, for love always remains both as a judgment on the adequacy of every partial achievement and as a challenge toward fuller approximation in the future" (*The Essential Reinhold Niebuhr,* pp. xvi-xvii). See also McCann, who puts it well: "The ethic of Jesus is possible insofar as we are free to aspire to it; it is impossible insofar as our finiteness precludes its perfect realization" ("Hermeneutics and Ethics," p. 42).

21. See David Kelsey's discussion of the biblical concept approach to Scripture in *The Uses of Scripture in Recent Theology* (Philadelphia: Fortress Press, 1975). Kelsey notes that "biblical concept theology" seeks to lay out "the distinctively biblical concepts of one thing and another. These concepts then serve as the basis for proposals about how Christians should think today" (pp. 24-25). Kelsey characterizes the approaches of H.-W. Bartsch, O. Cullmann, and G. E. Wright under the category of "biblical concept theology." I would largely place Reinhold Niebuhr's use of the Bible in this category as well, although he also fits in no small measure under the "symbolic" approach, for which Kelsey uses Tillich as a main representative (pp. 131 ff.). Tillich was Niebuhr's colleague at Union Theological Seminary for several years, and Niebuhr regularly notes his indebtedness to discussions with Tillich.

22. To an extent, Niebuhr's notions of prophetic religion and the love ethic of Jesus can also be seen as biblical concepts. But these two notions were much more highly abstracted and generalized in Niebuhr's thought, and they provided a macrostructure for his thought to a degree that was not true of other "biblical concepts" that he sought and employed.

23. See, e.g., the indexes to Niebuhr's *Nature and Destiny of Man,* vols. 1 and 2, for references.

24. E. A. Burtt, "Some Questions About Niebuhr's Theology," in *Reinhold Niebuhr,* ed. Kegley and Bretall, p. 358.

25. R. Niebuhr, "Reply to Interpretation and Criticism," in *Reinhold Niebuhr,* ed. Kegley and Bretall, p. 449.

26. See Rasmussen's comments in *Reinhold Niebuhr,* pp. 21-22.

27. It is striking that Niebuhr almost never begins by citing a biblical text followed by an exegetical analysis of it. Indeed, only very rarely does one find any real exegesis of biblical texts, with close attention given to literary form and context as well as to historical and social contexts.

28. R. Niebuhr, *Justice and Mercy,* p. 7. Niebuhr's illustrative use of Scripture also, of course, permeated his preaching. See the analysis of P. Scherer, "Reinhold Niebuhr—Preacher," in *Reinhold Niebuhr,* ed. Kegley and Bretall, pp. 311-32, esp. pp. 327-28.

29. R. Niebuhr, *Justice and Mercy,* p. 7.

30. R. Niebuhr, *The Nature and Destiny of Man,* 2:89.

31. Ibid., p. 106.

32. Ibid., p. 230.

33. Ibid., p. 254.

34. Ibid., p. 305. Reference to this citation from 1 Cor. 1:28 is not included in the Scripture index at the end of the volume.

35. R. Niebuhr, *Children of Light and Children of Darkness* (New York: Charles Scribner's Sons, 1944), pp. 81, 84. See also, e.g., ibid., pp. 151, 169-70; R. Niebuhr, *Interpretation of Christian Ethics,* pp. 71, 133. It must be noted that in appropriating these

biblical "confessions," Niebuhr rarely cites any reference for the biblical phrases used, nor does he seem to be aware of or particularly care about a phrase's original context.

36. R. Niebuhr, *Nature and Destiny of Man*, 2:271.

37. R. Niebuhr, *Justice and Mercy*, pp. 134–35.

38. R. Niebuhr, *Interpretation of Christian Ethics*, p. 37.

39. R. Niebhur, *Nature and Destiny of Man*, 2:152 (emphasis mine). See also vol. 2, p. 202, where he refers to the "historical relativities which are enshrined in a sacred canon."

40. R. Niebuhr, *Interpretation of Christian Ethics*, p. 37.

41. Ibid. Elsewhere, Niebuhr criticizes liberal Christianity for erroneously reducing scriptural revelation to the "history of man's quest for God or the record of man's increasingly adequate definitions of the person of God" (*Nature and Destiny of Man*, 2:136).

42. R. Niebuhr, *Nature and Destiny of Man*, 2:152.

43. R. Niebuhr, *Interpretation of Christian Ethics*, p. 94. Against Rom. 13, Niebuhr cites Luke 22:25, stating: "If it [Rom. 13] is compared with the words of Jesus, 'The kings of the Gentiles exercise lordship over them; and they that exercise authority upon them are called benefactors. But ye shall not be so; but he that is greatest among you, let him be as the younger; and he that is chief as he that doth serve,' one may observe a significant difference between the critical attitude of a prophetic religion toward the perils of power and the uncritical acceptance of the virtues of social power in a less prophetic type of religious thought" (p. 94).

44. R. Niebuhr, *Nature and Destiny of Man*, 2:270 n. 1.

45. Ibid.

46. As Niebuhr puts it: "The fact that it [Rom. 13] became a vehicle for a too uncritical devotion to government by its indiscriminate application in subsequent centuries illustrates one of the perils of Biblicism. Biblical observations upon life are made in a living relation to living history. When they are falsely given an eminence which obscures this relation, they can become the source of error and confusion" (ibid.).

47. R. Niebuhr, "An Answer to Karl Barth," in *Essays in Applied Christianity: The Church and the New World*, ed. D. B. Robertson (New York: Meridian Books, 1959), p. 179.

48. Ibid.

49. See ibid. Niebuhr also quips regarding the status of women that Barth seems at times "to deny the women in the name of St. Paul what he granted them in the name of Moses" (ibid., p. 181).

50. Ibid., p. 181.

51. R. Niebuhr, *Nature and Destiny of Man*, 2:152 (emphasis mine).

52. As D. P. McCann has observed, Niebuhr's "theoretical reflections consist in a few occasional essays and a number of tantalizing aphorisms" ("Hermeneutics and Ethics, p. 30). McCann argues that Niebuhr's hermeneutics employed "the mythical method," using a passing phrase from Niebuhr's *Interpretation of Christian Ethics*, p. 51.

53. See Tillich's *Systematic Theology* (Chicago: University of Chicago Press, 1951), 1:177. Niebuhr reveals much of his indebtedness to Tillich as well as his differences with Tillich in his essay "Biblical Thought and Ontological Speculation in Tillich's Theology," in *The Theology of Paul Tillich*, ed. Kegley and Bretall (New York: Macmillan, 1952), pp. 216–27.

54. R. Niebuhr, *Nature and Destiny of Man*, 2:289.

55. Ibid., p. 290.

56. Ibid., p. 296.

57. Ibid., p. 50.
58. Ibid., p. 289.
59. Ibid., pp. 50, 289.
60. Ibid., p. 136.
61. Ibid., pp. 50, 289.
62. Ibid., p. 94.
63. Ibid., p. 47.
64. R. Niebuhr, *The Irony of American History* (New York: Charles Scribner's Sons, 1952), p. 162.
65. R. Niebuhr, "As Deceivers, Yet True," in *Beyond Tragedy: Essays on the Christian Interpretation of History* (New York: Charles Scribner's Sons, 1947), pp. 3–24. Niebuhr apparently relied on the King James Version of 2 Cor. 6:8.
66. Ibid., p. 3. Niebuhr also claims that "the relation of time and eternity cannot be expressed in simple rational terms. It can be expressed only in symbolic terms" (ibid., p. 4).
67. Ibid., p. 9.
68. R. Niebuhr, *The Nature and Destiny of Man*, 2:136.
69. John Bennett, "Reinhold Niebuhr's Contribution to Christian Social Ethics," in *Reinhold Niebuhr*, ed. Landon, p. 61. In the discussion following the presentation of Bennett's paper on Niebuhr, Wilhelm Pauck commented: "Niebuhr speaks as a Christian, a very pragmatic Christian, and as a Protestant. But what his relation to the institutions of Protestantism, the ecclesiastical structure and the ecclesiastical procedures, is doesn't become plain, although he attacks . . . ecclesiastical monopolists and all the pretensions of churchmen and priests, and is always out for the hypocrites of all sorts. But what his own sense of the church is is barely intimated, or am I wrong there?" Bennett responded: "I think that's right" (p. 81).
70. Cartwright, "Practices, Politics, and Performance," p. 40.
71. R. Niebuhr, *Interpretation of Christian Ethics*, p. 23.
72. Ibid., p. 24.
73. Ibid., p. 28.
74. Ibid., p. 32.
75. R. Niebuhr, "The Problem of a Protestant Social Ethic," *Union Seminary Quarterly Review* 15 (1959): 11.
76. Robertson, ed., *Love and Justice*, p. 164.
77. R. M. Brown, ed., *The Essential Reinhold Niebuhr*, p. 228.
78. R. Niebuhr, "Literalism, Individualism, and Billy Graham," in *Essays in Applied Christianity*, ed. Robertson, p. 125 (from a subsection entitled "Barth's Attitude Toward Scripture," pp. 125–26). Niebuhr goes on to complain against Barth that "we are in danger of sacrificing one of the great achievements of 'liberal' theology—namely, the absolute honesty with which it encouraged the church to examine the Scriptural foundations of its faith. . . . this honesty . . . was not only an act of loyalty to the whole enterprise of modern culture; it was also a method of purifying the Christian faith" (pp. 125–26).
79. R. Niebuhr, *The Nature and Destiny of Man*, 2:202.
80. Robertson, ed., *Love and Justice*, p. 164.
81. The determination of the criteria involved in Niebuhr's concept of best judgment applies to the use not only of nonbiblical sources in Christian ethics but of biblical material as well.
82. As Niebuhr puts it in *Nature and Destiny of Man*: "It is necessary therefore to apply the Biblical doctrine to the facts of experience in order to establish its relevance"

(vol. 2, p. 107); and again, "our concern is . . . with the relevance of the Biblical doctrine of grace to the experiences of life. Does experience validate this . . . conception?" (2:119).

83. This criticism is also voiced by A. J. Burnstein, "Niebuhr, Scripture, and Normative Judaism," in *Reinhold Niebuhr*, ed. Kegley and Bretall, pp. 411–28; see esp. pp. 416–18.

84. H. N. Wieman, "A Religious Naturalist Looks at Reinhold Niebuhr," in *Reinhold Niebuhr*, ed. Kegley and Bretall, p. 339; see also pp. 340–42.

85. See, e.g., Emil Brunner's criticism of Niebuhr, where Brunner notes that "it would be difficult to determine just what Reinhold Niebuhr means by his equally crucial concept of the Biblical 'eschatological symbol'" ("Some Remarks on Reinhold Niebuhr's Work as a ChristianThinker," in *Reinhold Niebuhr*, ed. Kegley and Bretall, p. 31).

Chapter Three

1. See, e.g., R. Thiemann, ed., *The Legacy of H. Richard Niebuhr* (Minneapolis: Fortress Press, 1991); C. Scriven, *The Transformation of Culture: Christian Social Ethics After H. Richard Niebuhr* (Scottsdale, Pa.: Herald Press, 1988); J. Diefenthaler, *H. Richard Niebuhr: A Lifetime of Reflections on the Church and the World* (Macon, Ga.: Mercer University Press, 1986); D. C. Grant, *God the Center of Value: Value Theory in the Theology of H. Richard Niebuhr* (Fort Worth: Christian University Press, 1984); J. Irish, *The Religous Thought of H. Richard Niebuhr* (Atlanta: John Knox Press, 1983); D. Ottati, *Meaning and Method in H. Richard Niebuhr's Theology* (Washington, D.C.: University Press of America, 1982); L. Kliever, *H. Richard Niebuhr* (Waco, Tex.: Word Books, 1977); D. E. Fadner, *The Responsible God: A Study of the Christian Philosophy of H. Richard Niebuhr* (Missoula, Mont.: Scholars Press, 1975); J. W. Fowler, *To See the Kingdom: The Theological Vision of H. Richard Niebuhr* (Nashville: Abingdon Press, 1974); J. Godsey, *The Promise of H. Richard Niebuhr* (Philadelphia: Lippincott, 1970); L. Hoedemaker, *The Theology of H. Richard Niebuhr* (Philadelphia: Pilgrim Press, 1970); and P. Ramsey, ed., *Faith and Ethics: The Theology of H. Richard Niebuhr* (New York: Harper & Row, 1957).

2. See, e.g., H. R. Niebuhr, "Reformation: Continuing Imperative," *Christian Century* 77 (1960): 248–51.

3. In examining Niebuhr's approaches to Scripture I have relied primarily upon six of his eight books and on one essay. The books are *Christ and Culture* (New York: Harper & Brothers, 1951); *The Meaning of Revelation* (New York: Macmillan, 1941); *The Purpose of the Church and Its Ministry: Reflections on the Aims of Theological Education*, in collaboration with D. D. Williams and J. M. Gustafson (New York: Harper & Row, 1956); *Radical Monotheism and Western Culture* (New York: Harper & Brothers, 1960); *The Responsible Self: An Essay in Christian Moral Philosophy* (New York: Harper & Row, 1963); and the posthumous publication edited by his son R. Richard Niebuhr, *Faith on Earth: An Inquiry into the Structure of Human Faith* (New Haven: Yale University Press, 1989). I have also used his sociohistorical studies, *The Social Sources of Denominationalism* (New York: Henry Holt and Company, 1929; reprint, 1957) and *The Kingdom of God in America* (New York: Harper & Row, 1937), though reflections on or use of the Bible in constructive theological ethics plays relatively little role in either study. The one essay of which I have made significant use is Niebuhr's "Introduction to Biblical Ethics," the first chapter of the sourcebook he edited with Waldo Beach, *Christian Ethics: Sources of the Living Tradition*, 2d ed. (New York: Ronald Press, 1973) (1st ed., 1955). Of the fifteen chapters in the 1955 edition of the book, H. R. Niebuhr wrote only four: chap. 1 (on biblical ethics), chap. 8 and 9 (on Luther and Calvin, respectively), and chap. 13 (on

Jonathan Edwards). Only the chapter on biblical ethics does not contain a section of primary sources, presumably because Niebuhr felt it unnecessary to reprint the biblical materials. (On p. 13, n. 4, Niebuhr encourages the reader to read Exod. 20:22–23:33, Amos, the Sermon on the Mount, and Paul's letter to the Romans.) I have, of course, made use of many other articles and essays Niebuhr wrote, but those listed here were the most important primary sources for my examination of his uses of Scripture.

4. Eden Theological Seminary was his alma mater, from which he had graduated in 1915, and was part of the German Evangelical Synod of North America, to which he belonged. For the influence of the Evangelical Synod on Niebuhr, see esp. Diefenthaler, *H. Richard Niebuhr*, pp. 1–25.

5. H. R. Niebuhr and D. D. Williams, eds., *The Ministry in Historical Perspectives* (New York: Harper & Brothers, 1956); H. R. Niebuhr, D. D. Williams, and J. M. Gustafson, *The Advancement of Theological Education* (New York: Harper & Brothers, 1957).

6. I have found only two other examinations of Niebuhr's uses of Scripture: a section in W. C. Spohn's popular book *What Are They Saying About Scripture and Ethics?* (New York and Ramsay: Paulist Press, 1984), pp. 71–84; and the doctoral dissertation by B. T. Jordan, "The Use of Scripture in the Ethics of H. Richard Niebuhr" (Ph.D. diss., Emory University, 1974). Jordan approaches Niebuhr from the perspective of methodology in ethics. Though I have found his work of some help, I must confess some surprise upon realizing that Jordan does not deal with any of Niebuhr's concrete interpretations of biblical texts. Finally, see also E. L. Long's "The Relational Motif and the Bible," in his *A Survey of Christian Ethics* (New York: Oxford University Press, 1967), pp. 117–28.

7. H. R. Niebuhr, *Faith on Earth*, p. 21 n. 22.

8. See, e.g., H. R. Niebuhr's citations of Job and Isaiah in his *Radical Monotheism and Western Culture*, p. 51, the Psalms and Job on p. 124; Job in *Christ and Culture*, pp. 154, 199 (Gospel of John); the last chapter of Genesis in *Responsible Self*, p. 169, "Paul" (Gal. 2:20) on p. 156; Jesus' words on the cross (from Luke) in *Meaning of Revelation*, p. 89, and the Gospel of John on p. 115.

9. If we take a simple (and simplistic) look at Niebuhr's references to Scripture, the following information stands out. By my calcualtions, Niebuhr refers to the Bible 375 times in the eight books and one essay surveyed. Of these references, 146 are to Old Testament texts and 229 are to New Testament texts. The totals are somewhat deceptive, however, because 171 of the 375 references (some citations, some not) come from Niebuhr's thirty-five-page essay "Introduction to Biblical Ethics" (110 of the 146 Old Testament references and 61 of the 229 New Testament references).

E.g., out of 34 references to Amos, all but 2 come from Niebuhr's "Introduction to Biblical Ethics." Similarly, out of 31 references to Exodus, only 5 do not come from this essay. The story is somewhat different with the New Testament. Of the 47 references to Matthew, 21 come from this essay. Only 3 of the 47 references to John are from the essay, while 18 of the 31 references to Romans are found in it. Excluding this essay, then, Niebuhr refers to the Old Testament 36 times and to the New Testament 168 times in his eight books.

10. In H. R. Niebuhr's *Radical Monotheism and Western Culture*, there are fourteen references to Exodus, Deuteronomy, Job, Psalms, and Isaiah, emphasizing, not surprisingly, radical monotheism and the sovereignty of God.

11. H. R. Niebuhr, *The Purpose of the Church and Its Ministry*, p. 102. See also Niebuhr's reference to Old Testament texts as fundamental witnesses to God and God's relationship to humanity in *Meaning of Revelation*, pp. 42–44 (in relation to God's revelation to Moses in the burning bush story in Exod. 3).

12. *Responsible Self*, pp. 169–70.

13. Ibid., p. 170.

14. Ibid., p. 66.

15. Ibid., pp. 129–30.

16. Niebuhr is also critical of the general movement of Jewish faith from the time of Second Isaiah to the time of Ezra and Nehemiah. Indeed, he seems to see this movement as a general decline of faith away from radical monotheism to henotheism. In *Radical Monotheism and Western Culture*, Niebuhr states: "Evolutionary theory saw in the development of Israelite religion only upward movement from henotheism to monotheism; but the movement from Second Isaiah to Ezra and Nehemiah seems to run in the opposite direction" (p. 57).

17. H. R. Niebuhr, "Introduction to Biblical Ethics," pp. 31–36.

18. See, e.g., H. R. Niebuhr, *Responsible Self*, pp. 14, 60, 63, 66, 168.

19. H. R. Niebuhr, "Introduction to Biblical Ethics," p. 22.

20. H. R. Niebuhr, "The Social Gospel and the Mind of Jesus," ed. D. Yeager, *Journal of Religious Ethics* 16 (1988): p. 120. This previously unpublished essay was originally a paper read before the American Theological Society, New York, in 1933.

21. J. M. Gustafson, introduction to *Responsible Self*, pp. 6–41; esp. pp. 19–25.

22. Reflecting on the virtues of Jesus in *Christ and Culture*, Niebuhr writes rather strongly against liberal construals of Jesus' "love ethic": "The virtue of Christ which religious liberalism has magnified beyond all others is love. . . . Yet when we examine the New Testament and study its portraits of Jesus we become dubious of the descriptive value of such phrases as 'the absolutism and perfectionism of Jesus' love ethic' [with reference to Reinhold Niebuhr's 1935 *An Interpretation of Christian Ethics*, p. 39]. . . . Jesus nowhere commands love for its own sake, and nowhere exhibits that complete dominance of the kindly over the aggressive sentiments and emotions which seems indicated by the idea that in him and for him love 'must completely fill the soul.' . . . The virtue of love in Jesus' character and demand is the virtue of the *love of God and of the neighbor in God*, not the virtue of the love of love" (pp. 15–16). Similarly, H. Richard Niebuhr is critical of Reinhold Niebuhr's liberal portrait of Jesus in *Moral Man and Immoral Society* (1932). See H. R. Niebuhr's "The Social Gospel and the Mind of Jesus," pp. 118–19.

23. H. R. Niebuhr, *Purpose of the Church*, 43.

24. See esp. H. R. Niebuhr, *Meaning of Revelation*, pp. 44–66. See also L. A. Hoedemaker, "Revelation and the Duality of Internal and External History," in *Theology of H. Richard Niebuhr*, pp. 98–105 and H. Frei, "The Theology of H. Richard Niebuhr," in *Faith and Ethics: The Theology of H. Richard Niebuhr*, ed. P. Ramsey (New York: Harper & Row, 1957), pp. 89–91.

25. H. R. Niebuhr, *Meaning of Revelation*, p. 48.

26. See ibid., pp. 61–65. It is also important for Niebuhr to stress that persons do not have singular internal histories, "because their faiths are various and the events of life cannot be related to one continuing and abiding good" (p. 57).

27. Ibid., pp. 53–54. Similarly, Niebuhr writes: "We cannot point to Scriptures saying that what we mean can be known if men will but read what is there written. We must read the law with the mind of the prophets and the prophets with the eyes of Jesus; we must immerse ourselves with Paul in the story of the crucifixion, and read Paul with the aid of the spirit in the church if we would find revelation in the Scriptures. A history that was recorded forward, as it were, must be read backward through our history if it is to be understood as revelation" (p. 37).

28. H. R. Niebuhr, "Introduction to Biblical Ethics," pp. 11–13. See also *Kingdom of God in America*, where Niebuhr states: "[D]espite all its diversity the Bible has a certain unity—that not only of the Hebraic but also of the prophetic outlook on life. If its diversity fostered freedom, its unity gave direction to that freedom" (p. 203 n. 24).

29. H. R. Niebuhr, *Meaning of Revelation*, pp. 65–66.

30. H. R. Niebuhr, See *Responsible Self*, p. 169.

31. H. R. Niebuhr, "Introduction to Biblical Ethics," p. 22.

32. Ibid., p. 20.

33. Ibid., p. 33.

34. See H. R. Niebuhr, *Responsible Self*, pp. 166–67; H. R. Niebuhr, "Introduction to Biblical Ethics," p. 34.

35. H. R. Niebuhr, "Introduction to Biblical Ethics," p. 35. In his essay "The Social Gospel and the Mind of Jesus," Niebuhr also states: "There was *a social gospel in the mind of this Jesus* [in the synoptic Gospels]" (p. 125).

36. H. R. Niebuhr, *Meaning of Revelation*, p. 38.

37. H. R. Niebuhr, *Faith on Earth*, p. 87.

38. Ibid., p. 93. See also pp. 91, 94.

39. See H. R. Niebuhr, *Meaning of Revelation*, p. 29; for other allusions in Niebuhr to the Christ hymn in Phil. 2:5–11, see *Christ and Culture*, pp. 23 n. 27, 26; and *Radical Monotheism and Western Culture*, p. 59.

40. H. R. Niebuhr, "Introduction to Biblical Ethics," p. 42. Similarly, Niebuhr writes: "What Paul emphasizes is not . . . the fact that because God is the Creator of all men therefore all are brothers but rather that since Christ died and rose again for all men he has made all of them neighbors both by showing their common sinfulness and by calling all to newness of life" (p. 43).

41. H. R. Niebuhr, *Meaning of Revelation*, p. 63.

42. H. R. Niebuhr, *Purpose of the Church*, p. 87.

43. H. R. Niebuhr, *Faith on Earth*, p. 114.

44. Ibid., p. 117.

45. H. R. Niebuhr, "Introduction to Biblical Ethics," p. 10.

46. H. R. Niebuhr, *Purpose of the Church*, p. 119.

47. "In this communication between the Biblical and the modern communities the movement is not all one way; it is not simply the Bible that speaks to the theological student; he also speaks to the men of the Bible. Nothing is more evident from the history of Biblical interpretation in the Church and from the self-critical conversations of modern Biblical scholars than that the movement is reciprocal. New light does break forth from Scriptures as inquirers learn from their social and personal experience to ask new questions of the old communities and to read apparently familiar communications in a new setting" (ibid., p. 120).

48. H. R. Niebuhr, *Meaning of Revelation*, p. 81. Niebuhr continues: "To be sure, the labor of prophets and poets and priests who searched the memories of Israel and ordered them with the aid of the revelatory image was necessary before a unified understanding could be achieved. They had to carry the light of revelation into their past; revelation did not excuse the reasoning heart from toil but equipped it with the instrument whereby it could understand what it remembered. So the Scriptures were written not as the history of revelation only but as the history of Israel understood and unified by means of revelation" (p. 81, see also p. 97).

49. H. R. Niebuhr, *Responsible Self*, p. 143. See also p. 102, where he writes: "There is, however, another way of changing the patterns of interpretation—a method more

fitting to beings that have in every present an internal, remembered past which they cannot forget or leave behind. It is the way of *reinterpreting* the past. It recalls, accepts, understands, and reorganizes the past instead of abandoning it."

50. As Niebuhr states in his "Introduction to Biblical Ethics": "The Bible is the book in which the story of the self-disclosure of God, his nature and will, to Israel and to the world, is recorded" (p. 11).

51. Niebuhr continues: "Here the clear distinction is made between the particular intentions that guide a finite action and the divine intention that uses or lies behind such actions" (*Responsible Self*, p. 169).

52. Niebuhr continues: "The chapter represents, it seems to me, the logic of Hebrew ethics as that ethics runs through all the pages of Hebrew Scriptures and through the tragic, yet wonderful story of this people of God" (*Responsible Self*, p. 170). On Isa. 10 elsewhere in Niebuhr, see *Christ and Culture*, p. x; and "Introduction to Biblical Ethics," p. 28.

53. Niebuhr is quick to add, however: "As ethos of universal responsibility the ethos exemplified in Jesus Christ is not unique. It has affinities to other forms of universal ethics. Insistence on the absolute uniqueness of the Christian ethos has never been able to meet either the theoretical or the practical test" (*Responsible Self*, pp. 167–68).

54. Reflecting on a difference between Reinhold Niebuhr and H. Richard Niebuhr, Liston Pope commented in a remark addressed to Paul Tillich: "I once went with Richard Niebuhr to hear Reinhold Niebuhr speak. I suppose I should not quote Richard in his absence. But I am sure he has said this to Reinhold many times. I turned to him and said, 'What did you think of the lecture?' And he said, 'I don't see how Reinie talks so much about sin without talking more about grace' " (see the "Discussion" of Paul Tillich's essay "Sin and Grace in the Theology of Reinhold Niebuhr," in *Reinhold Niebuhr: A Prophetic Voice in Our Time*, ed. H. R. Landon [Greenwich, Conn.: Seabury Press, 1962], p. 50).

55. In presenting his definition of "Christ," Niebuhr emphasizes various virtues of Christ (love, hope, obedience, faith, humility) but devotes most of this section to criticizing and qualifying how these virtues have been developed in contemporary theology (*Christ and Culture*, pp. 11–29).

56. He also notes aspects of this approach in the book of Revelation.

57. H. R. Niebuhr, "Back to Benedict," *Christian Century* 42 (1925): 860–61; H. R. Niebuhr, W. Pauck, and F. P. Miller, *The Church Against the World* (Chicago: Willett, Clark & Co., 1935), esp. pp. 1–13 and 123–56. See also the discussion of Niebuhr's separatist approach in Kliever, *H. Richard Niebuhr*, pp. 48–52. See also the celebrated exchange between H. Richard Niebuhr and his brother Reinhold: H. Richard's essay "The Grace of Doing Nothing," *Christian Century* 49 (1932): 378–80, and Reinhold's response, "Must We Do Nothing?" *Christian Century* 49 (1932): 415–17.

58. H. R. Niebuhr, *Christ and Culture*, pp. 68, 71.

59. Ibid., p. 69, with reference to C. H. Dodd's *The Johannine Epistles* (London: Hodder & Stoughton, 1946).

60. Further, Niebuhr criticizes the denigration of reason in relation to revelation in this approach, which he sees as implicit in 1 John's contrast between the world of darkness and the realm of light, where Christians walk (*Christ and Culture*, pp. 76–77).

61. Niebuhr does note how the "Christ of Culture" type tends to distort the New Testament witness: "the cultural answers to the Christ-culture problem show a consistent tendency to distort the figure of the New Testament Jesus. . . . They take some fragment

of the complex New Testament story and interpretation, call this the essential characteristic of Jesus, elaborate upon it, and thus reconstruct their own mythical figure of the Lord. Some choose the opening verses of the Fourth Gospel, some the Sermon on the Mount, some the announcement of the kingdom, as the key to Christology. It is always something that seems to agree with the interests or the needs of their time. . . . Ultimately these fanciful descriptions are destroyed by the force of the Biblical story. With or without the official actions of bishops and councils, the New Testament witness maintains itself against them. In the second century the formation of the New Testament canon, in the nineteenth and twentieth the continuous work of Biblical scholars, make it evident that Jesus Christ is not like this" (ibid., pp. 108–9).

62. Ibid., p. 123. He continues: "[B]ut there are many statements in gospels and epistles which sound the *motif* or which can be interpreted, without violence to the text, as containing this solution [synthesist] of the Christ-and-culture problem. Among them are the following: 'Think not that I have come to abolish the law and the prophets [Matt. 5:17–19 (cf. 23:2), 22:21; Rom. 13:1, 6—with citations of each]' " (p. 123).

63. Regarding the inclusion of Paul under this type, Niebuhr writes: "Whether or not Paul may be counted a member of such a group, it is evident that its later representatives are his spiritual descendants, and that the *motif* is more pronouncedly present in his thought than are synthetic or radical, not to speak of cultural, tendencies" (ibid., p. 159).

64. Niebuhr goes on to treat Marcion's dualism as a distortion of Paul's and pays special attention to Luther as most representative of the dualistic type (which, of course, begs the question of whether Niebuhr too readily reads Paul through the eyes of Luther).

65. Ibid., pp. 185–88. Niebuhr also criticizes Paul's and Luther's dualism for too closely linking temporality or finiteness to sin, "as to move creation and fall into very close proximity, and in that connection to do less than justice to the creative work of God" (p. 188).

66. Following C. H. Dodd and the general consensus of the 1940s and 1950s in New Testament scholarship, Niebuhr clearly sees the Fourth Gospel as more heavily Hellenistic than Jewish.

67. Niebuhr concludes the chapter by considering Augustine and F. D. Maurice as other examples of the Christ the Transformer of Culture type. Regarding Maurice, Niebuhr writes: "He is above all a Johannine thinker, who begins with the fact that the Christ who comes into the world comes into his own, and that it is Christ himself who exercises his kingship over men" (*Christ and Culture*, p. 220).

68. Kliever, *H. Richard Niebuhr*, pp. 53–60.

69. H. R. Niebuhr, *Kingdom of God in America*, p. 109. It is interesting to note that in responding to a question regarding which books most shaped his vocational attitude and philosophy of life, Niebuhr listed ten titles, including Jonathan Edwards's *The Nature of True Virtue* (along with Bosanquet, Spinoza, Pascal, Otto, Barth, Calvin, Kant, Troeltsch, and Palgrave's *Golden Treasury of English Songs and Lyrics*) ("Ex Libris," *Christian Century* 79 [1962]: 754).

70. K. S. Latourette, ed., *The Gospel, the Church, and the World* (New York: Harper & Brothers, 1946), pp. 111–33.

71. H. R. Niebuhr, "Introduction to Biblical Ethics," pp. 10–11.

72. Ibid., p. 11.

73. H. R. Niebuhr, *Faith on Earth*, pp. 114–115.

74. Gustafson, introduction to *Responsible Self*, pp. 22–24.

75. H. R. Niebuhr, *Faith on Earth*, p. 115.

76. H. R. Niebuhr, "Reformation," p. 250. In the same context, he warns against the "deification of Scriptures and of the church."

77. Niebuhr notes this as well in *Kingdom of God in America*: "The equation of the Scriptures with the revealed will of God led to virtual denial of the living reality of God. . . . Moreover, the Scriptures taught the immediate activity of God through his Holy Spirit and criticized severely the worship of the letter" (p. 61).

78. H. R. Niebuhr, *Faith on Earth*, p. 115.

79. Ibid., pp. 115–16.

80. Ibid., p. 116.

81. Ibid.

82. H. R. Niebuhr, *Meaning of Revelation*, p. x.

83. H. R. Niebuhr, *Responsible Self*, p. 46.

84. H. R. Niebuhr, *Meaning of Revelation*, p. x.

85. Niebuhr further states: "The history of the inner life can only be confessed by selves who speak of what happened to them in the community of other selves" (*Meaning of Revelation*, p. 54).

86. See H. R. Niebuhr, *Faith on Earth*, p. 114. "For what are the Scriptures except the confession of trust in God and loyalty to him and the report of what happened to those who believed in him and were not put to shame?"

87. H. R. Niebuhr, *Meaning of Revelation*, p. 62.

88. Niebuhr clearly saw the limits even of his own approach to constructive Christian ethics: "It will not do to say that the analysis of all our moral life in general and of Biblical ethics in particular by means of the idea of responsibility offers us an absolutely new way of understanding man's ethical life or of constructing a system of Christian ethics. . . . But the approach to our moral existence as selves, and to our existence as Christians in particular, with the aid of this idea makes some aspects of our life as agents intelligible in a way that the teleology and deontology of traditional thought cannot do" (*Responsible Self*, p. 67).

89. Ibid., p. 162. Niebuhr also sees Isa. 10 as presenting a paradigm of the ethics of response.

90. H. R. Niebuhr, "War as the Judgment of God," *Christian Century* 59 (1942): 630–33; H. R. Niebuhr, "Is God in the War?" *Christian Century* 59 (1942): 953–955; and H. R. Niebuhr, "War as Crucifixion," *Christian Century* 60 (1943): 513–15. In addition to these essays, Niebuhr wrote two other war-related articles ten years earlier: "The Grace of Doing Nothing," *Christian Century* 49 (1932): 378–80; and "A Communication: The Only Way into the Kingdom of God," *Christian Century* 49 (1932): 447. On Niebuhr's war articles in particular, see R. B. Miller, "H. Richard Niebuhr's War Articles: A Transvaluation of Value," *Journal of Religion* 68 (1988): 242–62; and W. Spohn, "H. Richard Niebuhr: Interpreting Events," in his *What Are They Saying About Scripture and Ethics?* pp. 71–84.

91. H. R. Niebuhr, "War as the Judgment of God," p. 630.

92. Niebuhr clearly saw the war as God's judgment upon the self-preoccupations of the United States in particular: "Our nation . . . has demonstrated its profound preoccupation with its own prosperity, safety and righteousness, so that in its withdrawal from international responsibilities, in its tariff, monetary and neutrality legislation, it has acted always with a single eye to its own interests rather than to those of its neighbors in the commonwealth of nations" (ibid., p. 632).

93. H. R. Niebuhr, "War as Crucifixion," p. 513. See also his "War as the Judgment of God," where he writes "the suffering of innocence is used for the remaking of the guilty" (p. 631).

94. As B. T. Jordan notes, "Niebuhr is concerned to illumine contemporary experience by an analogical use of Biblical images" ("The Use of Scripture in the Ethics of H. Richard Niebuhr," p. 188).

95. H. R. Niebuhr, "War as Crucifixion," p. 515.

96. J. Cobb, *Living Options in Protestant Theology* (Philadelphia: Westminster Press, 1962), pp. 298–99.

97. H. R. Niebuhr, *Christ and Culture*, pp. 196–97.

98. H. R. Niebuhr, *Responsible Self*, p. 172.

99. Ibid., p. 173.

100. H. R. Niebuhr, "War as Crucifixion," p. 515.

101. H. R. Niebuhr, *The Responsible Self*, p. 177.

Chapter Four

1. See, e.g., the comments of C. Curran: "Häring's work stands as the most creative and important accomplishment in moral theology in this century" ("*Free and Faithful in Christ*: A Critical Evaluation," *Studia Moralia* 20 [1982] 145); or V. Macnamara, who states that "it is doubtful if anyone contributed more to the general spirit of renewal than Häring" (*Faith and Ethics: Recent Roman Catholicism* [Dublin: Gill & MacMillan; Washington, D.C.: Georgetown University Press, 1985], p. 33.

2. For a thorough overview of the development of moral theology, see esp. J. Mahoney, *The Making of Moral Theology: A Study of the Roman Catholic Tradition* (Oxford: Clarendon Press, 1987).

3. Curran notes that "no book of moral theology has been translated into more languages and used by more people than Häring's *Law of Christ*." ("*Free and Faithful in Christ*," p. 145). (It has been translated into eleven languages and has gone through eight editions in German, with the eighth appearing in 1967.) Similarly, R. M. Gula states that "the most significant work for the renewal movement was Bernard Häring's *The Law of Christ* . . . Few works were as popular as that one, and no one contributed more to the general spirit of renewal in moral theology than did Bernard Häring. This 'charter document' of moral theology retained an interest in the concerns of the manuals but approached these interests with a new spirit. Häring's work shows, if even at times in an uncritical fashion, what a moral theology might look like which returns to its sources, notably the Bible, and which is integrated with the great mysteries of faith" (*Reason Informed by Faith: Foundations of Catholic Morality* [New York and Mahwah, N.J.: Paulist Press, 1989], p. 29).

4. It is no accident that Häring was invited to serve as a *peritus*, an expert, at Vatican II, although moral theology was not high on the agenda of the Council and is referred to in only one brief passage from the documents, *Optatam totius* (Decree on Priestly Formation, promulgated on 28 October 1965), para. 16.

5. See, e.g., L. Abadamloora, "*Some Modern Attempts Towards Biblical Renewal in Moral Theology*" (Dissertatio ad Doctoratum in Facultate Theologiae Pontificiae Universitatis Gregorianae, Rome, 1975).

6. W. M. Abbot, ed., *The Documents of Vatican II* (New York: Crossroad, 1989), p. 452.

7. B. Häring, *My Witness for the Church*, trans. L. Swidler (New York and Mahwah, N.J.: Paulist Press, 1992), p. 60.

8. See, e.g., B. Häring, "The Role of the Catholic Moral Theologian," in *Moral Theology: Challenges for the Future*, ed. C. E. Curran (New York and Mahwah, N.J.: Paulist Press, 1990), p. 32; and B. Häring, *Free and Faithful in Christ*, 3 vols. (New York: Seabury Press, 1978–81), 1:7, 57, 101.

9. B. Häring, *The Law of Christ*, 3 vols., trans. E. Kaiser (Westminster, Md.: Newman Press, 1961–66), 1:viii. Along the same lines, he states elsewhere: "To present the specific characteristics and the content of the New Testament law is the task of moral theology as a whole" (ibid., 1:257).

10. I have been able to find only three works that examine Häring's use of Scripture: the doctoral dissertation of M. Clark, "The Use of Sacred Scripture in the Moral Theology of Father Bernard Häring, C.Ss.R." (Gregorian, 1979; see also now his short summary "The Major Scriptural Themes in the Moral Theology of Father Bernard Häring," *Studia Moralia* 30 [1992]: 3–16); a section from the doctoral dissertation of Abadamloora, "Some Modern Attempts Towards Biblical Renewal in Moral Theology," pp. 218–36; and a few pages in V. Macnamara's *Faith and Ethics* (pp. 33–35). But these studies deal only with Häring's *Law of Christ* and not with *Free and Faithful in Christ* (Clark's 1992 essay does incorporate some material from *Free and Faithful in Christ*). Many authors refer in a general way to Häring's biblical approach. See, e.g., R. Gula, *What Are They Saying About Moral Norms?* (New York and Mahwah, N.J.: Paulist Press, 1982), p. 29; and P. Lehmann, who from a Protestant perspective comments on Häring's emphasis on responsibility: "What impresses the reader is the conspicuously biblical way in which this interpretation of responsibility is worked out" (*Ethics in a Christian Context* [London: SCM Press, 1963], pp. 298–299).

11. Häring, *Law of Christ*, 1:8. In Häring's review of the history of moral theology, he regularly praises or criticizes significant authors for their use or neglect of Scripture. E.g., he commends Augustine and Gregory the Great for their attention to Scripture (ibid., p. 9). In particular, Häring praises the work of two nineteenth-century German moral theologians, John Michael Sailer and John Baptist Hirscher, for grounding their moral theology in the biblical material on the Sermon on the Mount and on the kingdom of God, respectively (ibid., pp. 23–26). He also commends F. Linsenmann as the most important continuator of the work of Sailer and Hirscher, in part because "we sense a genuine Pauline spirit" (ibid., p. 28). Linsemann receives even more attention in *Free and Faithful in Christ*, 1:53–54. Similarly, Häring praises the work of the twentieth-century moral theologian F. Tillmann, "whose moral teaching is based entirely on the inspired word," and who "radically eliminated on Biblical grounds" the false antithesis between a morality of minimal requirement and an asceticism for those seeking perfection that had so dominated the field before him (*Law of Christ*, 1:31–32).

12. Häring, *Law of Christ*, 1:xi.

13. Bernard Häring, letter to author, 16, July 1991.

14. Häring, *Law of Christ*, 1:257.

15. E.g., Häring makes 71 references to Proverbs in *Law of Christ* but only 5 references in *Free and Faithful in Christ*. Similarly, one finds 33 references to Sirach in *Law of Christ* but only 3 in *Free and Faithful in Christ*.

16. Häring makes the following comment in *Free and Faithful in Christ*: "Moral theology is interested not only in decisions and actions. It raises the question, 'What ought I to do?' but asks, first of all, 'What ought I to be; what kind of person does the

Lord want me to be?'" (1:85). Similarly, see "Role of the Catholic Moral Theologian," where Häring warns against "the chaos of a thousand do's and don'ts" (p. 42).

17. Häring refers to this passage ten times, more than any other in the Old Testament. See *Law of Christ,* 1:208, 258, 397; 2:xxix; 3:16; *Free and Faithful in Christ,* 1:14, 186, 226, 237, 423.

18. Häring, *Free and Faithful in Christ,* 1:340.

19. Ibid., p. 75. Häring cites John 15:12 sixteen times: *Law of Christ,* 1:3, 257; 2:13, 85, 89, 170, 360, 377; *Free and Faithful in Christ,* 1:16, 75, 126, 132, 237, 252, 305; 2:435. Häring refers nine times to Matt. 5:48: *Law of Christ,* 2:xxxii, 158, 418; *Free and Faithful in Christ,* 1:35, 75, 250, 341; 2:431, 454.

20. Häring, *Free and Faithful in Christ,* 2:542; 1:48.

21. Häring, "Role of the Catholic Moral Theologian," p. 37.

22. Häring refers to Rom. 8:2 seventeen times: *Law of Christ,* 1:xi, 238, 258, 259, 306; 2:xxxvii; 3:78, 194, 675; *Free and Faithful in Christ,* 1:128, 141, 249, 292, 344, 371, 384; 3:79. Häring has a similar emphasis on Rom. 6:14, with its language of no longer living under the law but under grace.

23. Häring refers to Gal. 6:2 nine times: *Law of Christ,* 1:257, 262; 2:75; *Free and Faithful in Christ,* 1:5, 17, 128, 386, 438; 2:456. He explicitly states that he derived the title for *Law of Christ* from Gal. 6:2 in *Free and Faithful in Christ,* 1:5, contrary to Raymond Collins's claim that the title comes from Rom. 8:2 (*Christian Morality: Biblical Foundations* [Notre Dame: University of Notre Dame Press, 1986], p. 22). J. Gustafson makes the same mistaken attribution in "The Changing Use of the Bible in Christian Ethics," in *Readings in Moral Theology,* no. 4, *The Use of Scripture in Moral Theology,* ed. C. E. Curran and R. A. McCormick (New York and Ramsey: Paulist Press, 1984), p. 147.

24. Häring cites John 1:14 thirteen times: *Law of Christ,* 1:63, 89; 2:xxix, xxx, xxxii, 8; 3:189, 549, 587; *Free and Faithful in Christ,* 1:107, 115; 2:104, 203.

25. Häring acknowledges that "to a great extent, the Bible is narrative theology, an unsystematized account of great events in the history of creation and salvation" ("Role of the Catholic Moral Theologian," p. 42), but his own writing does not develop the narrative character of the Bible.

26. See Häring, *Law of Christ,* 2:xxxii, 427; *Free and Faithful in Christ,* 1:115, 248, 422, 440; 2:429, 560.

27. Häring, *Free and Faithful in Christ,* 2:560.

28. Given Häring's attention to the nuances of translation, it is somewhat surprising that he rather anachronistically condemns apparently all modern forms of homosexuality, partly on the basis of Paul's negative reference to "homosexuality," without discussing what Paul may have meant by "homosexuality" in his own historical context. See Häring's brief discussion of homosexuality in *Free and Faithful in Christ,* 2:563–64.

29. Ibid., 1:7.

30. Ibid., p. 333.

31. Collins comments that prior to Vatican II, moral theologians would regularly appeal "to a scriptural passage, taken out of its biblical context, in order to provide a biblical warrant for or a scriptural confirmation in support of a moral judgment which had been essentially elaborated by means of a merely rational process" (*Christian Morality,* pp. 1–2). In a footnote to this observation Collins remarks: "Essentially this use of the Scriptures is to be found in the work of Bernard Häring, *The Law of Christ.* . . . it must be acknowledged that, apart from some significant exceptions (e.g., on the love of neighbor), the use of the Scriptures did not really enter the fabric of the exposition" (pp. 13–14 n. 2). Similar comments may be found in Gula, *Reason Informed by Faith,* where he

writes: "Even Bernard Häring's *The Law of Christ*, for example, which is monumental as a breakthrough in the renewal of moral theology, largely uses the proof-text method" (p. 166). Gula's comment even occurs in a section entitled "Pre-critical Use of Scripture."

32. See *Faith and Ethics*, pp. 33–35, for Macnamara's critical discussion of Häring's use of Scripture in *Law of Christ*.

33. Macnamara, *Faith and Ethics*, p. 34.

34. Ibid. See Häring, *Law of Christ*, 3:315, who in his use of Gen. 1:28 is citing a portion of the *Pastoral Constitution on the Church in the Modern World*, art. 50, which Macnamara does not mention.

35. See the discussion in MacNamara, *Faith and Ethics*, p. 34. The citation in Häring comes from *Law of Christ*, 3:316.

36. Bernard Häring, letter to author, 16 July, 1991. The English is his own.

37. Häring, *Law of Christ*, 2:xxxv.

38. See the comments of D. H. Kelsey on "biblical concept theology" in his *The Uses of Scripture in Recent Theology* (Philadelphia: Fortress Press, 1975), pp. 24–29, although Kelsey deals with Protestant theologians.

39. Vol. 3 of *Law of Christ* has no separate treatments of any biblical concept.

40. Indeed, it is interesting to note that of the journals and main works listed in the abbreviations at the beginning of *Law of Christ*, the only work that has any real connection to biblical studies is Kittel's *Theological Dictionary*. One finds no references to periodical literature in biblical studies.

41. Häring, *Free and Faithful in Christ*, 2:380.

42. Häring, *Law of Christ*, 1:423.

43. Häring, *Free and Faithful in Christ*, 3:225.

44. Ibid., 1:32–33.

45. Ibid., p. 33.

46. Ibid., 2:156.

47. Ibid., 3:229.

48. Ibid., 1:307.

49. See, e.g., *Law of Christ*, 1:124, where Häring cites 1 John 2:9 ("He who says that he is in the light, and hates his brother, is in the darkness still") and then comments: "Obviously the word *light* means more than the simple light of reason; it means the total splendor of grace proceeding from the light of knowledge in the Word."

50. There are hundreds of examples of cluster citations in Häring's work. See, e.g., *Law of Christ*, 2:xxix, xxxi, xxxvii, 18, 73–75, 93, 128, 131, 392, 406–7, 418–19, 500; 3:49, 145, 189–90, 229, 299, 316–18, 434–50, 483, 560, 577, 586, 617; *Free and Faithful in Christ*, 1:128–29, 131–32, 139, 148, 186–87, 226–27, 229, 237, 248, 256; 2:12, 42, 57, 78, 106, 154, 206, 219, 401, 412, 454; 3:175, 393–94, 396.

51. Häring, *Law of Christ*, 1:257.

52. Ibid., p. 251.

53. Ibid., p. 244.

54. Ibid., p. 251.

55. Ibid., p. 252.

56. Ibid., p. 257.

57. Ibid., p. 263.

58. Ibid., p. 403.

59. Ibid., 3:124.

60. Häring, *Free and Faithful in Christ*, 1:8.

61. Ibid., p. 11.

62. Ibid., p. 13. See also 1:61, where Häring cites Isa. 50:4–5 to show how Jesus is "the One who listens and can give the consoling and healing message."

63. Häring, *Free and Faithful in Christ*, 1:252.

64. Ibid., pp. 337–38. In the same place he writes: "Moral Theology is neither biblicistic nor a mere philosophical endeavor. It is either under the authority of the word of God or it is not theology at all. But the way it is guided by the Bible needs to be discovered by painstaking effort of research and reflection. The Bible offers much more than a moral code, something quite different from a list of ready-made norms, but nevertheless, does offer binding norms."

65. Ibid., p. 336.

66. Ibid., p. 335.

67. Ibid., pp. 201–2.

68. B. Häring, "The Normative Value of the Sermon on the Mount," *Catholic Biblical Quarterly* 29 (1967): 69–79. Already in *Law of Christ* (1:26), Häring had criticized most nineteenth-century works on moral theology for not according the Sermon on the Mount its rightful and authoritative place in moral reflection.

69. Häring, *Law of Christ*, 1:403. See also 3:78–79, where Häring states: "Surely Christian moral teachings should be as richly positive as is the Sermon on the Mount which holds forth the loftiest ideals for every Christian."

70. MacNamara continues: "One does not know how crucial Scripture is to his system or whether, in the end, he needs it at all. One does not know whether it is meant to give a general religious vision of life; or whether he sees himself as founding a moral argument on it; or whether it provides a context which influences judgment in an indirect way; or whether it is meant to give inspiration and motivation. This rather uncritical appeal to biblical morality was typical of the first enthusiasm of the renewal and did much to provoke a reaction. Twenty-five years later, a great deal will have been learned and we shall find Häring adverting to all of these problems and advocating a more nuanced use of Scripture" (*Faith and Ethics*, p. 35).

71. Häring, *Free and Faithful in Christ*, 1:334.

72. Ibid., 3:398.

73. McCormick's statement comes from his 1971 "Notes on Moral Theology" regarding an article by Häring on marriage. The citation is taken from McCormick's *Notes on Moral Theology: 1965 Through 1980* (Washington, D.C.: University Press of America, 1981), p. 340. One of my colleagues in the Department of Theological Studies at Loyola Marymount University, Dr. Marie Anne Mayeski, remarked to me that this kind of fuzziness was experienced by many Roman Catholics as wonderfully freeing and liberating after so many years of moral pronouncements that allowed little to no flexibility.

74. "Finally, theological hermeneutics, using all the resources of philosophy and of the anthropological sciences, should always take place within the faith community" (Häring, *Free and Faithful in Christ*, 1:338).

75. Similarly, in the third volume of *Law of Christ*, Häring states: "Our first interest is the dialogical character of living fellowship with God and neighbor" (3:3).

76. The following two sections are entitled "God's Word and Man's Response in the Old Testament" and "God's Word and Man's Response in Christ" (*Law of Christ*, 2:xxi-xxxv).

77. Häring, *Free and Faithful in Christ*, 1:59.

78. For Häring's comments on some specific interpretations and applications of Scripture, see, e.g., his comments on Luke 6:34 ff. regarding lending with interest (*Law*

of Christ, 3:452), his comments on Paul's teachings about sexuality (*Free and Faithful in Christ*, 2:503), and Jesus' sayings about divorce (*Free and Faithful in Christ*, 2:540–42).

79. Häring, *Free and Faithful in Christ*, 3:398. In this context Häring is discussing using the New Testament for deliberations about war and peace.

80. See, e.g., Häring's comments in *Free and Faithful in Christ*: "We cannot learn from traditional moral theology unless we are fully aware of the different contexts in which it served the Church and the consciences of the faithful" (2:285).

81. See Häring, *Law of Christ*, 3:561.

82. See, e.g., his references to biblical studies in *Free and Faithful in Christ*, 2:503, 540–42. See also Häring's use of the work of R. Bultmann (1:68, 76–77; 2:129–30), O. Cullmann (1:154), W. Eichrodt (1:362), E. Käsemann (1:24, 119, 123; 3:157), and H. Schlier (1:133).

Chapter Five

1. Regarding Ramsey's significance, Charles Curran writes: "The very fact that no Christian ethicist today can discuss politics, medicine, and genetics without grappling with the thought of Paul Ramsey indicates the importance that Ramsey has for his contemporaries" (*Politics, Medicine, and Christian Ethics: A Dialogue with Paul Ramsey* [Philadelphia: Fortress Press, 1973], p. 222. And in the editorial preface to the special-focus issue of the *Journal of Religious Ethics* devoted to Paul Ramsey (vol. 19, no. 2; 1991, p. ii) James Johnson refers to Ramsey as "one of the most creative and broadly influential Christian theological ethicists of this century." See also J. Allen, "Paul Ramsey and His Respondents Since *The Patient As Person*," *Religious Studies Review* 5 (1979): 89–95.

2. See Curran, *Politics, Medicine, and Christian Ethics*; J. T. Johnson and D. H. Smith, eds., *Love and Society: Essays in the Ethics of Paul Ramsey* (Missoula, Mont.: Scholars Press, 1974) (Ramsey responds to these essays in "Some Rejoinders," *Journal of Religious Ethics* 4 [1976]: 185–237). See also two recent books on Ramsey's ethics: D. Attwood, *Paul Ramsey's Political Ethics* (Lanham, Md: Rowman & Littlefield, 1992); and D. S. Long, *Tragedy, Tradition, Transformism: The Ethics of Paul Ramsey* (Boulder, Colo.: Westview Press, 1993).

3. James Gustafson has also written on Paul Ramsey's work as a benchmark for theological ethics in his *Ethics from a Theocentric Perspective* (Chicago: University of Chicago Press, 1984), 2:84–93. Here, Gustafson does make some helpful comments on Ramsey's use of the Bible. There is also a passing reference to Ramsey's approach to the Bible in E. L. Long's article "The Use of the Bible in Christian Ethics: A Look at Basic Options," *Interpretation* 19 (1965): 149–62. Long appears to link Ramsey to Adolph von Harnack's and A. C. Knudson's emphasis on love as a moral principle that permeates the teachings of Jesus (see pp. 154, 160). See also A. Tambasco's analysis of Ramsey's use of the Bible under the heading "Scriptural-Deontological Model" in *The Bible for Ethics: Juan Luis Segundo and First World Ethics* (Washington, D.C.: University Press of America, 1981), pp. 28–42; the brief discussion of Ramsey's use of the Bible for social ethics in J.I.H. McDonald, *Biblical Interpretation and Christian Ethics* (Cambridge: Cambridge University Press, 1993), pp. 147–50; and the brief section on Ramsey, "A Biblical Thinker," in Attwood's *Paul Ramsey's Political Ethics*, pp. 16–17.

4. R. McCormick, "A Commentary on the Commentaries," in *Doing Evil to Achieve Good: Moral Choice in Conflict Situations*, ed. P. Ramsey and R. McCormick (Chicago: Loyola University Press, 1978), pp. 206–7. For an overview of the ongoing debate between

Ramsey and McCormick, see L. S. Cahill, "Within Shouting Distance: Paul Ramsey and Richard McCormick on Method," *Journal of Medicine and Philosophy* 4 (1979): 398–418.

5. See also Charles Curran: "There is another difficulty with Ramsey's writings—his prose style. He has been criticized for his long, complicated sentences, his purple passages, and his rhetoric which seems to get in the way of his meaning. There is no doubt that Ramsey is more of a chore than reading many other writers in the field of ethics. . . . Sometimes it is the complexity of the argument itself which requires careful scrutiny, but Ramsey does add to the problems by the opaqueness of his prose" (*Politics, Medicine, and Christian Ethics*, p. 8).

6. P. Ramsey, *Basic Christian Ethics* (New York: Charles Scribner's Sons, 1950); hereafter cited as *BCE*. See now the reissue of this volume by Westminster/John Knox Press (1993) with a new preface by Stanley Hauerwas. See also a collection of Ramsey's most significant writings: *The Essential Paul Ramsey: A Collection*, ed. W. Werpehowski and S.D. Crocco, (New Haven: Yale University Press, 1994).

7. P. Ramsey, *Deeds and Rules in Christian Ethics*, Scottish Journal of Theology Occasional Papers, no. 11 (Edinburgh and London: Oliver & Boyd; New York: Charles Scribner's Sons, 1967; P. Ramsey, *The Patient as Person: Explorations in Medical Ethics* (New Haven: Yale University Press, 1970); P. Ramsey, *Speak Up for Just War or Pacifism: A Critique of the United Methodist Bishops' Pastoral Letter "In Defense of Creation"* (University Park: Pennsylvania State University Press, 1988; P. Ramsey, "Beyond the Confusion of Tongues," *Theology Today* 3, no. 4 (1947): 446–58; P. Ramsey, "The Biblical Norm of Righteousness," *Interpretation* 24, no. 4 (1970): 419–29.

8. Only *BCE* provides an index of biblical citations.

9. See *BCE*, pp. 16–17. This material can already be found in Ramsey's article, "Elements of a Biblical Political Theory," *Journal of Religion* 29 (1949): 258–83; esp. p. 280.

10. P. Ramsey, *Fabricated Man: The Ethics of Genetic Control* (New Haven: Yale University Press, 1970), p. 37.

11. Ramsey, *Speak Up for Just War or Pacifism*, p. 30.

12. Ramsey does, however, refer more to Matthew than to any other New Testament writing (forty-five references).

13. Ramsey states that Luke's version of the Last Supper is "the most ancient and reliable account" (*BCE*, p. 29). Ramsey also states that "if ever any consistent account [of Jesus' ethics] is to emerge, certain of the sayings attributed to him must be decisively rejected, at least as they are ordinarily understood. Only with bitter irony and indignation could the Jesus whom we otherwise know in our gospels have said concerning the religious leaders of his day, 'The scribes and the Pharisees sit on Moses' seat; so practice and observe whatever they tell you' " (Matt. 28:2–4) (*BCE*, pp. 54–55).

14. See *BCE*, pp. 62–63. Throughout this section of *BCE*, Ramsey draws on some of the standard New Testament studies of the day, e.g., T. W. Manson's *The Teachings of Jesus* (Cambridge: Cambridge University Press, 1939), and E. F. Scott's *The Ethical Teachings of Jesus* (New York: Macmillan, 1948).

15. See Ramsey's comments in "A Letter to James Gustafson," *Journal of Religious Ethics* 13 (1985): 71–100, esp. p. 75. Ramsey also published some popular articles on the Bible. See "Paul and Some of His Letters," a series of seven Sunday School lessons for adult classes published in *Crossroads* (Board of Christian Education of the Presbyterian Church of the U.S.A.), Apr.–June 1953, pp. 77–79; together with the exegesis of Scripture and instruction for teachers in *Westminster Teacher*, Apr.–June 1953.

16. "[T]he interpretation given in this book concerning the ethics of obedient love

does not rest on any merely *linguistic* study of the New Testament. It rests rather on a study of morality in the light of the religious *thought* of the New Testament" (*BCE*, p. xvii). J. Gustafson also calls attention to this feature of Ramsey's work: "In studying his work one must take very seriously the commitment he makes to Christian ethics being biblical ethics, and to obedient love as the central theme of biblical ethics" (*Ethics from a Theocentric Perspective*, 2:85–86).

17. See the comments of S. Davis, who notes that Ramsey's *BCE* responded to some of the problems he had with Protestant ethics, especially with Reinhold Niebuhr's *An Interpretation of Christian Ethics* (1935) ("'Et Quod Vis Fac': Paul Ramsey and Augustinian Ethics," *Journal of Religious Ethics* 19, no. 2 [1991]: 33).

18. See, e.g., Ramsey's statement in *BCE*, p. 147: "In the preceding chapter it was suggested that more of the Neo-Platonic ingredients ought to be jettisoned from Augustine's doctrine of love by submitting it again to the judgment of the New Testament norm of disinterested *agape*—love for neighbor."

19. "Christian Ethics Today," *Rockford College Alumni Magazine*, spring 1968, p. 3. Perhaps because this essay was for a general audience, Ramsey articulates his understanding of "biblical ethics" more clearly here than in many of his other essays addressed to a more academic audience. The bulk of this essay is repeated in Ramsey's article "The Biblical Norm of Rightousness," *Interpretation* 24 (1970): 419–29.

20. Ibid.

21. In this regard, Ramsey is very critical of Augustine's interpretation of Paul. Augustine saw "love of God" as humanity's love for God, whereas Ramsey argues that for Paul "love of God" refers to God's love for humanity. God's love is always the starting point. Thus, God provides the paradigm for human existence (see *BCE*, pp. 126–27). "Nothing is more striking than the way St. Augustine has of wrenching St. Paul's meaning completely around to his own Neo-Platonic notion of man's yearning for God. . . . For explicitly rejecting St. Paul's real meaning Augustine is not to be excused simply because of the ambiguity of the genitive 'the love of God' . . . , which modern translations of this verse uniformly render, 'God's love.' Paul's point of view should have been clear in any translation and in any language, for in Romans [5:5–8] he immediately goes on to speak of God showing *his* love for us in that while we were yet sinners Christ died for us (5:8). Plainly, God's love is shed abroad or poured into our hearts because he loves us, not first of all because he makes us by infusion lovers of himself. Augustine is not to be excused; he has to be explained, in that before coming to study the scriptures he already had learned too much of what love meant from the Platonists" (*BCE*, p. 127). See also Ramsey's critique of Augustine's interpretation of Matt. 5:39 ("if anyone strikes you on the right cheek . . .") in *BCE*, pp. 166–67.

22. Throughout his writings, Ramsey speaks of obedient love as the mark of the Christian approach to ethics. E.g., he states: "The central ethical notion or 'category' in Christian ethics is 'obedient love'—the sort of love the gospels describe as 'love fulfilling the law' and St. Paul designates as 'faith that works through love'" (*BCE*, p. xi). "In place of rules for conduct, instead of 'the law' which Christianity entirely finishes, comes not irregularity but self-regulation, and not merely the self-regulation of free, autonomous individuals but the self-regulation of persons unconditionally bound to their neighbors by obedient 'faith working through love'" (*BCE*, p. 78). Finally, on the last page of *BCE*, Ramsey writes: "In this book, the basic norm for Christian ethics has been called '*obedient*-love' because of its intimate association with the idea of 'covenant' and with the 'reign' of God. . . . Rightly grasped, the biblical idea of justice or Christian love may also be reduced to a simple corollary of the idea of covenant. And 'consenting' to the

sovereignty of God manifestly means acknowledging his righteousness or justice to be the sovereign rule of life. These two are, in fact, the same thing: obeying the covenant and doing justice, love for neighbor and fulfilling the law" (p. 388).

23. Ramsey, "Letter to James Gustafson," p. 74. Ramsey's quotation is from his own *BCE*, p. 2.

24. In his article "Elements of a Biblical Political Theory," Ramsey begins by stating: "Never imagine that you have rightly grasped a biblical idea until you have succeeded in reducing it to a simple corollary of the idea of 'covenant' " (p. 258). On Ramsey's use of the covenant theme, see e.g., Paul Nelson's "Fidelity to Covenant: Paul Ramsey Remembered," *Christian Century*, 107, 5 Dec. 1990, pp. 1131–34. The most extensive examination and critique of Ramsey's notion and use of "covenant" is P. T. McCormick's dissertation, "Paul Ramsey's Covenantal Ethics: An Investigation into His Medical Writings" (Rome, Gregorian University 1984), where McCormick places the covenant language of Ramsey's medical ethics in the larger context of his general ethics.

25. Ramsey, *Patient as Person*, p. xii.

26. In a 1984 letter responding to James Gustafson's portrayal of Ramsey's work, Ramsey states that Gustafson would have done better to characterize Ramsey's views as "covenant-ridden" rather than as being permeated by "love monism" ("Letter to James Gustafson," p. 74). Ramsey is responding to Gustafson's presentation of Ramsey's ethics in Gustafson's *Ethics from a Theocentric Perspective*, 2:84–93. Elsewhere, in a 1979 article commenting on the significance of biblical narrative for liturgy and ethics, Ramsey quips that "not everyone who today cries, 'Story, Story' in theology, or 'Covenant, Covenant' in ethics as I have, shall enter into the kingdom beyond the eclipse of Biblical narrative" ("Liturgy and Ethics," *Journal of Religious Ethics* 7 [1979]: 148). In his "Letter to James Gustafson," Ramsey states: "There has been less change over the years in the centrality of covenant and my understanding of it than developments in my understanding of Christian love" (p. 74).

27. P. Ramsey, "The Case of the Curious Exception," in *Norm and Context in Christian Ethics*, ed. G. H. Outka and P. Ramsey (New York: Charles Scribner's Sons, 1968), p. 125.

28. For an examination of Ramsey's covenant ethics as applied to his medical ethics, see D. H. Smith, "On Paul Ramsey: A Covenant-Centered Ethic for Medicine," in *Theological Voices in Medical Ethics*, ed. A. Verhey and S. E. Lammers (Grand Rapids: Eerdmans, 1993), pp. 7–29. See also the dissertation by P. T. McCormick, "Paul Ramsey's Covenantal Ethics." McCormick is appreciative but fairly critical of Ramsey's use of "covenant" as a guiding theme. "Ramsey has not critically analyzed covenant's ability or inability to effectively generate all the principles necessary for a complete and coherent Christian ethics. The superficial efficiency of covenant in seeming to serve Ramsey's primary ethical concerns has led him to prescind from critically examining the limits and problems of a covenantal ethic" (p. 27 from the *excerpta*). "Covenant serves Ramsey's occasional and polemical style more as a banner than a bedrock" (pp. 165–66). See his extensive substantive critique of Ramsey's use of covenant on pp. 27–160.

29. Ramsey, *Fabricated Man*, p. 38.

30. Ramsey, *Patient as Person*, p. xii.

31. See, e.g., Ramsey's statement that "throughout the Bible men are slanted in the direction of redemptive love where no love is due" (*BCE*, p. 34).

32. D. Smith has ably summarized this aspect of Ramsey's ethics. For Ramsey, the early Christians "regarded Jesus as the 'righteousness of God.' For them the center of the covenant was Jesus who both embodied and taught the importance of love. . . . The love

commandment, therefore, is the basic rule or principle of *Christian* morality" ("Paul Ramsey, Love, and Killing," in *Love and Society*, ed. Johnson and Smith, pp. 4–5).

33. E.g., regarding 1 Cor. 11:14, where Paul admonishes women to cover their heads in public worship, Ramsey writes: "Only when he [Paul] appeals in sub-Christian fashion to what 'nature itself teaches' does Paul adopt parochial standards about women's hairdress and such matters (I Cor. 11:14). The wonder is that Paul was so thoroughly emancipated from his Jewish background as not to appeal to Torah, or that under pressure of advising in church administration he did not 'lay down the law,' his own law or that which 'nature itself teaches,' more than he does. His exhortations generally have authority only as love's directions, and hold in view the needs and 'edification' or 'building up' of others. Christian love will not be limited by any previously existing regulation drawn from what society or 'surely nature itself' teaches, it will not conform to preconceptions about right and wrong or conventional codes of conduct with which authorities on good and evil happen to be prepossessed" (*BCE*, p. 78).

34. Ramsey sees the eschatological dimension of Christian faith as a fundamental orientation of Christian existence. He is particularly critical of theological ethics that tends to dismiss or misconstrue the character of the eschatological language found in the New Testament. E.g., Ramsey chides the Methodist bishops for smoothing over biblical eschatology and thus fundamentally confusing the eschatological peace spoken of in the book of Revelation with a this-worldly peace that disarmament might bring about (*Speak Up for Just War or Pacifism*, pp. 33–37).

35. In response to those who would dismiss Jesus' ethical teachings because of his apocalyptic eschatological approach, Ramsey states: "Whoever considers it a fault that the ethics of Jesus originated from connection with an apocalyptic view of the end of human history which modern men no longer find plausible, whoever as a consequence is tempted either to dismiss the ethic or to modernize Jesus' other views, should reflect that *genesis* has nothing to do with *validity*" (*BCE*, p. 41).

36. D. Smith, "Paul Ramsey, Love, and Killing," in *Love and Society*, ed. Johnson and Smith, p. 5.

37. See the discussion by Stanley Hauerwas in Ramsey's *Speak Up for Just War or Pacifism*, pp. 168–69.

38. Ramsey further states that "neighbor-centered preferential love and a Christian ethic of protection do have their beginning in him [Jesus], in spite of the effect of apocalypticism in expelling concern for the permanent organization of justice and making men well acquainted with the pure will of God in the case of a single neighbor" (*BCE*, p. 166).

39. Regarding the use of physical force in defending oppressed against oppressor, Ramsey is particularly critical of the biblical interpretation of the United Methodist bishops in their pastoral letter "In Defense of Creation." See esp. his discussion in "Biblical and Theological Foundations," in his *Speak Up for Just War or Pacifism*, pp. 19–39. In this section, Ramsey states: "The 'writer' chosen to do exegesis for the Bishops did not serve them well" (p. 28; also see p. 33).

40. J. Gustafson, "The Changing Use of the Bible in Christian Ethics," in *Readings in Moral Theology*, no. 4, *The Use of Scripture in Moral Theology*, ed. C. E. Curran and R. A. McCormick (New York and Ramsey: Paulist Press, 1984), p. 141.

41. Ramsey, "Beyond the Confusion of Tongues," p. 456.

42. Ibid., p. 455. In Ramsey's conclusion to this article, he states: "At best it may be a forlorn hope, but it is the world's last, that Biblical Christianity may again speak to every man in his own tongue, with his own understanding and psychological condition-

ing, so that men will say to each other, 'Are not all these who are speaking Galileans? And how is it that we hear, each of us in his own native language?' [Acts 2:7–8] Prerequisite to world understanding is that men should by personal appropriation of Christian truth speak both in his own and in another's language, and in the spirit of knowing they are known better than they know, bear witness no longer to themselves but to God in Christ" (p. 458).

43. This emphasis on relations between persons, which I have briefly discussed, is central to Ramsey's entire understanding of the task of theological ethics. The seeds for Ramsey's later work in medical ethics, e.g., which emphasizes the patient as person and the respect for personal rights and personal consent, can be traced directly back to his understanding of the Bible as personal address and personal dialogue between God and human beings. The authority of Scripture in medical ethics is also clearly stated in the introduction to Ramsey's *Ethics at the Edges of Life* (New Haven: Yale University Press, 1978): "I do not hesitate to write as a Christian ethicist. No more did I hesitate in my first major book on medical ethics to invoke ultimate appeal to scripture or theology" (p. xiii).

44. Ramsey, "Letter to James Gustafson," p. 78.

45. Ibid., p. 73.

In Ramsey's view, Gustafson relegates Scripture to a secondary status as a source for theological ethics. Indeed, for precisely this reason, Ramsey charges that Gustafson's *Ethics from a Theocentric Perspective* is more anthropocentric than theocentric: "I must say that your account of theocentric ethics remains strangely anthropocentric. Must this not necessarily be the case if the revelation to which Scripture and tradition both testify is less vital and informative in Christian theological ethics than [scientific information and human experience]? . . . Must this not necessarily be the case, if Scripture and tradition are subordinate sources?" ("Letter to James Gustafson," p. 73).

46. P. Lehmann, *Ethics in a Christian Context* (London: SCM Press, 1963), pp. 26–27 n. 1. In response to Lehmann's critique and his ethics in general, Ramsey wrote an essay, "The Contextualism of Paul Lehmann," in *Deeds and Rules in Christian Ethics*, pp. 49–103; see esp. pp. 51–52.

47. Gustafson, *Ethics from a Theocentric Perspective*, 2:86.

48. Ramsey, *Deeds and Rules in Christian Ethics*, pp. 51–52 n. 3.

49. This section of BCE was also published as "In This Is Love . . . ," *Motive* 11, no. 1 (1950): 21.

50. Ramsey, "Letter to James Gustafson," pp. 78–79.

51. See also Ramsey's "The Morality of Abortion," in *Life or Death: Ethics and Options*, ed. D. Labby (Seattle: University of Washington Press, 1968), pp. 60–93; "Reference Points in Deciding About Abortion," in *The Morality of Abortion: Legal and Historical Perspectives*, ed. J. T. Noonan, Jr. (Cambridge: Harvard University Press, 1970), pp. 60–100; "Abortion: A Review Article," *Thomist* 37 (1973): 174–226; and "Abortion: Last Resort," in *Ethics for Modern Life*, ed. R. Abelson and M. Frequegnon (New York: St. Martin's Press, 1977), pp. 61–75. Ramsey says little regarding the Bible in these essays.

52. Ramsey, "Liturgy and Ethics," p. 150.

53. Ibid., p. 160.

54. Ibid., p. 161.

55. Ibid., pp. 162–63.

56. Regarding Ramsey's understanding of biblical ethics, James Gustafson comments at length: "It is fair to raise the question of whether Ramsey's work is an accurate depiction of biblical ethics. . . . Ramsey is correct to say that the biblical writers 'view

ethics theologically as rooted in the nature and activity of God' [*BCE*, p. 1]. But two questions can be asked about this to which I have given different answers than he does. The first is internal to the Bible: Within the biblical accounts, is the nature and activity of God as exclusively in focus on God's love as Ramsey's argument claims? I believe that it is not. The second question is: Does such knowledge as human beings can have of God's nature and activity depend so exclusively on the biblical material as Ramsey's does?" "To establish that steadfast love is the central category of biblical ethics is an exegetical task. I have indicated that a question can be raised about whether Ramsey's view of biblical ethics is fully defensible. Work on the ethics in the Bible by biblical scholars could be adduced to show that the matter is more complex than Ramsey's position states." "Ramsey has stated that his way of working in ethics 'endeavors to stand within the way the Bible views morality.' Is biblical morality deontological? . . . The biblical writers were not ethical theorists. In both the moral writings in the Bible and in the theological backings that are given them there is a great variety. There are at least as many biblical grounds for saying that Christian ethics is teleological or an ethics of response as there are for saying that the biblical way of viewing morality is deontological." (Quotations from *Ethics from a Theocentric Perspective*, 2:86–87, 88, 89–90.)

57. E.g., D. Smith observes: "It is important that Ramsey's handling of conflict cases proceeds in great remove from his starting point, the Christian scriptures. Particular texts which bear on the morality of killing are never seriously considered" ("Paul Ramsey, Love, and Killing," in *Love and Society*, ed. Johnson and Smith, p. 7).

58. J. Gustafson, "A Response to Critics," *Journal of Religious Ethics* 13 (1985): 189. This Biblicism also gets expressed in Ramsey's somewhat uncritical reading of Scripture through the eyes of Augustine and, especially, Luther, which Ramsey readily admits (see, e.g., *BCE*, pp. xiii–xiv).

Chapter Six

1. In the process of reading Hauerwas, I have come largely to share an assessment voiced by Jeff Stout, an ethicist in the Department of Religion at Princeton University, who wrote the following in a 1987 review of one of Hauerwas's books. I cite him at length: "No one writing on related topics reads more widely or brings learning to bear on the moral life more creatively. Over the last decade, he has done more than anyone but the liberation theologians to set the agenda for Christian ethics. It is hard to imagine what recent work on character, the virtues, narrative, and the relation between the church and liberal society might look like in the absence of Hauerwas' influence. Indeed, it is hard to know whether these topics would seem as central as they do had Hauerwas not helped make them unavoidable. . . . Most distinguished ethicists polish gems. They take pride in well-rounded articles and precise lines of argument. They borrow technical innovations from neighboring disciplines in hope of keeping the cutting edge of inquiry sharp. Hauerwas, meantime, pans for gold. He often gives us the whole pan, sludge and all, leaving us to do the sorting. Each pan contains enough nuggets to attract a crowd of prospectors—all of them eager to size up the latest find. By the time the crowd assembles, Hauerwas is already working against the current farther upstream, following up a tip from somebody named MacIntyre or Yoder, staking out a new claim." See Stout's review of Hauerwas's *Suffering Presence: Theological Reflections on Medicine, the Mentally Handicapped, and the Church* (Notre Dame: University of Notre Dame Press, 1986), in *Theology Today* 44 (1987): 125.

2. S. Hauerwas, *A Community of Character: Toward a Constructive Christian Social*

Ethic (Notre Dame: University of Notre Dame Press, 1981), p. 1. Similar statements can also be found in his other writings. See, e.g., his preface to *The Peaceable Kingdom: A Primer in Christian Ethics* (Notre Dame: University of Notre Dame Press, 1983), p. xvi.

3. It is worth noting that Hauerwas's approach to his own writing has a strong, self-conscious communal dimension, to which his many collaborative writing projects and his long lists of acknowledgments in each book attest. He writes out of community for community, so that he can state: "The more I write the less I feel able to claim what I do as mine" (preface to *Against the Nations: War and Survival in a Liberal Society* [San Francisco: Harper & Row, 1985], p. viii). I stress this communal aspect of his writing because it so thoroughly permeates his approach to theological ethics and to the Bible as the church's Scripture.

4. *Truthfulness and Tragedy: Further Investigations in Christian Ethics* (Notre Dame: University of Notre Dame Press, 1977) does include an essay that has a section "Charity and the Gospel of Luke," pp. 135–39.

5. It should be noted, however, that Hauerwas's book *After Christendom? How the Church Is to Behave If Freedom, Justice, and a Christian Nation Are Bad Ideas* (Nashville: Abingdon Press, 1991) has but two references to specific biblical texts: once to John 18:33–38 (p. 91) and once to James 5:14–16 (p. 110). Aside from these citations, there is also a brief reference to Paul (p. 37). The lack of much reference to the Bible in this volume leads one to suspect that in his 1989 book *Resident Aliens: Life in the Christian Colony* (Nashville: Abingdon Press, 1989), coauthored with William Willimon, the much greater appeal to the Bible is perhaps due to Willimon's input. Willimon is, after all, the campus minister at Duke University and is responsible for regular preaching.

6. Hauerwas himself makes a similar observation at the very beginning of his essay "Salvation and Health: Why Medicine Needs the Church," in *Suffering Presence* (pp. 63–83), under the heading "A Text and a Story": "While it is not unheard of for a theologian to begin an essay with a text from the Scripture, it is relatively rare for those who are addressing issues of medicine to do so. However I begin with a text, as almost everything I have to say is but a commentary on this passage from Job 2:11–13" (p. 63; followed by the citation of the biblical passage). On the Bible and medical ethics, see further R. J. Mouw, "Biblical Revelation and Medical Decisions," *Journal of Medicine and Philosophy* 4, no. 4 (1979): 367–82.

7. See Hauerwas and Willimon, *Resident Aliens*, p. 54. Cf. pp. 66, 68; Hauerwas, *Peaceable Kingdom*, pp. 23–24.

8. Hauerwas refers to Ps. 13, 35, and 86 in this context (*Naming the Silences: God, Medicine, and the Problem of Suffering* [Grand Rapids: Eerdmans, 1990], pp. 42–43, 79–80; see also *Suffering Presence*, p. 66, where Hauerwas draws on Ps. 32 and 38 in discussing illness and human sin). See also Hauerwas and Willimon, *Resident Aliens*, p. 54; Hauerwas, *Peaceable Kingdom*, p. 23.

9. "I really do not know the 'text' of the Bible well" (Hauerwas, *Unleashing the Scripture: Freeing the Bible from Captivity to America* [Nashville: Abingdon Press, 1993], p. 9). See also his essay "The Church as God's New Language," in *Christian Existence Today: Essays on Church, World, and Living in Between* (Durham, N.C.: Labyrinth Press, 1988), p. 55. In private correspondence, Hauerwas has written that "when I started I simply did not know the Bible well enough to use it one way or the other" (letter to author, 17 Mar. 1992).

10. See, e.g., Hauerwas, Bondi, and Burrell, *Truthfulness and Tragedy*, p. 137; Hauerwas, *Community of Character*, pp. 53, 65, 92, 95, 136, 150, 224; Hauerwas, *Peaceable Kingdom*, pp. xviii, 27–28, 57, 62, 63, 81, 133; Hauerwas, *Suffering Presence*, p. 91; Hauerwas, *Christian Existence Today*, p. 61, 75, 101.

11. Hauerwas, *Peaceable Kingdom*, p. 76.

12. See, e.g., ibid., pp. 69, 77; Hauerwas, *Against the Nations*, p. 58; Hauerwas, *Christian Existence Today*, pp. 155, 157. See also his comments regarding seminary courses on the "Old Testament" in *Christian Existence Today*, p. 124.

13. Hauerwas, *Peaceable Kingdom*, p. 107. Hauerwas indicates (p. 168 n. 9) that in his thoughts on Israel he is borrowing from Paul van Buren's *A Theology of the Jewish-Christian Reality, Part 1: Discerning the Way* (San Francisco: Harper & Row, 1980). Elsewhere, Hauerwas states: "Ironically 'Orthodox christologies' and liberal Protestantism often attempt to give an account of Christianity that makes the continuation of the Jews irrelevant. Christian universalism is bought at the expense of Israel, and as a result Christians become accommodated to those stories of high humanism that ironically end up atheistic" (*After Christendom?* pp. 169–70 n. 24).

14. See esp. Hauerwas and Willimon, *Resident Aliens*, pp. 72–80.

15. See, e.g., Hauerwas, *Community of Character*, p. 47 (Mark 8:27–9:1); Hauerwas, *Peaceable Kingdom*, pp. 80–81 (Mark 8:34; 10:37–39, 42–45).

16. See esp. Hauerwas, Bondi, and Burrell, *Truthfulness and Tragedy*, pp. 135–40, where Hauerwas draws on such texts as Luke 4:18, 5:31–32, 6:20, 7:22, and a full citation of the parable of the Good Samaritan followed by the Mary and Martha story (10:25–42).

17. John 15:26–16:11 occurs as one of the readings from the lectionary cycle for a Pentecost sermon, a passage that receives little development in the sermon that follows. In the sermon "On Having the Grace to Live Contingently," from Hauerwas's *Unleashing the Scripture* (pp. 84–91), the lectionary reading is from John 3:14–21. Hauerwas uses the sermon in large part to argue against the generic and formulaic use of John 3:16.

18. Given all the charges that Hauerwas is "sectarian," it is interesting that he makes virtually no use of John, the Gospel that most biblical scholars identify as among the most "sectarian" writings of the New Testament.

19. See Hauerwas, *Peaceable Kingdom*, pp. 91–95 (a section subtitled "An Ethics of Salvation and Faith"). See also his extended discussion of Rom. 5:1–5 in his essay "On Developing Hopeful Virtues," *Christian Scholar's Review* 18, no. 2 (1988) 107–17.

20. Hauerwas, *Community of Character*, p. 71. See also his comments on the household codes of Eph. 5:21–6:9; Col. 3:18–4:1; and 1 Pet. 2:13–3:7 in *Community of Character*, pp. 58, 70, 190, 283 n. 20; and (with Willimon) *Resident Aliens*, pp. 152–55. Hauerwas notes his indebtedness to the interpretation of these passages offered by John Howard Yoder in the chapter "Revolutionary Subordination," *The Politics of Jesus* (Grand Rapids: Eerdmans, 1972), pp. 163–92. Hauerwas probably owes more of his thinking to John Howard Yoder than to any other single person. Indeed, Hauerwas states that "the best recent book that utilizes scripture for ethics is Yoder's *The Politics of Jesus*" (from "The Moral Authority of Scripture," in *Community of Character*, p. 239 n. 2).

21. Hauerwas states that "for Christian ethics the Bible is not just a collection of texts but scripture that makes normative claims on a community" (*Community of Character*, p. 56). Along similar lines, see Michael Goldberg's discussion of what he calls "master stories," stories that provide foundational community-shaping narratives, in *Jews and Christians, Getting Our Stories Straight: The Exodus and the Passion-Resurrection* (Nashville: Abingdom Press, 1985; reprint, Philadelphia: Trinity Press International, 1991), and also his *Theology and Narrative: A Critical Introduction*, 2d ed. (Philadelphia: Trinity Press International, 1991), p. 146. In the latter volume, Goldberg also discusses Hauerwas's work; see, e.g., pp. 173–78, 190–91, 235–38.

22. Hauerwas, *The Peaceable Kingdom*, p. 24. Hauerwas makes a similar statement in *Resident Aliens*: "The Bible is fundamentally a story of a people's journey with God" (p. 53).

23. Hauerwas, *Community of Character*, p. 64.

24. Hauerwas and Willimon, *Resident Aliens*, p. 97. Similarly, Hauerwas writes: "The role of the theological ethicist is to continually call us back to and seek a greater understanding of our sustaining story and the moral skills it provides for those people called Christian" (Hauerwas, Bondi, and Burrell, *Truthfulness and Tragedy*, p. 105).

25. Hauerwas, Bondi, and Burrell, *Truthfulness and Tragedy*, p. 137.

26. Ibid.

27. Already in his first book, *Vision and Virtue: Essays in Christian Ethical Reflection* (Notre Dame: Fides/Claretian, 1974), Hauerwas made the following comment on the story of the Good Samaritan in Luke 10: "Contrary to many assumptions, the principle 'love your neighbor as yourself' is not the moral 'upshot' of that story, nor is the story but an illustration of the principle, but the story is the moral meaning of the principle. Universal ethical principles become ethically significant only as we learn their meaning in stories" (pp. 115–16).

28. See, e.g., Hauerwas, *Community of Character*, p. 224; Hauerwas, *Peaceable Kingdom*, p. xviii.

29. See, e.g., Hauerwas, *Peaceable Kingdom*, pp. 29, 57, 81.

30. Ibid., p. 77. In drawing on the motifs of prophet, king, and priest, Hauerwas refers to E. J. Tinsley's book *The Imitation of God in Christ* (London: SCM Press, 1960). Similarly, "We Christians must recognize, by the very fact that we are a people of a book, that we are a community which lives through memory. . . . We test our memory with Scripture as we are rightly forced time after time to seek out new implications of that memory by the very process of passing it on" (Hauerwas, *Peaceable Kingdom*, p. 69).

31. Hauerwas, *Peaceable Kingdom*, p. 81.

32. E.g., Hauerwas is quite critical of Paul Ramsey's emphasis on covenant as a controlling concept: "Ramsey is a classical example of an ethicist exploiting the assumption that biblical theology is primarily a matter of locating the central 'biblical' concepts. Thus Ramsey stresses the centrality of love and covenant on the assumption that by doing so his ethic is thereby 'biblical' " (*Community of Character*, p. 241 n. 16).

33. Hauerwas, *Naming the Silences*, pp. 79–80. In this connection, Hauerwas also cites Job. See ibid., pp. 43–46; Hauerwas, *Suffering Presence*, pp. 63–82.

34. Hauerwas, *Community of Character*, p. 136.

35. Hauerwas, *Peaceable Kingdom*, p. 29. In Jesus' life, death, and resurrection, the early Christians had "found a continuation of Israel's vocation to imitate God and thus in a decisive way to depict God's kingdom for the world. Jesus' life was seen as a recapitulation of the life of Israel and thus presented the very life of God in the world" (ibid., p. 78). Similarly, Hauerwas states that the "temptation narratives are but a particularly concentrated example of how the early church understood Jesus' life as recapitulating the life of the Lord with Israel" (ibid., p. 79).

36. As Hauerwas puts it: "In effect the church is the extended argument over time about the significance of [Christ's] story and how best to understand it" (ibid., p. 107). For another vantage on the moral significance of remembering, see his essay "Remembering as a Moral Task: The Challenge of the Holocaust," reprinted in *Against the Nations*, pp. 61–90.

37. Hauerwas, *Peaceable Kingdom*, p. 76.

38. Hauerwas, *Community of Character*, p. 47.

39. Ibid., p. 48.

40. "It is in his cross that we learn we live in a world that is based on the presupposition that man, not God, rules" (ibid., p. 50). See also Hauerwas, *Vision and Virtue*, p. 117.

41. Hauerwas, *Peaceable Kingdom*, p. 87.

42. Hauerwas, "Epilogue: A Pacifist Response to the Bishops," in *Speak Up for Just War or Pacifism: A Critique of the United Methodist Bishops' Pastoral Letter "In Defense of Creation*," by P. Ramsey (University Park: Pennsylvania State University Press, 1988), p. 177.

43. Hauerwas, *Peaceable Kingdom*, p. 80.

44. Here, Hauerwas refers to Mark 8:34 and 10:45 (*Peaceable Kingdom*, p. 80).

45. Ibid., p. 76. As he states it in *Resident Aliens*: "The overriding political task of the church is to be the community of the cross" (p. 47).

46. Hauerwas, *Peaceable Kingdom*, p. 76.

47. Ibid., Emphasis his.

48. See, e.g., "The Nonresistant Church: The Theological Ethics of John Howard Yoder," in Hauerwas, *Vision and Virtue*, pp. 197–221; "Tragedy and Joy: The Spirituality of Peaceableness," in Hauerwas, *Peaceable Kingdom*, pp. 135–51; "Peacemaking: The Virtue of the Church," in Hauerwas, *Christian Existence Today*, pp. 89–97; and "Taking Time for Peace," also in *Christian Existence Today*, pp. 253–66.

49. Hauerwas, *Should War Be Eliminated?* (Milwaukee: Marquette University Press, 1989), p. 67 n. 30 (this passage was reprinted in *Against the Nations*, p. 205 n. 30). See also Hauerwas's chapter "The Politics of Justice: Why Justice Is a Bad Idea for Christians," in his *After Christendom?* pp. 45–68, and esp. his critique of G. Gutiérrez's notion of liberation as justice (pp. 50–58). See also his article "Some Theological Reflections on Gutiérrez's Use of 'Liberation' as a Theological Concept," *Modern Theology* 3, no. 1 (1986): 67–76.

50. Regarding the Resurrection, Hauerwas states: "Only if our Lord is a risen Lord . . . can we have the confidence and the power to be a community of forgiveness. For on the basis of the resurrection we have the presumption to believe that God has made us agents in the history of the kingdom. The resurrection is not a symbol or myth through which we can interpret our individual and collective dyings and risings. Rather the resurrection of Jesus is the ultimate sign that our salvation comes only when we cease trying to interpret Jesus' story in the light of our history, and instead we interpret ourselves in the light of his. For this is no dead Lord we follow but the living God, who having dwelt among us as an individual, is now eternally present to us making possible our living as forgiven agents of God's new creation" (*Peaceable Kingdom*, p. 90).

51. Ibid., p. 82. Hauerwas seeks to restore the cosmic drama of the apocalyptic writings in the Bible to a more significant place in Christian theological reflection. As he puts it: "While I have no wish to underwrite every form of speculation in Christian history inspired by apocalyptic, I do want to maintain that our faith—and in particular our holding up the lives of the saints—cannot make sense without the apocalyptic drama of the cosmos in conflict" (from one of Hauerwas's sermons, "On the Production and Reproduction of the Saints," in *Reformed Journal* 40 [1990]: 12; reprinted in *Unleashing the Scripture*, pp. 99–104).

52. Hauerwas, *Peaceable Kingdom*, p. 88. Further, "We must learn to see the world as Israel had learned to understand it—that is, eschatologically" (ibid., p. 82).

53. Hauerwas and Willimon, *Resident Aliens*, pp. 72–80.

54. Hauerwas, *Peaceable Kingdom*, pp. 72–95.

55. As Hauerwas puts it elsewhere: "The Sermon on the Mount does not encourage heroic individualism, it defeats it with its demands that we be perfect even as God is perfect, that we deal with others as God has dealt with us" (Hauerwas and Willimon, *Resident Aliens*, p. 77).

56. Hauerwas, *Peaceable Kingdom*, p. 85.

57. Ibid., p. 85. Elsewhere, Hauerwas states: "The Christian's task to care for the weak is but an aspect of his call to love God. Serving the weak in the name of man is not enough; God calls us to love and care for the weak just as He has loved and cared for us. Surely this is the force of Jesus' admonition to be perfect as his Father is perfect" (*Vision and Virtue*, p. 190).

58. "Thus, within a world of violence and injustice Christians can take the risk of being forgiven and forgiving. They are able to break the circle of violence as they refuse to become part of those institutions of fear that promise safety by the destruction of others. As a result, some space, both psychological and physical, is created where we can be at rest from a world that knows not who is its king" (Hauerwas, *Against the Nations*, p. 117). Hauerwas hastens to add that such rest does not imply a withdrawal from the world.

59. Hauerwas, *Peaceable Kingdom*, p. 83. "Put starkly, Jesus himself is the meaning and content of the kingdom" (Hauerwas, *Against the Nations*, p. 113).

60. Hauerwas, *Peaceable Kingdom*, p. 83. Thus, for Hauerwas, "the eschatological nature of the kingdom as embodied in the ministry of Jesus does have immediate ethical implications" (Hauerwas, *Against the Nations*, p. 117).

61. Hauerwas, "The Reality of the Kingdom," in *Against the Nations*, p. 111. See also Hauerwas's essay "The Reality of the Church: Even a Democratic State Is Not the Kingdom," in *Against the Nations*, pp. 122–31. For other evaluative comments Hauerwas makes about Rauschenbusch (both positive and negative), see his "Rauschenbusch on the Prophets," a subsection of the chapter "The Pastor as Prophet," in *Christian Existence Today*, pp. 152–57. See also the larger discussion of Rauschenbusch in *Against the Nations*, 107–121. For a helpful analysis of Rauschenbusch's use of Scripture, see the (unfortunately unpublished) Ph.D. dissertation of Allen Verhey, "The Use of Scripture in Moral Discourse: A Case Study of Walter Rauschenbusch" (Yale University, 1975).

62. Hauerwas's analysis of Luke's Gospel is a subsection (pp. 135–39) of his essay "The Politics of Charity," in Hauerwas, Bondi, and Burrell, *Truthfulness and Tragedy* (pp. 132–43).

63. Ibid., p. 135.

64. Ibid.

65. This observation regarding Luke's concern is a well-established consensus among New Testament scholars. See, e.g., my own essay " 'First to the Gentiles': A Literary Analysis of Luke 4:16–30," *Journal of Biblical Literature* 111 (1992): 69–86.

66. Hauerwas, Bondi, and Burrell, *Truthfulness and Tragedy*, p. 136.

67. Ibid., p. 137.

68. Ibid.

69. Ibid., p. 138. This argument is very similar to what Paul has to say in 1 Cor. 1:18–32 about God working through what is foolish and weak in the world.

70. Ibid.

71. Hauerwas and Willimon, *Resident Aliens*, p. 87.

72. Hauerwas, Bondi, and Burrell, *Truthfulness and Tragedy*, p. 138.

73. Thus, "*Scripture* makes sense only within the ongoing liturgical life of the church. It is inseparable from the church year" (Hauerwas and Long, "Interpreting the Bible as a Political Act," *Religion and Intellectual Life* 6 [1989]: 142).

74. Hauerwas writes that "without the liturgy the text of Scripture remains just that—text. . . . In effect, the worship of the church created Scripture" ("The Church as God's New Language," in *Christian Existence Today*, p. 64 n. 11).

75. Ibid., p. 55. Hauerwas prefaces the sermon with the following comments: "It is a bit unusual to begin a putatively scholarly essay with a sermon . . . Too often many of

us who have written about narrative end up using that emphasis to talk about how we should do theology if we ever get around to doing any. So I thought I would try to do a little by writing a sermon. Of course, since I was trained at Yale I am too insecure to let the sermon stand on its own, so it is followed by methodological commentary. Yet I believe if I have anything of value to say on these matters it is said in the sermon" (p. 47). See further Hauerwas's comments on preaching in the introduction to S. Hauerwas and W. H. Willimon, *Preaching to Strangers* (Nashville: Abingdon, 1992) (the introduction is by Hauerwas), pp. 1–13; as well as his own sermons in *Unleashing the Scripture.*

76. See, e.g., his occasional published sermons: "Hating Mothers as the Way to Peace," *Journal for Preachers* 11, no. 4 (1988): 17–21 (with Ezek. 33:1–11, Philem. 1:1–20, and Luke 14:25–33 as the texts); "On Being Dispossessed: Or This Is a Hell of a Way to Get Someplace," *Reformed Journal* 39, no. 1 (1989): 14–16 (with Gen. 3:8–19; Heb. 4:1–3, 9–13; and Mark 10:17–30 as the texts); "The August Partiality of God's Love," *Reformed Journal* 39, no. 5 (1989): 10–12 (with Ruth 2:1–13 and Matt. 22:32–46 as the texts); "On the Production and Reproduction of the Saints," *Reformed Journal* 40 (1990): 12–13 (with Dan. 7:1–3, 15–18; Eph. 1:11–23; and Luke 6:20–36 as the texts). These sermons are now reprinted in his *Unleashing the Scripture.* See also "A Pentecost Sermon," in "The Church as God's New Language," in his *Christian Existence Today*, pp. 47–54 (with Gen. 11:1–9, Acts 2:1–21, and John 15:26–16:11 as the texts). Finally, see his "A Sermon on the Sermon on the Mount" and "Discipleship as Interpretation: A Sermon" (with Isa. 25:6–9 and Luke 24:13–35 as the texts) in *Unleashing the Scripture.* In private correspondence, Hauerwas has stated regarding these last two sermons that he is "increasingly inclined to turn them into what I want to call Biblical Essays rather than sermons. Yoder has a quite wonderful account of what it means to do Biblical essays in that short book he wrote called *He Came Preaching Peace* that I admire deeply" (letter to author, 17 Mar. 1992).

77. Hauerwas, *Christian Existence Today*, p. 61.

78. Hauerwas, "The Ministry of a Congregation: Rethinking Christian Ethics for a Church-Centered Seminary," in *Christian Existence Today*, p. 124.

79. Hauerwas suggests that "part of the reason for the misuse of the scripture in matters dealing with morality is that the text was isolated from a liturgical context. . . . the shape of the liturgy over a whole year prevents any one part of scripture from being given undue emphasis in relation to the narrative line of scripture. The liturgy, in every performance and over a whole year, rightly contextualizes individual passages when we cannot read the whole" (*Community of Character*, p. 240 n. 9).

80. Hauerwas and Willimon, *Resident Aliens*, p. 162.

81. See, e.g., Hauerwas, *Community of Character*, p. 6; and "The Testament of Friends," *Christian Century* 107, n. 7 (1990): 212–16.

82. S. Hauerwas, *Character and the Christian Life: A Study in Theological Ethics* (San Antonio: Trinity University Press, 1975), p. 223.

83. Hauerwas and Willimon, *Resident Aliens*, p. 11.

84. Ibid., p. 12.

85. Ibid., pp. 146–47.

86. On Hauerwas as a "sectarian," see esp. J. Gustafson, "The Sectarian Temptation: Reflections on Theology, the Church, and the University," in *Proceedings of the Catholic Theological Society of America* 40 (1985): 83–94. See Hauerwas's response in his introduction to his collection of essays *Christian Existence Today*, pp. 1–21. See also the comments of M. Quirk, "Stanley Hauerwas' *Against the Nations*: Beyond Sectarianism," *Theology Today* 44, no. 1 (1987): 78–86; and Hauerwas's response in the same issue, "Will the Real Sectarian Stand Up?" *Theology Today* 44, no. 1 (1987): 87–94; as well as the appendix in

Hauerwas's *After Christendom?* (pp. 153–61) by David Toole, one of Hauerwas's graduate students at Duke, who in part addresses the issue of Hauerwas's "tribalism." Regarding tribalism, Hauerwas states: "We reject the charge of tribalism, particularly from those whose theologies serve to buttress the most nefarious brand of tribalism of all—the omnipotent state. The church is the one political entity in our culture that is global, transnational, transcultural. Tribalism is not the church determined to serve God rather than Caesar. Tribalism is the United States of America, which sets up artificial boundaries and defends them with murderous intensity. And the tribalism of nations occurs most viciously in the absence of a church able to say and to show, in its life together, that God, not nations, rules the world" (Hauerwas and Willimon, *Resident Aliens*, pp. 42–43).

87. See Hauerwas and Willimon, *Resident Aliens*, pp. 15–19. Similarly, Hauerwas writes that "first and foremost the community must know that it has a history and tradition which separate it from the world. Such separation is required by the very fact that the world knows not the God we find in the scripture" (*Community of Character*, p. 68).

88. Hauerwas, "The Moral Authority of Scripture: The Politics and Ethics of Remembering," in *Community of Character*, pp. 68–69. This chapter has been reprinted in C. E. Curran and R. A. McCormick, *Readings in Moral Theology*, no. 4, *The Use of Scripture in Moral Theology* (New York and Ramsey: Paulist Press, 1984), pp. 242–75. My page citations refer to the original publication.

89. Ibid., p. 69.

90. See esp. Hauerwas and Willimon, *Resident Aliens*, pp. 17–18, 21–22, 24, 27, 29–30, 37, 40, 42, 72, 76, 151.

91. See ibid., p. 22. Later in the same book (p. 72) Hauerwas writes: "The habit of Constantinian thinking is difficult to break. It leads Christians to judge their ethical positions, not on the basis of what is faithful to our peculiar tradition, but rather on the basis of how much Christian ethics Caesar can be induced to swallow without choking. The tendency therefore is to water down Christian ethics, filtering them through basically secular criteria like 'right to life' or 'freedom of choice,' pushing them on the whole world as universally applicable common sense, and calling that Christian.

"How bland and unfaithful such ethics appear when set next to the practical demands of the story" (followed by a citation of Jesus' Sermon on the Mount in Matt. 5).

92. Ibid., pp. 19, 24. "So the theological task is not merely the interpretive matter of translating Jesus into modern categories but rather to translate the world to him. The theologian's job is not to make the gospel credible to the modern world, but *to make the world credible to the gospel*" (p. 24).

93. Hauerwas notes that "most modern ethics begin from the Enlightenment presupposition of the isolated, heroic self, the allegedly rational individual who stands alone and decides and chooses. The goal of this ethic is to detach the individual from his or her tradition, parents, stories, community, and history, and thereby allow him or her to stand alone, to decide, to choose, and to act alone" (ibid., p. 79; see also pp. 19, 49, 80–81, 99–100, 156). See also Hauerwas, *After Christendom?* pp. 83–84.

94. Hauerwas and Willimon, *Resident Aliens*, p. 50.

95. Ibid., pp. 80–81.

96. The quotation is taken from Hauerwas's 1992 Sprunt Lectures, p. 36 of the unpublished manuscript. For an example of how "liberals" and "conservatives" have both approached the Bible in much the same manner, but with different ideologies to proof text, see my essay "The Bible and Public Policy," *Christian Century* 103, no. 6 (1986): 171–73. See also the many responses to my arguments there in "The Bible's Role in Public Affairs: Readers Respond," *Christian Century* 103, no. 13 (1986): 389–94.

97. This citation is from Hauerwas's 1992 Sprunt Lectures, p. 37 of the unpublished manuscript.

98. See Hauerwas, *Against the Nations*, p. 111.

99. On this point, see esp. Hauerwas's essay (with Steve Long), "Interpreting the Bible as a Political Act."

100. Hauerwas, "Moral Authority of Scripture," pp. 53–71. Unless otherwise noted, all references in this section come from "Moral Authority of Scripture." For the sake of convenience I have included the page references in the main body of the text after each citation.

101. Hauerwas states: "Where such a community does not exist the most sophisticated scholarly and hermeneutical skills cannot make scripture morally relevant" ("Moral Authority of Scripture," p. 54).

102. Hauerwas and Long, "Interpreting the Bible as a Political Act," p. 135.

103. Hauerwas's emphasis on the politics of Christian existence is evident in the chapter titles of his 1991 book *After Christendom?* The six chapters have the following titles: "The Politics of Salvation," "The Politics of Justice," "The Politics of Freedom," "The Politics of Church," "The Politics of Sex," "The Politics of Witness."

104. See Hauerwas, *Peaceable Kingdom*, p. 98. In "Moral Authority of Scripture," he writes: "The authority of scripture derives its intelligibility from the existence of a community that knows its life depends on faithful remembering of God's care of his creation through the calling of Israel and the life of Jesus" (p. 53).

105. See also Hauerwas, *Peaceable Kingdom*, p. 70.

106. For Hauerwas's extended critique of historical-critical biblical scholarship, see esp. *Resident Aliens*, pp. 161–64; for his linking of the approaches taken by biblical literalists and higher critics as two sides of the same coin, see Hauerwas and Long, "Interpreting the Bible as a Political Act." See also Hauerwas, *Unleashing the Scripture*, pp. 15–44.

107. Throughout "Moral Authority of Scripture," Hauerwas makes significant use of David Kelsey's *The Uses of Scripture in Recent Theology* (Philadelphia: Fortress Press, 1975), esp. pp. 198–201, on the distinction between the Bible as Scripture and as text.

108. Hauerwas, Bondi, and Burrell, *Truthfulness and Tragedy*, p. 39.

109. See part 1 of Hauerwas's *Unleashing the Scripture*, which is entitled "The Politics of the Bible: *Sola Scriptura* as Heresy?"

110. Hauerwas and Long, "Interpreting the Bible as a Political Act," p. 139.

111. Hauerwas, *Suffering Presence*, p. 56 n. 9.

112. Hauerwas, Bondi, and Burrell, *Truthfulness and Tragedy*, p. 140.

113. Hauerwas and Willimon, *Resident Aliens*, p. 53 (emphasis mine). Hauerwas can also personify Scripture by speaking of "the Bible's concern," of what "the Bible finds uninteresting," and of how "scripture wonders" about our preaching (ibid., pp. 22, 23, 164), though in private correspondence he states that "I wouldn't do it today. The Bible doesn't do anything but people using the Bible do many things" (letter to author, 3 June, 1992).

114. Hauerwas and Long, "Interpreting the Bible as a Political Act," p. 142.

115. See Hauerwas, *Peaceable Kingdom*, p. 70.

116. Hauerwas states, "Obviously I am convinced that the most appropriate image . . . for characterizing scripture, for the use of the church as well as morally, is that of a narrative or a story" ("Moral Authority of Scripture," p. 66). See also his essays "The Self as Story," in *Vision and Virtue*, pp. 68–89; "From System to Story: An Alternative Pattern for Rationality in Ethics" (with David Burrell) and "Story and Theology," both in *Truth-*

246 Notes to Pages 116–118

fulness and Tragedy (pp. 15–39 and 71–81, respectively); "A Story-Formed Community: Reflections on *Watership Down*" and "Jesus: The Story of the Kingdom," both in *Community of Character* (pp. 9–35 and 36–52, respectively); and "A Qualified Ethic: The Narrative Character of Christian Ethics," in *Peaceable Kingdom*, pp. 17–34.

117. Hauerwas, introduction to Hauerwas, Bondi, and Burrell, *Truthfulness and Tragedy*, p. 8. Elsewhere, Hauerwas states that "it is a mistake to assume that my emphasis on narrative is the central focus of my position—insofar as I can be said even to have a position. Narrative is but a concept that helps clarify the interrelation between the various themes I have sought to develop in the attempt to give a constructive account of the Christian moral life" (*Peaceable Kingdom*, p. xxv). As for where his emphasis on narrative comes from, Hauerwas answers: "I honestly do not know" (*Peaceable Kingdom*, p. xxv).

118. Hauerwas, *Peaceable Kingdom*, p. 24.

119. Ibid., pp. 24–25. Hauerwas notes: "By emphasizing the narrative character of our knowledge of God I mean to remind us that we do not know what it means to call God creator or redeemer apart from the story of his activity with Israel and Jesus" (ibid., p. 62).

120. Hauerwas, "Moral Authority of Scripture," p. 67. As M. Goldberg has observed, narrative is central for Hauerwas because it "provides a way of articulating the movement—the development—of both character and vision through time" (*Theology and Narrative*, p. 273 n. 63). See Goldberg's extended discussion of Hauerwas on narrative, pp. 173–78. See also the critique of Hauerwas's narrative approach by J. W. Robbins, "Narrative, Morality, and Religion," *Journal of Religious Ethics* 8 (1980): 161–76; Hauerwas's response, "The Church in a Divided World: The Interpretive Power of the Christian Story," originally published in *Journal of Religious Ethics* 8 along with the essay by Robbins and now reprinted in *Community of Character*, pp. 89–110; and G. Outka's critique, "Character, Vision, and Narrative," *Religious Studies Review* 6 (1980): 116–18.

121. Hauerwas, *Peaceable Kingdom*, p. 28.

122. Ibid.

123. Ibid., pp. 28–29 (emphasis his). Here again, we see the issue of truth raised by Hauerwas. As Goldberg has noted, Hauerwas has not sufficiently articulated his underlying hermeneutics in this regard: "Hauerwas is one of the few figures who has focused on the issue of truth for a narrative-based theology in any kind of direct or sustained fashion. However, he generally fails to spell out explicitly the hermeneutic on whose basis he makes his various theological and ethical claims" (*Theology and Narrative*, pp. 190–91). See also W. C. Spohn's brief treatment of Hauerwas regarding the biblical story and truth claims in *What Are They Saying About Scripture and Ethics?* (New York and Ramsey: Paulist Press, 1984), pp. 97–99.

124. Hauerwas, "The Church as God's New Language," in *Christian Existence Today*, p. 55. He states further that "the truth of the story we find in the gospels is finally known only through the kind of lives it produces. If such lives are absent then no amount of hermeneutical theory or manipulation can make those texts meaningful" (pp. 40–41). Finally, Hauerwas also writes that "we could easily forget that a biblical ethic requires the existence of a community capable of remembering in the present, no less than it did in the past. Where such a community does not exist the most sophisticated scholarly and hermeneutical skills cannot make scripture morally relevant" (*Community of Character*, p. 54).

125. Hauerwas, *Vision and Virtue*, p. 120. Along the same lines Hauerwas writes: "No doubt love has a central place in the Bible and the Christian life, but when it becomes the primary locus of the biblical ethic it turns into an abstraction that cannot be biblically

justified. Indeed when biblical ethics is so construed one wonders why appeals need be made to scripture at all, since one treats it as a source of general principles or images that once in hand need no longer acknowledge their origins. In fact, once we construe Christian ethics in such a way, we find it necessary to stress the 'uniqueness' of the 'biblical concept of love covenant,' or some other equally impressive sounding notion" (*Community of Character*, p. 58).

126. Hauerwas, *Vision and Virtue*, pp. 115–16. Regarding social ethics, Hauerwas writes: "Christian social ethics is not first of all principles or policies for social action but rather the story of God's calling of Israel and of the life of Jesus. That story requires the formation of a corresponding community which has learned to live in a way that makes it possible for them to hear that story" (*Christian Existence Today*, p. 101).

127. See Hauerwas, "Moral Authority of Scripture," p. 58.

128. See, e.g., Hauerwas, "Epilogue: A Pacifist Response to the Bishops," p. 164.

129. Hauerwas, "Jesus: The Story of the Kingdom," in *Community of Character*, p. 42. Similarly, "Jesus' identity is prior to the 'meaning' of the story" (p. 43).

130. Hauerwas and Willimon, *Resident Aliens*, p. 21.

131. Hauerwas, *Community of Character*, p. 52.

132. Ibid., p. 190.

133. Ibid., p. 92.

134. Hauerwas, "The Moral Authority of Scripture," p. 67. Hauerwas refers to "the main story line" of Scripture in the following context: "One of the virtues of calling attention to the narrative nature of scripture is the way it releases us from making unsupportable claims about the unity of scripture or the centrality of the 'biblical view of X or Y.' Rather, the scripture must be seen as one long, 'loosely structured non-fiction novel' that has subplots that at some points appear minor but later turn out to be central. What is crucial, however, is that the scripture does not try to suppress those subplots or characters that may challenge, or at least qualify, the main story line, for without them the story itself would be less than truthful" (p. 67).

135. Ibid., pp. 67–68. Of course, whether Jesus himself claimed to be the Messiah or whether this claim originated with the earliest church remains an issue of much debate.

136. Ibid., p. 59. See also Hauerwas's brief discussion of allegory as an attempt at renarration in *Unleashing the Scripture*, pp. 39–41.

137. Hauerwas, *The Peaceable Kingdom*, p. 98.

138. Hauerwas, "On Keeping Theological Ethics Imaginative," in *Against the Nations*, p. 58.

139. Hauerwas, *Peaceable Kingdom*, p. 71.

140. See, e.g., Hauerwas, *Character and the Christian Life*, pp. 196–97; Hauerwas and Willimon, *Resident Aliens*, p. 162; Hauerwas, *Naming the Silences*, p. 51. In *Unleashing the Scripture*, he writes that "all my theological formation took place in curricula shaped by Protestant liberalism. Yet such formation was more 'biblical' than I suspected because I now think it an advantage to learn Scripture through the work of Aquinas, Luther, Calvin, Barth, and Yoder" (p. 9).

141. It should be pointed out that in his discussion of Christian practical reasoning, Hauerwas explicitly notes his reliance on J. H. Yoder's essay "The Hermeneutics of Peoplehood: A Protestant Perspective," from Yoder's *The Priestly Kingdom: Social Ethics as Gospel* (Notre Dame: University of Notre Dame Press, 1984), pp. 15–45.

142. The story of Olin Teague is taken from Hauerwas's "Reconciling the Practice of Reason: Casuistry in a Christian Context," in *Christian Existence Today*, pp. 67–87;

esp. pp. 74–82. Unless otherwise noted, all page references in this section are to this essay. I do not know where Hauerwas gets the story of Olin Teague.

143. Hauerwas, *Community of Character*, p. 96.

144. Hauerwas, *Peaceable Kingdom*, p. 98.

145. Hauerwas and Willimon, *Resident Aliens*, p. 129.

146. Hauerwas, "Moral Authority of Scripture," p. 66.

147. See in particular B. Metzger's *The Canon of the New Testament: Its Origin, Development, and Significance* (Oxford: Oxford University Press, 1987), esp. pp. 271–75. For one example of the dispute over the canon, see my article "The Canonical Status of the Catholic Epistles in the Syriac New Testament," *Journal of Theological Studies* 38 (1987): 311–40.

148. Hauerwas, "Moral Authority of Scripture," p. 68.

149. See, e.g., Hauerwas, *Community of Character*, p. 92.

150. In one essay he does offer "criteria for judging among stories." These criteria, which he qualifies as neither complete nor unambiguous, are as follows: "Any story which we adopt, or allow to adopt us, will have to display: (1) power to release us from destructive alternatives; (2) ways of seeing through current distortions; (3) room to keep us from having to resort to violence; (4) a sense for the tragic: how meaning transcends power" ("From System to Story," with David Burrell, in *Truthfulness and Tragedy*, p. 35). Hauerwas has received sharp criticism regarding these criteria. E.g., M. Goldberg remarks that "other than the bare assertion of these criteria, he [Hauerwas] fails to support his claim for their necessity. Not only is it unclear why these criteria are ones that any justifiable narrative theology must employ, but also it is equally unclear . . . how such criteria are related to narrative in general" (*Theology and Narrative*, p. 237).

151. In private correspondence, Hauerwas responds: "You note that I give no rationale for choosing among the range when interpretations conflict. You are right [that] I don't and I never will. I can't imagine what such a rationale would look like capable of determining future possibilities of interpretation. Since, however, all interpretation occurs within contexts that are constrained I think that the range will always be controlled. Those that assume [that] this means there is no control at all fail to appreciate the fact that all interpretation is working already within some tradition that implies some constraints" (letter to author, 3 June 1992).

152. Hauerwas, "Reconciling the Practice of Reason," in *Christian Existence Today*, p. 82.

153. Hauerwas, "Character, Narrative, and Growth in the Christian Life," in *Community of Character*, p. 151. As Hauerwas notes, Gustafson has criticized him for not presenting "a way that the revelatory power of the biblical material can be confirmed in human experience (as the Niebuhrs do)" (*Christian Existence Today*, p. 6). In private correspondence, Hauerwas responds: "to let Gustafson ask the question in that way is already to have let him win the day. I do not think that kind of correlation makes any sense since I don't know what human experience means characterized apart from the gospel. I do talk about confirmations such as the Saints, the faithful churches, concrete practices and so on. [What] I simply will not do is privilege something called human experience that the Bible is supposed to confirm or illumine" (letter to author, 3 June 1992).

Chapter Seven

1. For a general assessment of the significance of Gutiérrez's work, see esp. R. M. Brown, *Gustavo Gutiérrez: An Introduction to Liberation Theology* (Maryknoll, N.Y.:

Orbis Books, 1990); M. Ellis and O. Maduro, eds., *The Future of Liberation Theology: Essays in Honor of Gustavo Gutiérrez* (Maryknoll, N.Y.: Orbis Books, 1989); and C. Cadorette, *From the Heart of the People: The Theology of Gustavo Gutiérrez* (Oak Park, Ill.: Meyer Stone Books, 1988). Although Gutiérrez considers himself a theologian, he sees himself first and foremost as a pastor engaged in ministry and only secondarily as a "professional" theologian. This self-understanding fits with his conviction that pastoral activity comes first, whereas theology is a second step (not secondary) that reflects on pastoral activity. See, e.g., G. Gutiérrez, *A Theology of Liberation*, 2d ed. (Maryknoll, N.Y.: Orbis Books, 1988), pp. 9–10; G. Gutiérrez, *On Job: God-Talk and the Suffering of the Innocent* (Maryknoll, N.Y.: Orbis Books, 1987), p. xiii.

2. Gutiérrez, *Theology of Liberation*, pp. xxix, 5.

3. For references to "the word of God" as a way of talking about the Bible, see, e.g., Gutiérrez, *Theology of Liberation*, pp. xxxiii, 32; G. Gutiérrez, *The Power of the Poor in History* (Maryknoll, N.Y.: Orbis Books, 1983), pp. 3–4, 102; G. Gutiérrez, *The Truth Shall Make You Free* (Maryknoll, N.Y.: Orbis Books, 1990), pp. 47, 88; G. Gutiérrez, *We Drink from Our Own Wells* (Maryknoll, N.Y.: Orbis Books, 1984), pp. 34, 95; Gutiérrez, *On Job*, p. xvii; and G. Gutiérrez, *The God of Life* (Maryknoll, N.Y.: Orbis Books, 1991), pp. 121, 189. I have not found any references to "the word of God" where Gutiérrez seems to be referring to something other than the Bible, although I would not conclude that Gutiérrez consciously restricts the term to the Bible exclusively.

4. For brief treatments of Gutiérrez's use of the Bible, see esp. R. M. Brown, *Gustavo Gutiérrez*, pp. 107–8; L. Boisvert, "Les images bibliques de Dieu dans l'oeuvre de Gustavo Gutiérrez," *Église et Théologie* 19 (1989): 307–21; and T. L. Schubeck, *Liberation Ethics: Sources, Models, and Norms* (Minneapolis: Fortress Press, 1993), pp. 151–71. Even the volume of essays in honor of Gutiérrez, *Future of Liberation Theology*, ed. Ellis and Maduro, includes no real discussion of Gutiérrez's biblical interpretation.

For discussions of biblical exegesis and Latin American liberation theology in general, see, e.g., C. Rowland and M. Corner, *Liberating Exegesis: The Challenge of Liberation Theology to Biblical Studies* (Louisville: Westminster Press/John Knox Press, 1989); L. Laberge, "L'éthique des théologiens de la libération et ses fondments bibliques," *Église et Théologie* 19 (1988): 373–400; A. F. McGovern, *Liberation Theology and Its Critics: Toward an Assessment* (Maryknoll, N.Y.: Orbis Books, 1989), pp. 62–82; and A. Tambasco, "First and Third World Ethics," in *Christian Biblical Ethics: From Biblical Revelation to Contemporary Christian Praxis, Method and Content*, ed. R.J. Daly (New York: Paulist Press, 1984), pp. 139–55.

For responses to uses of the Bible in Latin American liberation theology, see C. L. Nessan, *Orthopraxis or Heresy: The North American Theological Response to Latin American Liberation Theology* (Atlanta: Scholars Press, 1989), pp. 283–91, 377–81; and J. A. Kirk, *Liberation Theology: An Evangelical View from the Third World* (Atlanta: John Knox Press, 1979), pp. 45–194.

5. Gutiérrez also studied at the Gregorian University in Rome (1959–60). See R. M. Brown, *Gustavo Gutiérrez*, pp. 22–25.

6. Ibid., pp. 25–26.

7. This example shows that Gutiérrez can approach the Bible in terms of "biblical concept" theology. See D. H. Kelsey's discussion of this approach in his *The Uses of Scripture in Recent Theology* (Philadelphia: Fortress Press, 1975), pp. 24–29.

8. Gutiérrez, *We Drink from Our Own Wells*, p. 19. This comment occurs in the context of specific reference to Pss. 9 and 33.

9. See Gutiérrez, *On Job*, as well as the chapter "My Eyes Have Seen You," in Gutiérrez, *God of Life*, pp. 145–63, which was written after the commentary on Job.

Curiously, references to Job appear almost nowhere else in his writings. I have found only three other references to Job, all in *Theology of Liberation*, pp. 166 (twice), 229 n. 27.

10. See, e.g., various Vatican statements, especially the Congregation for the Doctrine of the Faith's "Ten Observations on the Theology of Gustavo Gutiérrez," p. 349; "Instruction on Certain Aspects of the 'Theology of Liberation,' " p. 397, and the more nuanced "Instruction on Christian Freedom and Liberation," p. 474, all found in A. T. Hennelly, ed., *Liberation Theology: A Documentary History* (Maryknoll, N.Y.: Orbis Books, 1990). In addition, see, e.g., A. Thiselton, *New Horizons in Hermeneutics: The Theory and Practice of Transforming Biblical Reading* (Grand Rapids: Zondervan, 1992), pp. 416–17; D. P. McCann, *Christian Realism and Liberation Theology: Practical Theologies in Creative Conflict* (Maryknoll, N.Y.: Orbis Books, 1981), p. 196; Kirk, *Liberation Theology*, pp. 63, 95–104, 147–52; and the general criticism of J. H. Yoder, "Probing the Meaning of Liberation," *Sojourners* 5, no. 8 (Sept. 1976): 26–29.

11. Christine Gudorf has made a similar observation in her article "Liberation Theology's Use of Scripture: A Response to First World Critics," *Interpretation* 41 (1987): 16–17.

12. Gutiérrez, *The Truth Shall Make You Free*, p. 29. See also, e.g., Gutiérrez, *Power of the Poor in History*, p. 219 n, 66: "Poverty is one of the earliest great biblical themes of the theology of liberation—see my *Theology of Liberation*, chap. 13, and the commentary on Matthew 25 in chap. 10. I apologize for this and other references to my own writings. Here it would scarcely be worth the trouble, were it not for friends who, naively 'buying' a distortion propagated by persons with other interests, have begun to repeat what they have heard to the effect that, in its beginnings, the theology of liberation was centered exclusively on the Old Testament theme of the exodus. This is altogether in error. (On the other hand, we are far from denying the central importance of the exodus theme throughout the Bible, and hence throughout theology.)" See also *The Truth Shall Make You Free*: "the exodus truly plays an important part in liberation theology. Its importance should not be exaggerated, however, since other themes and other passages of the Bible also have a decisive role in this theological approach" (pp. 118–19).

13. Gutiérrez has also reflected on Ecclesiasticus (Sirach) 34:18–22, a significant passage for Bartolomé de las Casas (who has been a powerful model for Gutiérrez), the sixteenth-century defender of a peaceful mission among the Indians amid the idolatry of gold and the oppression and massacre of Indian populations. This text was the scripture for de las Casas's 1514 Pentecost sermon in Cuba, which indicated his own conversion to the cause of the impoverished and oppressed peoples of the Indies. It is no accident that the center out of which Gutiérrez works in Lima is named after de las Casas, nor that Gutiérrez's personal heritage is itself partly Indian. See Gutiérrez's *Dios o el oro en las Indias* (Lima: CEP, 1989), pp. 126 ff., and his magnum opus on de las Casas, *En busca de los pobres de Cristo* (Lima: CEP, 1992). Elsewhere in his writings, Gutiérrez refers to Ecclus. 34:18–22 in *God of Life*, pp. 43, 130.

14. For another liberation approach to Matt. 25:31–46 comparable to that of Gutiérrez, see R. M. Brown, "Jesus' Vision: A Task for the Nations," in *Unexpected News: Reading the Bible with Third World Eyes* (Philadelphia: Westminster Press, 1984), pp. 127–41.

15. See, e.g., the following works by Gutiérrez: *Theology of Liberation*, pp. 85, 98, 112–13, 132, 177 n. 30; *Power of the Poor in History*, pp. 21, 33, 52, 96, 142, 162, 202; *We Drink from Our Own Wells*, pp. 38, 100, 104, 112; *On Job*, p. 40; *The Truth Shall Make You Free*, pp. 3, 5, 12, 36, 157, 160, 163–64, 171, 186; *God of Life*, pp. 74, 86–87, 114, 119, 122, 124, 128, 131–32.

16. Gutiérrez, *We Drink from Our Own Wells*, p. 104.

17. See, e.g., the following works by Gutiérrez: *Theology of Liberation*, p. 160; *The Truth Shall Make You Free*, pp. 156, 160, 166; *On Job*, p. 94; *God of Life*, pp. xv, 116, 122, 185, and esp. 132.

18. Gutiérrez, *Theology of Liberation*, p. 169. See esp. Gutiérrez's discussion of Matt. 5 in relation to Matt. 25 in *The Truth Shall Make You Free*, p. 160.

19. Gutiérrez, *The Truth Shall Make You Free*, p. 160.

20. Ibid., p. 163. See also his *God of Life*, pp. 118–28.

21. Gutiérrez makes use of the Luke 4 passage seventeen times. See, e.g., *Theology of Liberation*, pp. 96–97, 254 n. 43; *Power of the Poor in History*, pp. 14, 143, 149, 157, 207; *We Drink from Our Own Wells*, pp. 43, 100; *The Truth Shall Make You Free*, pp. 117, 173; *God of Life*, pp. 7, 103, 109.

22. See esp. Gutiérrez's comments on Mark 8:27–35 in *We Drink from Our Own Wells*, pp. 45–51; *God of Life*, p. 88. Gutiérrez clearly sees Mark 8:27–33 as a central passage in Mark's Gospel (e.g., *Theology of Liberation*, p. xxiv), but more as a witness to life in the face of suffering and death than a call to imitate Jesus' suffering and death as if this were the goal. Suffering and death is never an end in itself but only a consequence of being condemned by unjust powers for seeking the fullness of life which God promises here and now to God's people (see *We Drink from Our Own Wells*, p. 51).

23. The texts from the Passion narratives referred to are Matt. 26:73 (*Theology of Liberation*, p. xxxv; *God of Life*, p. 99); Matt. 27:49 (*On Job*, p. 97); Mark 14:9 (*God of Life*, p. 170); Mark 15:34 (*We Drink from Our Own Wells*, p. 131; *On Job*, p. 97); Luke 22:44–45 (*Theology of Liberation*, p. xxxi; *God of Life*, p. 47); John 18–19 (*The Truth Shall Make You Free*, p. 12); John 18:20 (*Theology of Liberation*, p. 133); John 18:36–37 and 19:5 (*God of Life*, p. 87); and John 19:19 (*God of Life*, p. 100).

24. See also the comments of R. M. Brown, *Gustavo Gutiérrez*, pp. 4–5, in a subsection entitled "Transition: Two Views of the Crucifix." For Gutiérrez's reflections on the resurrection of Jesus, see esp. his comments on 1 Cor. 15 in *We Drink from Our Own Wells*, pp. 56, 66–68, 121.

25. Interestingly, Gutiérrez makes only three references to Rom. 9–11 in all his writings. Gutiérrez has a significant discussion of Philemon in his *God of Life*, pp. 132–36. See also his essay "Haz más de lo que te pido: La Carta a Filemón," *Paginas* 9, no. 60 (Apr. 1984): 2, 43.

26. For James 2, see, e.g., *Theology of Liberation*, pp. 113, 116, 167; *Power of the Poor in History*, pp. 17, 19; *We Drink from Our Own Wells*, p. 91. For 1 John 3:14, see, e.g., *Theology of Liberation*, pp. 98, 113; and *Power of the Poor in History*, pp. 17, 37, 60, 105.

27. Gutiérrez, *The Truth Shall Make You Free*, p. 48. Similarly, Gutiérrez asserts "that we approach the Bible from our experience as believers and members of the church. It is in the light of that experience that we ask our questions" (*We Drink from Our Own Wells*, p. 34).

28. Gutiérrez, *Theology of Liberation*, p. xxxiii; see also p. xiii.

29. Gutiérrez, *Power of the Poor in History*, p. 4.

30. On the centrality of experience for Gutiérrez, both that of the biblical authors and that of contemporary readers, see Boisvert, "Les images bibliques de Dieu dans l'oeuvre de Gustavo Gutiérrez," pp. 318–20.

31. Gutiérrez, *The Truth Shall Make You Free*, p. 88.

32. Gutiérrez, *We Drink from Our Own Wells*, p. xix.

33. Gutiérrez, *On Job*, p. xviii.

34. Ibid., pp. 13, 16, 27, 47, 73.

35. Ibid., p. 31.

36. Ibid., p. 94.

37. See also the comments of L. Laberge on Gutiérrez's use of Job in "L'éthique des théologiens de la libération," pp. 397–99.

38. See, e.g., Gutiérrez, "Toward a Theology of Liberation," written in 1968 (in *Liberation Theology*, ed. Hennelly, pp. 62–76, esp. 71–72); Gutiérrez, "Notes for a Theology of Liberation," *Theological Studies* 31 (1970): 255–57; Gutiérrez, *Theology of Liberation*, pp. 86–101; Gutiérrez, *Power of the Poor in History*, pp. 11–12, 31–33.

39. On John 1, see, e.g., *Theology of Liberation*, pp. xvii, 108; *Power of the Poor in History*, pp. 13, 20, 32, 209; and *God of Life*, pp. 69, 81–84, 172. On Col. 1:15–20, see, e.g., *Theology of Liberation*, p. 90; *Power of the Poor in History*, p. 32; "Toward a Theology of Liberation," p. 72; and "Notes for a Theology of Liberation," p. 256.

40. Gutiérrez, *Theology of Liberation*, p. 93; also see Gutiérrez, "Notes for a Theology of Liberation," p. 257.

41. Gutiérrez, *Theology of Liberation*, p. 8.

42. Ibid., p. 113.

43. Ibid., p. 122.

44. Ibid., p. 135.

45. Ibid., p. 136.

46. Ibid., p. 93.

47. Ibid., p. 96.

48. Ibid., p. 97.

49. Gutiérrez, "Notes for a Theology of Liberation," p. 257.

50. Gutiérrez, *Theology of Liberation*, p. 88.

51. Gutiérrez, "Notes for a Theology of Liberation," p. 256.

52. Gutiérrez, *Theology of Liberation*, p. 167.

53. Ibid., p. 168.

54. Gutiérrez discusses "spiritual childhood" throughout his writings. See, e.g., *Power of the Poor in History*, p. 89; *The Truth Shall Make You Free*, pp. 160–64; *We Drink from Our Own Wells*, pp. 122–27 (part of a chapter entitled "Spiritual Childhood: A Requirement for Commitment to the Poor"); and *God of Life*, pp. 120–28.

55. Gutiérrez, *Theology of Liberation*, p. 171.

56. See, e.g., Gutiérrez, *Power of the Poor in History*, p. 89.

57. Gutiérrez, *Theology of Liberation*, p. 171.

58. Ibid., p. 169.

59. Gutiérrez, *The Truth Shall Make You Free*, p. 161.

60. Gutiérrez, *We Drink from Our Own Wells*, p. 127.

61. See ibid., pp. 126–27.

62. G. Gutiérrez, "The Irruption of the Poor in Latin America and the Christian Communities of the Common People," in *The Challenge of Basic Christian Communities*, ed. S. Torres and J. Eagleson (Maryknoll, N.Y.: Orbis Books, 1981), p. 121.

63. See, e.g., *Truth Shall Make You Free*, pp. 46–47; *We Drink from Our Own Wells*, p. 34; *On Job*, p. xvii; and *God of Life*, p. xvii.

64. Gutiérrez, *God of Life*, pp. xvi–xvii.

65. The notion of the Bible "reading us" and interrogating the reader can also be found, e.g., in S. E. Fowl and L. G. Jones, *Reading in Communion: Scripture and Ethics in Christian Life* (Grand Rapids: Eerdmans, 1991), pp. 42–43, 96–99, 140.

66. Gutiérrez, *The Truth Shall Make You Free*, p. 47.

67. Gutiérrez, *Power of the Poor in History*, p. 22.

68. Ibid., p. 204.

69. Gutiérrez, *God of Life*, pp. 57–58. Ironically, although in Luke 16 the rich man is nameless, church tradition quickly gave him the name Dives.

70. G. Gutiérrez, "Freedom and Salvation," in *Liberation and Change*, ed. R. H. Stone (Atlanta: John Knox Press, 1977), p. 90; almost exactly the same language can also be found in *Power of the Poor in History*, p. 18. See also C. Mesters's seminal essay "The Use of the Bible in Christian Communities of the Common People," in *Challenge of Basic Christian Communities*, ed. Torres and Eagleson, pp. 197–210; reprinted in Hennelly, ed., *Liberation Theology*, pp. 14–28. Mesters writes that: "the common people have entered the precincts of biblical interpretation and they are causing much shifting and dislocation. . . . the Bible itself has shifted its place and moved to the side of the poor. One could almost say that it has changed its class status" (p. 24).

71. Gutiérrez, "God's Revelation and Proclamation in History," in his *Power of the Poor in History*, pp. 3–4.

72. Gutiérrez, "Theology from the Underside of History," in his *Power of the Poor in History*, p. 208. Gutiérrez sees the direction taken by E. Cardenal in his four-volume *The Gospel in Solentiname* (Maryknoll, N.Y.: Orbis Books, 1976–82) as "a most fertile area for further investigation." He feels the same way about various materialist readings of the Bible, as long as they do not become mere intellectual readings (*Power of the Poor in History*, p. 220 n. 78). Elsewhere, Gutiérrez notes that the participation of the theologian in the plight of the poor is not just a theological fad, because "whatever the meaning of the 'death of theology' may be, a much more important and striking phenomenon has been the death of the theologian. I am not playing with words here. I am not speaking figuratively. I mean real deaths. The prophets, then Job, Paul, and so many others who attempted to interpret and proclaim the word of God, were theologians—and as theologians they were put to death. . . . But there is another meaning of the 'death of the theologian.' It is the one implied in the celebrated text of Paul [1 Cor. 1:18–19] . . . What is to be done away with is the intellectualizing of the intellectual who has no ties with the life and struggle of the poor—the theology of the theologian who reflects upon the faith precisely from the point of view of those from whom the Father has hidden his revelation" (*Power of the Poor in History*, pp. 102–3).

73. A recurring motif throughout Gutiérrez's writings is that in the Latin American setting, the primary contrast is between the wealthy and the poor, those who are treated as persons and those treated as nonpersons, whereas in the European and North American settings, the contrast has often been envisioned as being between the believer and the nonbeliever (esp. in the writings of such authors as Pascal and Bonhoeffer). See, e.g., *Power of the Poor in History*, pp. 57, 92, 193, 213; *The Truth Shall Make You Free*, pp. 7, 24–25; and *On Job*, p. 16. See also Cadorette, *From the Heart of the People*, pp. 8–9; and R. M. Brown, *Gustavo Gutiérrez*, pp. 85–93.

74. For Gutiérrez's views on violence, see *The Truth Shall Make You Free*, pp. 83–84 n. 21; and his comments on the violence of Camilo Torres in R. M. Brown, *Gustavo Gutiérrez*, p. 34.

75. See Gutiérrez's 1984 essay "Theology and the Social Sciences," in *The Truth Shall Make You Free*, pp. 52–84, esp. 60–63. For further analysis of Gutiérrez and Marxism, see Cadorette, *From the Heart of the People*, esp. chap. 4, "Marxism, Social Science, and Class Struggle," pp. 83–114. On dependency theory versus development theory, see Gutiérrez, *Theology of Liberation*, pp. 13–25, 49–57; Cadorette, *From the Heart of the People*, pp. 18–29; and R. M. Brown, *Gustavo Gutiérrez*, pp. 93–98.

76. On the *comunidades cristianas de base*, the "basic Christian communities," see esp. Torres and Eagleson, eds., *Challenge of Basic Christian Communities*, and particu-

larly Gutiérrez's essay in that volume, "The Irruption of the Poor in Latin America and the Christian Communities of the Common People," pp. 107–23.

77. See R. M. Brown, *Gustavo Gutiérrez*, pp. 38–39; and J. Eagleson and P. Sharper, eds., *Puebla and Beyond* (Maryknoll, N.Y.: Orbis Books, 1979), pp. 35–36.

78. Gutiérrez, *Power of the Poor in History*, p. 142.

79. Ibid., p. 115.

80. Gutiérrez, *The Truth Shall Make You Free*, p. 139.

81. "Ten Observations on the Theology of Gustavo Gutiérrez" is reprinted in English translation in Hennelly, ed., *Liberation Theology*, pp. 348–50. For the quotations, see pp. 349 and 350.

82. In *God of Life*, Gutiérrez calls the Beatitudes "the Magna Carta of the congregation (the church) that is made up of the disciples of Jesus" (p. 118).

83. On Latin American liberation theology hermeneutics in general, see, e.g., Kirk, *Liberation Theology*, pp. 61–65, 175–77, 185–94; M. L. Branson and C. R. Padilla, eds., *Conflict and Context: Hermeneutics in the Americas* (Grand Rapids: Eerdmans, 1986); and more recently Thiselton, *New Horizons in Hermeneutics*, pp. 411–70. From a Latin American perspective, see also, e.g., J. L. Segundo, *The Liberation of Theology* (Maryknoll, N.Y.: Orbis Books, 1976), pp. 7–38; S. Croatto, *Exodus: A Hermeneutics of Freedom* (Maryknoll, N.Y.: Orbis Books, 1981); S. Croatto, *Biblical Hermeneutics: Towards a Theory of Reading as the Production of Meaning* (Maryknoll, N.Y.: Orbis Books, 1987); C. Boff, *Theology and Praxis: Epistemological Foundations* (Maryknoll, N.Y.: Orbis Books, 1987); as well as a critique of Croatto in J. L. Segundo's "Faith and Ideologies in Biblical Revelation," in *The Bible and Liberation: Political and Social Hermeneutics*, ed. N. Gottwald (Maryknoll, N.Y.: Orbis Books, 1983), pp. 482–96, esp. 486–87. On Gutiérrez's focus on Jesus in his hermeneutics, see Gutiérrez, "Freedom and Salvation," p. 83. See also his *Power of the Poor in History*, pp. 15, 61; and *The Truth Shall Make You Free*, p. 3.

84. Gutiérrez, *Power of the Poor in History*, p. 15.

85. Ibid., p. 13.

86. Ibid., pp. 61 . . . 15. This formula of the hermeneutical circle is found several times in slightly different form in Gutiérrez's writings. See also his "Freedom and Salvation," p. 83.

87. "A Discussion of Gustavo Gutiérrez's Work (Lyons, 1985)," in *The Truth Shall Make You Free*, pp. 46–47. The question was posed in the context of a 1985 discussion of Gutiérrez's work before the theological faculty of the Catholic Institute of Lyons, where he had earlier done his theological studies.

88. Ibid., pp. 47–48.

89. As Gutiérrez puts it in his essay "God's Revelation and Proclamation in History," in *Power of the Poor in History*: "For some, the effort to read the Bible may be directed toward simply adapting its message and language to men and women of today. For others, however, it is a matter of reinterpretation. We reinterpret the Bible, from the viewpoint of our own world—from our personal experience as human beings, as believers, and as church. This approach is more radical. It goes more to the roots of what the Bible actually is, more to the essence of God's revelation in history and of God's judgment on it.

"Let us try to understand the Bible . . . in the following pages using this second approach. And let us start out with Christ, the fulfillment of the promise of the Father, for this is the only way to grasp the profound unity of the Old and New Testaments. Our reading, then, will be *christological*" (p. 4).

90. Gutiérrez writes that authentic reading of the Bible "will also be a reading *in faith*. It will not be a reading done by trained specialists, but by a community that knows itself to be the subject of the word's intercession, that recognizes Christ as Lord both of history and its own life" (ibid.). See also *God of Life*, pp. xvi–xvii.

91. See, e.g., *Power of the Poor in History*, pp. 4, 18, 21, 101, 208; *The Truth Shall Make You Free*, p. 48. See also R. M. Brown, "The Bible—and a 'Militant Reading,' " in his *Gustavo Gutiérrez*, pp. 107–9. It should be noted that the original Spanish word used, "*militante*," has a less confrontational connotation than the English word "militant." It might be more appropriate to translate the term as "activist."

92. Gutiérrez, *Power of the Poor in History*, p. 4. Later in the same volume, he writes, "The social appropriation of the gospel is a reading of the gospel in solidarity with the struggles of the poor. It is a militant reading of the Bible. The interpretation that the poor give their life situations opens a rich vein for the understanding of the gift of God's kingdom. A point of departure in that life situation will enable the theologian to take into account the data of modern scientific exegesis and give it a new, radical dimension" (p. 101). See also *The Truth Shall Make You Free*, p. 48.

93. Gutiérrez, *The Truth Shall Make You Free*, p. 48.

94. Gutiérrez, *Power of the Poor in History*, p. 4. See also Gutiérrez's comments on the dialogue between past history and present history in all biblical interpretation in *God of Life*, pp. xvi–xvii.

95. Gutiérrez, *God of Life*, p. 118.

96. For Gutiérrez's use of James 2:14–26, see *Theology of Liberation*, pp. 113, 150; *Liberation and Change*, p. 89; *Power of the Poor in History*, p. 17; *The Truth Shall Make You Free*, p. 99; and *We Drink from Our Own Wells*, p. 91. Interestingly, Gutiérrez makes no reference to Paul's statements in Rom. 4 and Gal. 3 that Abraham was reckoned righteous on the basis of his faith and not his works.

97. This is the title of chap. 7 in *God of Life* (pp. 118–39), one of the places where Gutiérrez most clearly articulates the significance of his reading of the Bible for Christian praxis.

98. See, e.g., *Theology of Liberation*, pp. 118–19; *We Drink from Our Own Wells*, pp. 107–13; *On Job*, pp. xi–xiv, 16, 82, 87, 94, 103; *God of Life*, pp. 154, 161; and *The Truth Shall Make You Free*, p. 164 and p. 36, where Gutiérrez states: "in the Bible as a whole, two approaches are taken to the mystery of God: gratuitousness and resultant obligation. The saving love of God is a gift, but its acceptance entails a commitment to one's neighbor. Christian life is located between the gratuitous gift and the obligation." See similarly Gutiérrez's use of Matt. 5:10 in *The Truth Shall Make You Free*, p. 162.

99. Gutiérrez, *God of Life*, pp. 118–28. See further Gutiérrez's article, "Ser discípulo según Mateo," *Páginas* 11, no. 76 (Apr. 1986): 2, 46–47. Regarding the contrast between the Lukan and the Matthean Beatitudes, Gutiérrez comments: "The Beatitudes in Luke put the emphasis on the gratuitousness of the love of God, who has a predilection for the poor. The Beatitudes in Matthew fill out the picture by specifying the ethical requirements that flow from this loving initiative of God" (*The Truth Shall Make You Free*, p. 164).

100. Gutiérrez, *God of Life*, p. 121.

101. Ibid., p. 131.

102. Ibid., p. 135. See further Gutiérrez's article "Haz más de lo que te pido," pp. 2, 43.

103. Gutiérrez, *God of Life*, pp. 135–36.

104. Ibid., pp. 137–38.

105. Hennelly, ed., *Liberation Theology*, pp. 349–50. See Schubeck's positive evaluation of Gutiérrez's use of Scripture in *Liberation Ethics*, pp. 167–71.

106. Hennelly, ed., *Liberation Theology*, p. 407.

107. For Gutiérrez's comments on the Exodus, see, e.g., *Theology of Liberation*, pp. 69, 86–93, 101; *Power of the Poor in History*, pp. 5–9, 219 n. 66; *The Truth Shall Make You Free*, pp. 27–29, 118–19; *We Drink from Our Own Wells*, pp. 11, 73; and *God of Life*, pp. 4, 50.

108. Gutiérrez, *The Truth Shall Make You Free*, pp. 118–19.

109. N. Gottwald's "social revolution model" of the Exodus and conquest traditions would be very helpful here, because in this model, the Canaanites are not conquered but participate in social and political liberation along with the "Israelites." See, e.g., Gottwald's *The Tribes of Yahweh: A Sociology of the Religion of Liberated Israel, 1250–1050 B.C.E.* (Maryknoll, N.Y.: Orbis Books, 1979) and *The Hebrew Bible: A Socio-literary Introduction* (Philadelphia: Fortress Press, 1985), pp. 261–76; as well as his essay "The Exodus as Event and Process: A Test Case in the Biblical Grounding of Liberation Theology," in *Future of Liberation Theology*, ed. Ellis and Maduro, pp. 250–60.

110. Gutiérrez, *Power of the Poor in History*, p. 115. On p. 120, Gutiérrez speaks about maintaining "faithfulness to Medellín," clearly showing that the documents from this General Conference of Latin American Bishops are paradigmatic for his view of appropriate biblical interpretation.

111. Gutiérrez, *The Truth Shall Make You Free*, p. 139.

112. Gutiérrez, *God of Life*, p. 87.

Chapter Eight

1. I should state at the outset that I have have felt more of an outsider in relation to the traditions and experiences that have shaped Cone's life and work than in relation to those of any of the other theologians examined in this book. I can safely say that I have never felt so "white" as when reading through James Cone's writings! I am then also mindful of some of Cone's words that bear directly on my goal as a white scholar to understand and to critically discuss Cone's work: "The time has come for white Americans to be silent and listen to black people. . . . Whatever blacks feel toward whites or whatever their response to white racism, it cannot be submitted to the judgments of white society" (*Black Theology and Black Power* [New York: Seabury Press, 1969], p. 21). Cone also states that "no white person who is halfway sensitive to black self-determination should have the audacity to speak for blacks. That is the problem! *Too many whites think they know how we feel about them.* If whites were really serious about their radicalism in regard to the black revolution and its theological implications in America, they would keep silent and take instructions from blacks" (ibid., p. 62).

2. J. H. Cone, *God of the Oppressed* (San Francisco: Harper, 1975), p. 6.

3. On the significance of the Bible in the black church in general, see, e.g., M. G. Cartwright, "Ideology and the Interpretation of the Bible in the African-American Christian Tradition," *Modern Theology* 9, no. 2 (1993): 141–58; P. J. Paris, "The Bible and the Black Churches," in *The Bible and Social Reform*, ed. E. Sandeen (Philadelphia: Fortress Press; Chico, Calif.: Scholars Press, 1982), pp. 133–54; R. A. Bennett, Jr., "Black Experience and the Bible," *Theology Today* 27 (1971): 422–33.

4. J. H. Cone, "Christian Theology and Scripture as the Expression of God's Liber-

ating Activity for the Poor," in *Speaking the Truth: Ecumenism, Liberation, and Black Theology* (Grand Rapids: Eerdmans, 1986), p. 4. This essay has been published with slight variations in four different places. It was originally presented in 1975 at the annual meeting of the Society for the Study of Black Religion and later appeared as "What Is Christian Theology?" in *Encounter* 43 (1982): 117–28. It was published under the title "Christian Theology and Scripture as the Expression of God's Liberating Activity for the Poor," in *Speaking the Truth* (1986), pp. 4–16; and in *Bangalore Theological Forum* 22, no. 2 (June 1990): 26–39. Most recently, it has appeared as "Theology, the Bible, and the Poor," in *Standing with the Poor*, ed. P. Parker (Cleveland: Pilgrim Press, 1992), pp. 82–92.

5. Ibid., p. 5.

6. Cone, *God of the Oppressed*, p. 8. Emphasis his.

7. Nearly all of Cone's reflections on the Bible occur in his first four books (*Black Theology and Black Power; A Black Theology of Liberation* [Philadelphia and New York: Lippincott, 1970; reprint, Maryknoll, N.Y.: Orbis Books, 1990]; *The Spirituals and the Blues* [New York: Seabury Press, 1972; reprint, Maryknoll, N.Y.: Orbis Books, 1991]; and *God of the Oppressed*). His last four books (*My Soul Looks Back*, [Nashville: Abingdon Press, 1982; reprint, Maryknoll, N.Y.: Orbis Books, 1986]; *For My People: Black Theology and the Black Church* [Maryknoll, N.Y.: Orbis Books, 1984]; *Speaking the Truth*; and *Martin and Malcolm and America: A Dream or a Nightmare* [Maryknoll, N.Y.: Orbis Books, 1991]) refer very rarely to discrete biblical texts. This is illustrated in part by tabulating references to biblical texts. In his first four books, Cone refers to biblical texts 336 times, whereas in his last four books, Cone refers to biblical texts 34 times. It is important to note in this connection that his first four books are much more constructive in scope, whereas his last four books are more reflections on and analytical descriptions of the course of black theology.

8. For these topics, see the following works by Cone: *Black Theology and Black Power*, p. 44 (within a general section entitled "The Righteousness of God and Black Power," pp. 43–47), *A Black Theology of Liberation*, pp. 46–48, 114–19; *Spirituals and the Blues*, pp. 54–56; *God of the Oppressed*, pp. 164–77, 62–83 (this essay also appeared separately as "Biblical Revelation and Social Existence" in *Interpretation* 28, no. 4 [1974]: 422–40); *For My People*, pp. 63–68; *A Black Theology of Liberation*, pp. 31–33. Cone has also offered significant reflections on the Bible in his essay "Christian Theology and Scripture as the Expression of God's Liberating Activity for the Poor."

9. For Isa. 40:1–5, see Cone, *God of the Oppressed*, pp. 71–72, 109, 171, 173; for Isa. 53, see ibid., pp. 170–77. Cone also uses Isaiah to show God's righteousness, e.g., Isa. 42:1 (ibid., pp. 74–75, 172–73). Cone refers several times to Amos, stressing God's call to justice and righteousness. See, e.g., ibid., pp. 66–67, 154; and Cone, *Speaking the Truth*, pp. 41–42.

10. On Exod. 14:11–15, see Cone, *God of the Oppressed*, pp. 93, 161; Cone, *Spirituals and the Blues*, pp. 34, 92; and Cone, *Speaking the Truth*, p. 34. On Exod. 15:1–3, see *God of the Oppressed*, pp. 63, 164; Cone, *A Black Theology of Liberation*, p. 47; and *Spirituals and the Blues*, p. 92. On Exod. 19:4–6, see *God of the Oppressed*, pp. 64, 119, 233; Cone, *Black Theology and Black Power*, p. 44; *A Black Theology of Liberation*, p. 2; and *Speaking the Truth*, p. 41.

11. For the quotations, see the following works by Cone: *Black Theology and Black Power*, pp. 44, 64, 68, 104; *God of the Oppressed*, p. 63; *Martin and Malcolm and America*, p. 165. On his references to "the God of Exodus," see, e.g., *Spirituals and the Blues*, p. 90; *God of the Oppressed*, pp. 62, 64, 82, 100; and *Speaking the Truth*, p. 12. For other examples of the importance of the Exodus to Cone, see, e.g., *Black Theology and Black*

Power, pp. 44, 63–64; *A Black Theology of Liberation*, pp. 1–2, 29, 47–48, 53, 68, 104–5, 128; *Spirituals and the Blues*, pp. 60, 90; *God of the Oppressed*, pp. 60–66, 68, 73, 80, 82, 92, 100, 164; *My Soul Looks Back*, pp. 24, 104; *For My People*, pp. 62, 65; *Speaking the Truth*, pp. 5, 12, 91, 94, 100, 102; *Martin and Malcolm and America*, pp. 125–26, 164–65.

12. See Cone, *Black Theology and Black Power*, p. 45; Cone, *God of the Oppressed*, p. 69; and Cone, *Spirituals and the Blues*, p. 92.

13. Cone, *Spirituals and the Blues*, p. 56. Cone also links Habakkuk closely to Job. On Job and Habakkuk, see *God of the Oppressed*, pp. 166–70; *Black Theology and Black Power*, p. 97; *A Black Theology of Liberation*, p. 79; *Spirituals and the Blues*, pp. 54–56, 62, 64.

14. See the following works by Cone: *God of the Oppressed*, pp. 47, 75, 136, 173; *A Black Theology of Liberation*, p. 3; *Black Theology and Black Power*, p. 35; *For My People*, pp. 32, 80; *Speaking the Truth*, pp. vii, 123; *Martin and Malcolm and America*, p. 143. See also the related passage from Luke 7:22: "And he [Jesus] answered them, 'Go and tell John what you have seen and heard; the blind receive their sight, the lame walk, the lepers are cleansed, the deaf hear, the dead are raised, the poor have good news brought to them.' " (See *God of the Oppressed*, pp. 76, 173; *Black Theology and Black Power*, p. 36.)

15. Cone, *God of the Oppressed*, p. 75. Emphasis his.

16. Ibid., p. 76. Similarly, Cone links Luke 4:18–19 to the "primary definition of the church," which is "not its confessional affirmations but rather its political commitment on behalf of the poor" (*Speaking the Truth*, p. 123).

17. Cone, *Black Theology and Black Power*, p. 59.

18. Cone, *God of the Oppressed*, p. 136.

19. Ibid., p. 150.

20. Ibid., p. 151. On Mark 10:42–45, see also ibid., pp. 80, 173; and Cone, *Speaking the Truth*, p. 124.

21. Cone, *God of the Oppressed*, p. 224.

22. See, e.g., Cone, *Speaking the Truth*, p. 110 (also pp. 14, 120); Cone, *God of the Oppressed*, p. 225; and Cone, *My Soul Looks Back*, p. 105. In addition to 1 Cor. 1:26–28, Cone also cites Gal. 5:1 in several places: *God of the Oppressed*, pp. 176, 233; *A Black Theology of Liberation*, p. 128; and *Black Theology and Black Power*, p. 39.

23. Cone, *Speaking the Truth*, p. 24.

24. See, e.g., T. Hoyt, "Black Theology's Roots in Scripture," *Ecumenical Trends* 16 (1987): 172–76; R. A. Bennett, "Biblical Theology and Black Theology," *Journal of the Interdenominational Theological Center* 3 (1976): 1–16.

25. Cone, *God of the Oppressed*, p. 63.

26. Cone, *For My People*, p. 65.

27. Cone, *A Black Theology of Liberation*, p. 68.

28. Cone, *Black Theology and Black Power*, p. 43.

29. Ibid., p. 44.

30. Ibid., p. 45.

31. See, e.g., Cone, *A Black Theology of Liberation*, pp. 66–74.

32. Ibid., p. 70.

33. Cone, *For My People*, p. 65. Similarly, in *God of the Oppressed*, Cone states: "The biblical emphasis on God's continuing act of liberation in the present and future means that theology cannot merely repeat what the Bible says or what is found in a particular theological tradition. Theology must be prophetic, recognizing the *relativity* of human speech, but also that God can use human speech at a particular time for the

proclamation of his Word to the suffering poor. As theologians, therefore, we must take the risk to be prophetic by doing theology in the light of those who are helpless and voiceless in the society" (p. 82).

34. Cone, *Speaking the Truth*, p. 5.

35. Cone, *Spirituals and the Blues*, p. 37; see also Cone, *God of the Oppressed*, p. 18.

36. See, e.g., the following works by Cone: A *Black Theology of Liberation*, pp. xix, 22–33, 36, 38, 60, 114; *Spirituals and the Blues*, p. 37; *God of the Oppressed*, pp. 6, 8–9, 17–18, 30–32, 111; *My Soul Looks Back*, p. 59; *For My People*, pp. 28, 152, 165; *Speaking the Truth*, pp. 4, 7, 138; *Martin and Malcolm and America*, p. 250.

37. Cone, *God of the Oppressed*, pp. 35–36. See also Cone's essay, "Black Theology and Black Liberation," originally published in *Christian Century* in 1970 and reprinted in J. Cone and G. Wilmore, *Black Theology: A Documentary History*, Vol. 1, 1966–1979 (Maryknoll, N.Y.: Orbis Books, 1993), pp. 106–13, esp. 110–12. Responding to critics who have called into question Cone's emphasis on Scripture, Cone responds: "At this writing, I cannot change my emphasis on Jesus Christ and Scripture, because the emphasis seems to be a decisive ingredient of the black experience as I and others have lived it in North America" (*God of the Oppressed*, p. 253 n. 38).

38. As Cone puts it in a discussion of the identity of Jesus, in *God of the Oppressed*: "Who Jesus is for us today is not decided by focusing our attention exclusively on either the social context alone or the Bible alone but by seeing them in dialectical relation. The true interpretation of one is dependent upon viewing it in the light of the other. We must say unequivocally that who Jesus Christ is for black people today is found through an encounter with him in the social context of black existence. But as soon as that point is made, the other side of this paradox must be affirmed; otherwise the truth of the black experience is distorted. The Jesus of the black experience is the Jesus of Scripture. The dialectic relationship of the black experience and Scripture is the point of departure of Black Theology's Christology" (p. 113).

Or again: "To summarize: the dialectic between the social situation of the believer and Scripture and the traditions of the Church is the place to begin the investigation of the question, Who is Jesus Christ for us today? Social context, Scripture, and tradition operate together to enable the people of God to move actively and reflectively with Christ in the struggle of freedom" (p. 115).

39. Cone, A *Black Theology of Liberation*, p. 31.

40. Ibid., p. 31. Emphasis his.

41. Ibid., pp. 32–33.

42. Cone, *God of the Oppressed*, p. 112.

43. Cone, A *Black Theology of Liberation*, p. 31; see also p. 45; and Cone, *Spirituals and the Blues*, p. 37; Cone, *God of the Oppressed*, pp. 58, 110–12.

44. Cone, A *Black Theology of Liberation*, p. 83.

45. Ibid., p. 7.

46. Ibid., p. 32. Emphasis his. Similarly, Cone states that "it is most difficult to make first-century New Testament language relevant to a contemporary 'world come of age.' Jesus did not give us a blueprint for identifying God and his work or for relevant human involvement in the world. But this is the never-ending task of theology and the Church" (*Black Theology and Black Power*, p. 49).

47. Cone articulates six sources of black theology: black experience, black history, black culture, revelation, Scripture, and tradition. See A *Black Theology of Liberation*, pp. 23–35.

48. Ibid., p. 32. See also Cartwright, "Ideology and the Interpretation of the Bible in the African-American Christian Tradition," pp. 141–58.

49. See Cone, *Speaking the Truth*, p. 94. On Ps. 68:31, see A. Raboteau, " 'Ethiopia Shall Soon Stretch Forth Her Hands': Black Destiny in Nineteenth Century America," University Lecture in Religion, Arizona State University, 27 Jan. 1983. (In the 1930s this passage was even used as the headline of a newspaper sports story on Joe Louis's boxing victory over a much ballyhooed Italian fighter (see Raboteau). On this and other significant Old Testament texts, see, e.g., C. B. Copher, "The Black Presence in the Old Testament," and R. C. Bailey, "Beyond Identification: The Use of Africans in Old Testament Poetry and Narratives," both in *Stony the Road We Trod: African American Biblical Interpretation*, ed. C. Felder (Minneapolis: Fortress Press, 1991), pp. 146–64, 165–84.

50. Such an interpretation can be seen, e.g., in the comments of ex-slave John Bates: "My uncle, Ben, he could read de Bible, and he allus tell us some day us be free. And Massa Henry laugh, 'Haw, haw, haw.' And he say, 'Hell, no, yous never be free. Yous ain't got sense 'nuf to make de livin', if yous was free.' Den, he takes de Bible 'way from Uncle Ben and say it put de bad ideas in he head, but Uncle gits 'nother Bible and hides it, and Massa never finds out." Cited in D. N. Hopkins, "Slave Theology in the 'Invisible Institution,'" in D.N. Hopkins & G. Cummings, eds., *Cut Loose Your Stammering Tongue: Black Theology in the Slave Narratives*, ed. D. N. Hopkins and G. Cummings (Maryknoll, N.Y.: Orbis Books, 1991), p. 1; also see D. N. Hopkins, *Shoes That Fit Our Feet: Sources for a Constructive Black Theology* (Maryknoll, N.Y.: Orbis Books, 1993) p. 13.

51. Cone, *God of the Oppressed*, p. 31.

52. For treatments of Cone's hermeneutics, see A. Thiselton, *New Horizons in Hermeneutics: The Theory and Practice of Transforming Biblical Reading* (Grand Rapids: Zondervan, 1992), pp. 419–23; and J. L. Segundo, "The Hermeneutic Circle," in his *Liberation of Theology* (Maryknoll, N.Y.: Orbis Books, 1976), pp. 25–38. For an overall analysis of Cone, see R. Burrow, Jr., *James H. Cone and Black Liberation Theology* (Jefferson, N.C.: McFarland, 1994).

53. Cone, *A Black Theology of Liberation*, p. 35.

54. Ibid., p. 38. Emphasis his.

55. Ibid., p. 113.

56. Cone, *God of the Oppressed*, p. 258 n. 4, where he also states, "I contend that the Jesus of the Gospels cannot be separated from the 'real' Jesus."

57. Cone, *A Black Theology of Liberation*, p. 115.

58. Ibid., p. 118.

59. Cone, *God of the Oppressed*, p. 115. He continues: "If we do not take the historical Jesus seriously as the key to locating the meaning of Christ's presence today, there is no way to avoid the charge of subjectivism, the identification of Christ today with a momentary political persuasion. Although it cannot 'prove,' by historical study alone, that Jesus is the Christ, the historical record provides the essential datum without which faith in Christ is impossible" (p. 116).

60. Ibid., p. 120. And again: "The truth of Jesus Christ stands or falls on the historical validity of the biblical claim that Jesus identifies with the poor and the outcasts. That historical fact alone does not provide the evidence that Jesus is the Christ, for the same could be said of other people in history; but without this historical fact, the claim that God has come to liberate the weak in Jesus is sheer illusion" (p. 261 n. 5).

61. Cone, *A Black Theology of Liberation*, p. 120. Emphasis his.

62. Cone, *Black Theology and Black Power*, p. 68. He continues: "To suggest that

Christ has taken on a black skin is not theological emotionalism. If the Church is a continuation of the Incarnation, and if the Church and Christ are where the oppressed are, then Christ and his Church must identify totally with the oppressed to the extent that they too suffer for the same reasons persons are enslaved. . . . Therefore Christ is black because he is oppressed, and oppressed because he is black. And if the Church is to join Christ by following his opening, it too must go where suffering is and become black also" (p. 69).

63. Cone, A *Black Theology of Liberation*, p. 123. See also A. Cleage, *The Black Messiah* (New York: Sheed & Ward, 1968). For an important analysis of Cone, Cleage, and Joseph Washington, see William R. Jones, "Theodicy and Methodology in Black Theology: A Critique of Washington, Cone, and Cleage," *Harvard Theological Review* 64 (1971): 541–57 (also reprinted in Cone and Wilmore, *Black Theology*, 1:141–52).

64. Cone, *God of the Oppressed*, p. 135.

65. Ibid., p. 136.

66. Cone, A *Black Theology of Liberation*, p. 6. In the same volume Cone states: "White theologians would prefer to do theology without reference to color, but this only reveals how deeply racism is embedded in the thought forms of their culture. To be sure, they would *probably* concede that the concept of liberation is essential to the biblical view of God. But it is still impossible for them to translate the biblical emphasis on liberation to the black-white struggle today" (p. 64).

67. Cone, *Black Theology and Black Power*, p. 151. See also pp. 147–48. In his book *For My People*, Cone reflects as follows on the claim that Jesus is black: "In place of the white Jesus, we insisted that 'Jesus Christ is black, baby!' . . . Whites thought that blacks had lost their religious sanity. It was one thing to identify liberation as the central message of the Bible, but something else to introduce color into christology.

" . . . The vehement rejection of the black Jesus by whites merely reinforced the determination of black clergy radicals to develop a christology that took seriously Jesus' blackness—both literally and symbolically. The literal significance of Jesus' blackness meant that he *was not* white! He was a Palestinian Jew. . . . By making this point, black clergy radicals wanted to show that the so-called scientific biblical exegesis of white scholars frequently was not scientific at all.

" . . . The major importance of the claim that 'Jesus is black' rested on the symbolic meaning of that affirmation. . . . The blackness of Jesus had definite political implications that we derived from the New Testament witness. It was our way of saying that his cross and resurrection represented God's solidarity with the oppressed in their struggle for liberation" (pp. 66–67).

68. Cone, *Martin and Malcolm and America*, pp. 166–68.

69. Cone, *Black Theology and Black Power*, p. 2.

70. Reflecting on the development of African American theology in the 1970s and early 1980s Cone laments that "today we black theologians seem to have forgotten our own theological history. Black theology is in danger of becoming respectable in a corrupt church and in seminaries that favor the privileged. . . . We have not remained on the cutting edge of history but have turned the revolution we started into a church social and cocktail party among black and white academic elites" (*For My People*, pp. 198–99). And in *My Soul Looks Back*, he writes: "Black theology's chief task is not to be an *academic* discipline, as white theology has largely become. Black theology must be a *church* discipline, true to itself only when validated in the context of people struggling for the freedom of the oppressed" (p. 77).

71. Cone, A *Black Theology of Liberation*, p. 116.

72. Cone, *For My People*, p. 67.

73. Cone, *Black Theology and Black Power*, p. 88.

74. "It is so easy to make his [Jesus'] name mean intellectual analysis, and we already have too much of that garbage in seminary libraries. What is needed is an application of the name to concrete human affairs" (Cone, *A Black Theology of Liberation*, p. 38).

75. Ibid., p. 117. Elsewhere, Cone comments: "Because most biblical scholars are the descendants of the advantaged class, it is to be expected that they would minimize Jesus' gospel of liberation for the poor by interpreting poverty as a spiritual condition unrelated to social and political phenomena" (*God of the Oppressed*, p. 78).

76. Cone continues: "to hear the message of Scripture is to hear and see the truth of God's liberating presence in history for those who are oppressed by unjust social structures" (*God of the Oppressed*, p. 200).

77. Ibid., p. 201.

78. Ibid., p. 203.

79. P. Williams, "James Cone and the Problem of a Black Ethic," *Harvard Theological Review* 65 (1972): 483–94.

80. Cone, *God of the Oppressed*, p. 205. See also Cone's critique of Major Jones's *Christian Ethics for Black Theology* (Nashville: Abingdon Press, 1974) in *God of the Oppressed*, pp. 270–71 n. 14.

81. Cone, *God of the Oppressed*, p. 207.

82. Ibid..

83. Ibid., p. 208.

84. Ibid.

85. Ibid., pp. 206–17.

86. Ibid., p. 224. Similarly, "the question is not what Jesus *did*, as if his behavior in first-century Palestine were the infallible ethical guide for our actions today. We must ask not what he did, but what is he *doing*—and what he did becomes important only insofar as it points to his activity today. To use the Jesus of history as an absolute ethical guide for people today is to become enslaved to the past, foreclosing God's eschatological future and its judgment on the present. It removes the element of risk in ethical decisions and makes people slaves to principles" (p. 222).

87. Cone, *A Black Theology of Liberation*, p. 6.

88. See N. Gottwald, *The Hebrew Bible: A Socio-literary Introduction* (Philadelphia: Fortress Press, 1985), pp. 261–76.

89. Robert Allen Warrior, "Canaanites, Cowboys, and Indians: Deliverance, Conquest, and Liberation Theology Today," *Christianity and Crisis* 49 (1989–90): 261–65.

90. James Cone, letter to author, 13 Dec. 1993. Cone continues: "I have also been influenced by Delores Williams, my colleague at Union, who also points out the limitations of the Exodus as the only key for understanding the black religious experience, especially black women. See esp. her *Sisters in the Wilderness: The Challenge of Womanist Godtalk* (Orbis, 1993)."

91. In private correspondence (letter to author, 13 Dec. 1993), Cone has responded as follows: "I do not reject John, especially those parts that show Jesus' identity with the poor. But I do prefer the other three gospels for many of the reasons you suggested. Any passage of scripture that is not life-giving is rejected. Blacks have always been very selective in their use of scripture. See Howard Thurman's well-known reference to his grandmother's rejection of Paul as one of many such instances. (H. Thurman, "Jesus—An Interpretation" in *Jesus and the Disinherited*, p. 30f)."

92. James Cone, letter to author, 13 Dec. 1993.

93. Cone's response to this question is fairly straightforward: "I think your role is to take sides with the voiceless people of the world. It is time for *all* scholars in religion to expose the conservative nature of their disciplines and the roles they play in reinforcing the status quo that oppresses the poor. Scientific research that does not empower the poor people is pointless and often oppressive. When you begin to take sides for the poor and against those who ignore them in biblical scholarship, you will begin to express a solidarity that empowers poor blacks and others" (letter to author 13 Dec. 1993).

Chapter Nine

1. Already in her first book, *The Church Against Itself* (New York: Herder & Herder, 1967), Ruether poses the question: "does one ever meaningfully investigate any historical problem unless one has in it something at stake?" (p. 33). For her most complete statement regarding the relationship between her own experience and the development of her theology, see *Disputed Questions: On Being a Christian* (Maryknoll, N.Y.: Orbis Books, 1989). For a general overview of Ruether's theology, see W. M. Ramsay, *Four Modern Prophets* (Atlanta: John Knox Press, 1986), pp. 71–87. For a thorough treatment of her christology in particular, see M. H. Snyder, *The Christology of Rosemary Radford Ruether: A Critical Introduction* (Mystic, Conn.: Twenty-Third Publications, 1988).

2. T. Clarke-Sayer, "The Bible and the Religious Left: An Interview with Rosemary Radford Ruether," *Witness* 66, no. 3 (1983): 8. Elsewhere, Ruether has commented that "when I read the Bible for the first time I did so with the apparatus of historical-critical thought. After certain initial shocks to my inherited model of Christ, this came to seem the natural way to decipher the Bible. I had relatively little baggage of a precritical biblical schooling to discard" (*Disputed Questions,* p. 30).

3. I have relied principally on fourteen books and three articles by Ruether as the basis for my research on her use of the Bible. They are as follows:

The Church Against Itself (New York: Herder & Herder, 1967)

Communion Is Life Together (New York: Herder & Herder, 1968)

Disputed Questions: On Being a Christian (Maryknoll: Orbis Books, 1989; repr. Nashville: Abingdon, 1982)

"Feminist Hermeneutics, Scriptural Authority, and Religious Experience: The Case of the *Imago Dei* and Gender Equality," in *Radical Pluralism and Truth,* ed. W. G. Jeanrond and J. L. Rike (New York: Crossroad, 1991), pp. 95–106

"Feminist Interpretation: A Method of Correlation," in *Feminist Interpretaion of the Bible,* ed. L. Russel (Philadelphia: Westminster, 1985), pp. 111–24

From Machismo to Mutuality, with Eugene Bianchi (New York: Paulist Press, 1976)

"Feminism and Patriarchal Religion: Principles of Ideological Critique of the Bible," in *Journal for the Study of the Old Testament* 22 (1982): 54–66

Gaia and God (San Francisco: HarperCollins, 1992)

The Liberating Bond, with Wolfgang Roth (New York: Friendship Press, 1978)

Liberation Theology (New York: Paulist Press, 1972)

Mary—The Feminine Face of the Church (Philadelphia: Westminster, 1977)

New Woman/New Earth (New York: Seabury Press, 1975)

The Radical Kingdom (New York: Harper & Row, 1970)

Sexism and God-Talk (Boston: Beacon Press, 1983)
To Change the World (New York: Crossroad, 1981)
Women-Church (San Francisco: Harper & Row, 1985)
WomanGuides (Boston: Beacon Press, 1983)

4. One striking feature of Ruether's *Communion Is Life Together* is the inclusion of various songs for the children to sing at the end of each lesson (e.g., "He's Got the Whole World in His Hands," "This Land Is Your Land," "Go Down Moses," "O Freedom," "Where Have All the Flowers Gone?" "If I Had a Hammer," "Were You There?" "We Gonna Sit at the Welcome Table," and "Come by Here" ("Kum bah yah"). It is no accident that Ruether includes various spirituals and folk songs associated with the Civil Rights movement, given her own involvement in the movement and her experience of teaching at Howard Divinity School. (When the book was published, it came with a record of the various songs, so that the students could hear the music and sing along.)

5. Ruether, *Disputed Questions*, p. 31.

6. The notion of dialectic is crucial to Ruether's understanding of Christian existence and to her theology. She begins *Church Against Itself* by stating: "The theological tradition in which these essays stand is that of modern dialectical theology or crisis theology" (p. 1). Similarly, she characterizes her ecclesiology as dialectical (p. 13). Ruether also characterizes the relationship of church to society as "dialectical" (*Liberation Theology*, pp. 154–55) and speaks of "the prophetic dialectic of judgment and promise" (*Disputed Questions*, p. 32). She states: "I would regard my own mode of thinking as dialectical" (*Disputed Questions*, p. 141). Ruether also emphasizes the dialectic of the church as historical institution and the church as spirit-filled community, especially in developing how women should relate to the historic church. See *Women-Church*, pp. 31–32, 37.

Ruether is also critical of some expressions of dialectical theology. E.g., she sees James Cone's "formal dialectic between white and black" as failing to "satisfy the Biblical concept of Election and Exodus. . . . Cone's oppressor/oppressed dialectic offers no comparable concept of fidelity of the elect people to an intrinsic standard of righteousness, which would judge themselves, and not merely judge others" (*Liberation Theology*, p. 138).

7. R. R. Ruether, "Feminism and Patriarchal Religion: Principles of Ideological Critique of the Bible," pp. 55–56. See also her article, "Religion and Society: Sacred Canopy vs. Prophetic Critique," in *The Future of Liberation Theology: Essays in Honor of Gustavo Gutiérrez*, ed. M. Ellis and O. Maduro (Maryknoll, N.Y.: Orbis Books, 1989), pp. 172–76.

8. Ruether, "Religion and Society," p. 59.

9. See, e.g., Phyllis Bird, "Images of Women in the Old Testament," in *Religion and Sexism: Images of Woman in the Jewish and Christian Traditions*, ed. R. Ruether (New York: Simon & Schuster, 1974), pp. 41–88.

10. See, e.g., R. R. Ruether and E. C. Bianchi, *From Machismo to Mutuality: Essays on Sexism and Woman-Man Liberation* (New York: Paulist Press, 1976): "However much women may now chuckle over the fact that Adam appears something of a passive personality, in the fall the mythology that made man first in creation but woman first in sin was not intended to praise woman's wit" (p. 13). See also Ruether, *Women-Church*, p. 137.

11. Ruether, "Feminism and Patriarchal Religion," p. 57.

12. Ibid., pp. 58–59.

13. Ibid., p. 59.

14. See, e.g., Ruether, *Disputed Questions*, p. 93; Ruether, *Sexism and God-Talk*, p. 157.

15. Ruether, "Feminism and Patriarchal Religion," p. 60; Ruether, *Sexism and God-Talk*, p. 24.

16. Ruether, "Feminism and Patriarchal Religion," p. 60; Ruether, *Sexism and God-Talk*, p. 25.

17. See, e.g., Ruether, "Feminism and Patriarchal Religion," p. 61; Ruether, *Sexism and God-Talk*, p. 25; Ruether, *WomanGuides*, p. 196; Ruether, *Gaia and God*, p. 300, n. 12; Ruether, *Disputed Questions*, p. 93; Ruether, *To Change the World*, p. 20; Ruether, "Feminist Interpretation: A Method of Correlation," p. 121.

18. See, e.g., Ruether, "Feminism and Patriarchal Religion," p. 61; Ruether, *Mary—The Feminine Face of the Church*, pp. 33, 87; Ruether, *Sexism and God-Talk*, pp. 25, 153.

19. See, e.g., Ruether, "Feminism and Patriarchal Religion," p. 61; Ruether, *Sexism and God-Talk*, p. 26; and Ruether, *New Woman/New Earth*, pp. 45, 58.

20. See, e.g., Ruether, "Feminism and Patriarchal Religion," p. 62; Ruether, *Sexism and God-Talk*, p. 26; Ruether, *Disputed Questions*, pp. 34, 62; Ruether, *To Change the World*, p. 35; Ruether, "Feminist Interpretation," p. 118; Ruether, *Gaia and God*, p. 120.

21. Ruether, "Feminism and Patriarchal Religion," p. 62; Ruether, *Sexism and God-Talk*, pp. 26–27.

22. See, e.g., Ruether, "Feminism and Patriarchal Religion, p. 63; Ruether, *Sexism and God-Talk*, p. 27; Ruether, *New Woman/New Earth*, p. 66, Ruether, *To Change the World*, p. 35; and Ruether, *Disputed Questions*, p. 62.

23. See, e.g., Ruether, "Feminism and Patriarchal Religion," pp. 63–64; Ruether, *Sexism and God-Talk*, p. 29; Ruether, *Mary*, p. 83; Ruether, *To Change the World*, p. 54; and Ruether, *New Woman/New Earth*, p. 65.

24. Ruether, "Feminism and Patriarchal Religion," p. 65.

25. Ruether, *Sexism and God-Talk*, p. 32.

26. Ruether, *Liberation Theology*, p. 33.

27. On Christianity and the status quo, see Ruether, *To Change the World*, p. 26.

28. Ruether, *Communion Is Life Together*, p. 14.

29. Ibid., p. 28.

30. Ruether and Roth, *Liberating Bond*. Roth, a professor of Old Testament interpretation at Garrett Evangelical Theological Seminary, where Ruether also teaches, wrote the first six chapters under the heading "Covenant—The Biblical Story." Ruether wrote the second six chapters under the heading "Covenant—The Impact of a Motif."

31. Ruether and Roth, *Liberating Bond*, p. 49.

32. Ibid., p. 91. This emphasis on covenant communities explains Ruether's interest in various radical Christian communities throughout church history, most of which had a strong sense of communal covenant (e.g., the Ecological New Covenanters, the Shakers, the Anabaptist tradition). On the Ecological New Covenanters, who emphasize the covenant not only between humanity and God but also between humanity and nature, see ibid., p. 50.

33. Ruether, *Women-Church*, pp. 122–25.

34. Ibid., p. 122.

35. Ruether commends the Shakertown Pledge as a good starting point for discussing specific commitments (ibid., p. 123).

36. Ibid., p. 124.

37. Ibid., pp. 192–200.

38. Ruether, *Gaia and God*, pp. 205–28. See also Ruether's article "The Biblical

Vision of the Ecological Crisis," *Christian Century* 95 (1978): 1129–32, where she articulates "a covenantal vision" in keeping with the prophetic vision of the Hebrew Bible (p. 1131). In this connection, she cites Isa. 24 at length as an expression of the broken covenant between humanity and the natural world. She concludes: "In the biblical view, the raping of nature and the exploitation of people in society are profoundly understood as part of one reality, creating disaster in both. We look not to the past but to a new future, brought about by social repentance and conversion to divine commandments, so that the covenant of creation can be rectified and God's Shalom brought to nature and society" (p. 1132).

39. Ruether, *Gaia and God*, p. 9.

40. Ibid., p. 210.

41. Ibid., p. 211.

42. Ibid., p. 227.

43. Ruether, *WomanGuides*, pp. 161–62. The sermon ("WomanChurch as a Feminist Exodus Community") was originally given at the WomanChurch Speaks conference in Chicago in November 1983.

44. Ruether, *Sexism and God-Talk*, p. 205. See also her article "'Basic Communities': Renewal at the Roots," *Christianity and Crisis* 41 (1981): 234–37. Ruether particularly notes the rediscovery of Scripture in the basic Christian communities, looking at such communities in Latin America, Italy, and Holland.

45. Ruether, *Women-Church*, p. 62.

46. Ruether, *To Change the World*, p. 69. Ruether makes much the same point in *Sexism and God-Talk*, pp. 254–56.

47. Ruether, *To Change the World*, p. 68. Ruether notes (p. 80 n. 32) that J. H. Yoder has also argued for the Jubilee messianic vision as more representative of Jesus' teaching than the apocalyptic vision. See Yoder, "The Implications of the Jubilee," in his *The Politics of Jesus* (Grand Rapids: Eerdmans, 1972), pp. 64–77.

48. Ruether, *WomanGuides*, pp. 195–97, 202–5, 264.

49. As Ruether states: "Jesus' own vision of the Kingdom of God as release of captives, remissions of debts, and provision of daily bread may have had more to do with the Jubilee pattern than with the apocalyptic doctrine of the end point of history later incorporated into the Gospels" (*Sexism and God-Talk*, p. 256). See also Ruether, *Gaia and God*, p. 214.

50. See Ruether, *Gaia and God*, pp. 20, 276 nn. 9–10.

51. Ibid., p. 213.

52. Regarding the early Christian portrayals of Jesus as the Davidic Messiah, Ruether writes: "Although these visions of the Davidic Messiah, as well as the Apocalyptic Messiah, came to be attached to the figure of Jesus, the first-century prophet from Nazareth, it would seem that his own vision was far from these ways of thinking" (*WomanGuides*, p. 108). See also Ruether, *Sexism and God-Talk*, pp. 119–20.

53. See, e.g., Ruether, "Mistress of Heaven: The Meaning of Mariology," in *New Woman/New Earth*, pp. 36–62; Ruether, "Mariology as Symbolic Ecclesiology: Repression or Liberation?" in *Sexism and God-Talk*, pp. 139–58; and, of course, her book *Mary*.

54. See Ruether, *New Woman/New Earth*, p. 46.

55. This kind of doctrine can be seen, e.g., in Pope John Paul II's encyclical "Mulieris Dignitatem" (On the Vocation and Dignity of Women), *Origins* 18, no. 17 (1988): 262–83.

56. *New Woman/New Earth*, p. 55.

57. Ibid., p. 58.

58. Ruether, *Sexism and God-Talk*, p. 154. As Ruether puts it elsewhere, "The Magnificat at least opens up the possibility of a Christian interpretation of redemptive community as a community of liberation for all, starting with women of the poorest and most despised classes" (*WomanGuides*, p. 159).

59. Ruether, *WomanGuides*, pp. 165–66, 185.

60. Ruether, *To Change the World*, p. 1. See, e.g., Ruether's review of E. Schillebeeckx's *Christ: The Experience of Jesus as Lord* (New York: Crossroad, 1980) in *Religious Studies Review* 9 (1983): 42–44.

61. Ruether, *Church Against Itself*, p. 40. Of course, in the 1990s there is yet another new quest pressing on in search of the historical Jesus. See, e.g., M. Borg, *Jesus in Contemporary Scholarship* (Valley Forge, Pa: Trinity Press International, 1994).

62. As Ruether puts it, "It is crucial that the Jesus who points beyond himself to the coming one should not be overlooked and obliterated in our moving on to proclaim him as the Christ, for his statement of his own self-understanding is both necessarily different from and a necessary precondition of our understanding of him and thus our new self-understanding in him" (*Church Against Itself*, pp. 46–47).

63. The notion of "iconoclasm" is very important for Ruether and runs throughout her writings. E.g., the "biblical God is a God who, by nature, speaks through the iconoclastic prophet," and Christianity's problem "lies in its forfeiting of its iconoclastic responsibility" (*Church Against Itself*, p. 202). The synoptic Gospels show "a startling element of iconoclasm toward the traditional subordination of women in Jewish life" (*New Woman/New Earth*, p. 63). As for Jesus, his "vision of the kingdom is one of radical social iconoclasm" (*To Change the World*, p. 17), and he is "the prophetic iconoclastic Christ" rather than an imperial or androgynous Christ (*To Change the World*, pp. 47, 53). Further, "Jesus proclaims an iconoclastic reversal of the system of religious status," and the role played by women in earliest Christianity "is an intrinsic part of the iconoclastic, messianic vision" (*Sexism and God-Talk*, pp. 135–36). And, finally, the image of the church as spirit-filled community leads to an egalitarianism that "can, at times, be set in an iconoclastic relation to the hierarchies of established religious and civil institutions" (*Women-Church*, p. 22).

64. Ruether, "Feminism and Patriarchal Religion," pp. 62–63.

65. Ruether, *To Change the World*, p. 17.

66. For Ruether's use of Matt. 20:25–28 elsewhere, see, e.g., *Mary*, p. 83; *To Change the World*, p. 54; *Sexism and God-Talk*, p. 29; *New Woman/New Earth*, p. 65; and "Feminism and Patriarchal Religion," pp. 63–64.

67. Ruether, *Sexism and God-Talk*, p. 5. Elsewhere, Ruether states: "Instead of the concept of God as Father providing a pattern for setting up a group of 'fathers' in the church who lord it over the laity, the way husbands lorded over wives in Jesus' society, the God whom Jesus is speaking about is One who creates a community of equals, a community of brothers and sisters" (*Mary*, p. 84).

68. Ruether, *New Woman/New Earth*, p. 66.

69. Ruether, *To Change the World*, p. 14. In the same place, she continues: "There is little trace in the more clearly historical sayings of Jesus of a predominant concern with eschatological features of resurrection, life after death and a transcendent world beyond history."

70. Ibid. On the centrality of the Lord's Prayer in Ruether's theology, see also her *Communion Is Life Together*, p. 35; and *Gaia and God*, p. 214.

71. Ruether, *To Change the World*, p. 15.

72. Ibid.

73. Ibid.

74. Ibid., p. 23.

75. Ruether, *Disputed Questions*, p. 72. See also Ruether, *To Change the World*, pp. 42–43.

76. Ruether notes that this "proleptic understanding of Jesus' messianic identity . . . has been particularly renewed in liberation theologies. It is the exegesis that best translated the New Testament experience" (*To Change the World*, pp. 42–43).

77. Ruether, *Sexism and God-Talk*, p. 114.

78. Ibid.

79. Ibid., p. 122.

80. Ibid., p. 135.

81. Ruether, *Gaia and God*, p. 253.

82. Ruether, *New Woman/New Earth*, p. 67.

83. Ruether, *Sexism and God-Talk*, p. 3.

84. Ibid., p. 137.

85. Ruether comments that "what we see here is an ongoing process of *kenosis* and transformation. God's power no longer remains in Heaven where it can be used as a model of the 'thrones of the mighty.' In the iconoclastic and messianic prophet, it has been emptied out into the human situation of suffering and hope" (ibid., p. 157). See also *WomanGuides*, pp. 108–9, 120, where Ruether contrasts "Kenosis Christology: Christ as Servant" with "Logos Christology: Christ as Cosmic Lord."

86. For Ruether's use of Gal. 3:28, see, e.g., *Mary*, p. 86; *New Woman/New Earth*, pp. 67–68; *Sexism and God-Talk*, pp. 26, 33, 127, 199; *Women-Church*, p. 46; *Disputed Questions*, p. 123; *To Change the World*, p. 47; Ruether and Bianchi, *From Machismo to Mutuality*, p. 135; Ruether and Roth, *Liberating Bond*, p. 85.

87. Ruether, *Gaia and God*, p. 127.

88. R. R. Ruether, "The Subordination and Liberation of Women in Christian Theology: St. Paul and Sarah Grimké," *Soundings* 61 (1978): 168.

89. Ibid., p. 170.

90. Ibid., p. 171.

91. Ibid., p. 173.

92. See Sarah Grimké's "Epistle to the Clergy of the Southern States" (1836), in *The Public Years of Sarah and Angelina Grimké*, ed. L. Ceplair (New York: Columbia University Press, 1989), pp. 90–115.

93. See Sarah Grimké's "Letters on the Equality of the Sexes and the Condition of Women" (1838), in S. Grimké, *Letters on the Equality of the Sexes*, ed. E. A. Bartlett (New Haven: Yale University Press, 1988), pp. 31–103.

94. See further Ruether's comments on Mary the mother of Jesus and on Mary Magdalene in her article "What Do the Synoptics Say? The Sexuality of Jesus," *Christianity and Crisis* 38 (1978): 134–37.

95. Ruether, *The Church Against Itself*, p. 226.

96. "What have been called the objective sources of theology, Scripture and tradition, are themselves codified collective human experience" (Ruether, *Sexism and God-Talk*, p. 12).

97. Ibid.

98. Ruether, *Church Against Itself*, p. 226.

99. Ruether, *Sexism and God-Talk*, pp. 12–13. Similarly, see Ruether's article "Feminist Interpretation," pp. 111–16.

100. Ruether, *Sexism and God-Talk*, p. 13.

101. Ruether, "Feminist Hermeneutics, Scriptural Authority, and Religious Experience," p. 101.

102. "Although the New Testament preserves remnants of this earlier [egalitarian] role of women, the authority of these stories as the basis for gender equality has been erased or marginalized. Instead, the canon is shaped to direct us to read the understanding of the church from texts such as Ephesians 5 and I Timothy. Here the patriarchal hierarchy of men over women is set forth as the model for interpreting the relationship of Christ and the church" (Ruether, *Women-Church*, p. 48).

103. Ruether, *Sexism and God-Talk*, p. 34.

104. *Religion and Sexism*, p. 121. Elsewhere, Ruether states: "There are two ways of making the Bible into a tool of the status quo. One is the fundamentalist way of picking out a certain series of things in the Bible, excluding all the prophetic material, and then using it in a very literalistic way to support patriarchy or creationism or whatever. The other way is the historical-critical method, which is the academic establishment's way of making the Bible something that ordinary people are not equipped to read accurately" ("The Bible and the Religious Left," p. 8).

105. Ruether, *WomanGuides*, p. 247. In the same place, she comments: "Every new upsurge of the liberating spirit must challenge the efforts of fossilized religious authority to 'close the canon,' to declare that God has spoken once and for all in a past time and 'his' words are enshrined in a final and definite form in a past collection of texts, and therefore, that all true theology is confined to circumscribed commentaries on these past texts. It is ironic that Christianity particularly has attempted to cut off all further revelatory experience and declare that God's final word is spoken in Jesus, even to the exclusion of any word from God spoken before Jesus. Jesus alone becomes the one word from God. This is ironic because it was key to Jesus' own message that revelation was not closed and that he spoke 'with authority,' as a prophet, and not 'as the scribes and the Pharisees,' those who were confined merely to commentary on past texts" (p. 247).

106. See also Ruether, *Women-Church*, p. 135.

107. This rite is from ibid., p. 137.

108. On feminist hermeneutics in general, see, e.g., P. Trible, "Feminist Hermeneutics and Biblical Studies," *Christian Century* 99 (1982): 116–18; E. Schüssler Fiorenza, "A Feminist Critical Hermeneutics of Liberation," in *In Memory of Her* (New York: Crossroad, 1983), pp. 26–36; M. A. Tolbert, ed., *The Bible and Feminist Hermeneutics*, Semeia 28 (Chico, Calif.: Scholars Press, 1983) (esp. Tolbert's article "Defining the Problem: The Bible and Feminist Hermeneutics," pp. 113–26); C. Osiek, "The Feminist and the Bible: Hermeneutical Alternatives," in *Feminist Perspectives on Biblical Scholarship*, ed. A. Yarbro Collins (Chico, Calif.: Scholars Press, 1985), pp. 93–106; A. Thiselton, *New Horizons in Hermeneutics: The Theory and Practice of Transforming Biblical Reading* (Grand Rapids: Zondervan, 1992), pp. 430–62; E. Schüssler Fiorenza, "The Hermeneutical Space of a Feminist Rhetoric of Liberation," part 2 of *But She Said: Feminist Practices of Biblical Interpretation* (Boston: Beacon Press, 1992), pp. 77–163.

109. See Ruether, *Sexism and God-Talk*, p. 135.

110. Ibid., p. 24.

111. Ibid., p. 24 (emphasis mine).

112. "The renewal of the prophetic meaning of religious language from its ideological deformations is the creative dynamic of Biblical faith. This rediscovery of prophetic content, and its discerning reapplication to new social situations, is precisely what the Bible calls 'The Word of God.' This, in other words, is the critical principle that Biblical faith applies to itself. It is the hermeneutical principle for discerning prophetic faith

within Scripture as well as for the ongoing interpretation of Scripture as critique of tradition" (ibid., p. 31).

113. Ibid. Elsewhere, Ruether states: "The Bible can be appropriated as a source of liberating paradigms only if it can be seen that there is a correlation between the feminist critical principle and that critical principle by which biblical thought critiques itself and renews its vision as the authentic Word of God over against corrupting and sinful deformations. It is my contention here that there is such a correlation between biblical and feminist critical principles. This biblical critical principle is that of the prophetic-messianic tradition" ("Feminist Interpretation," p. 117).

114. "Feminist theology is not asserting unprecedented ideas; rather it is rediscovering the prophetic context and content of Biblical faith itself when it defines the prophetic-liberating tradition as norm" (Ruether, *Sexism and God-Talk*, p. 31).

115. Ruether, *To Change the World*, p. 5.

116. Ruether, "Feminist Interpretation," p. 122.

117. "Clarified hermeneutics lies in being conscious of the questions one brings from one's own situation and the response that one reads from the scripture, either negatively or positively, about these concerns" (Ruether, *To Change the World*, p. 3).

118. Ibid., p. 4.

119. Ibid., p. 5. Similarly, "There is a hermeneutic circle with our own past experiences and thoughts, just as with the historical past. What our past means at any given time is always conditioned by the present questions that we bring to it" (Ruether, *Disputed Questions*, p. 12).

120. "The circle from experience to experience, mediated through instruments of tradition, is thus completed when the contemporary community appropriates the foundational paradigm as the continuing story of its own redemption in relation to God, self, and one another" (Ruether, *Sexism and God-Talk*, p. 16).

121. E. Achtemeier, "The Impossible Possibility: Evaluating the Feminist Approach to Bible and Theology," *Interpretation* 52, no. 1 (1988): 54.

122. For an even more reactionary approach to Ruether, and other feminists, see the rather frightful book by Donna Steichen, *Ungodly Rage: The Hidden Face of Catholic Feminism* (San Francisco: Ignatius Press, 1991).

123. Schüssler Fiorenza, *In Memory of Her*, p. 19.

124. In *Sexism and God-Talk*, Ruether writes: "But even when biblical texts are most clearly in this prophetic mode, not all dimensions of unjust relations may be discerned. The prophet may see clearly the injustice of master-slave relations, of male-female relations in patriarchal, slave-holding society, or else ameliorate these relations in more conventional ways that still take the basic system for granted.

"The vision of the world rectified may also degenerate into a vision of world reversal, or 'revenge theology,' that merely makes of the presently poor and weak new imperial powers triumphing over their former enemies. In significant parts of the Scriptures, both Old and New Testament, the prophetic vision evaporates, allowing God again to become simply the sanctifier of the existing social order, as in much of the law codes and the New Testament household codes. Even at its best, prophetic insight has some limitations of the sociology of consciousness of its spokesmen (generic not intended)" (pp. 33–34).

125. "Review Symposium," *Horizons* 1, no. 2 (1984): 148.

126. Ibid., p. 149.

127. C. Christ, "A Spirituality for Women," in *Laughter of Aphrodite: Reflections on a Journey to the Goddess* (San Francisco: Harper & Row, 1987): 63. This entire chapter

from Christ's book is a response to an article by Ruether, "A Religion for Women: Sources and Strategies," *Christianity and Crisis* 39 (1979): 307–11.

128. Ruether, "Religion for Women," p. 309.

129. Christ, *Laughter of Aphrodite*, p. 62.

130. Ruether, *Sexism and God-Talk*, p. 27.

131. R. Chopp, "Seeing and Naming the World Anew: The Works of Rosemary Radford Ruether," *Religious Studies Review* 15, no. 1 (1989): 11.

132. Ruether, *Sexism and God-Talk*, p. 24.

Chapter Ten

1. On the Sermon on the Mount in general, see L. Cahill, "The Ethical Implications of the Sermon on the Mount," *Interpretation* 41 (1987): 144–56; W. Carter, *What Are They Saying About Matthew's Sermon on the Mount?* (New York: Paulist Press, 1994); and esp. H. D. Betz's exhaustive *The Sermon on the Mount* (Minneapolis: Fortress Press, 1995).

2. See chapter 2, n. 19 above.

3. B. Häring, "The Normative Value of the Sermon on the Mount," *Catholic Biblical Quarterly* 29 (1967): 72.

4. S. Hauerwas, *The Peaceable Kingdom: A Primer in Christian Ethics* (Notre Dame: University of Notre Dame Press, 1983), p. 85.

5. Ibid., p. 83.

6. G. Gutiérrez, *A Theology of Liberation*, 2d ed. (Maryknoll, N.Y.: Orbis Books, 1988), p. 169.

7. G. Gutiérrez, "The Irruption of the Poor in Latin America and the Christian Communities of the Common People," in *The Challenge of Basic Christian Communities*, ed. S. Torres and J. Eagleson (Maryknoll, N.Y.: Orbis Books, 1981), p. 121.

8. J. Cone, *Black Theology and Black Power* (New York: Seabury Press, 1969), p. 2.

9. I have found only one reference to the Sermon on the Mount in all of the writings of Ruether that I have examined: a reference to Matt. 6:9–13 (the Lord's Prayer) in *Gaia and God* (San Francisco: HarperCollins, 1992), p. 214 (in the chapter "Healing the World: The Covenantal Tradition").

10. It is important to note that Hauerwas is quite critical of Gutiérrez's theological approach. See esp. *After Christendom? How the Church Is to Behave If Freedom, Justice, and a Christian Nation Are Bad Ideas* (Nashville: Abingdon Press, 1991), pp. 50–58.

11. See esp. E. Schüssler Fiorenza's 1987 Society of Biblical Literature presidential address: "The Ethics of Biblical Interpretation: Decentering Biblical Scholarship," *Journal of Biblical Literature* 107 (1988): 3–17; and part 3 ("Participation in Meaning") of J. I. H. McDonald's *Biblical Interpretation and Christian Ethics* (Cambridge: Cambridge University Press, 1993), pp. 163–246.

12. Schüssler Fiorenza, "Ethics of Biblical Interpretation," p. 17.

13. To be sure, many biblical scholars have self-consciously taken on this task. See, for but one example, the popular but very useful book by V. P. Furnish, *The Moral Teaching of Paul: Selected Issues*, 2d ed. (Nashville: Abingdon Press, 1985). One place where I have sought to use the Bible in constructive theological ethics is in my article "How to Decide? Homosexual Christians, the Bible, and Gentile Inclusion," *Theology Today* 51 (1994): 219–34.

14. On the "polyphonic" character of the biblical witness, see, e.g., W. Meeks, "The

Polyphonic Ethics of the Apostle Paul," *Annual of the Society of Christian Ethics* (1988): 17–29; and the reflections of P. Ricouer, "Toward a Hermeneutic of the Idea of Revelation," in *Essays on Biblical Interpretation*, ed. L. S. Mudge (Philadelphia: Fortress Press, 1980), pp. 73–118.

BIBLIOGRAPHY

Abadamloora, L. "Some Modern Attempts Towards Biblical Renewal in Moral Theology." Dissertatio ad Doctoratum in Facultate Theologiae Pontificiae Universitatis Gregorianae, Rome, 1975.

Abbot, W. M., ed. *The Documents of Vatican II.* New York: Crosssroad, 1989.

Achtemeier, E. "The Impossible Possibility: Evaluating the Feminist Approach to Bible and Theology." *Interpretation* 52, no. 1 (1988): 45–57.

Allen, J. "Paul Ramsey and His Respondents Since *The Patient as Person.*" *Religious Studies Review* 5 (1979): 89–95.

Attwood, D. *Paul Ramsey's Political Ethics.* Lanham, Md.: Rowman & Littlefield, 1992.

Bailey, R. C. "Beyond Identification: The Use of Africans in Old Testament Poetry and Narratives." In *Stony the Road We Trod: African American Biblical Interpretation*, ed. C. Felder. Minneapolis: Fortress Press, 1991.

Beach, W., and H. R. Niebuhr, eds. *Christian Ethics: Sources of the Living Tradition.* 2d ed. New York: Ronald Press, 1973 (original ed. 1955).

Bennett, J. "Reinhold Niebuhr's Contribution to Christian Social Ethics." In *Reinhold Niebuhr: A Prophetic Voice in Our Time*, ed. H. R. Landon. Greenwich, Conn.: Seabury Press, 1962.

Bennett, R. A. "Biblical Theology and Black Theology." *Journal of the Interdenominational Theological Center* 3 (1976): 1–16.

Bennett, R. A. "Black Experience and the Bible." *Theology Today* 27 (1971): 422–33.

Betz, H. D. *The Sermon on the Mount.* Minneapolis: Fortress Press, 1995.

Birch, B. *Let Justice Roll Down: The Old Testament, Ethics, and Christian Life.* Louisville: Westminster Press/John Knox Press, 1991.

Birch, B., and L. Rasmussen. *Bible and Ethics in the Christian Life.* Rev. and exp. ed. Minneapolis: Augsburg, 1989.

Bird, P. "Images of Women in the Old Testament." In *Religion and Sexism: Images of Woman in the Jewish and Christian Traditions*, ed. R. Ruether. New York: Simon & Schuster, 1974.

Boff, C. *Theology and Praxis: Epistemological Foundations.* Maryknoll, N.Y.: Orbis Books, 1987.

Boisvert, L. "Les images bibliques de Dieu dans l'oeuvre de Gustavo Gutiérrez." *Église et Théologie* 19 (1989): 307–21.

Borg, M. "Portraits of Jesus in Contemporary North American Scholarship." *Harvard Theological Review* 84 (1991): 1–22.

Borg, M. *Jesus in Contemporary Scholarship*. Valley Forge, Penn.: Trinity Press International, 1994.

Branson, M. L. and C. R. Padilla, eds. *Conflict and Context: Hermeneutics in the Americas*. Grand Rapids: Eerdmans, 1986.

Brown, C. C. *Niebuhr and His Age: Reinhold Niebuhr's Prophetic Role in the Twentieth Century*. Philadelphia: Trinity Press International, 1992.

Brown, R. M. *Gustavo Gutiérrez: An Introduction to Liberation Theology*. Maryknoll, N.Y.: Orbis Books, 1990.

————. *Unexpected News: Reading the Bible with Third World Eyes*. Philadelphia: Westminster Press, 1984.

————, ed. *The Essential Reinhold Niebuhr*. New Haven: Yale University Press, 1986.

Brunner, E. "Some Remarks on Reinhold Niebuhr's Work as a Christian Thinker." In *Reinhold Niebuhr: His Religious, Social, and Political Thought*, ed. C. W. Kegley and R. W. Bretall. New York: Macmillan, 1956.

Burnstein, A. J. "Niebuhr, Scripture, and Normative Judaism." In *Reinhold Niebuhr: His Religious, Social, and Political Thought*, ed. C. W. Kegley and R. W. Bretall. New York: Macmillan, 1956.

Burrow, R., Jr. *James H. Cone and Black Liberation Theology*. Jefferson, N.C.: McFarland, 1994.

Burtt, E. A. "Some Questions About Niebuhr's Theology." In C. W. Kegley and R. W. Bretall, eds., *Reinhold Niebuhr: His Religious, Social, and Political Thought*. New York: Macmillan, 1956.

Cadorette, C. *From the Heart of the People: The Theology of Gustavo Gutiérrez*. Oak Park, Ill.: Meyer Stone Books, 1988.

Cahill, L. S. "Within Shouting Distance: Paul Ramsey and Richard McCormick on Method." *Journal of Medicine and Philosophy* 4 (1979): 398–418.

Cahill, L. "The Ethical Implications of the Sermon on the Mount" *Interpretation* 41 (1987): 144–56.

Cardenal, E. *The Gospel in Solentiname*. 4 vols. Maryknoll, N.Y.: Orbis Books, 1976–82.

Carter, W. *What Are They Saying About Matthew's Sermon on the Mount?* New York: Paulist Press, 1994.

Cartwright, M. G. "Ideology and the Interpretation of the Bible in the African-American Christian Tradition." *Modern Theology* 9, no. 2 (1993): 141–58.

————. "The Practice and Performance of Scripture: Grounding Christian Ethics in a Communal Hermeneutic." In *The Annual of the Society of Christian Ethics, 1988*, ed. D. M. Yeager. Washington, D.C.: Georgetown University Press, 1988.

————. "Practices, Politics, and Performance: Toward a Communal Hermeneutic for Christian Ethics." Ph.D. diss., Duke University, 1988.

Chopp, R. "Seeing and Naming the World Anew: The Works of Rosemary Radford Ruether." *Religious Studies Review* 15, no. 1 (1989): 8–11.

Christ, C. *Laughter of Aphrodite: Reflections on a Journey to the Goddess*. San Francisco: Harper & Row, 1987.

Clark, M. "The Use of Sacred Scripture in the Moral Theology of Father Bernhard Häring, C.Ss.R." Ph.D. diss., Gregorian, 1979.

————. "The Major Scriptural Themes in the Moral Theology of Father Bernhard Häring." *Studia Moralia* 30 (1992): 3–16.

Clarke-Sayer, T. "The Bible and the Religious Left: An Interview with Rosemary Radford Ruether." *Witness* 66, no. 3 (1983): 8–9, 17–18.

Cleage, A. *The Black Messiah.* New York: Sheed & Ward, 1968.

Cobb, J. *Living Options in Protestant Theology.* Philadelphia: Westminster Press, 1962.

Collins, R. *Christian Morality: Biblical Foundations.* Notre Dame: University of Notre Dame Press, 1986.

Cone, J. H. "Biblical Revelation and Social Existence." *Interpretation* 28, no. 4 (1974): 422–40.

———. "Black Theology and Black Liberation." In *Black Theology: A Documentary History.* Vol. 1, 1966–1979, ed. J. H. Cone and G. Wilmore. Maryknoll, N.Y.: Orbis Books, 1993.

———. *Black Theology and Black Power.* New York: Seabury Press, 1969.

———. *A Black Theology of Liberation.* Philadelphia and New York: Lippincott, 1970. Reprint, Maryknoll, N.Y.: Orbis Books, 1990.

———. *For My People: Black Theology and the Black Church.* Maryknoll, N.Y.: Orbis Books, 1984.

———. *God of the Oppressed.* San Francisco: Harper, 1975.

———. *Martin and Malcolm and America: A Dream or a Nightmare.* Maryknoll, N.Y.: Orbis Books, 1991.

———. *My Soul Looks Back.* Nashville: Abingdon Press, 1982. Reprint, Maryknoll, N.Y.: Orbis Books, 1986.

———. *Speaking the Truth: Ecumenism, Liberation, and Black Theology.* Grand Rapids: Eerdmans, 1986.

———. *The Spirituals and the Blues.* New York: Seabury Press, 1972. Reprint, Maryknoll, N.Y.: Orbis Books, 1991.

———. "What Is Christian Theology?" *Encounter* 43 (1982): 117–28.

Cooper, J. W. *The Theology of Freedom: The Legacy of Jacques Maritain and Reinhold Niebuhr.* Macon, Ga.: Mercer University Press, 1985.

Copher, C. B. "The Black Presence in the Old Testament." In *Stony the Road We Trod: African American Biblical Interpretation,* ed. C. Felder. Minneapolis: Fortress Press, 1991.

Crenshaw, J. L., and J. T. Willis, eds. *Essays in Old Testament Ethics.* New York: KTAV, 1974.

Croatto, S. *Biblical Hermeneutics: Towards a Theory of Reading as the Production of Meaning.* Maryknoll, N.Y.: Orbis Books, 1987.

———. *Exodus: A Hermeneutics of Freedom.* Maryknoll, N.Y.: Orbis Books, 1981.

Curran, C. "*Free and Faithful in Christ:* A Critical Evaluation." *Studia Moralia* 20 (1982): 145–75.

———. *Politics, Medicine, and Christian Ethics: A Dialogue with Paul Ramsey.* Philadelphia: Fortress Press, 1973.

Curran, C. E., and R. A. McCormick, eds. *Readings in Moral Theology* No. 4, *The Use of Scripture in Moral Theology.* New York and Ramsey: Paulist Press, 1984.

Daly, R. J., et al. *Christian Biblical Ethics: From Biblical Revelation to Contemporary Praxis, Method and Content.* New York and Ramsey: Paulist Press, 1984.

Davis, S. " 'Et Quod Vis Fac': Paul Ramsey and Augustinian Ethics." *Journal of Religious Ethics* 19, no. 2 (1991): 31–69.

Diefenthaler, J. H. *Richard Niebuhr: A Lifetime of Reflections on the Church and the World.* Macon, Ga: Mercer University Press, 1986.

Dodd, C. H. "The Ethics of the New Testament." In *Moral Principles of Action*, ed. R. N. Anshen. New York: Harper & Row, 1952.

Eagleson, J. and P. Sharper, eds. *Puebla and Beyond*. Maryknoll, N.Y.: Orbis Books, 1979.

Ellis, M., and O. Maduro, eds. *The Future of Liberation Theology: Essays in Honor of Gustavo Gutiérrez*. Maryknoll, N.Y.: Orbis Books, 1989.

Fadner, D. E. *The Responsible God: A Study of the Christian Philosophy of H. Richard Niebuhr*. Missoula, Mont.: Scholars Press, 1975.

Fey, H. E., ed. *How My Mind Has Changed*. New York: Meridian Books, 1961.

Fowl, S. E., and L. G. Jones, *Reading in Communion: Scripture and Ethics in Christian Life*. Grand Rapids: Eerdmans, 1991.

Fowler, J. W. *To See the Kingdom: The Theological Vision of H. Richard Niebuhr*. Nashville: Abingdon Press, 1974.

Fox, R. W. *Reinhold Niebuhr: A Biography*. New York: Pantheon, 1985.

Frei, H. "The Theology of H. Richard Niebuhr." In *Faith and Ethics: The Theology of H. Richard Niebuhr*, ed. P. Ramsey. New York: Harper & Row, 1957.

Furnish, V. P. *The Moral Teaching of Paul: Selected Issues*. 2d ed. Nashville: Abingdon Press, 1985.

———. *Theology and Ethics in Paul*. Nashville: Abingdon Press, 1968.

Gaudin, G., and D. J. Hall, eds. *Reinhold Niebuhr (1892–1971): A Centenary Appraisal*. Atlanta: Scholars Press, 1994.

Godsey, J. *The Promise of H. Richard Niebuhr*. Philadelphia: Lippincott, 1970.

Goldberg, M. *Jews and Christians, Getting Our Stories Straight: The Exodus and the Passion-Resurrection*. Nashville: Abingdon Press, 1985. Reprint, Philadelphia: Trinity Press International, 1991.

———. *Theology and Narrative: A Critical Introduction*. 2d ed. Philadelphia: Trinity Press International, 1991.

Gottwald, N. "The Exodus as Event and Process: A Test Case in the Biblical Grounding of Liberation Theology." In *The Future of Liberation Theology*, ed. M. Ellis and O. Maduro. Maryknoll, N.Y.: Orbis Books, 1989.

———. *The Hebrew Bible: A Socio-literary Introduction*. Philadelphia: Fortress Press, 1985.

Gottwald, N. *The Tribes of Yahweh: A Sociology of the Religion of Liberated Israel, 1250–1050 B.C.E.* Maryknoll, N.Y.: Orbis Books, 1979.

Grant, D. C. *God the Center of Value: Value Theory in the Theology of H. Richard Niebuhr*. Fort Worth: Christian University Press, 1984.

Grimké, S. "Epistle to the Clergy of the Southern States" (1836). In *The Public Years of Sarah and Angelina Grimké*, ed. L. Ceplair. New York: Columbia University Press, 1989.

———. "Letters on the Equality of the Sexes and the Condition of Women" (1838). In *Letters on the Equality of the Sexes*, ed. E. A. Bartlett. New Haven: Yale University Press, 1988.

Gudorf, C. "Liberation Theology's Use of Scripture: A Response to First World Critics." *Interpretation* 41 (1987): 5–18.

Gula, R. M. *Reason Informed by Faith: Foundations of Catholic Morality*. New York and Mahwah, N.J.: Paulist Press, 1989.

———. *What Are They Saying About Moral Norms?* New York and Mahwah, N.J.: Paulist Press, 1982.

Gustafson, J. "The Changing Use of the Bible in Christian Ethics." In *Readings in Moral*

Theology. No. 4, *The Use of Scripture in Moral Theology*, ed. C. E. Curran and R. A. McCormick. New York and Ramsey: Paulist Press, 1984.

Gustafson, J. "A Response to Critics." *Journal of Religious Ethics* 13 (1985): 185–209.

———. *Ethics from a Theocentric Perspective*. 2 vols. Chicago: University of Chicago Press, 1981–84.

———. "The Place of Scripture in Christian Ethics: A Methodological Study." *Interpretation* 24 (1970): 430–55.

———. "The Sectarian Temptation: Reflections on Theology, the Church, and the University." *Proceedings of the Catholic Theological Society of America* 40 (1985): 83–94.

Gutiérrez, G. *Dios o el oro en las Indias*. Lima: CEP, 1989.

———. *En busca de los pobres de Cristo*. Lima: CEP, 1992.

———. "Freedom and Salvation." In *Liberation and Change*, ed. R. H. Stone. Atlanta: John Knox Press, 1977.

———. *The God of Life*. Maryknoll, N.Y.: Orbis Books, 1991.

———. "Haz más de lo que te pido: La Carta a Filemón." *Páginas* 9, no. 60 (Apr. 1984): 2, 43.

———. "The Irruption of the Poor in Latin America and the Christian Communities of the Common People." In *The Challenge of Basic Christian Communities*, ed. S. Torres and J. Eagleson. Maryknoll, N.Y.: Orbis Books, 1981.

———. "Notes for a Theology of Liberation." *Theological Studies* 31 (1970): 243–61.

———. *On Job: God-Talk and the Suffering of the Innocent*. Maryknoll, N.Y.: Orbis Books, 1987.

———. *The Power of the Poor in History*. Maryknoll, N.Y.: Orbis Books, 1983.

———. "Ser discípulo según Mateo." *Páginas* 11, no. 76 (Apr. 1986): 2, 46.

———. *A Theology of Liberation*. 2d ed. Maryknoll, N.Y.: Orbis Books, 1988.

———. "Toward a Theology of Liberation" (July 1968). In *Liberation Theology: A Documentary History*, ed. A. T. Hennelly. Maryknoll, N.Y.: Orbis Books, 1990.

———. *The Truth Shall Make You Free*. Maryknoll, N.Y.: Orbis Books, 1990.

———. *We Drink from Our Own Wells*. Maryknoll, N.Y.: Orbis Books, 1984.

Häring, B. *Free and Faithful in Christ*. 3 vols. New York: Seabury Press, 1978–81.

———. *The Law of Christ*. 3 vols. Trans. E. Kaiser. Westminster, Md.: Newman Press, 1961–66.

———. *Toward a Christian Moral Theology*. Notre Dame: University of Notre Dame Press, 1966.

———. *My Witness for the Church*. Trans. L. Swidler. New York and Mahwah, N.J.: Paulist Press, 1992.

———. "The Normative Value of the Sermon on the Mount." *Catholic Biblical Quarterly* 29 (1967): 69–79.

———. "The Role of the Catholic Moral Theologian." In *Moral Theology: Challenges for the Future*, ed. C. E. Curran. New York and Mahwah, N.J.: Paulist Press, 1990.

Harries, R., ed. *Reinhold Niebuhr and the Issues of Our Time*. Grand Rapids: Eerdmans, 1986.

Hauerwas, S. *After Christendom? How the Church Is to Behave If Freedom, Justice, and a Christian Nation Are Bad Ideas*. Nashville: Abingdon Press, 1991.

———. *Against the Nations: War and Survival in a Liberal Society*. San Francisco: Harper & Row, 1985.

———. "The August Partiality of God's Love." *Reformed Journal* 39, no. 5 (1989): 10–12.

———. *Character and the Christian Life: A Study in Theological Ethics*. San Antonio: Trinity University Press, 1975.

——. *Christian Existence Today: Essays on Church, World and Living in Between.* Durham, N.C.: Labyrinth Press, 1988.

——. *A Community of Character: Toward a Constructive Christian Social Ethic.* Notre Dame: University of Notre Dame Press, 1981.

——. "Hating Mothers as the Way to Peace." *Journal for Preachers* 11, no. 4 (1988): 17–21.

——. *Naming the Silences: God, Medicine, and the Problem of Suffering.* Grand Rapids: Eerdmans, 1990.

——. "On Being Dispossessed: Or This Is a Hell of a Way to Get Someplace." *Reformed Journal* 39, no. 1 (1989): 14–16.

——. "On Developing Hopeful Virtues." *Christian Scholar's Review* 18, no. 2 (1988): 107–17.

——. "On the Production and Reproduction of the Saints." *Reformed Journal* 40 (1990): 12–13.

——. "Epilogue: A Pacifist Response to the Bishops." In *Speak Up for Just War or Pacifism,* by P. Ramsey. University Park: The Pennsylvania State University Press, 1988. pp. 149–82.

——. *The Peaceable Kingdom: A Primer in Christian Ethics.* Notre Dame: University of Notre Dame Press, 1983.

——. *Should War Be Eliminated?* Milwaukee: Marquette University Press, 1989.

——. "Some Theological Reflections on Gutiérrez's Use of 'Liberation' as a Theological Concept." *Modern Theology* 3, no. 1 (1986): 67–76.

——. *Suffering Presence: Theological Reflections on Medicine, the Mentally Handicapped, and the Church.* Notre Dame: University of Notre Dame Press, 1986.

——. "The Testament of Friends." *Christian Century* 107, no. 7 (1990): 212–16.

——. *Unleashing the Scripture: Freeing the Bible from Captivity to America.* Nashville: Abingdon Press, 1993.

——. *Vision and Virtue: Essays in Christian Ethical Reflection.* Notre Dame: Fides/Claretian, 1974.

——. "Will the Real Sectarian Stand Up?" *Theology Today* 44, no. 1 (1987): 87–94.

Hauerwas, S., with R. Bondi and D. B. Burrell. *Truthfulness and Tragedy: Further Investigations in Christian Ethics.* Notre Dame: University of Notre Dame Press, 1977.

Hauerwas, S., and S. Long. "Interpreting the Bible As a Political Act." *Religion and Intellectual Life* 6 (1989): 134–42.

Hauerwas, S., and W. H. Willimon. *Preaching to Strangers.* Louisville: Westminster Press/John Knox Press, 1992.

——. *Resident Aliens: Life in the Christian Colony.* Nashville: Abingdon Press, 1989.

Hays, R. B. *Community, Cross, New Creation: New Testament Ethics.* New York: HarperCollins, 1996.

——. "Scripture-Shaped Community: The Problem of Method in New Testament Ethics." *Interpretation* 44 (1990): 42–55.

Hempel, J. *Das Ethos des Alten Testaments.* Berlin: Alfred Töpelmann, 1964.

Hennelly, A. T., ed. *Liberation Theology: A Documentary History.* Maryknoll, N.Y.: Orbis Books, 1990.

Hoedemaker, L. *The Theology of H. Richard Niebuhr.* Philadelphia: Pilgrim Press, 1970.

Hopkins, D. N. *Shoes That Fit Our Feet: Sources for a Constructive Black Theology.* Maryknoll, N.Y.: Orbis Books, 1993.

Hopkins, D. N., and G. Cummings, eds. *Cut Loose Your Stammering Tongue: Black Theology in the Slave Narratives.* Maryknoll, N.Y.: Orbis Books, 1991.

Houlden, J. L. *Ethics and the New Testament.* Baltimore: Penguin Books, 1973.

Hoyt, T. "Black Theology's Roots in Scripture." *Ecumenical Trends* 16 (1987): 172–76.

Irish, J. *The Religious Thought of H. Richard Niebuhr.* Atlanta: John Knox Press, 1983.

Janzen, W. *Old Testament Ethics.* Louisville: Westminster Press/John Knox Press, 1994.

John Paul II. "Mulieris Dignitatem" (On the Vocation and Dignity of Women). *Origins* 18, no. 17 (1988): 262–83.

Johnson, J. "Editor's Note: Special Focus Issue: The Ethics of Paul Ramsey." *Journal of Religious Ethics* 19, no. 2 (1991): ii–iii.

Johnson, J. T. and D. H. Smith, eds. *Love and Society: Essays in the Ethics of Paul Ramsey.* Missoula, Mont.: Scholars Press, 1974.

Jones, M. *Christian Ethics for Black Theology.* Nashville: Abingdon Press, 1974.

Jones, W. R. "Theodicy and Methodology in Black Theology: A Critique of Washington, Cone, and Cleage." *Harvard Theological Review* 64 (1971): 541–57.

Jordan, B. T. "The Use of Scripture in the Ethics of H. Richard Niebuhr." Ph.D. diss., Emory University, 1974.

Kaiser, W. *Toward Old Testament Ethics.* Grand Rapids: Zondervan, 1983.

Kegley, C. W., and R. W. Bretall, eds. *Reinhold Niebuhr: His Religious, Social, and Political Thought.* New York: Macmillan, 1956.

Kelsey, D. H. *The Uses of Scripture in Recent Theology.* Philadelphia: Fortress Press, 1975.

Kirk, J. A. *Liberation Theology: An Evangelical View from the Third World.* Atlanta: John Knox Press, 1979.

Kliever, L. H. *Richard Niebuhr.* Waco, Tex.: Word Books, 1977.

Laberge, L. "L'éthique des théologiens de la libération et ses fondments bibliques." *Église et Théologie* 19 (1988): 373–400.

Latourette, K. S., ed. *The Gospel, the Church, and the World.* New York: Harper & Brothers, 1946.

Lehmann, P. *Ethics in a Christian Context.* London: SCM Press, 1963.

Long, D. S. *Tragedy, Tradition, Tranformism: The Ethics of Paul Ramsey.* Boulder, Colo.: Westview Press, 1993.

Long, E. L. *A Survey of Christian Ethics.* New York: Oxford University Press, 1967.

———. "The Use of the Bible in Christian Ethics: A Look at Basic Options." *Interpretation* 19 (1965): 149–62.

Macnamara, V. *Faith and Ethics: Recent Roman Catholicism.* Dublin: Gill & MacMillan; Washington, D.C.: Georgetown University Press, 1985.

Mahoney, J. *The Making of Moral Theology: A Study of the Roman Catholic Tradition.* Oxford: Clarendon Press, 1987.

Marxsen, W. *New Testament Foundations for Christian Ethics.* Minneapolis: Fortress Press, 1993.

McCann, D. P. "The Christian Element in Christian Realism." In *The Bible in American Law, Politics, and Political Rhetoric,* ed. J. T. Johnson. Philadelphia: Fortress Press; Chico, Calif.: Scholars Press, 1985.

———. *Christian Realism and Liberation Theology: Practical Theologies in Creative Conflict.* Maryknoll, N.Y.: Orbis Books, 1981.

———. "Hermeneutics and Ethics: The Example of Reinhold Niebuhr." *Journal of Religious Ethics* 8, no. 1 (1980): 27–53.

McCormick, P. T. "Paul Ramsey's Covenantal Ethics: An Investigation into His Medical Writings." Excerpta ex dissertatione ad Doctoratum in Facultate Theologiae Pontificiae Universitatis Gregorianae, Rome, 1984.

McCormick, R. A. *Notes on Moral Theology: 1965 Through 1980*. Washington, D.C.: University Press of America, 1981.

McDonald, J.I.H. *Biblical Interpretation and Christian Ethics*. Cambridge: Cambridge University Press, 1993.

McGovern, A. F. *Liberation Theology and Its Critics: Toward an Assessment*. Maryknoll, N.Y.: Orbis Books, 1989.

McInery, W. F. "Scripture and Christian Ethics: An Evaluative Analysis of the Uses of Scripture in the Works of Walter Rauschenbusch." Ph.D. diss., Marquette University, 1983.

Meeks, W. *The Origins of Christian Morality: The First Two Centuries*. New Haven: Yale University Press, 1993.

———. "The Polyphonic Ethics of the Apostle Paul." *Annual of the Society of Christian Ethics* (1988): 17–29.

Mesters, C. "The Use of the Bible in Christian Communities of the Common People." In *The Challenge of Basic Christian Communities*, ed. S. Torres and J. Eagleson. Maryknoll, N.Y.: Orbis Books, 1981.

Metzger, B. *The Canon of the New Testament: Its Origin, Development, and Significance*. Oxford: Oxford University Press, 1987.

Meyer, D. *The Protestant Search for Political Realism, 1919–1941*. Middletown, Conn.: Wesleyan University Press, 1988.

Miller, R. B. "H. Richard Niebuhr's War Articles: A Transvaluation of Value." *Journal of Religion* 68 (1988): 242–62.

Mott, S. C. "The Use of the New Testament for Social Ethics." *Journal of Religious Ethics* 15 (1987): 225–60.

Mouw, R. J. "Biblical Revelation and Medical Decisions." *Journal of Medicine and Philosophy* 4, no. 4 (1979): 367–82.

Nelson, P. "Fidelity to Covenant: Paul Ramsey Remembered." *Christian Century* 107 (1990): 1131–34.

Nessan, C. L. *Orthopraxis or Heresy: The North American Theological Response to Latin American Liberation Theology*. Atlanta: Scholars Press, 1989.

Neuhaus, J. R., ed. *Reinhold Niebuhr Today*. Grand Rapids: Eerdmans, 1989.

Niebuhr, H. R. "Back to Benedict." *Christian Century* 42 (1925): 860–61.

———. *Christ and Culture*. New York: Harper & Brothers, 1951.

———. "A Communication: The Only Way into the Kingdom of God." *Christian Century* 49 (6 Apr. 1932): 447.

———. *Faith on Earth: An Inquiry into the Structure of Human Faith*. Ed. R. R. Niebuhr. New Haven: Yale University Press, 1989.

———. "The Grace of Doing Nothing." *Christian Century* 49 (1932): 378–80.

———. "Introduction to Biblical Ethics." In *Christian Ethics: Sources of the Living Tradition*, ed. W. Beach and H. R. Niebuhr. 2d ed. New York: Ronald Press, 1973.

———. "Is God in the War?" *Christian Century* 59 (1942): 953–55.

———. *The Kingdom of God in America*. New York: Harper & Row, 1937.

———. *The Meaning of Revelation*. New York: Macmillan, 1941.

Niebuhr, H. R. *The Purpose of the Church and Its Ministry: Reflections on the Aims of Theological Education*. In collaboration with D. D. Williams and J. M. Gustafson. New York: Harper & Row, 1956.

———. *Radical Monotheism and Western Culture (with Supplementary Essays)*. New York: Harper & Brothers, 1960.

———. "Reformation: Continuing Imperative." *Christian Century* 77 (1960): 248–51. Reprinted in H. E. Fey, ed. *How My Mind Has Changed* (New York: Meridian Books, 1961), pp. 69–80.

———. *The Responsible Self: An Essay in Christian Moral Philosophy.* Introduction by J. M. Gustafson. New York: Harper & Row, 1963.

———. "The Social Gospel and the Mind of Jesus." Ed. D. Yeager. *Journal of Religious Ethics* 16 (1988): 115–27.

———. *The Social Sources of Denominationalism.* New York: Henry Holt and Company, 1929. Reprint, New York: Meridian Books, 1957.

———. "War as Crucifixion." *Christian Century* 60 (1943): 513–15.

———. "War as the Judgment of God." *Christian Century* 59 (1942): 630–33.

Niebuhr, H. R., W. Pauck, and F. P. Miller. *The Church Against the World.* Chicago: Willett, Clark & Co., 1935.

Niebuhr, H. R. and D. D. Williams, eds. *The Ministry in Historical Perspectives.* New York: Harper & Brothers, 1956.

Niebuhr, H. R., D. D. Williams, and J. M. Gustafson. *The Advancement of Theological Education.* New York: Harper & Brothers, 1957.

Niebuhr, R. *Beyond Tragedy: Essays on the Christian Interpretation of History.* New York: Charles Scribner's Sons, 1947. Original 1937.

———. "Biblical Thought and Ontological Speculation in Tillich's Theology." In *The Theology of Paul Tillich,* ed. C. W. Kegly and R. W. Bretall. New York: Macmillan, 1952.

———. *Children of Light and Children of Darkness.* New York: Charles Scribner's Sons, 1944.

———. *Christianity and Power Politics.* New York: Charles Scribner's Sons, 1940. Reprint, Hamden, Conn.: Archon Books, 1969.

———. "The Conflict Between Nations and Nations and Between Nations and God." In *Love and Justice,* ed. D. B. Robertson, Gloucester, Mass.: Peter Smith, 1976. Originally published in *Christianity and Crisis,* 5 Aug. 1946.

———. *Faith and History.* New York: Charles Scribner's Sons, 1949.

———. *An Interpretation of Christian Ethics.* 1935. Reprint, New York: Crossroad and Seabury Press, 1979.

———. *The Irony of American History.* New York: Charles Scribner's Sons, 1952.

———. *Justice and Mercy.* Ed. U. M. Niebuhr. New York: Harper & Row, 1974.

———. *Moral Man and Immoral Society.* New York: Charles Scribner's Sons, 1932.

———. "Must We Do Nothing?" *Christian Century* 49 (1932): 415–17.

———. *The Nature and Destiny of Man.* 2 vols. New York: Charles Scribner's Sons, 1941–43.

———. "The Problem of a Protestant Social Ethic." *Union Seminary Quarterly Review* 15 (1959): 1–11.

———. *Reflections on the End of an Era.* New York: Charles Scribner's Sons, 1934.

Ogletree, T. *The Use of the Bible in Christian Ethics.* Philadelphia: Fortress Press, 1983.

Optatam Totius (Decree on Priestly Formation). In *The Documents of Vatican II,* ed. W. M. Abbot. New York: Crossroad, 1989.

Osborn, E. *Ethical Patterns in Early Church Thought.* New York and Cambrige: Cambridge University Press, 1976.

Osiek, C. "The Feminist and the Bible: Hermeneutical Alternatives." In *Feminist Perspectives on Biblical Scholarship,* ed. A. Yarbro Collins. Chico, Calif.: Scholars Press, 1985.

Ottati, D. *Meaning and Method in H. Richard Niebuhr's Theology.* Washington, D.C.: University Press of America, 1982.

Outka, G. H. "Character, Vision, and Narrative." *Religious Studies Review* 6 (1980): 116–18.

Paris, P. J. "The Bible and the Black Churches." In *The Bible and Social Reform*, ed. E. Sandeen. Philadelphia: Fortress Press; Chico, Calif.: Scholars Press, 1982.

Quirk, M. "Stanley Hauerwas' *Against the Nations:* Beyond Sectarianism." *Theology Today* 44, no. 1 (1987): 78–86.

Ramsey, P. *Basic Christian Ethics.* New York: Charles Scribner's Sons, 1950.

———. "Beyond the Confusion of Tongues." *Theology Today* 3, no. 4 (1947): 446–58.

———. "The Biblical Norm of Righteousness." *Interpretation* 24, no. 4 (1970): 419–29.

———. "The Case of the Curious Exception." In *Norm and Context in Christian Ethics*, ed. P. Ramsey and G. H. Outka. New York: Charles Scribner's Sons, 1968.

———. "A Christian Approach to the Question of Sexual Relations Outside Marriage." *Journal of Religion* 45 (1965): 100–18.

———. "Christian Ethics and the Future of Humanism." In *God, Man, and Philosophy*, ed. C. W. Grindell. New York: St. John's University Press, 1971.

———. *Christian Ethics and the Sit-In.* New York: Association Press, 1961.

———. "Christian Ethics Today." *Rockford College Alumni Magazine*, spring 1968, pp. 3–6, 23.

———. *Deeds and Rules in Christian Ethics.* Scottish Journal of Theology Occasional Papers, no. 11. Edinburgh and London: Oliver & Boyd. New York: Charles Scribner's Sons, 1967.

———. "Elements of a Biblical Political Theory." *Journal of Religion* 29 (1949): 258–83.

———. *The Essential Paul Ramsey: A Collection.* Ed. W. Werpehowski and S. D. Crocco. New Haven: Yale University Press, 1994.

———. *Ethics at the Edges of Life.* New Haven: Yale University Press, 1978.

———. *Fabricated Man: The Ethics of Genetic Control.* New Haven: Yale University Press, 1970.

———. "Faith Effective Through In-Principled Love." *Christianity and Crisis* 20 (1960): 76–78.

———. "The Great Commandment." *Christianity and Society* 8 (1943): 29–35.

———. "How Shall We Sing the Lord's Song in a Pluralistic Land? The Prayer Decisions." *Journal of Public Law* 13 (1964): 353–400.

———. "In This Is Love . . . " *Motive* 11, no. 1 (1950): 21.

———. "A Letter to James Gustafson." *Journal of Religious Ethics* 13 (1985): 71–100.

———. "Liturgy and Ethics." *Journal of Religious Ethics* 7 (1979): 139–71.

———. "The Manger, the Cross, and the Resurrection." *Christianity and Crisis* 3 (1943): 2–5.

———. "Marriage, Law and Biblical Covenant." In *Religion and the Public Order*, ed. D. A. Giannella. Chicago: University of Chicago Press, 1964.

———. *The Patient as Person: Explorations in Medical Ethics.* New Haven: Yale University Press, 1970.

———. "Paul and Some of His Letters." *Crossroads* (Board of Christian Education of the Presbyterian Church of the U.S.A.), Apr.–June 1953.

———. "Political Repentance Now." *Christianity and Crisis* 28 (1968): 247–252.

———. "Protestant Casuistry Today." *Christianity and Crisis* 23 (1963): 24–28.

———. "Responsible Parenthood: A Response to Fr. Bernhard Häring." In *The Vatican*

Council and the World of Today. Providence, R.I.: Office of the Secretary, Brown University, 1966.

———. "Some Rejoinders." *Journal of Religious Ethics* 4 (1976): 185–237.

———. *Speak Up for Just War or Pacifism: A Critique of the United Methodist Bishops' Pastoral Letter "In Defense of Creation."* University Park: Pennsylvania State University Press, 1988.

———. "The Status and the Advancement of Theological Scholarship." *Christian Scholar* 47 (1964).

———. "Teaching 'Virtue' in the Public Schools." In *Religion and the Public Order*, ed. D. A. Giannella. Chicago: University of Chicago Press, 1964.

———. "Theological Studies in College and Seminary." *Theology Today* 17 (1960).

———. "A Theory of Virtue According to the Principles of the Reformation." *Journal of Religion* 28 (1948).

———. "Two Concepts of General Rules in Christian Ethics." *Ethics* 76 (1966).

———. ed. *Faith and Ethics: The Theology of H. Richard Niebuhr.* New York: Harper & Row, 1957.

Ramsey, P., and R. McCormick, eds. *Doing Evil to Achieve Good: Moral Choice in Conflict Situations.* Chicago: Loyola University Press, 1978.

Ramsey, W. M. *Four Modern Prophets.* Atlanta: John Knox Press, 1986.

Rasmussen, L., ed. *Reinhold Niebuhr: Theologian of Public Life.* London: Collins, 1989.

Ricouer, P. "Toward a Hermeneutic of the Idea of Revelation." In *Essays on Biblical Interpretation*, ed. L. S. Mudge. Philadelphia: Fortress Press, 1980.

Robbins, J. W. "Narrative, Morality, and Religion." *Journal of Religious Ethics* 8 (1980): 161–76.

Robertson, D. B. *Reinhold Niebuhr's Works: A Bibliography.* Boston: G. K. Hall, 1979.

———. ed. *Essays in Applied Christianity: The Church and the New World.* New York: Meridian Books, 1959.

———. *Love and Justice: Selections from the Shorter Writings of Reinhold Niebuhr.* Gloucester, Mass.: Peter Smith, 1976.

Rowland, C., and M. Corner. *Liberating Exegesis: The Challenge of Liberation Theology to Biblical Studies.* Louisville: Westminster Press/John Knox Press, 1989.

Ruether, R. R. "'Basic Communities': Renewal at the Roots." *Christianity and Crisis* 41 (1981): 234–37.

———. "The Biblical Vision of the Ecological Crisis." *The Christian Century* 95 (1978): 1129–32.

———. "The Bible and the Religious Left: An Interview with Rosemary Radford Ruether by Tony Clarke-Sayer." *Witness* 66, no. 3 (1983): 8–9, 17–18.

———. *The Church Against Itself.* New York: Herder & Herder, 1967.

———. *Communion Is Life Together.* New York: Herder & Herder, 1968.

———. *Disputed Questions: On Being a Christian.* Nashville: Abingdon Press, 1982. Reprint, Maryknoll, N.Y.: Orbis Books, 1989.

———. "Feminism and Patriarchal Religion: Principles of Ideological Critique of the Bible." *Journal for the Study of the Old Testament* 22 (1982): 54–66.

———. "Feminist Hermeneutics, Scriptural Authority, and Religious Experience: The Case of the *Imago Dei* and Gender Equality." In *Radical Pluralism and Truth*, ed. W. G. Jeanrond and J. L. Rike. New York: Crossroad, 1991.

———. "Feminist Interpretation: A Method of Correlation." In *Feminist Interpretation of the Bible*, ed. L. Russell. Philadelphia: Westminster Press, 1985.

———. *Gaia and God*. San Francisco: HarperCollins, 1992.

———. *Liberation Theology*. New York: Paulist Press, 1972.

———. *Mary—The Feminine Face of the Church*. Philadelphia: Westminster Press, 1977.

———. *New Woman/New Earth*. New York: Seabury Press, 1975.

———, ed. *Religion and Sexism: Images of Woman in the Jewish and Christian Traditions*. New York: Simon & Schuster, 1974.

———. *The Radical Kingdom*. New York: Harper & Row, 1970.

———. "Religion and Society: Sacred Canopy vs. Prophetic Critique." In *The Future of Liberation Theology: Essays in Honor of Gustavo Gutiérrez*, ed. M. Ellis and O. Maduro. Maryknoll, N.Y.: Orbis Books, 1989.

———. "A Religion for Women: Sources and Strategies." *Christianity and Crisis* 39 (1979): 307–11.

———. Review of E. Schüssler Fiorenza's *In Memory of Her*. *Horizons* 1, no. 2 (1984): 146–50.

———. *Sexism and God-Talk*. Boston: Beacon Press, 1983.

———. "The Subordination and Liberation of Women in Christian Theology: St. Paul and Sarah Grimké." *Soundings* 61 (1978): 168–81.

———. *To Change the World*. New York: Crossroad, 1981.

———. "What Do the Synoptics Say? The Sexuality of Jesus." *Christianity and Crisis* 38 (1978): 134–37.

———. *Women-Church*. San Francisco: Harper & Row, 1985.

———. *WomanGuides*. Boston: Beacon Press, 1983.

Ruether, R. R., and E. C. Bianchi. *From Machismo to Mutuality: Essays on Sexism and Woman-Man Liberation*. New York: Paulist Press, 1976.

Ruether, R. R., and W. Roth. *The Liberating Bond: Convenants—Biblical and Contemporary*. New York: Friendship Press, 1978.

Sakenfeld, K. "Feminist Perspectives on Bible and Theology." *Interpretation* 42, no. 1 (1988): 5–18.

———. "Feminist Uses of Biblical Materials." In *Feminist Interpretation of the Bible*, ed. L. Russell. Philadelphia: Westminster Press, 1985.

Schnackenburg, R. *The Moral Teaching of the New Testament*. New York: Herder & Herder, 1965.

Schrage, W. *The Ethics of the New Testament*. Philadelphia: Fortress Press, 1987.

Schubeck, T. L. *Liberation Ethics: Sources, Models, and Norms*. Minneapolis: Fortress Press, 1993.

Schüssler Fiorenza, E. *But She Said: Feminist Practices of Biblical Interpretation*. Boston: Beacon Press, 1992.

———. *In Memory of Her*. New York: Crossroad, 1983.

———. "The Ethics of Biblical Interpretation: Decentering Biblical Scholarship." *Journal of Biblical Literature* 107 (1988): 3–17.

Scriven, C. *The Transformation of Culture: Christian Social Ethics After H. Richard Niebuhr*. Scottsdale, Pa.: Herald Press, 1988.

Segundo, J. L. "Faith and Ideologies in Biblical Revelation." In *The Bible and Liberation: Political and Social Hermeneutics*, ed. N. Gottwald. Maryknoll, N.Y.: Orbis Books, 1983.

———. *The Liberation of Theology*. Maryknoll, N.Y.: Orbis Books, 1976.

Siker, J. S. "The Bible and Public Policy." *Christian Century* 103, no. 6 (1986): 171–73.

———. "The Canonical Status of the Catholic Epistles in the Syriac New Testament." *Journal of Theological Studies* 38 (1987): 311–40.

————. " 'First to the Gentiles': A Literary Analysis of Luke 4:16–30." *Journal of Biblical Literature* 111 (1992): 69–86.

————. "How to Decide? Homosexual Christians, the Bible, and Gentile Inclusion." *Theology Today* 51 (1994): 219–34.

————. "Uses of The Bible in the Theology of Gustavo Gutiérrez: Liberating Scriptures of the Poor." *Biblical Interpretation* 4, no. 1 (1996): 40–71.

Sleeper, C. F. *The Bible and the Moral Life.* Louisville: Westminster Press/John Knox Press, 1992.

Smith, D. H. "On Paul Ramsey: A Covenant-Centered Ethic for Medicine." In A. Verhey and S. E. Lammers, eds., *Theological Voices in Medical Ethics.* Grand Rapids: Eerdmans, 1993. Pp. 7–29.

Snyder, M. H. *The Christology of Rosemary Radford Ruether: A Critical Introduction.* Mystic, Conn.: Twenty-Third Publications, 1988.

Spohn, W. C. *What Are They Saying About Scripture and Ethics?* New York and Ramsey: Paulist Press, 1984.

Steichen, D. *Ungodly Rage: The Hidden Face of Catholic Feminism.* San Francisco: Ignatius Press, 1991.

Stone, R. H., ed. *Faith and Politics: A Commentary on Religious, Social, and Political Thought in a Technological Age.* New York: George Braziller, 1968.

————. *Liberation and Change.* Atlanta: John Knox Press, 1977.

Stout, J. "Review of S. Hauerwas, *Suffering Presence* (Notre Dame, Ind.: University of Notre Dame Press, 1986)." *Theology Today* 44 (1987): 125.

Tambasco, A. *The Bible for Ethics: Juan Luis Segundo and First World Ethics.* Washington, D.C.: University Press of America, 1981.

————. "First and Third World Ethics." In *Christian Biblical Ethics: From Biblical Revelation to Contemporary Christian Praxis, Method and Content.* ed. R. J. Daly. New York: Paulist Press, 1984.

Thiemann, R., ed. *The Legacy of H. Richard Niebuhr.* Minneapolis: Fortress Press, 1991.

Thiselton, A. *New Horizons in Hermeneutics: The Theory and Practice of Transforming Biblical Reading.* Grand Rapids: Zondervan, 1992.

Tillich, P. "Sin and Grace in the Theology of Reinhold Niebuhr." In *Reinhold Niebuhr: A Prophetic Voice in Our Time,* ed. H. R. Landon. Greenwich, Conn.: Seabury Press, 1962.

————. *Systematic Theology.* Vol. 1. Chicago: University of Chicago Press, 1951.

Tolbert, M. A., ed. *The Bible and Feminist Hermeneutics.* Semeia 28. Chico, Calif.: Scholars Press, 1983.

Trible, P. "Feminist Hermeneutics and Biblical Studies." *Christian Century* 99 (1982): 116–18.

Verhey, A. *The Great Reversal: Ethics and the New Testament.* Grand Rapids: Eerdmans, 1984.

————. "The Use of Scripture in Ethics." *Religious Studies Review* 4 (1978): 28–39. Reprinted in C. E. Curran and R. A. McCormic, eds., *Readings in Moral Theology,* no. 4, *The Use of Scripture in Moral Theology* (New York and Ramsey: Paulist Press, 1984), pp. 213–41.

————. "The Use of Scripture in Moral Discourse: A Case Study of Walter Rauschenbusch." Ph.D. diss., Yale University, 1975.

Warrior, R. A. "Canaanites, Cowboys, and Indians: Deliverance, Conquest, and Liberation Theology Today." *Christianity and Crisis* 49 (1989–90): 261–65.

Wieman, H. N. "A Religious Naturalist Looks at Reinhold Niebuhr." In *Reinhold Niebuhr*, ed. C. W. Kegley and R. W. Brettall. New York: Macmillan, 1956.

Williams, D. *Sisters in the Wilderness: The Challenge of Womanist Godtalk*. Maryknoll, N.Y.: Orbis Books, 1993.

Williams, P. "James Cone and the Problem of a Black Ethic." *Harvard Theological Review* 65 (1972): 483–94.

Yoder, J. H. *The Politics of Jesus*. Grand Rapids: Eerdmans, 1972.

———. *The Priestly Kingdom: Social Ethics as Gospel*. Notre Dame: University of Notre Dame Press, 1984.

———. "Exodus: Probing the Meaning of Liberation." *Sojourners* 5, no. 8 (Sept. 1976): 26–29.

INDEX TO MODERN AUTHORS

SUBJECT INDEX

Second Isaiah, 61, 70, 128, 152
Sermon on the Mount, 10, 28, 50, 51, 61, 71–74, 77, 78, 82, 99, 103, 104, 110, 145, 164, 203–208
Servant Songs, 61, 70, 81
sin, 5, 10–12, 14, 25, 28, 35, 39–41, 62, 65, 82, 85, 172, 174, 182, 194, 198
situation ethics, 72, 83
slavery, 33, 37, 40, 50, 135, 145, 150, 153, 159, 163, 166, 172, 181, 188
Spirit, 16, 30, 33, 41, 42, 52, 61, 62, 73, 76, 104, 125, 127, 129, 135, 137, 148, 151, 158, 164, 176, 180, 185, 187, 190, 192, 193, 206, 207
suffering, 19, 55, 58, 62, 70, 81, 98, 101, 130, 132, 149–151, 153, 155, 156, 159, 161, 186, 194
symbol, 8, 11–13, 19, 21, 28, 102, 108, 130, 158, 180, 191

telling the story, 48, 117, 152–155
temple, 32, 50, 90, 177, 195
Ten Commandments, 15, 50
Torah, 10, 100, 101, 152
transformation, 28, 32–34, 37, 41–43, 52, 54, 55, 104, 108–110, 126, 130, 142, 183, 184, 186, 187, 189, 200, 205

Vatican II, 59, 60, 126, 208
virtue, 16, 17, 68, 98

war, 5, 10, 54, 55, 58, 65, 80, 81, 89, 180
women, 17, 18, 57, 70, 85, 125, 171, 174, 177, 178, 180, 181, 183–188, 190–199, 207, 208
worship, 22, 41, 65, 106, 107, 143, 176

INDEX OF SCRIPTURE